Rebellion From the Roots
Indian Uprising in Chiapas

John Ross

Common Courage Press   Monroe, Maine

Cover photo by Douglas Engle, AP Wide World Photos

Author photo by Richard Gibson

Cover design by Matt Wuerker

Library of Congress Cataloging-in-Publication Data
Ross, John.
Rebellion from the roots : Indian uprising in Chiapas / John Ross.
p.   cm.
Includes Index.
ISBN 1-56751-043-4 (cloth). — ISBN 1-56751-042-6 (paper)
1. Chiapas (Mexico)—History—Peasant Uprising, 1994.
2. Mayas—Mexico—Government relations.
3. Ejército Zapatista de Liberación Nacional (Mexico).
4. Mexico—Politics and government—1988-
I. Title.
F1256.R7 1995
972'.75--dc20   94-38143
CIP

Common Courage Press
P.O. Box 702
Monroe, ME 04951
207-525-0900 fax: 207-525-3068

First Printing

Contents

Acknowledgments	5
¡Feliz Año Nuevo, Cabrones!	7
The NAFTA Connection	23
What Washington Knew and When	37
502 Years of Warning	53
Straw Just Waiting to Burn	63
The War in Chiapas	83
Bad Blood, Unquiet Bones	113
"¡Alto Al Masacre!"	141
The Crimes of Mi General	155
Photos	187
The Specter of Chinameca	201
Conversations in the Cathedral	217
Back to the Jungle	251
Into the Zapatista Zone	269
A Bullet From Within	303
Ballots or Bullets?	331
¡Locura!	363
The End of the Beginning	377
Index	405

To Amado Avendaño and all the journalists, national and international, who went to the roots of this rebellion and told the truth, a profound debt of gratitude.

—John Ross

For a long time, this town has existed where the men are Zapatistas, the women are Zapatistas, the kids are Zapatistas, the chickens are Zapatistas, the stones are Zapatistas, everything is Zapatista. And in order to wipe out the Zapatista Army of National Liberation, they will have to wipe this piece of territory from the face of the earth—not just destroy it but erase it completely because there is always the danger from the dead below...

—Subcomandante Marcos
to *Proceso*
(August 8th, 1994)

Acknowledgments

The author wishes to thank (not in order of importance and/or the alphabet) Blanche Petrich, Sandina Robbins, Gray Newman, Ted Bardacke, Adolfo Gilly, Antonio García de León, Antonio Turok, Imagenlatina, Jan De Voss, Herman Bellinghausen, Roberto Garduño, Elio Henríquez and the reporters at *La Jornada* and *El Tiempo,* Jaime Aviles, Francisco Gómez-Maza, Dolia Estévez and the reporters at *El Financiero*, the staff of *Proceso*, León Lazaroff, Michael McCaughan, Douglas Engle, Michael Tangeman, Marcia Perskie, Frank Bardacke, Kate Doyle, Ross Rogers, Medea Benjamen, Ellen Lutz, Ramsey Clark, Andrew Mutter, Dr. Tom Crane, Felicia Oldfather, Richard Gibson, Roger Maldonado, Lucas Mazere, Father Jorge Trejo, Father Pablo Romo, Pedro Moctezuma, Miguel Angel Vázquez-Sánchez. Araceli Burguete, Génaro Dominguéz, Dante Ross, Alan Hynds, John Womack, the nanas and tatas of Santa Cruz Tanaco, Major Rolando, Captain Irma, Subcomandante Marcos, Common Courage Press, and, most emphatically, E. Bell, for their contributions and assistance in compiling and publishing *Rebellion From the Roots*.

¡Feliz Año Nuevo, Cabrones!

The din of rockets and strings of firecrackers, pistol shots, and churchbells, faded fast in the frigid night. Not ten minutes after midnight, bundled-up revelers were toddling off to the warmth of their comfortable homes and expensive hotel rooms and the privacy of their own parties. The New Year's Eve cold stabbed at the bones "like all the devils," as Marcos would tell. The empty, stone streets of the old royal city glistened with icy mist. A few desultory tourists drained the last of their bottles under the yellow vapor lamps in the 31st of March Plaza.

The pitch black night suddenly came alive with darting shadows at precisely 00:30, New Year's Day, the day of Hix on the Tzeltal calendar. The slap slap of rubber boots against the slick pavement echoed throughout the silent neighborhoods on the periphery of town. Sleepy dogs stirred in their patios, stretched and bayed, the howling catching from block to block, barrio to barrio. Across the narrow Puente Blanco, down the rutted Centenary Diagonal, up General Utrilla from the marketplace, dark columns jogged in military cadence. With their features canceled behind ski masks and bandannas that left their breath hanging in the still mountain air like vapors from a past many never considered present, men and women without faces advanced on the strategic center of San Cristóbal de las Casas, the capital of the Mayan highlands in Mexico's southernmost state of Chiapas.

Just a half-hour before, the New Year had detonated in the boom of bottle rockets, muffling the moves of the interlopers on the outskirts of town. One group had busied itself felling stout pine trees on the north end of the Pan American Highway in an effort to blockade the sole paved road up from Tuxtla Gutiérrez, the state capital 60 miles northwest. Two other detachments had secured the PEMEX gas stations at both ends of San Cristóbal. An attack team had been dispatched to take the public justice ministry headquarters south of the city, at María Auxiliadora. Now short figures, wrapped in black wool chujs (serapes) and carrying a motley array of weapons that ranged from AK-15s and UZIs to axes and sledgehammers, entered the 31st of March Plaza, surrounded the Municipal Palace and its tiny unguarded police station, and began to smash down its doors with their "marros" (sledges)—the weapon of the Indian street laborers of San Cristóbal.

Inside the police precinct, the phone was ringing urgently. One of the ski-masked rebels reached for it. "Jefe, armed men are attacking the public ministry building," Samuel Moreno, the lone judicial police agent on duty at María Auxiliadora, yelled into the phone. "We are informed. Do not worry. Everything is under control. Adios," responded a slightly nasal, world-weary voice, and the receiver was returned to its cradle. Then the rebel leader, whom all of Mexico would soon know as "Subcomandante Marcos," let loose with a great soul-shaking guffaw: "¡Feliz Año Nuevo, Cabrones!" (Happy New Year, Jerks!)

* * *

In their ramshackle office-home down potholed Venustiano Carranza street in the Barrio of San Diego, Amado Avendaño and Concepción Villafuerte were about to crawl into bed when someone started pounding on the office door. The middle-aged owner-editors of a tiny, crusading San Cristóbal daily, El Tiempo, the Avendaños are understandably leery about latecallers. *El Tiempo* prides itself on covering the indigenous communities surrounding the city and is not popular with high-born "authentic coletos," the white and light-skinned bourgeoisie who control this tradition-bound, tourist-minded city. "We have had some unpleasant visitors here," the balding Avendaño explains. "Some have left behind their marks"—he points to a bullet-scarred street wall.

Still, Amado responded to the insistent knocking and the visitor proved to be Mercedes Osuna, a pal of one of the Avendaños' three daughters. "Please excuse the disturbance, Licenciado," she stammered, using the title by which all college-educated Mexicans are respectfully referred to, "but I have just driven back from the San Ramón neighborhood and I saw a lot of armed man with their faces covered up, coming into town..." The editor thanked the young lady, wished her a prosperous New Year, and bolted the door. "To tell you the truth, I thought she had had a little too much to drink at her New Year's dinner..."

But Avendaño, ever the newshound, got on the phone anyway, ringing up General Gastón Menchaca, then commander of Rancho Nuevo, the headquarters of the 31st Military Zone eight miles south of San Cristóbal. Menchaca was sleepy. No, he knew nothing about armed men with their faces covered coming into the city. No, no one else had called, he was the first. Prospero New Year's, Licenciado. Good night.

* * *

Despite the biting cold and the lateness of the hour, the 3lst of March Plaza was a beehive of bellicose activity. The masked invaders swarmed over the Municipal Palace, carrying out furniture and files to barricade the streets surrounding the square. Others slapped up leaflets on walls from one end of the plaza to the other and stuffed propaganda under the doors of all the surrounding businesses. "They were very well prepared," recalls "José Luis" (not his real name), night clerk at the Posada Santa Clara, a fashionable five-star inn on the southwest corner of the square. José Luis had locked the huge doors at the first sign of trouble. Now he studied the leaflet that had just been shoved under the portals. The paper said it was a declaration of war against the government. Later, the state judicial police in Tuxtla would call the hotel for a first-hand report and José Luis would read the leaflet to them: "We declare war against the Mexican Federal Army, the basic pillar of the dictatorship under which we suffer. We will advance on the capital, defeating the federal army as we march forward." The declaration of war was signed by the Zapatista Army of National Liberation. E. Z. L. N.

For a handful of adventurous tourists, the Zapatistas' New Year's eve assault on the royal city was the high point of their visit to Los Altos of Chiapas. Although warned by the rebels to get out, that there was going to be a big battle, the Italians perched up on the kiosk, sipping from small flasks against the cold. "We stayed up all night drinking coffee and smoking cigarettes and watching them smashing down the doors," Canadian Philip McDonald later told reporters, sounding like he was having the time of his life.

Antonio Turok, an artful San Cristóbal photographer who makes a living shooting local Mayans, piled out of "El Circo" around 1:30 A.M., "medio bolo" (half drunk) he says, walked a block to the plaza, watched the masked men tear down the front door of the Municipal Palace, finally found his car, and motored out to Amado Avendaño's place to inform the Licenciado of what was happening downtown.

¡Feliz Año Nuevo, Cabrones!

For the Avendaños, New Year's Eve would be the first of many long nights on the phone or out in the print shop in back, writing, tearing up, and re-writing tomorrow morning's edition. The calls were already starting to come in from correspondents in outlying municipalities. Three police officers had been gunned down in Las Margaritas, 40 miles southeast, after armed men—their faces covered too—had attacked the government palace there with sledgehammers. Was there a generalized uprising in the Altos of Chiapas? Don Amado called the Bishop, Samuel Ruiz, and spoke with Don Samuel's vicar and alter ego, Gonzalo Ituarte. Ituarte knew nothing about the masked men. Then the editor rang the General back. Menchaca's tone had hardened in the past hour: yes, he had been informed of the coordinated attacks in San Cristóbal and Las Margaritas, yes, the military was monitoring the situation closely, no, he did not know who the transgressors were. Click.

Now Turok was banging on the door. "Licenciado!" the sandy-haired photographer shouted, "there are armed men in the plaza." "Yes, I know," smiled Amado, "come in..." Doña Concha was making fresh coffee.

* * *

For the families of President Carlos Salinas and his hand-picked successor Luis Donaldo Colosio, New Year's Eve was like a fine cigar, a moment of quiet reflection upon the good fortune the international community had bestowed upon them both in 1993 and the even rosier prospects for the coming fiscal and political year. After a bitter, nerve-wracking floor fight in the U.S. Congress, the North American Free Trade Agreement would, at last, kick in by morning. NAFTA, or the "Tratado de Libre Commercio—the "TLC," as it is known south of the Rio

11

Grande—would be the fulcrum that would springboard Mexico from the third world to the first one. The treaty was the linchpin of neo-liberal reforms that had won the balding, diminutive president accolades in the economic community around the world. For five industrious years, Salinas had privatized virtually the entire economy and sold off thousands of state-owned enterprises to syndicates of his favorite entrepreneurs. His bold leadership was credited with rekindling the "Mexican Miracle" and creating 24 Mexican billionaires. Moreover, triple-digit inflation had been reduced to a single cipher and, although foreign debt totaled $130 billion, payments accounted for only a third of the gross internal product. The Mexican stock market remained one of the hottest in the world, having sucked in $60 billion foreign investor dollars during the Salinas years. Sure, there were soft spots up ahead—the California recession had seeped south and growth for the last quarter of '93 was reportedly negative—but the cash flow remained sweet and the long-range forecast was glowing.

Barred by the constitution from succeeding himself, Salinas would now pass on his legacy to his political son, Luis Donaldo Colosio, an acolyte so cloned of his boss that political columnists wagged he was "Salinas with hair." A protégé of the president since Salinas headed the budget ministry, Colosio had been chosen as his mentor's successor through arcane political rituals known as the "dedazo" or "big fingerpoint" and the "destape" ("the unveiling"), in which the outgoing chief of state imposes his choice upon the nation. Since 1929, both the president and his heir have been distinguished members of the state party, now known as the Institutional Revolutionary Party, the longest-running political dynasty on the planet. For the past six and a half decades, in 11 previous presidential contests, the PRI has never lost the office and the balloting scheduled for the third week of August 1994 would be no exception.

According to published reports, Carlos Salinas, his wife Cecilia Occeli, and their three teenaged children—one of them named for Mexican revolutionary martyr Emiliano Zapata—had invited Diana Laura and Luis Donaldo, ten-year-old Maríana and eight-year-old Luisito to spend New Year's Eve at the exclusive Pacific resort of Huatulco, a magnificent tourist "megadevelopment" overlooking nine fragile bays on the coast of impoverished Oaxaca state.

All that day, the families had swum and sunbathed on the pristine, private beach below the presidential guest-house on swank Tangalunda Bay. Now, at the stroke of midnight, the first families raised glasses of Dom Pérignon (or so reported *El Financiero*, January 16th) to celebrate the long-awaited arrival of NAFTA and 1994, strolled out on the terrace, and sat down under the stars to a tradition-al dinner of roast turkey, "relleno de picadillo," black olives, and "romeritos," a confection of shrimp and swamp grass that is de rigueur at the Mexican New Year's feast. By the third bottle of Dom Pérignon, the mood had grown mellow. A luxury yacht rolled invitingly on the tropical swells at anchor in Tangalunda and a post-midnight cruise was contemplated.

Just before 2 A.M., a military attaché stepped onto the terrace and handed the President a card. Carlos Salinas frowned, excused himself, and went inside to receive an urgent call on his confidential cellular phone.

The Secretary of Defense, General Antonio Reveillo Bazán, was on line from Mexico City. "I have just spoken with the commander of the 31st Military Zone and he has informed me that an armed force, calling itself the Zapatista Army of National Liberation, has entered San Cristóbal de las Casas, Chiapas and declared war on the military and the government..."

"Are you sure?" the startled president is reported to have responded. "Please investigate this and keep me informed." Then, Mexico's young and thoroughly modern president slowly returned to the terrace to announce, discreetly, that the party was over.

* * *

For the first three centuries of its municipal life, San Cristóbal de las Casas did business as "Ciudad Real," the royal city, a heavily fortified outpost of the Spanish Crown, the administrative and commercial center of Los Altos of Chiapas. In the royal city, wealth was concentrated in the strong boxes and vaults of the light-eyed conquerors, men and women who built many churches to pave their way to heaven but enslaved the conquered without a Christian qualm.

Today, crowning the Mayan Indian highlands of Chiapas like a priceless tiara, San Cristóbal is a small, elegant city filled with scores of jewelbox churches and chapels, boutiques, cafés, and fine hotels with impressive patios. The European conquerors come as tourists now. The Sunday market here is asterisked in the guidebooks for its colorfully costumed indígenas hawking their huipiles and handsome weavings and hand-sewn dolls at a price that the international tourist set can readily afford.

Unlike the founding bishop of the city, Bartolomé de las Casas, the priest who accompanied Columbus on his third voyage to the New World and spent the rest of his days trying to stave off the genocide of the native peoples of the Americas whose souls he had come to redeem, the pale-complexioned upper crust of San Cristóbal—the "authentic coletos"—have rarely been kind to their Indians. Even today, indígenas will step deferentially into the gutter to allow the highborn to traverse the narrow sidewalks unimpeded by the barefooted rabble.

San Cristóbal has been cruel to its Indians," Subcomandante Marcos admonished the few "coletos" who dared venture into the plaza on New Year's morn. "You deserve what is happening..."

"We're not all bad here," a well-dressed matron spoke in a small voice on the edge of the assembly of the curious that had gathered that first morning to gawk at the rebels.

Even in their most fretful nightmares of being overrun by the "Indiada" (the Indian hordes), the good burghers of San Cristóbal never believed this day would come. Now, at dawn in the center of their fortress city, the rebels raised their black flag with the red star and the letters "E," "Z," "L," "N" emblazoned upon the standard—the initials of an insurgent Indian army, named, as are many independent campesino groups in Mexico, for the Nahua Indian Emiliano Zapata, executed by his government in April 1919, because he refused to lay down the arms he had taken up to rescue his village's communal lands.

The new Zapatistas milled around under the eaves of the Government Palace, their faces covered with red handkerchiefs ("paliacates") and black ski masks, their hand-sewn uniforms strikingly uniform—black or dark olive pants and café-colored shirts and their trademark rubber boots. Some were armed with long guns, others with revolvers, and still others with no guns at all. Crews had been dispatched to expropriate victuals from government stores and medicines from the Bios pharmacy one block west of the plaza. The confiscated merchandise was piled up on tables under the porticos of the damaged palace. Armed Indian rebels stood over early-morning bonfires, kindled from the furniture hauled out of the government offices and the papers of the municipal archives.

Around 10:30 New Year's morning, Justus Fenner

rushed into the plaza in panic. A history buff, Fenner had dedicated years of his life to sifting through the San Cristóbal Municipal Archives. Like many elites in Chiapas, the archivist is of Germanic extraction and his native sense of order was jolted by what he now saw spread before him: the town's historical documents dumped ankle-deep in the patio of the Palacio Municipal. Fuming, Fenner walked up to the young Indians who patrolled the area and began to lecture them in his guttural-inflected Spanish. Didn't they know the very history of their grandfathers was contained in this sea of papers they had flung in the streets? Here was the whole sad story of how the Europeans and the mestizos had swindled the Indians out of their lands and their forests. In these documents was the only legal proof of their very existence.

The shorthaired German's argument was convincing. "We too respect the history of the people and we are not fighting against them. This archive shows us the historical struggle and the advancement of the people and we will not destroy it," a comandante instructed in his own patchy Spanish. The door of the Archive was shuttered and guards posted to make sure no further documents leaked out.

Three days later, Fenner sadly laments, in a frenzy to cleanse San Cristóbal of the taint of rebellion, the Mexican military, which would soon occupy these streets, scooped up all the papers still on the ground, trucked them off to the municipal cemetery, and burnt them in the landfill just beyond.

* * *

By noon on New Year's Day, the 31st of March Plaza was thrumming with locals and international tourists, many of them of the Bohemian persuasion, for whom this old stone city has always been a source of fascination.

Whether they were prisoners of or witnesses to the revolution preoccupied the visitors. A group of Italian tourists was said to be particularly anxious.

The Comandantes appeared on the high-windowed balcony, Comandante Felipe—"Jelipe" to his compañeros—pushed to the rail and revealed the origins of the Zapatista Army of National Liberation. "We are the product of 500 years of struggle," the small Tzeltal warrior told the onlookers, reading the opening words of the *Declaration of the Lacandón Jungle*, a document that highlights the continuing cruel exploitation of the indigenous peoples throughout Mexican history. Accusing the government of rank treachery, Jelipe demanded the resignation of President Carlos Salinas, the substitution of a transitional government, and declared war—in the name of the EZLN—on the Mexican Federal Army. "Today we say Basta Ya! Enough!" shouted the Comandante.

Jelipe was followed to the rail by other ski-masked leaders—Uno, Virginia, Ovidio—who declaimed the laws of the revolution and the Zapatistas' succinct eleven-word program: "Trabajo, Tierra, Techo, Pan, Salud, Educación, Democracia, Libertad, Paz, Independencia, and Justicia" (work, land, shelter, bread, health, education, democracy, liberty, peace, independence, and justice). "To live for the fatherland or die for liberty!" the Indians gesticulated from the balcony. Then, clad in his black chuj, redtipped bandaleros crisscrossed on his chest, and cradling his trademark short-barreled shotgun, Subcomandante Marcos summoned the public to dialogue.

The first questions came from so deep in the crowd that Marcos had a hard time catching the drift. The Subcommander descended into the street to facilitate the interchange. Tourists pressed in around him, demanding to know if they were free to leave. "We have reservations to visit the ruins at Palenque," one Swiss couple pleaded. "Please forgive us," Marcos responded, "this is a revolution." But some tourists were not at all satisfied with this answer. The Italians had already contacted their embassy and the embassy had filed a complaint with the national human rights commission, somebody said. Reluctantly, Marcos asked for a notebook and began scrawling out what he called "salvaconductas"—safe conduct passes. "Take these to our roadblock at kilometer 78 and maybe they will let you through..." he ventured hopefully.

"Why do you wear that ski mask," a feminine voice called out. "Actually, only the most handsome of us are required to wear them, for our own protection," bantered the Zapatista spokesperson. Schulamis Hirsch, a tourist from Mexico City who had come to San Cristóbal to whitewater raft on the Usumacinta river down below in the jungle, asked if she could snap the Subcomandante's photo. "But of course!" he laughed—in English! "What a perfect showman!" Hirsch told a *Proceso* reporter.

Amado Avendaño had been on the story since early morning. Arriving just after 8 A.M. with his notebook in hand, he approached the plaza cautiously, offering a cheery "Buenos Dias compañeros" to the young sentries posted at the corners. He was looking for a leader. "Hola, Licenciado Avendaño," a ski-masked Zapatista, bandaleros crossed over his chuj, offered his hand. Don Amado was startled by the name recognition. He and Marcos stood in the plaza and talked. "I am not a comandante," the rebel insisted and he escorted Amado to the patio of the trashed Municipal Palace where the editor was introduced to several older Zapatistas. "My jefes..." Marcos explained. "My elders..."

A handful of newshounds, trapped in the royal city by the holidays and the uprising, pressed Marcos about the roots of the rebellion. "We have been training for ten years," the

Subcommander told Gianni Prociettis, an Italian freelancer who later sold the interview to *"L'Unitá,"* the Rome-based left-wing paper. "Today, we have taken four cities in Chiapas because there are no conditions for free elections in this country. This is a warning to the government that we are fed up with the lack of democracy." Marcos reiterated the demand for Salinas's resignation. A "transitional government," must be appointed to oversee the August elections.

The Subcomandante said he was a "ladino" (non-Indian), one of three within the Zapatista ranks. The General Command of the Clandestine Revolutionary Indigenous Committee (CCRI), which he served, was composed of Tzotzil, Tzeltal, Chol, Tojolabal, Mam, and Zoque speakers, and he had been chosen to communicate their directives because he had "facility with Castilla (Spanish)" but the collective "spoke with one heart." He was just "the Subcomandante," he confessed—the occupation of San Cristóbal was actually directed by a woman, Comandante Ana María.

"Today, the white people of San Cristóbal respect the Indians because they have guns in their hands," Marcos told Avendaño and his colleagues. Noting that the Zapatistas had done little damage to the royal city, Marcos warned that if there was retaliation against the Indian people here after the Zapatistas left, "we will return and take San Cristóbal de las Casas apart stone by stone..."

By mid-afternoon, the Zapatistas' tone had grown ominous. A few minutes after 2 P.M., the first government response to the rebel uprising appeared on the horizon: four light-framed Mexican Air Force fighters, flying in from the west, dipped low in formation as if to salute, and circled back in the direction of the military airbase down in Tuxtla. "Pilatus," Marcos observed darkly, correctly identifying their Swiss manufacturer as he traced the vapor trails hanging in the mountain sky.

REBELLION FROM THE ROOTS

* * *

All New Year's afternoon, the radio crackled with rebel voices. The EZLN had seized XEOCH, the state government transmitter located next door to the Ocosingo market, 60 kilometers northeast Sandwiched in between the "rancheros" (country music), Zapatista DJs did the play-by-play. The Ocosingo Ranchers Association's slaughterhouse had been burnt down. The local Banamex bank branch was being expropriated. All prisoners, except narcotics traffickers and murderers, will be released from the jails. Tenants who have lived in one place for 15 years no longer need to pay rent. Wife-beaters will be tracked down and severely punished. All families were asked to take in the homeless Indian children who roam the cities of the Altos. Marcos stood in the plaza of San Cristóbal and explained to Amado Avendaño why so many of the troops appeared to be children no older than 14. "Children grow up fast in the jungle where we live..."

News of the uprising had been on the wire since daylight and national and international correspondents were already winging in to Tuxtla from the center of the country. What Subcomandante Marcos was telling reporters in the Plaza of San Cristóbal on New Year's afternoon, would be looked at closely in the capitals of several countries, notably Mexico City and Washington D.C., signatories, along with Canada, to the historic North American Free Trade Agreement that had become an irrevocable reality at one minute past midnight, the hour of the uprising. The Subcomandante was questioned about the timing. "Of course what we are doing here today has to do with the 'Tay Ele Say' (TLC)," he responded, laying out how cheap U.S. grains that NAFTA would pour into Mexico would obliterate the possibilities of commercializing Mayan Corn. The Mayans are known as the Men of Corn.

¡Feliz Año Nuevo, Cabrones!

"To us, the free trade treaty is the death certificate for the ethnic peoples of Mexico," the ski-masked Zapatista lamented, a pull quote that made the overnight AP wire and jolted Washington awake on the bleak, snowbound Sunday morning of January 2nd.

Other stunning appraisals that Subcomandante Marcos had to offer should have been of equal interest to those who control the pursestrings of the New North American Economic Order. "The whole neo-liberal project that Carlos Salinas represents is put in jeopardy by our challenge," he told *L'Unitá*. Would the EZLN's denunciation of NAFTA invoke U.S. intervention? "The end of the Cold War gives the U.S. no pretext for this," responded the masked man, putting a spin on the first post-Cold War uprising of the Latin American poor, that Washington would soon be weighing.

The time for interviews was running short. Dusk had put a chill touch on the energies of the onlookers. All morning and afternoon, they had sensed they were watching history happen and now they were a little weary of the responsibility that entailed. The outside world had discovered San Cristóbal's private New Year's revolution and the threat to public security that the self-proclaimed Zapatistas represented was being broadcast to a state and national audience. Chiapas government radio counted the number of rebels in San Cristóbal as "200, mostly Guatemalans" and led by a green-eyed foreigner who speaks four languages. The government radio charged that San Cristóbal's liberationist Bishop, Samuel Ruiz, and his nuns and priests, had incited the uprising. The theme was reprised on the national screen on *24 Hours*, the giant Televisa conglomerate's most-watched newshour. Under the baton of Jacobo Zabludowsky, the venemous, archly pro-government news director, Televisa reporters accused two of Bishop Ruiz's

21

lieutenants, Pablo Romo and Joel Padrón, of being the ring-leaders of what the military was inflexibly labeling "the transgressors of the law" and "professionals of violence."

Great activity was reported at Tuxtla's civilian and military airports. Army Fusilier Paratroopers were being dropped in to safeguard the state's vulnerable dam system north of Tuxtla from rebel attack. "The rebels are fine," Peter Morris, a traveling Brit on holiday in San Cris, told Reuters, "but I'm getting out of here before the soldiers come..."

As night draped itself over the colonial city, Marcos returned to the balcony for what he called a last press conference. He had announcements: In addition to the occupation of the municipalities of San Cristóbal, Ocosingo, Las Margaritas, and Altamirano, the rebels had taken Chanal to the south and were marching on Comitán. Tourists would be free to leave at 7:30 the next morning for Tuxtla only, the Subcommander told the hundred or so hardy souls who remained in the plaza, emphasizing that the Zapatistas were complying with a request faxed to the General Command in care of the Municipal Palace by the National Human Rights Commission (CNDH), asking the safe passage of foreign tourists. Finally, Marcos announced that the Zapatistas would be leaving too, early the next morning, and that the Army would soon be in San Cristóbal: "We have stayed too long waiting for a political response from the government." Two shots rang out just below the plaza as if to fine-tune the uncertainty of the moment. An informal "toque de queda" (curfew) had been imposed by the comandantes. It was time for the public to go home and stay there because the soldiers were going to come soon. Marcos warned: "Go home and don't open your doors..."

The NAFTA Connection

The 30-hour occupation of San Cristóbal de las Casas had been a masterstroke of armed public relations, a "poem," Marcos styled it in his first interview one month later with the national daily *La Jornada*. By Monday morning, Subcomandante Marcos's poem was pulsing over power centers in Mexico City and Washington D.C. like a pounding post-New Year's hangover. Who were those masked men, where had they come from, and what exactly did they want?

The answer to most of these questions had been available for months as close as the corner news stand. Initial notice of the mysterious guerrilleros, who magically emerged from the Lacandón jungle on New Year's morning, had come March 28th, 1993 when the charred and dismembered remains of two missing army officers were found buried in a shallow grave near a clandestine sawmill outside of the Tzotzil-speaking hamlet of San Isidro Ocotal, 15 miles south of San Cristóbal. On a Saturday morning, one week previous, Second Captain Marco Antonio Romero and Air Force Lieutenant Porfirio Millán had set off from Rancho Nuevo in full military dress for what their widows describe as a "hike" up to the joint U.S.-Mexico radar installation atop the Cerro de los Extranjeros (Stranger Hill) above Ocotal. Some close to the case suggest villagers mistook the officers for the newly-created and deeply despised Chiapas state forestry patrols—a state-wide timber-cutting ban, enforced by the patrol, is broadly opposed by impoverished Indian and mestizo farmers. Other sources conjecture that the unlucky officers had encountered a detachment of Zapatistas returning from a training session held in the region March

12th-18th, 1993—an event of which the authorities had previous notice.

The Mexican military's response to the killings was swift and brutal. 400 troops from the 24th Motorized cavalry, stationed in Comitán, sealed off the village and swept through the 40-family settlement, rousting all the men from their homes. "Do you play the guitar?" soldiers asked Carmelino González, 23. "No? What a pity that you won't be able to play us a tune while we rape your wife..."

In a preamble to the interrogation sessions the military would sponsor in rural hamlets in the wake of the January 1st Zapatista attack, soldiers marched the men of the village to the town basketball court, forced them to lie face down on the ground, and beat them with rifle butts for hours—one man was allegedly held with his face buried in an ant hill for 20 minutes. 13 blindfolded villagers were then taken up the highway to Rancho Nuevo, the 31st Military Zone headquarters, where they were tortured into verbally confessing to the murders.

Terrified relatives hurried into San Cristóbal to inform the Catholic diocese's human rights office—the Fray Bartolomé de las Casas Human Rights Center—of what was happening to their men. When the 13 suspects were finally brought before a civil judge on April 4th, Pablo Romo, a slim, ascetic Dominican who heads the Fray Bartolomé Center, intervened on the Indians' behalf, arguing that the confessions had been extracted by torture and that no representative of the civil justice system had been present to record them, as the law prescribes. Moreover, contrary to new judicial regulations, the proceedings were being conducted in Spanish when the accused spoke only Tzotzil. The Public Justice Minister had no recourse but to release the Indians.

Outside the public ministry offices below María

Auxiliadora hill, the same building torched January 1st by the Zapatistas, dozens of villagers from Ocotal and their supporters joyously celebrated the release of their men while the military brass seethed with resentment.

General Miguel Godínez, commander of the Seventh Military Region, which oversees the 31st Zone, was particularly incensed by the display. Godínez, an affable, animated officer, who once headed the presidential security apparatus, had breakfasted with San Cristóbal's Catholic Bishop Samuel Ruiz on the very morning that the bodies had been located. The General had come calling to appeal to Don Samuel, one of Latin America's most hardcore liberation theologists and no friend of the military, to help find the officers, who had then been missing for a week. Now their bodies had been discovered and Godínez claimed to have evidence that the soldiers had been burnt alive. To the General's dismay, the Bishop's priests were actively defending the murderers and had even conspired to secure their release.

The enraged General retaliated. Troops and state public security police were sent back into Ocotal and a neighboring rancho, Mizitón, twice in April and again in early May but found the villages deserted each time. Many of the Indians in Ocotal and Mizitón were said to be affiliated with ANCIEZ, the Emiliano Zapata National Alliance of Independent Farmers, the militant campesino grouping which transformed itself into the Zapatista Army of National Liberation in the spring of 1993. Now, it was speculated, the villagers had gone off to "the mountains of the Southeast" to join the Zapatistas.

* * *

How long had Mexican authorities known about the EZLN's existence prior to their astonishing New Year's

Day debut? In December 1992, more than a year before the rebels' surprise takeover of six municipalities in Los Altos of Chiapas, what one police agent described, in a report to Las Margaritas municipal authorities, as "a black bi-motor Cessna" put down on a jungle airstrip "somewhere in the Lacandón jungle" and unloaded a shipment of arms that were distributed in 23 nearby ejidos (rural communal production units) in Las Cañadas, the heart of Zapatista territory. The unidentified police informant, who had managed to infiltrate a guerrilla unit, wrote Las Margaritas municipal officials in early March that he had "seen" his weapon and that it would cost him five million old pesos (about $1,300 USD—double what Zapatista weapons usually go for). The informant pleaded with the municipal government to send him the money right away so he wouldn't be suspected of being a spy and "be burnt." "The war is growing near," he wrote Las Margaritas municipal president Romeo Suárez Culebro, in a March 18th 1993 letter obtained by *Proceso* magazine.

By early May, General Godínez had become convinced that the guerrilla was preparing to pounce. 4,000 troops were moved into the municipalities of Ocosingo, Las Margaritas, and Altamirano, all of which converge on the Lacandón rain forest, within scant miles of the Guatemalan border. Field headquarters were established near the Nazareth petroleum drilling compound at the gateway to the Cañadas.

On May 22nd, elements of the 83rd Infantry Battalion operating between La Garrucha and Pataté Viejo in the Sierra of Corralchén south of Nazareth, engaged an undetermined number of armed men at a hollow known as Las Calabazas in a firefight that left one soldier dead and one wounded. A May 31st Secretary of Defense (SEDENA) bulletin listed one unidentified civilian as being killed in the attack. The firefight lasted all afternoon and into the night, the first encounter between two armies that would meet again with the New Year. The Zapatistas, whose forest this is, moved easily through the midnight mountain mists. The soldiers stumbled blindly around in the dark.

The next morning, troops tracking rebels fleeing into the mountains blundered into a fully-stocked guerrilla training camp. The six huts and four caves that served as storehouses were bristling with guns and ammunition and canned food. Uniforms were neatly hung or bagged, the café-colored shirts bore the legend "EZLN 5th Regiment" and a logo of a rifle. Propaganda "of a type used by the Guatemalan guerrillas" was confiscated. In one cleared area, stones had been stacked up to represent a tank—a tube was even protruding from the cairn. A wooden mock-up target of a military transport bus, labeled the 83rd Infantry battalion, was thoroughly perforated by bullets.

But the centerpiece of the camp, later described by *La Jornada* ace reporter Blanche Petrich as "a work worthy of Hollywood cinematographers," was a movie set-like facsimile of the municipal palace in Ocosingo, a stage that was framed by the crossings of four avenues hacked from the jungle, each clearly labeled with its own true name. To add a further fillip of reality, Marcos told Petrich, a motorcycle was carried in over the mountains and parked in front of the facsimile government building.

Five months later, on January 1st and 2nd 1994, the Zapatista Army of National Liberation attacked and sacked the Ocosingo municipal palace, a scenario for which the rebels had long been preparing.

* * *

By the morning of May 23rd, 4,000 troops were combing the Sierra of Corralchén. Skirmishes were reported all day and on three subsequent days. A bombing near the ejido of Morelia was noted in the Chiapas state press. "The Army proceeded as it should have, tracking the guerrilla and trying to finish us," concedes Marcos—but the Zapatistas were already out of the area, he swears. "We left immediately." The Subcommander insists the military inflicted multiple casualties upon itself as confused columns clashed repeatedly in the surrounding hillside jungle. A dozen soldiers were killed and six gravely wounded by the friendly fire, he says. "Our people in Garrucha saw them airlifting the body bags out..."

News of the fighting was not a well-kept secret. Beginning May 25th, details of the fighting in the jungle had filtered out to the state capital where Tuxtla's 12 daily newspapers front-paged the story Following reports of the bombing incident, students at the Tuxtla campus of the state university marched to protest the military action in the Lacandón. The gravity of the situation was impressed upon the civilian population of Las Margaritas, Ocosingo, and Altamirano by the establishment of heavily armed military roadblocks thrown up at key access points to the region.

By May 24th, the military was storming neighboring ejidos, dragging Tzeltal-speaking farmers out of their huts for interrogation on the town basketball courts as up in Ocotal. In Pataté Viejo, a hamlet of 23 families, Manuel Clara Ruiz had the misfortune to run right into the federal troops as he returned from the mountains with a .22 in his hand. "I had gone up there to kill a gato montez (bobcat) that had eaten 40 of my brother's chickens," Clara later told his lawyer. Eight Tzeltal villagers from Pataté were trussed up and transported to the field headquarters at Nazareth where helicopters flew them to the state's maximum security prison in Tuxtla. The men were joined in

Cerro Hueco (Hollow Hill) penitentiary by two itinerant Guatemalan second-hand clothing salesmen who had been grabbed at a roadblock when the public bus on which they were traveling from ejido to ejido, hawking their wares, was halted by soldiers—not an unusual event in their own guerrilla-riddled republic. In Tuxtla, all ten Mayan Indians were brought before Military Prosecutor Hans Karl Hahns Arias and charged with treason. Treason is defined under the Mexican Constitution as "an armed plot, fomented by foreigners, to violate the independence of the republic," and is the one crime in Mexico still officially punishable by death.

*　*　*

Public record of the existence of the Zapatistas was cemented May 26th when the Civil Justice Ministry ("Ministerio Publico") sent investigator José Luis Estrada to the scene of the first firefight at Las Calabazas to probe the death of the civilian casualty. The unidentified dead man was described as being outfitted in dark trousers, a café-colored shirt, a telltale Zapatista red bandanna knotted around his neck—comrades in the fifth regiment operating out of La Garrucha would later identify the dead man as a Zapatista lieutenant, Rafael. A second rebel was wounded in the battle of Las Calabazas.

Estrada's findings were recorded in a public ministry pre-Investigation document ("averiguación previa") numbered 8491CAJ41 BZ1993, that notes the discovery of four caves containing 27 automatic weapons and 15 handguns, trenches, barracks, "playing fields," uniforms, mockup military vehicles, wooden bazookas, a copy of *Vanguard*—an ejido newspaper—a color television set, radio communication equipment, and the skull of a small child. The report concluded that there was "clear evidence

of the existence of an armed group advised by foreigners."
The "ocular" investigation, Estrada notes in the document,
was interrupted by an outbreak of gunfire between the military and the rebels.

The Zapatistas had reflexively gone to red alert the
moment the military moved into the Sierra of Corralchén
and now the discovery of their training camp would surely
make their presence known to the world. The General
Command of the Clandestine Indigenous Revolutionary
Committee convened deep in the jungle and debated the
merits of moving up the date of the insurrection the EZLN
had planned for later in the year.

Then, on May 26th, four days after the first outbreak
of fire, the 83rd Infantry battalion was abruptly pulled out
of the Corralchén and the troops returned to Nazareth. By
June 3rd, helicopters had lifted the last troops out of the
drilling station and flown them back to Rancho Nuevo and
Ocosingo. Marcos was flabbergasted by the army's retreat.
"This could not have been just a military error," he told
Proceso. "This was a political decision and it was made
very high in the regime. I'm sure the decision had to be
made in the office of the President of the Republic. There is
no other explanation..."

The decision to withdraw the troops was made, figures Marcos, because an unpredictable U.S. Congress
would soon confront the North American Free Trade
Agreement.

* * *

As the Army backed off from engagement, the threat
of a resurgent guerrilla movement in southern Mexico
evaporated from the news. The vanishing act was facilitat-
ed by the May 24th assassination of Mexico's second leading Catholic churchman, Cardinal Juan Jesús Posadas,

blown away at the Guadalajara airport, allegedly by gunsels in the employ of the Tijuana drug cartel—Cardinal Posadas was once Bishop of Tijuana. The graying Prince of the Church, who was in full regalia with a great pectoral cross flattened upon his chest, was shot a reported 14 times in the thorax area from five feet away while perched in the backseat of his chauffeur-driven white Gran Marquis sedan, a land yacht much favored by Mexican mafiosi. The assassination was a case of mistaken identity, Mexico's Attorney General Jorge Carpizo explained. As the nation gasped in disbelief at the slaughter in Guadalajara, the guerrillas slipped back into the oblivion of their jungle. Had anything really happened in the Sierra of Corralchén?

The Public Ministry's report reached interim Governor Elmar Setzer's desk in early June and was sent on to his political godfather, Patrocinio González Garrido, the Secretary of the Interior and a former Chiapas governor himself. As Interior ("Gobernación") Secretary, González oversaw the nation's internal security and was regarded as among the three most powerful people in Mexico. The report of the sighting of guerrillas in his home state apparently did not arouse much enthusiasm on Patrocinio's part. The public ministry report languished on his desk for three months. *Proceso* writer Jorge G. Castañeda says it is inconceivable that the document was not seen by someone in the Salinas braintrust—most probably by then-chief advisor (some say Salinas's Svengali) José Córdoba Montoya, a French-born, Stanford-educated economist who, among myriad functions, was liaison on security matters for the President. Nonetheless, the existence of the public ministry's report remained a state secret until the document was finally made public August 7th, after being "obtained" by *Proceso*.

González grew short-tempered when asked to respond

to the leak of the report. "Whoever circulates this false rumor will cause grave prejudice to development because the release can halt foreign and domestic investment in the agricultural sector. The Mexican government discounts the presence of a guerrilla movement in Chiapas," the native-born Chiapaneco told the Spanish news agency EFE August 11th. The statement contrasts sharply with one Patrocinio, then Governor of Chiapas, had made two years previous when, on the eve of the Quincentennial of Columbus's arrival in the New World, armed insurgency was heavily rumored in Los Altos. "My government, the Attorney General, and the Army will act swiftly to disarticulate the guerrilla," Patocinio woofed to the press.

* * *

Proceso magazine is not a lunatic fringe publication. Each Monday morning, 100,000 readers in every capital and provincial city of the nation, line up to buy this outspoken, ill-designed, independent weekly. Directed by the reclusive Julio Scherer, *Proceso* is, by far, the hottest-selling political publication in the country. Scherer does it without government advertising, the lifeblood of Mexican print media, which has been denied the owner-editor since President José López Portillo perceived a disrespectful reference on its pages in the late 1970s. As a unique, and often lonely, voice in a media that has been in the PRI's hip pocket for six and a half decades, *Proceso* has its finger on what's really happening in Mexico long before its competitors. To find out what is really going down here, perusing *Proceso* is a must.

In recent years, the magazine's savvy investigative reportage has buoyed its stock on the international market. Now, each week, *Proceso* is available at better international news stands in Madrid, New York City, Los Angeles,

San Francisco, and, of course, Washington D.C.—in addition to the kiosk right down the street from the U.S. embassy on the Paseo de Reforma, in Mexico City. It is strongly suspected that both the U.S. Ambassador and President Carlos Salinas himself receive advance copies hot off the press early each Sunday morning.

Between the incident in San Isidro Ocotal (reported April 5th) and the publication of the public ministry report and its outfall in September, *Proceso* ran no fewer than seven dispatches that speculated on the guerrilla presence in the Lacandón jungle of Chiapas.

But Scherer was not alone in pursuing news of the rebels' existence. In October, *La Jornada*, a ten-year-old "pluralistic" national daily, sent its San Cristóbal correspondent Elio Henríquez, an Avendaño son-in-law, to hunt down the as-yet-unnamed Zapatistas. Ranchers in Las Margaritas told Henríquez about night marches by the rebels and played recordings of guerrilla citizen band broadcasts. An Evangelical preacher testified that the Zapatistas were worrying his flock. Antonio Hernández, of the independent campesino group CIOAC, fretted that his largely Tojolabal base was being invited to join. "Everyone knows they are out there," a soldier at a military roadblock declared to Henríquez. Aaron Gordillo, the director of the local ranchers' association in Las Margaritas, even reported a tall "gringo" had been sighted among the rebel ranks. Henríquez wrote of general war "psychosis" in the zone.

Ladino landowners—the "finqueros" or estate-owners, of Las Margaritas, Altamirano, and Ocosingo—had been fearful of the coming "Indiada" since the Quincentennial. The marking had generated marches and protests in Chiapas as the event had all over Indian Mexico. Ranchers and their wives had written one governor after another about the rising guerrilla threat to their peace and safety. One matron complained to Henríquez that she had communicated the danger directly to Luis Donaldo Colosio, when he barnstormed the region on a pre-campaign swing. The soon-to-be-PRI presidential candidate promised to investigate. No investigation was made. The rebel maneuvers continued.

* * *

Just how much the Mexican government actually knew about the Zapatista Army of National Liberation's operations in the months—and years—preceding New Year's Day 1994 was made perfectly clear during a January 7th press briefing at the Secretary of Interior's Bucareli Street offices in central Mexico City. Undersecretary of the Interior Socorro Díaz, a general's daughter and a staunch Salinas loyalist, presented an astonishing 28-page investigative report, compiled by Interior and the Secretary of Defense. The presentation confirmed that Zapatista activities had been monitored since 1990, detailed their attack plans, gave the location of their training bases, and even the hours at which the "transgressors" trained. The report pinpointed not only the Zapatista stationary bases but also their mobile encampments where the General Command is concentrated. The intelligence report called attention to community safe houses where "revolutionary propaganda" films were shown, but did not list the films. An inventory of the EZLN's arsenal was attached. So were the frequencies and hours at which the "extremists" transmitted on civil bands—the Zapatistas' use of "alleycat" antennas was pointed out. The deluge of details only reaffirmed what had long been suspected: the military had had full knowledge of Zapatista operations for many months prior to January 1st.

There are two possible explanations as to why Carlos Salinas did not move immediately to crush the guerrillas when they were caught off guard last May, writes Castañeda, Mexico's most oft-quoted political "oracle." One is military inefficiency: the message just never went up the chain of command—not a very likely scenario given the sensitivity of the southern border. "Deliberate omission" is the other alternative. "To have entered the jungle in full force would have had international repercussions. Salinas and his advisers decided to postpone the confrontations until after NAFTA was functioning and the August elections had taken place," he wrote in *Proceso*, January 10th 1994.

Marcos and other EZLN officers suggest that the Zapatistas, sensing they were being discounted by the Mexican government because passage of NAFTA by the U.S. Congress was Salinas's abiding consideration, selected January 1st, the very day his pet treaty took effect, to retaliate for being ignored for so long.

Whatever the underlying rationale for selecting the date, Marcos's New Year's Day caper and his comments to reporters in the San Cristóbal plaza, to the effect that the free trade treaty meant the end of the line for Mexico's Indian peoples, would soon have the phones of NAFTA's congressional boosters ringing off the hook.

What Washington Knew and When

John Horton's curious, out-of-print, espionage thriller *The Return of Inocencio Brown* comes to dénouement in the Mayan highland city of San Cristóbal de las Casas when Central Intelligence Agency operatives clink glasses with their Mexican counterparts after finally conceding that the Cuban revolutionary cell they had both been chasing through the Chiapas rain forest was only a figment of their fevered imaginations. "But that was fiction," protests the author, a retired Company man, on the phone from his Virginia home. Horton knows how to sort fact from fiction with élan. As lead CIA Mexico analyst, John Horton earned his 15 minutes of fame in Bob Woodward's once hot-selling *Veil*, a charged account of Reagan era Irangate chicanery and William Casey's last days at the CIA. It was Horton who shortstopped an alarmist 1984 appraisal, prepared by in-house terrorism guru Brian Latell, that placed Mexico on the brink of revolutionary chaos. The report had been submitted at Casey's instigation, to bolster the Old Man's case against Mexico's pals, the hated Sandinistas who, in that era of last gasp Cold War posturing, were just two days' drive from Harlingen Texas. In the Latell-Casey scenario, Mexico was the last big chip to fall in the global domino match between East and West. The collapse of Mexico would have the reds toasting marshmallows right on the White House front lawn.

Now Horton is retired and writes novels based on true-life adventures he can only get past the CIA censors wrapped as fiction. A sometime visitor in Chiapas, Horton was shaken by the misery and the fury of that region's

native peoples when he came through in '92. He is not surprised by the troubles with the Zapatistas. The conditions
are ripe for revolution in Oaxaca and Guerrero too, John
Horton tells Dolia Estévez, the resourceful Washington
correspondent for the Mexico City daily *El Financiero*.
Unlike Latell and Casey, the retired spy isn't crying wolf.

* * *

What did Washington know about the Zapatista
Army of National Liberation, when did Washington know
it, and why wasn't anyone told? This convoluted inquiry is
best answered by reviewing how the U.S. government in
general, and the neophyte Clinton administration in particular, learned of the Indian rebellion brewing in the
Lacandón rain forest months before January 1st, 1994.

U.S. government intelligence-gathering in Mexico
operates through both state-to-state contacts and independent fact-finding. Diplomatic channels are the most public
link between capitals but do not often feature frank discus-
sions of sensitive national security issues, such as guerrilla
activities in the jungle of Chiapas—particularly when dis-
closure might damage common commercial concerns as
was the case in the summer of 1993, with negotiations on
the three side accords to the North American Free Trade
Agreement winding down and NAFTA poised to hit the
floor of the U.S. Congress by autumn. Nonetheless, one
anonymous State Department source in Mexico tells me
that the fact or fiction of guerrilla activity in the Lacandón
was raised at least once at a high diplomatic level, prior to
the November 17th House of Representatives vote on
NAFTA. "The Mexicans told us that it wasn't happening,"
the embassy official remembers.

During the summer of 1993, then-U.S. Ambassador
John Negroponte, finishing up his fourth year as overseer

of the forbidding embassy behind the prison bar-like gates on bustling Paseo de Reforma, was spending a lot of his waking hours peddling a NAFTA-ized Mexico to U.S. Congressional reps, potential investors, and stateside manufacturers considering relocating "south of the border." In his pitch to Chamber of Commerce luncheons, congressional smokers, and conclaves of industrialists, Negroponte harped on the social and economic stability the reform-minded Salinas regime had achieved, the new "Mexican Miracle." But Negroponte ("Blackbridge") is less a high-powered salesman for free market reforms than a crafty diplomat with dark antecedents. Negroponte shuttled between Saigon and Phnom Penh during the 1969 Cambodian incursion and was "pro-consul" in Honduras when Tegucigalpa was the main frame of the CIA-sponsored Contra counter-revolution in Nicaragua. The Ambassador maintains close ties to the intelligence community.

The U.S. embassy in Mexico City has always held strong cards in this suit. With one of the biggest staffs of any State Department enterprise outside of Washington and the largest physical plant of any U.S. outpost in the Western Hemisphere, the block-wide bunker-style installation was designed to counter Soviet expansion into the Americas in the 1950s and '60s. The national security threat presented by the phantasmagoria of red revolution on the U.S. southern border, has kept the intelligence mills humming on Reforma for 40 years. Now, as the red menace fades to black, the mission of U.S. intelligence assets in Mexico has turned to other hot button issues—drugs and immigration, to name two themes that are not always handled through diplomatic channels.

One back channel link between U.S. intelligence gatherers and their Mexican counterparts, is located right on the roof of the Reforma complex. Up there, a nest of satellite radar dishes are said to be the brains of an early warning drug interdiction tracking system, reportedly operated by Mexican technicians but supervised by U.S. military intelligence. The system, reported the *Los Angeles Times'* Marjorie Miller in 1991, links up radar tracking outposts and spotter aircraft throughout southern Mexico, up Caribbean flyways from Colombia, and on the Central American isthmus, with a particular eye to northern Guatemala, presently a key transshipment point for close to 70 tons of Colombian cocaine (DEA estimates) heading north annually.

Stopping the flow of drugs north to the U.S. has been one area of improvement in cooperation between Washington and Mexico City in recent years. Forged during the Bush-Salinas co-presidencies, the developing antidrug cooperation has been much more military than civilian. The underlying reason for military intelligence linkup, says Dr. Sergio Aguayo, who researches security matters at the prestigious Colegio of Mexico, is that Washington wants to circumvent dependence on corrupt Mexican police to stop the drug flow through the country. Bringing the Mexican military on line was greatly enhanced by President Salinas's 1990 elevation of the drug war to national security status, thereby greenlighting the deployment of about a fifth of the Mexican Army and Navy— about 30,000 troops—to make war on drugs. Indeed, it was Salinas's upgrading of drug enforcement cooperation that convinced the Bush White House that Mexico was ready for full-fledged membership in the North American community.

The marriage of military intelligence assets has had its ups and downs. Mexico's closed, xenophobic military institutions are traditionally distrustful of U.S. overtures—if only because the United States has invaded the country they are sworn to defend, on at least three occasions. The Pentagon has sought to melt the Generals' reserve by gifting them with choice hardware. Since 1990, the U.S. has sold Mexico $40 million a year in licensed military equipment under military assistance credit programs. Another $25 million worth of war materials has come in drug enforcement credits with an additional $20 million obtained through State Department narcotics eradication grants, according to Kate Doyle of the privately-funded Washington-based National Security Archives. Mexican officers are encouraged to train in the U.S.—from 1984 to 1993, 725 military officers went north for advance training under the IMET program—150 in 1993 alone.

Sometimes U.S. efforts to strengthen ties with the Mexican military have been effective and sometimes they have flopped badly. November 7th, 1991, was not a good day in this developing alliance. On that morning, the U.S.-controlled radar system, with its command post reportedly right on the roof of the Mexico City embassy, picked up a suspected drug plane, winging north over Guatemala. For reasons that will be made clear, U.S. military intelligence asked Mexican Federal Judicial Police to tail the plane to its destination—but distrust of the federal police drug enforcement units caused the DEA to put up its own craft in order to track the police tracking the smugglers. When the drug plane finally put down on the Plain of Snakes near Tlaxicoyán in southern Veracruz, the "judiciales" went in after the narcos. As the police bailed out of their plane, Mexican Army troops, stationed on the ground to unload the cocaine, opened fire, killing seven police officers. The DEA, hovering overhead, filmed the one-sided battle in its entirety and later turned over 14 video cassettes to the National Human Rights Commission to force the only recommendation that government body has ever issued criticizing the activities of the Mexican military.

* * *

Such discouraging indicators have led Washington to sharpen its own independent intelligence gathering in southern Mexico. 45 Drug Enforcement Administration agents operate in country, with Mexican government permission, and the agency has developed an extensive network of informants in narco-zones throughout the nation. One growing area of concern: the Guatemalan border, across which flows about a third of the cocaine entering the U.S. yearly. It is widely believed that the DEA was instrumental in detaining drug kingpin "Chapo" Guzmán on that border at the Ciudad Hidalgo-Tecún Umán crossing in June 1993, days after the assassination of Cardinal Posadas in Guadalajara. DEA assets in the region are described as sophisticated and include fly-over satellite surveillance and electronic eavesdropping capabilities as well as ground-level informants.

For several years, the Zapatista Army of National Liberation has been training, running guns, transmitting radio messages, and occasionally clashing with the Mexican military in the sensitive eastern corner of this much-surveilled border. What did the DEA know about the Zapatistas? Did, for example, the DEA audit EZLN broadcasts prior to January 1st, 1994? Yes but, one informed source retorts. The drug agency's alibi for failing to signal the developing rebellion: it thought the Zapatistas were narcos.

Marcos offers confirmation of this confusion—but elevates the misunderstanding to government strategy. The Salinas government kept denying our existence, he told Blanche Petrich, so when the EZLN General Command received word that the military would launch a major anti-drug operation in the first weeks of the New Year, the Zapatistas struck first. "They would have liquidated us and said we were narcos, just like Chapo Guzmán," the ski-masked leader reflects. "We had to declare ourselves first..." The Zapatistas have actively denounced Mexican government efforts to tie them to drug syndicates ever since.

Besides military intelligence and drug enforcement agents, Washington has one other asset in southern Mexico (although an increasingly dubious one)—the Central Intelligence Agency. Both John Stockwell and Ralph McGehee, ex-spooks who have turned on the Company, insist that the CIA presence in the region is substantial: Chiapas is an oil-producing region—Mexico's last confirmed land-based deposits with perhaps over a hundred exploration sites in the Lacandón jungle alone. And oil always piques CIA interests, the two former agents concur.

The mix of drugs, oil, and guerrillas—the Guatemalan URNG operates across the Usumacinta—makes the eastern Guatemalan border a hot one, so hot that McGehee, the author of *Deadly Deceits*, thinks the Agency has close support teams in the area. The CIA has a long and twisted history of cooperation with Guatemalan security structures that began with the overthrow of the Arbenz government in 1954. In the early 1980s, as Mam and Kanjobal Indians fled north to Chiapas to escape the murderous "Kaibil" units of the Guatemalan Army, Bill Casey grew apoplectic that guerrilla elements were passing themselves off as refugees with the ultimate goal of destablizing Mexico and preaching the overthrow of the Yanqui Imperialists. CIA assets were upgraded in the region, the agent affirmed to Estevez.

Watching Chiapas from both sides of the Guatemala-Mexico border during the summer off 1993, one is hard put to explain how the CIA could have failed to notice that something was brewing in the jungle. In fact, CNN reported in mid-January, soon after the rebellion kicked in, that the Guatemalan military had been feeding certain U.S. embassy contacts intelligence regarding arms movement into Chiapas for many months.

Even if Langley—the headquarters of the CIA—was somehow left out of these loops, there was still one more channel through which Agency analysts could have accessed intelligence regarding the coming Zapatista rebellion—the corner news stand. Actually, Company readers didn't even have to journey to the corner to find out what was coming down in the Lacandón rain forest. The Central Intelligence Agency is a longtime subscriber to the Foreign Broadcast Information Service, which, five days a week, provides up-to-the-minute translations of *Proceso*, *La Jornada*, *El Financiero*, and dozens of other pertinent Mexican publications, many of which carried ample coverage of events in the jungle of Chiapas during the summer of 1993.

Some Mexico watchers, like Tulane University professor Roderic I. Camp, believe the CIA—like the DEA—just read the material wrong. Others such as Georgetown University Mexicologist John Bailey, attribute the omission to the Agency's disorientation as the result of the disappearance of the Soviet menace, a disarray that prevented the spooks from recognizing the first post-Cold War uprising of the Latin poor when it was staring them right in the face. Still others, like this author, think the CIA is guilty of deliberate omission.

On November 17th, 1993, several days after an intelligence briefing in which Agency officials made no mention of a guerrilla resurgence in southern Mexico, Dan Glickman, the Kansas Republican head of the House CIA oversight subcommittee, cast his vote in favor of the North American Free Trade Agreement. Later, he would tell

Estévez that the CIA estimates of Mexico's internal stability were "overly optimistic." Other Congressional voices were less charitable. One aide to Congressman Robert Torricelli, the outspoken New Jersey Democrat who heads the House Western Hemispheric Affairs Subcommittee, wondered out loud if the CIA estimates were compromised to fit the Clinton administration's commitment to the passage of NAFTA. Torricelli's subcommittee would later hold hearings on the Chiapas rebellion, at the conclusion of which the issue of deliberate omission by the CIA remained muffled in murkiness. What did the White House know and when? "We keep asking the White House this," Torricelli told me in San Cristóbal in May. "We don't get a credible answer..."

One of those charged with engineering the suspected omission was CIA terrorism expert Brian Latell, whose 1984 scenario wrongly predicted Mexico's collapse within five years. In November, just before NAFTA came to the House floor, Latell went up to the Hill for a closed door session—not to warn of the impending uprising in Chiapas but, rather, to plead with undecided congressional reps to pass the trade treaty or risk a social and political explosion in Mexico.

* * *

The 13-hour November 17th House of Representatives floor debate on the fate of NAFTA was one more crucial test of the Clinton White House's juice on the Hill. The NAFTA vote came on the heels of the administration's one-vote victory on a tax hike and the nearly as-slim margin on the budget, and was the first in a fall season that was calculated to culminate in the great Health Care debate. In the short, harrowing life of Bill Clinton's presidency, cajoling Congress into voting up NAFTA could be decisive in its tenuous hold on power.

The November 17th vote was the ultimate test for a pipe dream first hatched by Carlos Salinas and George Bush at the Lyndon B. Johnson Space Center in Houston in December 1988 while both winning candidates were waiting in the wings to assume the presidencies of their respective countries. The North American Free Trade Agreement was formally proposed by Bush, Salinas, and Canada's then-Prime Minister Brian Mulroney in November 1990 and negotiations on the economic integration of the northern half of the Americas began forthwith. For two years, the tri-partite talks that would lead to the creation of a 360 million-member consumer market stretching from the Yukon to the Yucatán, chugged along swimmingly. Then the politically unthinkable happened: against all odds, George Bush was evicted from the White House. NAFTA appeared to be on the rocks.

Fearful of alienating Big Labor—which opposed the trade treaty because it portended massive job loss to starvation-wage Mexico—Bill Clinton had straddled the fence on NAFTA until very, very late in his campaign. Finally, with just three weeks left until election day, the Arkansas Governor announced, during a North Carolina University speech, conditional support—but only if side agreements were negotiated dealing with labor conditions and protection of the environment. In March 1993, five months after Clinton's startling upset of Bush and in spite of Mexico's strenuous objections, the three North American would-be free trade partners went back to the bargaining table. By August, the two parallel agreements, plus a third focused on import surges, were signed, sealed, and delivered to the White House. A strategy for moving the enhanced NAFTA through Congress in time to meet the mandated January 1st 1994 start-up date was thrashed out.

What Washington Knew and When

Despite intense and expensive lobbying by 400 major U.S. corporations, banded together behind the banner of "U.S. NAFTA," plus a $24 million slush fund dispensed by the Salinas administration to contract Washington super-insiders like Burston-Marsteller, imagemakers to Third World despots, NAFTA faced a rough uphill battle in the House. Because the treaty was a matter of tariffs, the House had first crack at ratification and thus controlled its destiny.

To many U.S. citizens, NAFTA looked like the unmaking of the American Dream. Times were particularly tough in California and the Rust Belt and the agreement could only torque things tighter by shipping what few manufacturing jobs that remained, south to Mexico. The AFL-CIO made defeat of NAFTA a last-ditch stand in the fight to assert its fading influence with the Clinton White House. The administration began counting congressional heads one by one, beseeching and besieging uncommitted representatives to commit. Many Democrats were leery because of anti-NAFTA sentiments and threatened voter retaliation back home. As the Free Trade bandwagon inched tremulously uphill, it certainly did not need notice of an Indian guerrilla rebellion in southern Mexico to sidetrack it from its still uncertain climb to the top.

In its final hours, the selling of NAFTA became a frenzied media extravaganza. The deal finally came down to single combat between two of the most undistinguished public spokespersons on the North American continent: Veep Al Gore and the pint-sized, maverick Texas billionaire H. Ross Perot. Millions of viewers in NAFTA's three proposed signatory countries hunkered over brews in neighborhood taverns or lounged at home glued to the tube to watch the debate. Pundits were fascinated to discover that so many North Americans could be galvanized by a trade

47

issue—but NAFTA was more than that. The argument over the merits of free trade was mostly about class, as in the working class vs. the ruling one, and the NAFTA controversy featured the first public discussion of the class struggle to be openly displayed in the USA since the Great Depression.

Arrayed against the 400 mightiest corporations in America, their eight-page pull-out sections in the *New York Times*, and a primetime shower of pro-NAFTA TV spots featuring the likes of Lee Iaccoca, was an uneasy coalition of labor activists, environmentalists, human rights advocates, and freelance lefties, whose message of monumental job loss and environmental Armageddon struck a chord in the maw of a country where millions were living on the brink of the abyss. Anti-NAFTA crusaders staged spirited daily demos, hauled around inflated dolphins, disrupted public meetings, and threatened their congressional reps with mayhem if they dared to vote the treaty up.

Print and electronic media expended enormous amounts of space on NAFTA in the run-up to the showdown House vote. For months, the Big Four of U.S. Journalism—the *New York Times*, the *Washington Post*, the *Los Angeles Times*, and the *Wall Street Journal*—x-rayed impacts on both sides of the border. Every facet of Mexico's social and economic fabric seemed to come under scrutiny in the media's rush to get to know its formerly distant neighbor and soon-to-be North American trading partner. Mexico City-based freelancers suddenly found themselves in urgent demand, cranking out background pieces explaining the Mexicans to their new associates. The selling of NAFTA was good for everybody's business.

But despite the heavy news flow out of Mexico during the prelude to the vote, reports of a growing guerrilla threat in southern Mexico did not make the wire services.

What Washington Knew and When

One reason was timing: the May 22nd firefight with the Zapatistas had been eclipsed by the May 24th assassination of Cardinal Posadas in Guadalajara. "We read the reports of the fighting in the jungle but then the Cardinal was killed and we all went to Guadalajara instead—it was a bigger story," explained one colleague, a veteran Mexico correspondent for a prominent Texas paper, who I bumped into in San Cristóbal during the first days of the rebellion. "To tell you the truth, we blew the story. Now we're here trying to catch up with it..." he confessed.

* * *

During the first weeks of the Zapatista uprising, San Cristóbal was peopled with delegations of "observers." One five-person team, holed up at Na'Bolom, the eco-tourist inn and Lacandón research center, was sent in January 4th by the U.S. embassy to "evaluate" the situation and assist tourists trapped in the war zone. The group reportedly included military intelligence and CIA personnel.

Milling about the patio of the pseudo-colonial Mazariegos Hotel prior to a press conference by human rights workers, I asked one of the embassy men why he thought the U.S. press did not pick up the Zapatista story while NAFTA was still hanging fire in Washington. What did he think would have been Congress's reaction to such a sign of mounting instability south of the border?

"Ross Perot just didn't do his homework," postulated Ross Rodgers, a pleasant U.S. "political officer" who will never give me a deep background interview again. What had the embassy known about the coming Zapatista uprising before January 1st?

"You have to understand that our resources are limited. We have a part-time consular office in Oaxaca and one in Mérida but no one here in Chiapas. We have to depend on non-government sources and those sources told us there was no guerrilla threat..."

Wasn't the presence of the guerrillas amply covered in the Mexican press?

"Yes, but the information was confused." Rodgers said the embassy made its call based on the findings of a Minneapolis human rights group, the Minnesota Advocates for Human Rights. A team of observers from the group was in the Cañadas region on the day of the May 24th arrests in Pataté Viejo and spoke with General Godínez at the base camp near the Nazareth drilling compound. The Minnesota Advocates report, published in August 1993, does not focus exclusively on events in Chiapas but it does quite legibly state that the group "has no information about whether there has actually been guerrilla activity" in the state.

During our impromptu tête-a-tête, Rodgers underscored that the Clinton administration strongly supported NAFTA because "we think it is a good thing for both countries." The embassy handled many calls for information about social tensions in Mexico from both pro- and anti-NAFTA members of Congress prior to November 17th, "but not one of them ever asked us about the guerrilleros," Rodgers smiled, playing the Clinton administration's patented "don't ask, don't tell" gambit.

After a 13-hour debate that began promptly at 9 A.M. on Wednesday morning, November 17th and did not wind down until near midnight, the North American Free Trade Agreement squeaked through the House by 34 votes, most of them Republicans whose "Yeas" had been purchased at the last minute by the White House promise of pork barrel patronage for their pet district projects. From the House rostrum that day, Carlos Salinas was lauded as a champion of liberal reform who had brought economic stability and social justice to Mexico. No hint of insurrection in Mexico was uttered, even by Salinas's harshest critics in the U.S. Congress. Would the votes have been there if the developing Zapatista rebellion had been public knowledge?

Ross Rodgers best framed the response: "It is my impression that if Congress had known about the guerrillas on November 17th, NAFTA would have been dead...."

502 Years of Warning

If, in the autumn of 1993, the United States Congress remained uninformed about the possibility of an Indian rising in Chiapas, it was not for lack of warning. 502 years of warnings...

"Tierra! Tierra!" whooped lookout Juan Rodrigo Bermeo from the crows nest of the caravel Pinta on a starry after-midnight in October of 1492 and, with his sighting, the fate of the indigenous peoples of the Americas was sealed. Columbus's logbooks tell us that the first blood was spilled when the invaders set foot upon the white beach at Guanahani Island on the morning of October 12th and the Arawaks, drawn by the glint of steel swords under the tropical sun, rushed forward to touch the razor-sharp blades, slicing open their fingers. The open veins of Latin America have never been stanched.

"I seized by force the several Indians in order that they might learn from us," Cristóbal Colón (Columbus) wrote his Queen as he careened around the Caribbean, sowing terror, slavery, disease, and massacre wherever his ships put in. But the European invasion also planted other seeds, more dangerous seeds. The seeds of rebellion.

The human cost of the European conquest of the "New World" was horrific. When quantified, the genocide becomes a multiple of the Holocaust by ten. The bearded palefaces, with their cannons and their horses, their whips and crosses and, most of all, their plague, spread the stench of death throughout this luckless landmass they would soon call America. "Another more terrible weapon against the naked Indians," wrote the priest Bartolomé de las Casas, who sailed the ocean sea with Columbus, "was the ferocious greyhounds which, when released and told 'at

him!', in an hour tore over a hundred Indians to pieces..."
Of an estimated 100 million indigenous peoples who populated the Western Hemisphere from the Arctic to Tierra del Fuego before the Conquest, 40 million resisted the genocide and survive today.

The Dead did not go quietly. Furious, messianic rebels arose and resisted the invaders until the last defender of their nation was consumed. The memories of the martyrs were kept alive from house to house and generation to generation. Viceroys and Archbishops trembled whenever reminded of the vivid hatred of their subjects. "Indians are forbidden to wear the dress of the country which serves only to remind them of what the ancient Incas wore and brings back memories that cause them to feel more and more hatred for the ruling nation," the Governor of Cuzco decreed in 1781. Naked or clothed, the uprisings of the Indians were unceasing. One Tupac Amaru after another led their neo-Inca armies against the Crown in the High Andes. Tupac Katari and his warrior compañera Bartolina Sisa rose in resistance in Bolivia. Far north, on the Yucatán peninsula of Mexico, the Mayan rebel Jacinto Canek was led into the public square in Mérida with a paper crown upon his head that read: "Risen against God and King," and was slowly broken into body parts by iron rods, his flesh fed to the flames of the Inquisition. But the insurrectionary spirit of his people remained unquenchable.

The cycle of Indian rebellion and retaliatory massacre, uprising, revenge, repression, and uprising again, persisted long after independence from European domination. Violent revolt against the criollo overlords has been a chronic condition in the Americas ever since. In our own gore-encrusted century, the Mexican revolution of 1910-1919 began as an insurrection of landless Indian campesinos. Before the bloodletting had run its course, more than a million native peoples would be gone. The 1932 massacre of 30,000 farmers, El Salvador's last Indians, was another high point of contemporary genocide. The Guatemalan Guerrilla Army of the Poor calculates that an Indian died every hour between 1982 and 1988, resisting the rulers with which that majority indigenous nation is cursed.

* * *

On October 12th, 1992, the indigenous peoples of the Americas celebrated this inextinguishable history of resistance from one tip of the continent to the next. The militant mood that marked the marches and the rallies that day had been building for much of the previous decade. When, in 1984, Spanish King Juan Carlos de Borbón proposed that the Quincentennial anniversary of Columbus's brutal "discovery" of the Americas be celebrated as an "Encounter of Two Worlds," the hemisphere's indigenous peoples were perplexed that 500 years of their suffering could be neutralized to a mere "encounter." Councils were held every year to determine an appropriate response. While some saw the anniversary as a time to mourn or to seek reconciliation with the Conquistadores, more radical indigenous leaders like the Guatemalan Quiché, Rigoberta Menchú argued for a celebration of "500 Years of Indigenous, Black, and Popular Resistance." The decision to organize such a counter-Quincentennial was taken at the massive conclave of America's Indians in Guatemala City on October 12th, 1991.

The Indians' Quincentennial would not only remember past resistance but protest how the victors had rewritten history. Spain, the mother of much of this mischief, was hosting a multi-billion dollar mega-fiesta featuring a super-techno World's Fair and the Summer Olympic Games to white out the stain of genocide. Replicas of Columbus's ships would sail the bounding main again, putting into key American ports, accompanied by majestic flotillas of Tall Ships. Two all-star Christopher Columbus film bios were set for Quincentennial release and a California wine bottled for the festivities. In Columbus, Ohio, funds were subscribed to erect a football-field-high statue of the city's namesake to tower above that mecca of the midwestern industrial plain.

Closer to the ground in the Americas, the mood of Indian peoples was more combative than celebratory. Quincentennial protests were planned everywhere. In April, widespread rioting broke out at the opening of "Expo '92" in Seville, Spain, held on the site of the monastery from which Columbus had planned his voyages. Visiting Quechuas were held responsible. A Native American tribunal in Minnesota delivered a verdict convicting Columbus of genocide and terrorism. In Managua, Menchú, soon to be awarded the Nobel Peace Prize, rallied tens of thousands of indígenas and their supporters from 24 Latin countries that still had native populations and stirred the embers of 500 more years of "Indigenuos, Black, and Popular Resistance." Indians blocked Ecuadoran highways, clashing repeatedly with troops as they marched from the Amazon to the Andes. Bombs tore open statues of the Conquistadores in Colombia and Chile and security forces were placed on maximum alert in Bolivia. In Venezuela, Guajiro Indians attempted to assassinate then-president Carlos Andrés Pérez during a public ceremony. The U.S. State Department issued travel advisories and cautioned personnel to stay off the streets of Latin capitals.

Tensions were particularly scary in the Dominican Republic where Pope John Paul put down to celebrate 500 years of the Christian Evangelization of the Americas before an audience of the continent's Cardinals and Bishops. The Pontiff would also officiate at the inauguration of the just-completed Columbus Lighthouse, a 100-foot-tall laser-lit cross that could be seen 150 miles out to sea, and dimmed the lights of the Dominican Republic whenever it was turned on, so much juice did the monument suck up. "La Cruz de Colón" had cost the fifth poorest nation in Latin America $100 million USD. Impoverished colonies had been torn down around the monument and a wall erected to shield visitors from the unsightliness of what remained of the neighborhood. Rioting and bombings were expressions of the evictees' rage. On October 12th, the military was given shoot-to-kill orders as John Paul's Popemobile coasted through the streets of Santo Domingo on his way to ignite Columbus's cross.

* * *

The survival of Indian Mexico testifies to 500 years of dogged resistance to premeditated genocide. In the first third of a century of invasion—from the Good Friday morning in April 1519 that Hernán Cortez landed on the shores of Veracruz through the census of 1552—Mexico's Indian population was reduced to a tenth of its pre-Conquest numbers, calculates the anthropologist Gonzalo Aguirre Beltrán—as many as 12 million Native Mexicans may have perished. In just a few months in 1545, some 845,000 deaths from smallpox were recorded by the Crown's beancounters. Those who did not die from the pox starved to death in melancholy or were hung from trees as rebels.

The resistance of the Aztec-Mexicas of Tenochtitlán, the island-state that is today Mexico City, vibrates throughout all of Mexico's history. When Cuauhtémoc ("the Descending Eagle"), the brave nephew of the third Moctezuma, was finally captured on August 13th, 1521, the Tlaxcaltecas marked in their histories that "the end of the Mexicans had come" (The Tlaxcalteca Codex). Nonetheless, the young warrior's bones continue to rattle the national conscience. Hanged by Cortez in the distant Mayan territory of Tabasco, Cuauhtémoc's remains were smuggled back to his birthplace in the Nahua Sierra Madre of Guerrero. For four centuries, the Nahuas of Ixcateopán hid his bones until a town priest got drunk and blabbed to a Mexico City reporter.

In Tenochtitlán, Cuauhtémoc is not forgotten. Each August 13th, "cempaxochitl" (marigold) flowers are piled in front of an auto repair shop in the Perelvio colony of Mexico City—the exact spot on which Cuauhtémoc was captured. And in the great plaza that has been at the heart of political life in Mexico since Cuauhtémoc's time—the Zócalo—jaguar and eagle warriors burn copal and consecrate their dances to his spirit. On the brink of the 21st century, Mexico still has many sons who proudly wear Cuauhtémoc's name.

Despite its mestizo patina, Mexico, with the largest indigenous population in Latin America—40% of the continent's 40 million indígenas—remains a very Indian nation. Clustered in 56 distinct cultures and a hundred variations of language, the nation's Indian population exceeds the six million counted by the government's National Indigenous Institute—the INI parameters do not take into account Indians who have lost their language or their land or those mestizos who are reaching for their Indian roots. Genaro Domínguez, the driving force behind the independent National Coordinating Body of Indian Peoples (CNPI) insists that the indigenous population of Mexico totals 20 million, a high-end estimate. What is more statistically verifiable is that the birthrate of Mexico's Indians is growing much faster than the non-Indian population—a third of the nation's indígenas are not yet 18. At this pace, Mexico's native population is expected to finally reach its pre-Conquest census of 16 million early in the next century.

This young, angry generation inhabits a landscape that anthropologist Guillermo Bonfils calls "Mexico Profundo" or Deep Mexico, an unseen and unheard-from nation buried in the remote sierras and deserts of the nation or the less distant but equally out-of-sight "lost cities" ("ciudades perdidas") seething on the outer rims of urban magnets like Mexico City. The citizens of Deep Mexico suffer the highest malnutrition, disease, and infant mortality rates, their average life span is five years less than in non-Indian Mexico and, for the living, life is often like a jail—a quarter of the nation's prisoners are indígenas in a country in which Indians officially account for a tenth of the population. Most of the 15 million Mexicans who live in what the United Nations terms "extreme poverty," a condition in which one earns less in a day than the cost of daily nutritional requirements, are concentrated in the 803 predominantly indigenous municipalities on Mexico's political map.

Racism in Mexico is not much communicated in polite political discourse but it is as pervasive as apartheid under the Afrikaners. Television screens display white people rocking out, draining cokes, lobbing tennis balls, and the message seems to be that darker-skinned Mexicans are excluded from the fun. The presidents have European-sounding names like "De la Madrid" and "De Gortari," are birthed and groomed in walled enclaves peopled by their pink-faced peers, attend prestigious U.S. and European universities, are never out of sight of their personal security escort. The educated upper class has contact with the Indian poor mostly through its maids and a patriotic zest for folklore and the wonderful hand-embroidered "huipiles" (Mayan gowns) available in San Angel's better ethnic-oriented boutiques. Mexico's nostalgia for its Indian past is well-documented in Diego Rivera's epic murals and the monolithic National Anthropological Museum out in the capital's smog-damaged Chapúltepec Park, a mausoleum of Indian culture.

But the remembrances of the past are often pitted against the prospects for the future. Indian people stand resolutely in the path of what passes for progress in modern Mexico, refusing to give up lands for hydroelectric dams or environmental reserves or cattle ranching expansion or shopping centers. They are not very adept consumers. Attached as indigenous peoples are to a distinct place and long-standing traditions, Indian communities are the polar opposite of the global economy in which the Mexico of Carlos Salinas de Gortari has inserted itself.

Making the indígenas into museum pieces has long been the nation's solution to the Indian Question. From independence in 1821 onwards, "Mexicanizing" the Indians has been public policy. Benito Juárez, the country's first constitutional president and a Zapotec from the Sierra of Oaxaca, sent pacified Indian troops to pacify those who had risen in rebellion. After the revolution, the official line became "Indigenismo," a half-hearted effort to rescue the folkloric in the fading memories of more than 50 cultures. Marketing Mexico's Indians as tourist attractions—such as the "Mundo Maya" (Mayan World) megaproject which threatens to do in Chiapas, Tabasco, and the Yucatán—is the free market face of the racism and exploitation that pervades the modern Mexican Miracle.

* * *

Five centuries of accumulated anger, despair, and resistance broke from the throat of Mexico in one enormous "Basta Ya!" as the Quincentennial dawned over the Americas. Thousands of Mixes and Zoques, Zapotecs, Mixtecos, Amuzgos, Tlapanecos, and Nahuas took to the roads of Oaxaca, Guerrero, and Puebla, slowly advancing on Mexico City's Zócalo. Runners from nations as diverse as the Diné and the Quechua had departed from Alaska and Machu Picchu months earlier and now crossed through northern and southern Mexico to meet up first at Teotihuacan, the sacred city just outside of the capital, and then, the next morning, in the Zócalo of Tenochtitlán, the seat of Aztec-Mexica dominion. In that great plaza on the eve of October 12th, 1992, dozens of Indians on hunger strike huddled in the rain under plastic in front of the Metropolitan Cathedral, once a Mexica temple, while on the enormous stone expanse that forms the floor of the plaza, troupes of plumed "concheros" danced to the four cardinal points of the universe and white-clad mestizos offered damp copal and prayed for the coming of the Sixth Sun.

All over Mexico, October 12th, 1992, was a riotous indictment of 500 years of invasion, enslavement, and ethnocide. Just as they have every year for the past ten "Days of the Race" as Columbus Day is known in Mexico, Domínguez's Pan-Indian CNPI attacked the sole statue of Cristóbal Colón in Mexico City, a hulking bronze figure anchored on a traffic island in the middle of Reforma boulevard. "Colón al Paradón!" ("Columbus to the firing squad!") the Indians hooted and, failing to disassemble the Captain of the Ocean Sea, hung a sign around his neck that read "Discovery is Extermination!." The CNPI was followed to the monument by several dozen Mohawk-sporting "punkis" who pelted poor Columbus with balloons that splattered red paint all over his pedestal.

7,500 marchers, not a few of them elderly and barefoot, were led into the Zócalo by a group of Mayan "Men of Corn" from the Xi'Nich ("ant"), a Chiapas campesino cooperative. The protesters swirled and chanted, set off rockets, climbed the Cathedral, blew conch shells, and pounded on drums. Speaker after speaker mounted the podiums to denounce the government's policy of neglect and repression. One banner, carried by Nahuas from the Zongolica Sierra of Veracruz, encapsulated the mood: "They have pulled down our forests, cut our branches, burnt our trunks, but they could not kill our roots."

That evening, Televisa's *24 Hours*, with the sneering anchorman Jacobo Zabludowsky insinuating subversion, reported on some of the more militant outpourings of passion and rage against the Quincentennial afoot in the land. In Morelia, Michoacán, a state where the leftist leader Cuauhtémoc Cárdenas has much strength, a mob had pulled down a statue of the Spanish viceroy, and in San Cristóbal de las Casas, 10,000 Mayan Indians had similarly demolished the figure of Diego de Mazariegos, the European destroyer of the people known as the Chiapas.

Straw
Just Waiting to Burn

"Sticks and stones will rise up in struggle...dogs will bite their masters...those who borrowed thrones must throw up what they swallowed....very sweet, very tasty was what they swallowed but they will vomit it up...the usurpers will depart to the limits of the waters...then there will be no more devouring of man..." prophesied the Chilam Balam, the dictations of the old gods, memorized to the tongue, written down in secret, and carefully hidden by the Mayan priesthood from the intrusions of their new masters.

"We found a large number of these books of characters but since they contained nothing more than superstitions and lies of the devil, we burnt them," boasted Diego de Landa, Bishop of the Yucatán, in 1566.

For the Mayan peoples of southeastern Mexico, prophecy was a serious business. The future that was always coming was first narrated by the gods to the Jaguar Priests—the Chilam Balams—and the words echoed down the centuries in poetry and song and secret ceremony, underground waters coursing deep canyons until they would emerge fullstream in the sunlight as explosions of social discontent and religious exaltation that no one can ever quite explain.

Prophecy and uprising are twin signatures of modern Mayan history. When Jacinto Canek rose on the Yucatán in 1721, half the Mayan nation had already been extinguished by the plague and the sword and the Inquisition. Those who survived heard the voice of the Chilam Balam and took counsel to restore the old gods. In 1847, the talking crosses spoke at Chan Santa Cruz and the Mayans rose against the criollo aristocracy once again. The War of the Castes drenched the Mayan peninsula with the blood of tens of thousands of Indian rebels, and when the killing was done, the peace of the dead returned to the Yucatán. But the river of rebellion cuts deep channels in the Mayan southeast.

From its first days, the Conquest pushed inland, driving the Indians deep into the jungles and mountains for sanctuary. In the eastern jungles, the Lacon-Tums resisted the Europeans from the day they first saw the whites of each other's eyes in 1529 and the guerrilla war lasted two centuries. Pedro de Alvarado marched to the western limits of the Mayan lands in 1522, conquering the Soconusco and, ultimately, Guatemala. Luis Marín slashed south in 1524, subjugating the "Quelenes" (Tzotziles) of the highlands and decimating the fierce Zoctones (or Chiapa), cleansing their cities with fire and smashing their idols: "We found things much worse than the sodomy they practiced," wrote Marín in his *Book of Acts*. Behind Marín came Diego de Mazariegos, the Crown's clean-up man, whose duty it was to pacify the conquered, subdue hostile hold-outs, extract tribute to the Spanish kings, and prepare the way for colonization. In 1528, Mazariegos put an end to lingering resistance, cornering the last band of Chiapas at the Sumadero river canyon, above what is now the Tuxtla Gutiérrez state capital, "They fought until they could no longer raise their arms," Guillermo Bonfils recounts, and then, rather than submit to the rule of the Invaders, the last Chiapas threw their women and children into the swirling river below and then themselves disappeared below the white waters forever.

The jungles and the highlands of Chiapas did not lack for prophets and divinely-inspired rebellions were cyclical.

From 1531 through 1821, for nearly three centuries, Chiapas was a province of the Audiencia of the Capitanía of Guatemala and all its roads and lines of communications led south towards the imperial capital. The province of Chiapas had much more in common with the provinces of Salvador, Honduras, Costa Rica and Nicaragua than with the center of Mexico. Then, as now, Chiapas pertained more to Central America than to the Mexican mainland to which it is attached on the north and the east.

Described by visitors as a re-creation of a Spanish medieval city, Ciudad Real was the arm of the Crown in the region of the Chiapas. The Royal Treasury of Guatemala placed its offices there to exact tribute from its new subjects. In order to safeguard the tribute-takers, troops were stationed and the fortress-like city bristled—much as today—with military might. The Church held court in the great golden Cathedral of what is now San Cristóbal and blessed the systematization of conquest.

The royal city's first bishop, the same Bartolomé de las Casas, who had accompanied Columbus on his third voyage, nearly upset the neatness of this schema. A fierce opponent of the enslavement of the natives, the Dominican ordered his priests to deny the sacraments to those who held Indian slaves (De las Casas was a proponent of the importation of African Blacks for that purpose). Needless to say, the Bishop was not a popular personage among the great landowners of the Chiapas. In 1546, under threat of death, De las Casas fled to Honduras and the Conquest of Chiapas was back on track.

There were, of course, ephemeral deviations. The Chamulas rose against Marín in 1524 and were never quite subdued again. The Lacon-Tums slaughtered priests and taxmen at Pochotla in 1542. The roots of rebellion ran underground all the way to the Yucatán and grew strong in

65

REBELLION FROM THE ROOTS

Los Altos.

The end of the 17th century and the first third of the next one were a particularly restless period in the highlands and jungles of Chiapas, filled with "riots, supernatural acts, paranoiac persecutions by Ecclesiastical authorities, and messianic movements that left a profound mark upon ritual memory," writes Antonio García de León in his monumental *Resistance and Utopia* (Era, 1985). One recurring motif in this period was the apparitions of Virgins and Saints in the forest, spectral light darting from their extra-corporeal presences. The Church's dismissal of such miracles further infuriated the Indians.

In 1712, Salvador Gómez, "La Gloria," and 3,000 "Soldiers of the Virgin" rose against Church and Crown at Cancuc north of the royal city, and the so-called "rebellion of the Tzeltal republic" spread to Ocosingo and 20 more towns like wildfire or the plague. "La Gloria," an itinerant Tzeltal prophet who claimed to have been taken into the sky and advised by the Saints to ordain priests and found a new Catholic Church, ruled in union with the seer María Candelaria. Together, they led their Indian army against the conquerors, slaughtering priests and tax collectors and carrying the old deities back into the churches. With their prophets leading them towards glory, the Indians marched armed only with hoes and machetes upon Ciudad Real, which they had renamed Jerusalem, believing that their mission was so consecrated that lead bullets would not pierce them. As the good burghers of the royal city cowered in their Cathedral, certain that their throats would soon be slit, Spanish troops reached the highlands, first securing San Cristóbal from the fanatic Indians, and then sweeping north towards Cancuc, cutting off the ears of suspected rebels by the roadside, before beheading the visionary leaders of the rebellion.

The revolution dipped underground again, grew strong in the dark caverns, erupted anew in Chamula, the last city to submit to Spanish domination. The year was 1868 and three green stones fell from the sky near Tjazaljemel, a sign. Augustina Gómez Checheb wrapped them in linen and placed them in a wooden box and the stones began to talk, another sign. "The old gods assured victory—the return to the past became the project for the future," writes Bonfils in *Deep Mexico*. Said to have been incited by Ignacio Galindo, an anarchist from far-off Nayarit who was known to drift about Los Altos in a hot air balloon, the Chamula uprising took its cue from Yucatán's War of the Castes in which Galindo had fought, in the Army of the Mayans. Galindo, his wife, and a young follower—ladino outside agitators much as Marcos is today (but renamed as living saints by the Indians)—joined forces with Checheb and her protector, the cacique Pedro Díaz Cuscat, and organized an army to, once again, storm the citadel of San Cristóbal. Checheb's 12-year-old brother was crucified to insure victory.

Land hunger propelled the Chamulas forward as much as did their talking stones and living Saints. The criollos of San Cristóbal so dominated cultivable land in these high pine mountains that the holdings of Chamulans—much as they still are today—were measured in rows and not hectares. But armed only with green stones and an abiding hunger, the Chamulans could not take the former royal city for long. The rule of law returned with a vengeance to make certain the Indians would not rise again for a long time to come. Galindo's saintly body and the corpses of those who had dared to follow him, were left to rot in the plaza of San Cristóbal as a reminder to those who plotted fresh rebellion.

REBELLION FROM THE ROOTS

* * *

The watershed Mexican revolution of 1910-1919 was inspired by the ardor of Mexico's indigenous peoples to reclaim their ancestral lands but such demands were muzzled in Chiapas. Wrenched free from Guatemala in 1821 and annexed to Mexico City three years later by fragile lines of authority, Chiapas was too far south, too much a part of Central America, too hermetically sealed off from the center of the country, to be quickly infected by the fever of agrarian revolution. Power in Chiapas was condensed to a tiny elite class of white "finqueros" (the "finca" is the Central American equivalent of the Mexican "hacienda" or great estate), augmented by a handful of wealthy German coffee growers who were granted lands in the Soconusco in the 19th century. The Lords of Chiapas directed the affairs of their state much as the Spanish Crown had done in the centuries before them. The Indians belonged to the fincas and, by the Spanish laws of "encomienda" and "peataje," were obligated to serve their masters under the pain of the rawhide whip and the noose. The "derecho de la noche," the right of the finqueros to violate Indian women who worked their ranches and estates, is not unknown today in some backwaters of the state. Refusal to work the "trabajo de balde," free labor required by the finquero in return for permission to farm a garden plot, led to corporal punishment. Those who dared to rebel were pressganged and marched off in chains to the Lacandón jungle to fell the enormous mahogany and cedar forests in the "monterías" (slave labor logging camps).

Squatting by the side of the highway outside of Ocosingo just this year, Elias, a bilingual teacher in his 30s, recalled his father being flogged with a dried bull penis by the Patrón and his mother's fingers being burnt by a cruel mistress—"she has been paralyzed ever since. Come to my house and I will show you," Elias invited *La Jornada* reporter Roberto Garduño. Helicopters circled menacingly overhead. "We keep getting hit in the head but that doesn't mean we're so stupid that we forget the proclamations of our ancestors. How could the Zapatistas not rise up? This is 1994. The prophecies say everything will change for us this year..." Significantly, in January 1994, an image of the Holy Child, emitting darting rays of spectral light "rayos lucentes," was seen in the woodlands of the Lamantán ejido near Las Margaritas.

Despite the living resentments of its poor, the Mexican revolution did not visit Chiapas until 1914 and then only in appearance. Landowners banded together to prevent the spread of general uprising to the region, explains Araceli Burguete, a San Cristóbal sociologist who was driven from her home after being shot in 1987. The ruling elites, known as "mapaches" or "raccoons," for the figurative masks they wore, passed themselves off as "Zapatistas" although the only similarity the Zapatistas of Chiapas shared with the impoverished campesinos of the rest of Mexico was their distaste for Emiliano Zapata's arch-nemesis and eventual assassin, Venustiano Carranza, who had himself promulgated a wide-ranging agrarian reform. Zapata and Carranza were both assassination victims by 1920 and the Mapaches of Chiapas struck a deal with the Generals in command of the revolutionary government by which the "reparto"—or distribution of land to those who work it—would not be applied to Chiapas. Instead, an unofficial dispensation, allowing each elite family to hold up to 20,000 acres (8,000 hectares), was granted. "Here, there was only the counter-revolution," says Burguete.

The frustrations of the indigenous farmers of Chiapas—roughly a third of the state's 3.1 million population—have simmered underneath since the revolution was denied. When, at last, the "reparto" did come to Chiapas in the 1930s, during the progressive-minded presidency of Lázaro Cárdenas, the generals who administered the land distribution passed out to the Tzotzil, Tzeltal, Tojolabal, Chol, Zoque, and Mam peoples of the southeast, the worst lands on the sides of mountains so steep that campesinos had to tie themselves to trees to plow, while the ranchers continued to hold great swathes in the rolling valleys.

By the 1960s, the demand for land in the highlands had become so explosive that the National Indigenous Institute began settling the landless of Los Altos in the lowland Lacandón, a short run "safety valve" solution that only led to increased social turmoil and environmental devastation. Land hunger remained the detonating issue—in Chiapas, the average arable plot farmed by half the indigenous campesinos is less than 2.5 acres while ladino ranchers are known to run a single prize bull on 30 acres of prime grazing land.

The underground river of resentment burst through the subsoil again at San Andrés Larrainzar in the spring of 1974, the Tzotziles rushing from house to house, threatening to cut the throats of the ladino landowners with their machetes unless they abandoned their farms and ranches. No more than a dozen died but Cancuc and Chamula are never far from memory in Los Altos of Chiapas. The ladinos packed up and left.

Other manifestations of indigenous rage were more politically than physically vindictive. Militant, left national campesino organizations like the Communist Party-inspired CIOAC and the neo-Zapatista Coordinating Body of the Plan of Ayala (CNPA) built rural bases throughout the state, seized fincas, and occupied them until they were violently expelled by the military. The 1980 massacre at

Golonchán, under the command of General Absalón Castellanos, was one high-water mark of the repression.

During the governorship of General Castellanos (1982-88), the military and state security forces combined with the ranchers' private militias, the notorious "White Guards" ("Guardias Blancas"), to suppress land takeovers and murder independent campesino leaders. Names like Andulio Gálvez and Sebastián Núñez and Arturo Albores still live on the walls of Comitán and Simojovel and Venustiano Carranza to remind the campesinos that the war of Chiapas is hardly done with yet. But then, the Mayans of Los Altos and the Lacandón do not much have to be reminded that their resistance to the Conquest has never ended. "Sticks and stones will rise up in struggle: spoke the Chilam Balam, "the dogs will bite their masters..."

* * *

Zooming in from the satellite flyover, one finds Chiapas in the southeast corner of Mexico, a 74,000 square kilometer bulge (3.8% of Mexico's total land surface) of mountains and tropical forests, butt up against the Gran Petén of Guatemala on the south and the Pacific to the west. 9.7% of all rainfall in Mexico falls on Chiapas, an entity that produces 20% of the nation's energy needs, including 45% of its hydroelectric capacity. 92,000 barrels of oil and 516 million cubic feet of natural gas are daily extracted from the subsoils of Chiapas. 3.2 million Mexicans—many of them boomtime latecomers—inhabit this resource-rich state. A third of all Chiapanecos are members of ten Mayan cultures, concentrated in Los Altos and the Lacondon, the two poorest of Chiapas's eight geographical sections. The shocking disparities between the indigenous peoples and the rest of the state's citizens in

71

economic and political standing, has long fostered tinder-box tensions. Zoom the satellite picture a little closer to the ground and scan the dry, combustible grasses of Indian Chiapas. It looks like straw just waiting to burn...

The radiograph of impoverishment here has been printed out in reams of statistics compiled by Pronasol, the Salinas administration's "Solidarity" anti-poverty program. Although the state generates nearly half of Mexico's energy needs, 63% of the homes in Chiapas do not have electrici-ty. 90% of the homes in which the 1.2 million indigenous peoples of the state reside do not have potable water. Although Chiapas produces 28% of the nation's meat sup-ply, 90% of the indigenous communities censused rarely eat meat. Chiapas has the highest illiteracy percentages—30%—of Mexico's 31 states and the federal district. Salaries are three times lower than the national average and 40% of the farmers of Chiapas realize only $1.74 USD a day, half the Mexican minimum wage. 64,000 Chiapas families, almost all of them Mayan Indians, farm coffee, a crop that has lost 60% of its value on the international market since prices crashed in 1990.

An x-ray of the physical body yields more bad news. More people die in Chiapas than in any other Mexican political entity—the state has the highest total deaths per 100,000 citizens in the union. These numbers are nour-ished by infant mortality indicators double the national average (66 vs. 33 per 1,000) for the deaths of children five years of age and under. There are .54 doctors for each 1,000 patients in Chiapas—compare this to the belea-guered island-nation of Cuba which has 3.7 doctors for the same number of citizens. A third of all adult deaths are due to curable infectious diseases according to harried public health authorities.

"Where I live, everyone dies of illness—they die without anyone having to kill them," a Zapatista captain told Herman Bellinghausen, editor of *Ojarasca*, a journal of indigenous interest, as the two conversed outside of Guadalupe Tepeyac, a jungle hamlet 10 kilometers from the Guatemalan border. A controversial "Solidarity" hospital has recently been built in Guadalupe Tepeyac. In August 1993, with the Zapatistas afoot in the surrounding jungle, Carlos Salinas and his political heir, Luis Donaldo Colosio, helicoptered into Guadalupe Tepeyac to dedicate the facility. After the ribbon-cutting, hospital equipment was removed from the building and trucked back to the state capital at Tuxtla Gutiérrez, claims Subcomandante Marcos.

* * *

The abundance of death in Chiapas is matched by a startling scarcity of liberty. Since 1929, the ruling party has looked upon Chiapas, and neighboring Tabasco and Veracruz, as its "green reserve," year in and year out delivering not quite 100% of its votes to the imperial rule of the ruling PRI. The Institutional Party's "aplanadora" (steamroller) guarantees it virtually every elected municipal, state, and federal office in Chiapas. On January 1st, 1994, the ruling party controls the governor's mansion, all of the state's two senators and nine federal deputies, 19 out of 24 members of its state legislature, and 111 out of 112 municipal presidencies. This arrangement is called, in Institutional Party argot, a "carro completo" or a "full car."

On a cool spring day in 1988, PRI presidential hopeful Carlos Salinas came to the Plaza of San Cristóbal, wrapped in a black chuj not unlike the one Subcomandante Marcos would affect in the same square six years later. The former skinflint budget minister proclaimed his "solidarity" with "los que menos tienen" ("those who have the least"—a "Solidarity" slogan). To a select gathering of bussed-in PRI campesinos ("accarreados"—those who are driven in), the future president explained how he would "modernize" their ejidos. If one is to believe the 1988 election results, such stumping paid off handsomely for the PRI—no state gave Salinas a greater percentage of its vote. In the municipalities of Ocosingo and Palenque, 218,000 votes were cast for the PRI and less than 4,000 for left-opposition candidate Cuauhtémoc Cárdenas. The totals represented 102% of registered votes. 10 municipalities apparently gave Salinas all their votes: "zapatos" or "shoes" such wipe-outs are called. One town, Tila, near the Tabasco line, was swept 12,070 to zero by Carlos Salinas.

"We have never voted here," a Tzeltal farmer on the Morelia ejido outside Altamirano told me this spring. "There is no voting booth here—never has been one...every election day, the PRI would come and take our voting cards and go vote for us in Altamirano..."

The eccentricities of the Mexican electoral calendar inflicted both a presidential and a gubernatorial vote upon Chiapanecos in 1988. The PRI awarded the governor's job to one Patrocinio González Blanco Garrido, whose father, Salomán Blanco, had also once been governor of the state—so power flows in the kingdom of Chiapas. Another illustrious ancestor was Patrocinio's uncle Tomás Garrido Canabal, governor of neighboring Tabasco, whose pathological pogrom against the Catholic clergy inspired Graham Greene's *The Power and The Glory*.

Salinas's halcyon years at the helm of the nation were also Patrocinio's years as lord of Chiapas—the two have firm family ties that date back to their fathers: González is married to the daughter of Antonio Ortíz Mena, the dean of Mexico's bankers, and Ortiz Mena is the uncle of Salinas's highborn wife, Cecilia Occeli. In a tiny closed world of arranged marriages and strict family loyalties, Patrocinio and Carlos call each other cousin.

Despite his aristocratic lineage, the bald-pated Patrocinio González was seen as a progressive when juxtaposed against his predecessor, the tyrannical General Castellanos. The new governor's gleaming dome was seen as the light at the end of the tunnel by many Chiapanecos in 1988, particularly those dissidents released from Cerro Hueco prison by his inauguration day pardon.

The blood of Tomás Canabal pounded in Patrocinio's veins. His late uncle's celebrated disdain far the Romish Church immediately got the Governor into hot water with the state's Catholic hierarchy. One of González's initiatives was to ram the first-ever Mexican abortion-on-demand law through the state legislature, a thrust that enraged Chiapas's three Catholic bishops, most prominently the noted liberation theologist Samuel Ruiz, who displayed gruesome full-color photos of aborted fetuses in front of the San Cristóbal Cathedral, while nuns and priests solicited signatures to demand suspension of the abortion law.

Patrocinio's feuds with Don Samuel, the notorious Red Bishop of the Mayan highlands, are legendary. Patrocinio's police jailed the Bishop's priests for inciting land takeovers—the Governor had one trouble-making, Belgium-born padre thrown out of the country. Don Samuel issued pastoral letters decrying the Governor's aggressions against those who had the least.

Patrocinio's high-handed management of the state's tinder-box tensions extended well beyond the Church. During his years in office, 700 indigenous campesinos were jailed, often in Cerro Hueco, for crimes relating to land ownership, estimates Antonio Hernández of the left agricultural workers' group CIOAC—CIOAC leadership was seriously split by the Governor's Machiavellian carrot (Solidarity funds) and stick (police repression) manipulations. Other vulnerable sectors fared no better during Patrocinio's reign. 12 lethal assaults were reported against local newsgatherers (two were murdered), records the Chiapas chapter of the Union of Democratic Journalists (UPD), and 16 homosexuals (perhaps as many as 25), almost all of them Tuxtla Gutiérrez transvestites, were murdered with police-caliber slugs to the head, without anyone ever being charged. "We thought he was a very charming man," remembers Pepe Covarrubias of the Gay Cultural Circle, who was invited in to discuss the then-unsolved killings with Patrocinio. In January '94, in part due to the Zapatista uprising, Ignacio Flores Montiel, Patrocinio's state security force chief and his father's long-time bodyguard, was taken into custody at the Tuxtla airport while trying to flee the country and charged with, among other crimes, having covered up the killings of the homosexuals.

Early in 1993, Carlos Salinas surprised the nation by firing his powerful Secretary of the Interior Fernando Gutiérrez Barrios, a national security-oriented politico with designs on the presidency. Cousin Patrocinio was asked to assume the position. While the rest of the nation shuddered at the prospect of having such a hardliner as head of Mexico's internal security apparatus, Chiapas breathed a sigh of relief—but relief proved only momentary. The appointment of Patrocinio's "compadre"—extended family brother—as interim governor, boded more of the same for the poor of Chiapas. Patrocinio would continue to control Chiapas through the puppet administration of his substitute, the extravagantly European-named Elmar Setzer Marseille.

Straw Just Waiting to Burn

* * *

On the eve of the 500th year of the European Invasion of Indigenous America, the enigmatic masked man whom all Mexico now recognizes as Subcomandante Marcos sat down at a battered Olivetti portable "somewhere in the Lacandón jungle" and pounded out a treatise describing the social and physical landscape of his adopted state. What the Subcomandante entitled "The Southeast in Two Winds, A Storm, and A Prophecy" but issued on Econet as "A Reality Tour of the Heart of Chiapas," is an instructive vision of that conflictive state as the Quincentennial approached.

"Let's suppose that you decide to visit the state of Chiapas. Let's suppose that you drive the Pan-American Highway. Several kilometers beyond the state of Oaxaca you will see a big sign that reads 'Welcome to Chiapas'. Welcome to Chiapas—the poorest state in Mexico," Marcos writes in his anti-travelogue.

"Let's suppose that you drive on down to Tuxtla Gutiérrez, the state capital. Tuxtla is primarily a large warehouse for products from other parts of the state. You go on to Chiapa de Corso, without noticing the Nestlé plant there, and begin to climb into the mountains. You have entered another world: an Indigenous world in which millions live.

"If Tuxtla is a large warehouse, San Cristóbal is a large market. From many different routes, wood, coffee, cloth, handicrafts, fruits, vegetables, corn—the tribute of the indigenous Tzeltales, Tzotziles, Choles, Zoques, and Tojolabales—reaches capitalism. This is the poorest region of the poorest state in the country. In San Cristóbal de las Casas, you can buy or sell anything, except indigenous dignity. Here, everything is expensive except death.

"Continue along the road, the proud result of tourist infrastructure. In 1988, there were 6,270 hotel rooms, 139 restaurants, and 42 travel agents in the state. This year, one million tourists visited Chiapas and left $81 million USD in the hands of the restaurant and hotel owners. There are 70 hotel rooms for every 1,000 tourists but only three hospital beds for every 10,000 Chiapas residents.

"Drive on and notice the police officers in berets jogging along the shoulder of the road...leaving San Cristóbal, you will see the world-famous caves, surrounded by leafy forest. Do you see the sign? This national park is administered by the Army!

"Do you see the modern buildings, nice homes, paved roads? Is it a university? Workers' housing? No, look at the sign next to the cannons: General Army Barracks of the 31st Military Zone.

"Go to the famous Lacandón forest of Ocosingo, but on the way be sure not to look to your right at kilometer seven. You will see another magnificent construction with the noble symbol of "Solidarity" on the facade. This new building is a jail, a gift of President Salinas. Now peasants will not have to go all the way to Cerro Hueco....

"Continue on to Oxchuc to look at the beautiful waterfalls where the Jacaté river begins. Drive on until you reach Ocosingo, 'the door to the Lacandón forest'... Take a quick look around the city. What are the principal points of interest? The two large buildings at the entrance are brothels, next door is a jail, the building beyond is a church. This one is a beef-processing plant, that one an army barracks. Over there is the courthouse, the municipal palace, and way over there is Pemex. The rest are small, piled-up houses that crumble when the huge Pemex trucks go by.

"Do not follow the road that goes to San Quintín, in

front of the Montes Azules reserve. Do not walk for three eight-hour days to the poor, small community of San Martín. Do not approach that shed that is falling apart and is called a school. Do not look at the groups of children, riddled with tapeworms and lice, half-naked. Do not look at the young bi-lingual teachers who work for miserable wages. Do not look at the AIDS prevention posters, the only thing the government sends these children.

"Better to move on, return to the paved roads. Do you see the National Indigenous Institute as you leave the city? Do you see those pick-up trucks? They are given on credit to indigenous peasants. They only take unleaded gasoline because it is better for the environment. There is no unleaded gas in Ocosingo.

"The government is worried about the peasants. Evil tongues say that the government's Solidarity help is really intended to buy indigenous peoples' loyalties, but these are just rumors, surely. The Citizens' Defense Committee? It consists of heroic cattle ranchers, merchants, and corrupt union bosses...

"Let's go to Yajalón—so modern it even has a gas station. Look, there is a bank, over there by the army—it looks like another hacienda. Ah, there goes an indigenous march. It is going 1,100 kilometers to Mexico City. There, the government will receive the indígenas' petitions. Yes, that is all.

"Do you want to go to other places? Throughout Mexico, you will see the same things. The colors will change—the languages, the countryside, the names—but the people, the exploitation, the misery, and the death are the same.

"It will not always be this way. There are other winds beginning to blow."

REBELLION FROM THE ROOTS

* * *

500 years after Columbus drew his first Indian blood on Guanahani, Chiapas was crackling hot. State security police rushed from one community to another, stomping down hot spots only to have the grass ignite in the next municipality. In April, campesinos battled the state police near the exquisite Mayan ruins in Palenque over land expropriated for the tourist megaproject "Mundo Maya." Over 200 Choles were thrown in jail—the Xi'Nich set off on its 1,100-kilometer march to the capital of the republic and, as Marcos reports, received no response from their government. Earlier that spring, the ANCIEZ, from which the Zapatistas would soon bloom, had briefly seized the Ocosingo municipal palace, sharpening tensions with the region's ranchers. Land takeovers led to armed confrontations. "The only thing you can accuse the ranchers of doing is defending their property," Patrocinio declared from the safety of the State house. In the Dodge City-like ambiance of Las Margaritas and Altamirano, the ranchers tuned in their CB radios and audited what they perceived to be plans for armed insurrection, timed for October 12th, and they took out large newspaper advertisements in the *Diaro del Sureste* ("Southeast Daily") to advise the general populace that the Red Apocalypse was coming.

Although, as usual, the pro-Patrocinio press accused Samuel Ruiz of fomenting Bolshevik-Indian revolution, the truth was a little less toothrattling. What Don Samuel had in mind was celebrating Mass—although, afterwards, the faithful were not dissuaded from attending the march through San Cristóbal, planned by the "Common Front of Social Organizations—500 Years of Struggle and Resistance of the Chiapas People." Prominent among the march organizers was the CIOAC's Antonio Hernández and Domingo López Angel, the outspoken leader of the

CREACH, Tzotziles expelled from Chamula because they embraced evangelical beliefs—politics and prophecy keep blending in the Altos of Chiapas. At a press conference on the eve of the Quincentennial, the organizers estimated 5,000 indígenas would march to mark five centuries of painful resistance. 17 social associations from 32 communities in the municipalities around San Cristóbal would participate. Angel predicted the mood would be militant.

"Something could happen here," Patrocinio warned *La Jornada*'s Henríquez, inviting all sides to step back and reflect. "I want it clearly established that the Governor will use public force to guarantee order and the rule of law." The authentic "coletos" locked their solid oak front doors and shuttered their windows in anticipation of the long-awaited "Indiada" that was coming on the morrow.

Despite Patrocinio's stern admonitions, state and municipal police stood helplessly on the sidelines October 12th, 1992, as 10,000 enraged Indians marched through the cold stone streets of colonial San Cristóbal, screaming "Colón Al Paradón!" and other even more colorful invectives within earshot of the hated "coletos." The marchers' numbers were swollen beyond the wildest estimates of the organizers by the arrival of 5,000 militants from the ANCIEZ organization, who reportedly had expropriated buses and trucks to travel up from the edge of the Lacandón to demonstrate their own techniques of resistance. Many members of the ANCIEZ contingent carried bows and arrows and marched, one observer remembers, with a certain military precision to their configurations.

Beyond Santo Domingo church, outside the local archeological museum, the marchers abruptly halted in front of a statue of the Conquistador Diego de Mazariegos, exterminator of the Chiapas. Ropes were fastened around the Spaniard's neck and ANCIEZ members smashed at his pedestal with sledgehammers. Within ten minutes, the Indian killer was pulled to the ground as thousands of indígenas cheered. Then, with practiced moves, says another observer, the ANCIEZ contingent hoisted de Mazariegos's bronze corpse up on their shoulders "just like he was a 'muertito' (little dead one)" and stomped off down the cobbled street to the Plaza of the 31st of March where a can of gasoline was produced. Although repeated attempts to melt the old man were unsuccessful, de Mazariegos was so charred by the experience that he never again stood on his still-vacant pedestal.

By the next morning, the ANCIEZ too was gone, pulling back to the jungle just as their next avatar, the Zapatista Army of National Liberation, would escape two years and 81 days later. Amado Avendaño remembers that the last ANCIEZ organizers disappeared quietly from San Cristóbal in February 1993, four months later, reportedly after a secret council in Sabanillas. The organization made one final brief appearance under the ANCIEZ insignia at a march in Tuxtla in April, then slipped back into the jungle. In May, there was the first deadly confrontation with the Army in the Sierra of Corralchén. The war would soon begin.

The War in Chiapas

On the first morning that the military unsealed the roads out of San Cristóbal, we encounter five Tzotzil women walking single file along an uninhabited stretch of Highway 188, hunting down a strayed cow. Two of the women are leading black dogs on long strands of bright green ribbon. They all chatter excitedly in Tzotzil—the women have just found a corpse and want to take us into the cool pine forest to view the remains. The dogs dash eagerly ahead, smitten with the scent of decaying meat. The dead man is splayed on the forest floor. He has been thoroughly eaten by animals and birds of prey and only his grisly ribcage and the skeletal structure of his skull are still intact. Like all the half-eaten dead in this land where los "Muertitos" get up and dance every Day of the Dead, he seems to be grinning.

Someone in our crew speculates the dead man has been here since the Battle of Rancho Nuevo, ten days previous. He is clearly a Zapatista—the white bones in his pant legs are still planted in black rubber boots, the footwear so emblematic of this ragtag army.

We turn back to the highway, leaving the dead Zapatista to mulch with the generations of bones that rattle beneath the military base. Rancho Nuevo, the campus-like site of the 31st military Zone of the Mexican Army, was built upon a Tzotzil graveyard.

* * *

The war in Chiapas was joined soon after 7 A.M. on Sunday, morning, January 2nd, 1994, 12 kilometers south of San Cristóbal, at Rancho Nuevo. The 500 Zapatistas

83

(the EZLN had arrived with only 400 fighters) who marched out of the old colonial city in the dank mists before dawn, leaving the Municipal Palace smoldering behind them, dug themselves in to the north and south of the base, first feinting an attack from the north and then opening fire from the south side of the neatly-landscaped installation. "An army that is hungry for weapons and ammunition must go where these things are," Subcomandante Marcos later reminisced.

Reduced to a skeleton crew by holiday leave, as few as 180 men may have been on duty at Rancho Nuevo the morning after New Year's. Lieutenant Colónel Pablo Ruiz, the subcommander of the base, is hesitant to divulge the true strength of his forces that day but does concede that his men "faced a rain of bullets" from the perimeter and "cruel exchanges" between the Army and the guerrilleros cost him "valiant soldiers." The gunfire continued on and off all morning with both sides taking pains to haul away their dead and wounded—Ruiz is angered that one of his dead was apparently set afire by the EZLN forces.

The other Subcommander, Marcos, says only that the federal troops fought well. Like his Institutional Army counterpart, the Zapatista military strategist is reluctant to divulge how many combatants the EZLN lost at the Battle of Rancho Nuevo.

Both sides were quick to call up reinforcements. Helicopter gunships were sent in from Tuxtla in the west. Seven kilometers down 188, a sinuous two-lane blacktop that slices north towards Ocosingo, young Zapatista troops stormed the Social Readaptation Center #5, the local "Cereso." a jail built by the Solidarity program. The inmates, 173 men and five women, virtually all of them Mayan Indians, had been awaiting liberation since Zapatista broadcasts had begun the previous morning, promising that the prisons would be emptied out. Those guards who had not fled in terror at the news tore off their uniforms and tried to pass themselves off as prisoners. Now the newly-freed inmates turned the jail upside down, strewing Christmas ornaments everywhere, carrying off the food and the medicines and what rusty weapons they could find on the premises. One group of young men sped up 188 in a commandeered microbus towards Rancho Nuevo when they were strafed head-on by a Huey gunship roaring down the valley to cut them off, the first aerial attack of the war. 14 young men, presumably rebels, were killed in the confrontation, their mangled bullet-riddled bodies dumped on the roadside and deliberately allowed to rot there for days, reporters said, as a warning to other "transgressors of the law."Ten days later, the death van was still tilting precariously on the shoulder, dried pools of blood spread like blooming roses on the glass-strewn surfaces of the interior, mute testimony to what happens to those who would rebel against the rulers of Chiapas. A century and more after the Chamula uprising was crushed, Ignacio Galindo's corpse left to decompose upon the San Cristóbal plaza, the Mexican military was still deploying such terror tactics to discourage popular support.

As night fell, the rebels re-initiated their offensive. Marcos's strategy was to draw the enemy out to the perimeter of the base where Zapatista snipers picked them off from concealed positions in the hills fronting Rancho Nuevo. Meanwhile, EZLN commandos reportedly circled to the undefended rear of the base and penetrated the fence—the hit on the armory yielded 180 automatic weapons and an undisclosed number of grenades, a rebel dispatch boasted four days later.

After securing the safety of the weapons cache, "we did what a good army does when it has accomplished what it came to do—run." But the retreat from Rancho Nuevo was not so orderly as the Subcommander might have planned. Marcos was forced to jettison his battered old Olivetti—"I had brought it along to write out orders—this was before the days of the communiqués," he told avant-garde playwrite Vicente Leñero. "I'll have to ask General Godínez for it back one of these days..."

By daylight on Monday morning, the Subcomandante and the troops under his command, were already moving southeast, climbing the alpine ridge above Ocotal—where the first run-in with the military had occurred in March—breaking through the surrounding hump-backed hills at Chanal, and dropping down into the tropical jungle of "Las Cañadas," the canyons, the EZLN's base area 150 kilometers from Rancho Nuevo as the crow and the Zapatista Army flies. Having rolled into San Cristóbal the night before, 5,000 Mexican troops were right behind them.

Zapatista forces occupying Las Margaritas, Altamirano, Ocosingo, Oxchuc, and Huixtán were ordered to withdraw by Monday afternoon at the latest. Outside of Huixtán near noon, a team of reporters from *Excelsior* and *El Tiempo* was stopped and relieved of their press passes and a total of 700 new pesos (about $250 USD) in cash. War taxes, the young Zapatista told the reporters, collected under the revolutionary laws promulgated in the Declaration of the Lacandón Jungle.

Despite the tactical retreat of the Zapatistas, the reinforced defenders of Rancho Nuevo continued to take incoming fire for ten days. SEDENA issued daily bulletins from Mexico City that reported fire on the base from the surrounding hills, a threat deemed grave enough to require the relentless pounding of outlying communities by ground artillery and the Mexican Air Force, to root out suspected guerrilla nests.

The War in Chiapas

* * *

Ocosingo, 60 kilometers below San Cristóbal to the north, a crumbling commercial center of 50,000 that bills itself as "the Gateway to the Lacandón Jungle," was a key piece in the Zapatistas' military gamble. The city had long been fingered as the rebels' target. Discovery of the mock-up of Ocosingo Municipal Palace by the Army when it hit the training camp in the Sierra of Corralchén had tipped the EZLN hand to alarmed city officials, months before. The massing of Zapatista elements December 30th at San Miguel ejido on the Ocosingo edge of the jungle seemed to confirm that attack was imminent—General Godínez had even met with municipal officials after aerial reconnaissance substantiated the Zapatista concentration of forces. But Godínez was under strict orders not to publicly admit the existence of the guerrilla—technically the Zapatistas did not yet exist. Instead of strengthening the tiny Ocosingo military garrison, scores of civilian state security forces would be sent in to repel a possible rebel offensive

Godínez's preoccupation with a strike upon Ocosingo by the non-existent Zapatistas opened the way for the unimpeded surprise occupation of San Cristóbal, affirms Marcos.

Armed with a threadbare military library, a dog-eared Pentagon manual, a Mexican Army manual of more recent extraction, a volume by an unidentified French general, and the lessons of Mexican history, Marcos borrowed a page from the latter to capture the royal city. The model was Francisco Villa's occupation of Ciudad Juárez on the Texas border in 1911 when the federal troops were tricked into thinking that the Villistas were about to pounce on Chihuahua City 300 miles south. "They say we learned from the Farabundo Martí in Salvador or the Guatemalans but our tactics are purely Mexican, borrowed from Pancho

Villa and Emiliano Zapata," Marcos told Blanche Petrich.

Ocosingo, with its murderous White Guards, equally brutal (and often interchangeable) police, and smug, racist ranching elite, had to be punished by the Zapatistas. The EZLN mobilized 1,200-1,500 fighters for the January 1st offensive. 400 were sent to take San Cristóbal and smaller detachments assigned to occupy the three other municipalities. At least 300 rebels were sent against Ocosingo, infiltrating the city after 2 A.M. on New Year's morn. But police resistance, boosted by the state security detachment headquartered in the Municipal Palace, was much stiffer than up in San Cristóbal. Murderous gunfights broke out as the rebels advanced from block to block through the darkened city. "We were at our end-of-the-year dinner here in the Church convent and someone came to tell us that armed men had entered Ocosingo. We turned on the citizen band radios the taxis use here and listened the rest of the night," recalls Father Jorge Trejo, one of four priests assigned to San Jacinto de Polonia parish, located at the far end of the plaza from the municipal palace. "Around 4 o'clock, the shooting died down and we thought the men had left. But at 6 A.M., when I went to open the church doors, I saw that the rebels had taken up positions around the plaza. There were hundreds of them. 'Shut the doors, Padre, and get back inside' one young man told me..."

The face-off in Ocosingo plaza went on for hours; exchanges of gunfire between the Zapatistas and the 30 to 40 police holed up in the Palacio, were intermittent. "The atmosphere was very special, like a fiesta," Trejo remembers. "Young men brought crates of soft drinks for the Zapatistas..." In between the bursts of gunfire, the townspeople and the rebels shared cigarettes together. A lot of the bystanders had been drinking. Finally, near 3 P.M., the Zapatistas shooed away the drunks and launched their final assault on the palace. Four police officers—two state and two municipal—were killed. Their comrades, stripped to the waist in the heat of the firefight, slowly emerged from the town hall with their hands in the air.

By New Year's afternoon, Ocosingo was under Zapatista control and the fiesta of vindication commenced, the sledgehammers smashing huge, jagged holes in the whitewashed walls of the town hall. The Zapatistas set up shop in the municipal market and the adjacent open air "tianguis" (bazaar) and invited their new neighbors in to dialogue. The rebels had seized the state radio transmitter to broadcast their revolutionary laws and spin ranchero hits for their new fans. The municipal jail was emptied out—despite the injunction against releasing murderers, one person reportedly cut loose was an American, Leo Bruce, accused of killing his Indian common-law wife. The government ISSTE and CONASUPO supermarkets were sacked and an unquantified amount of money expropriated from the local branch of Banamex. The Calzimoda shoe-store was pillaged and the beef processing plant torched. Five members of the Solórzano ranching family were taken hostage.

The mood was still festive the next noon when Rodolfo Reyes Aguilar, a portly *El Financiero* stringer and Juan Carlos Cárdenas, one of *El Tiempo*'s eyes and ears in Ocosingo, were conducted into the market. Refrescos (soda pop) were offered. Reyes had driven in with four battalions (500 men each) from the 30th military Zone in Villahermosa, Tabasco, 200 miles to the east. The troops were now encamped just outside of town. 14 Mexican Air Force planes were in the air and paratroopers would soon be dropping into Ocosingo.

Although the EZLN had reportedly blown up the bridges at La Florida and La Virgen to prevent the rapid movement of reinforcements from Palenque, the military had circumvented the roadblock. Now, Brigadier General Juan López Ortiz ordered his troops to advance on Zapatista positions from the east, cutting off their escape routes back to the jungle. The rebels, concentrated in the flatlands around the public market—a dark, narrow warren of booths—were caught in a rat trap by the military advance. Worse, the civilian population was sandwiched in between.

The troops, armed with mortars and heavy artillery, bore down on the public market. The first shots were fired by the rebels at 3:15 on Reyes' watch. Reyes and Juan Carlos scrambled for cover behind Army lines. The first helicopter swung in low, reconnoitering the distances, circled back towards the hills, and roared in again, blazing machine-gun tracers. "You better get out of here before the good stuff begins," a soldier shouted at the reporters. The two retreated uphill and took refuge in the home of Juan Carlos's aunt.

The fighting in the Ocosingo municipal market was the heaviest of the war. "We were pissed off at the soldiers," Captain Laura told reporters later. "They had humiliated us often and now we wanted to humiliate them." Although the military's big guns were neutralized by the closeness of the combat, the rockets fired by the gunships screamed overhead. "I've never heard such a terrible noise," Major Rolando, a young Zapatista officer told me later. Mortars and fragmentation grenades hurled by the ground troops turned the market into a living hell. The surviving Zapatistas were forced to seek refuge in the surrounding barrio of San Sebastián.

By 8:20 that evening, Rodolfo Reyes seized upon a lull in the action to inspect the damage. Hugging the bullet-scarred walls in the dark, the stringer counted 15 bodies in the market area. Returning to Juan Carlos's house, Reyes was ambushed by soldiers and long guns placed under his nose. He would have been dead meat if one of the grunts had not remembered the "gordo" who had come in from Villahermosa with the troops.

Death was fresh enough the next morning to not yet trouble the nose. The market was strewn with dead Zapatistas—a Reuters' reporter counted 22 bodies, confirming what Reyes had seen in the dark. Nine bodies were found huddled in the market's sewers—dozens of Zapatistas trapped inside the market, had escaped through the Ocosingo drainage system. The bodies of seven young men lay in the market patio—five of the men appeared to have had their hands tied behind their backs. Each had been forced to kneel before being shot once, a "tiro de gracia" (coup de grâce) to the base of the skull. Months after the killings, there is still no official determination as to who the young men were, what they were doing, where they were found, and whether they were civilians or Zapatista rebels. More pertinently, who shot the young men remains shrouded in government and military obfuscation.

Undaunted by the deaths of their comrades, the rebels fought from house to house and the Army responded in kind, insuring that the number of civilian dead would be high. Matilde Vázquez was cut down when a shard of shrapnel pierced her abdomen after a fragmentation grenade landed atop her flimsy roof in the San Sebastián neighborhood. The mother of two was bleeding badly but her husband, Armando García, couldn't even put his head out of the door to scream for help because the bullets were flying everywhere. Finally, he managed to dump his dying wife into a wheelbarrow and, waving a white cloth, cut down back allies to take her two kilometers to the Coplamar IMSS clinic, the Ocosingo hospital, built by solidarity conveniently right next to the town cemetery.

Many victims were being treated, recalls Armando. An IV was attached to Matilde's arm. Then a group of soldiers broke into the clinic, looking for wounded Zapatistas. Armando pulled the IV from his wife's arm and put Matilde back into the wheelbarrow. "I thought we both would be killed if we stayed," he later told *La Jornada* reporter Roberto Garduño. What happened to between eight and 11 patients and visitors after Armando and Matilde left the IMSS has not yet been clarified by the Mexican government. Without proper medical attention, Matilde Vázquez died of her wounds two weeks later.

The battle for Ocosingo continued throughout Monday. Zapatista snipers fired from the rooftops and down below, the soldiers raced through the neighborhoods, kicking in doors and ransacking private homes, hunting the hidden rebels. HUEYs and P-7 Pilatus fighters streaked in from the hills, strafing rooftops and firing on Father Trejo's church, an alleged hotbed of Liberationist priests and nuns. The Padres were not pleased by the barrage. Father Pablo Ibarrarán picked up the phone to complain to the military but the phones were dead. A near-by parishioner got through. "Pinche Cura!" Reyes reports General David Rivera expectorated when he slammed down the phone, "fucking priest! He's got nine rebels hiding in that church!"

Again on the morning of the 4th, the remaining rebels tried to fight their way out of town. The civilian population, caught in the crossfire between the Army and the Zapatistas, continued to suffer grievously. The reek of death was not only above ground that Tuesday. A freshly dug common grave in the Coplamar cemetery would later yield 11 bodies. The military claims the cadavers were those of rebels buried by the EZLN. Edgar Salazar, a hospital worker forced by the military to dig the grave adjacent to the cemetery wall on late Monday afternoon, remembers that at least five of the 11 victims he buried were either wrapped in hospital sheets or were wearing hospital tags. Eight of the victims were shot inside the hospital and three in the street, Genaro Morena Santiago, the municipal grave digger told me later on. "I know. I had to dig them up..."

What happened after Armando García left the clinic with his dying wife in a wheelbarrow, remains as much of a mystery as the authorship of the killings in the marketplace. Wounded civilians, their families waving white flags, who tried to reach the IMSS were reportedly turned away by gunfire. Clinic workers claim they were taken hostage by the soldiers. Reporters who sought to enter the IMSS on January 4th were run off by the troops but later discovered a bloodstained mattress in the IMSS garbage, suggesting that patients had indeed been massacred in their beds.

Many civilians had been slain as the Zapatistas fought their way out of Ocosingo and the sacrifice troubled Marcos months after the battle. In an effort to limit civilian losses, Zapatista snipers, covering the rebel pullout, were forced to stay in fixed positions, "suicide for a sniper," Marcos told Leñero. "The worst thing for a guerrillero is to bring harm upon the civilian population—that hurts more than being captured by the enemy," the Subcomandante confessed.

As the Zapatista fled towards San Miguel and the jungle, the zopilotes (buzzards) settled in on big black wings. In front of the blasted Municipal Palace, troops yelled at small Tzeltal women to stand back as they checked their identity cards and asked the whereabouts of their husbands and sons and brothers. Some were dead. Others had run with the Zapatistas. "These rebels are just kids who haven't killed anyone yet," the Second Sergeant told reporter Linaloe Flores. The leathery, 19-year veteran of the Infantry had led the assault on the Palace that recaptured it from the Zapatistas Sunday night. Still, the Second Sergeant confessed, the Battle of Ocosingo had been worth it, the battle of his life. The last time he could remember having so much fun was back in Guerrero, in December 1974, when he was just a kid and the troops had chased Lucio Cabañas and his embattled Party of the Poor through the Sierra north of Acapulco.

Who won the Battle of Ocosingo? "If we had gone at it one on one ("tu y tu")" says Major Rolando, "we would have won—but we weren't expecting the pinche helicopters..." "Our troops did what they had to do—die for the people," Marcos sighs, conceding about 40 Zapatista casualties—Rolando puts the figure at 22. The military reported only six deaths in Ocosingo and 29 soldiers wounded—but stories of at least 180 body bags stored in a Tuxtla gymnasium commandeered by the military were common in the highlands in January.

But the big loser was the civilian population of this down-at-the-heels jungle city. 47 bodies were exhumed in Ocosingo and 30 more shipped to Tuxtla. Father Trejo thinks 150 were killed in all, the bloodiest fighting of this short, deadly war.

* * *

According to the London-based Institute for International Strategic Studies, the Mexican military structure is the second largest numerically of any Latin power (Behind Brazil)—175,000 troops spread in 36 regions and three branches of service. For the past six decades, the military has been content to serve the civil authority it brought to power in the 1910-1919 revolution, in exchange for an ample degree of autonomy to run its own affairs. Despite its reduced size, the Mexican military is one of the most xenophobic in the Americas, concludes Roderic I. Camp, the Tulane University professor who has been drawing a bead on this institution for a quarter of a century without much success in penetrating the armed forces' tightly-guarded reserve. What makes reading the Mexican military so difficult, considers the author of *Generals In The Palace* is that, despite the Generals' rabidly nationalist mindset, the institution often acts out of self-interest and its own internal logic when taking sides on national issues.

During the Salinas years, the military has buttered its bread with the presidency by performing political tasks usually assigned to civilian security forces: the arrest of Joaquín "La Quina" Hernández Galicia, an allegedly corrupt union leader who, it is reported, financed rival Cuauhtémoc Cárdenas's presidential bid in 1988; the breaking of a miners' strike so that the mine could be privatized and sold to a Mexican metals tycoon; post-electoral mobilizations to discourage Cárdenas supporters from protesting fraud in state elections. But for the most part, the military's attention has been keyed on the drug war—to the delight of Mexico's new trading associates in Washington. To this end, the Generals have been armed to their dentures through U.S. military credits. The drug war has greatly elevated the profile of the youngest branch of the Mexican armed forces, the air force—a service that in 1995 will become independent of the Secretary of Defense. On the eve of the air war over Chiapas, the Mexican Air Force's inventory included over 80 U.S.-supplied helicopter transports and gunships, mostly HUEYs, in addition to some 45 jet trainers and 69 troops transport planes. The frontline strike force was composed of 75 Swiss-made P-7 jet trainers, converted and customized to kill.

The skies were alive over Chiapas from the first morning of the Zapatista uprising. 14,000 troops had been rounded up in the center of the country and airlifted in newly-acquired Hercules transports to Tuxtla's military and civilian airbases. Paratroopers were dropped in to secure Chiapas's three huge dams on the western edge of the war zone—Angostura, Chicoasén, and Malpaso. The three dams, plus a fourth under construction on the Grijalva, provide nearly half of Mexico's hydro-electric power, in addition to supplying juice to northern Guatemala. The P-7s and the HUEYs were active over Ocosingo, in an effort to dislodge rebel snipers from fixed positions on January 2nd and 3rd. In Los Altos, HUEY gunships opened up on the commandeered minibus January 2nd. By late Tuesday afternoon, January 4th, P-7s, based at Rancho Nuevo, were strafing surrounding hillsides in a coordinated offensive to flush the guerrillas from their nests. Civilian populations at Corralitos and San Antonio de los Baños, on María Auxiliadora mountain, appeared to have been deliberately targeted.

Despite warnings from the military that they were entering an active war zone, journalists ventured up the mountain Wednesday morning to inspect the damage. In San Antonio de los Baños, a collection of 40 Tzotzil families, only dogs and chickens scratched and sniffed at the empty streets. Suddenly, the tense mountain silences were perforated by jet fighters streaking in from the west and strafing the forests on the edge of town. The flash and boom rattled teeth as the rockets plowed into the hillside. Sandina Robbins, of MONITOR radio, dove for cover in a nearby house. Inside the wooden hut, five Tzotzil women gasped for breath but insisted they were not afraid. One pulled out her voter identification card, the new kind, with one's picture imprinted upon it, and shook it at the screaming heavens: "Somos del PRI," she hollered back in halting Spanish, "we're from the PRI!" "Somos del PRI, del PRI, del PRI..." her compañeras chorused.

As the planes hit the hillsides up above, tensions on the ground were on a hair-trigger. Troops occupying the plaza of San Cristóbal were now bivouacked behind sand-bagged machine-gun emplacements. That morning, a blue "combi"—Volkswagen van collective taxi—that had allegedly tried to run a military roadblock heading south in front of Rancho Nuevo, was hit by at least 100 rounds from both sides of the highway. By the time reporters got to the crime scene, a rusty .38 had been wedged in the driver's hand. Four people were counted dead inside. Straw on the bodies of the dead indicated that they had been removed from the vehicle and rearranged to justify the Army's barrage. A 10-year-old girl in a pink dress, now blooming with bloodstains, slumped in the backseat. The Army insisted the four were fleeing guerrilleros.

Journalism was a hazardous profession to practice in the highlands of Chiapas during the early days of the war. On Monday the 3rd, Ismael Romero, a reporter dispatched by *La Jornada* to cover the insurrection, was hit and seriously wounded by unknown snipers while driving east on Highway 188—three other reporters riding in the caravan received lighter wounds. On Wednesday January 5th, a crew from the U.S.-based Univisión Spanish-language news was raked by air force fire as they interviewed terrified campesinos in Corralitos. Breathing hard, the debonair star reporter Bruno López pointed at a rocket that had smashed into the forest just meters away, and then at the Univision van, a taped "T.V." marking clearly visible on its roof.

The airwar spread east on the 6th. In Tenejapa, a community thought to harbor Zapatista cadre, the P-7s and helicopter gunships raked the surrounding hillsides.

"They look beautiful," one Indian farmer, who had never seen an airplane this close before, marveled to the *San Francisco Chronicle*'s David Luhnow, "but the sound they make is like death..."

Farther to the south, on the ejido of Nuevo San Carlos, near Altamirano, Augustín Lorenzo and his large family had run out of food after four days of sticking close to the house. The bean field was just 700 meters away and, for now, the skies appeared clear of warclouds. His eldest daughter and a cousin volunteered to help the Tzeltal campesino. Five-year-old Augustín Jr. fussed when the three set out—he wanted to tag along and "chupar caña," suck the sugar cane whose season it was. His father went back and fetched the disconsolate youngster.

After they had picked the beans and cut the cane, the family rested on the bank of the San Carlos River that weaves through the ejido, scanning the skies for signs of danger. Three planes, apparently returning to San Cristóbal, broke the bucolic silence. Abruptly, one of the P-7s peeled out of formation and doubled back towards Nuevo San Carlos. A terrified Augustín watched it drop three "bultos" (packages) several hundred yards away. He lost consciousness after the explosion.

When the farmer regained his senses perhaps an hour later, Rosa was still unconscious and he was bleeding badly from a shrapnel wound in the neck. Young Augustín, his son, was dead. Days later, Lorenzo's family attempted to take him to the San Carlos hospital that the nuns of St. Vincent operate under watchful eyes in Altamirano, but soldiers detained the grieving father as a suspected Zapatista.

The War in Chiapas

* * *

January 6th is the equivalent of Christmas in the Spanish-speaking world. Called Epiphany on the Christian calendar and the Day of the Kings ("Los Reyes") in Spain and Hispanic America, the celebration marks the arrival of the three wise men from the orient, bearing gifts to the infant Jesus. Everywhere in Mexico, it is a day when the "chicos" ("the small ones") receive their gifts. This January 6th, the Salinas government offered gifts to the "chicos" of the Zapatista Army of National Liberation: a ceasefire if the rebels would turn in their guns, release all their prisoners, take off their masks, and identify their leaders. Those Indians, who had been "tricked" into participating in the war would be granted pardons. The bombing would continue if the rebels refused to comply with the terms of surrender.

And for the "chicos" of the press, there was a present too: the sealing off of the war zone for their own protection. Every day for a week thereafter, correspondents penned up in San Cristóbal drove out to the roadblocks and were denied access to the highways beyond by surly soldiers with itchy fingers on the triggers of their French- and Israeli-made weapons.

Faced with a news blackout, illuminated once a day by a SEDENA press release fired off from Mexico City, reporters turned their binoculars on the nearby hills. Air force planes repeatedly punished Tzontehuitz, a peak near Chamula from which a gargantuan television tower spires spookily into the mountain mists. According to the Secretary of Defense, hundreds of Zapatistas had tried, time and time again, to take the installation. Multiple forays were also flown southeast towards the "Hill of Strangers" above Ocatál where the military and the U.S. share a vital radar facility, and over which Marcos and his men had disappeared on the run for the jungle January 3rd.

It was on this hill's wooded flanks that the Mexican Army may have suffered its most serious casualties of the War in Chiapas. Although unrecorded in the SEDENA daily bulletins, as many as 30 soldiers were either bush-whacked by a Zapatista ambush or flattened by air force planes that mistakenly hit their troop convoy January 7th. Confirmation of the tragedy was made impossible by the military quarantine but months after the rumored incident, the hillside still featured 500 meters of scorched meadow up near the radar station. The "friendly fire" hypothesis is bolstered by other observed evidence of military careless-ness. Reporters versed in the field of war wrote mordant notes of military ineffectiveness. Thomas Long, *San Francisco Examiner* Salvador correspondent who, like other Central American vets, drove in from the south to cover the hostilities, was amazed by the poor marksman-ship of ground batteries as he witnessed the big guns zero in on bombed areas, from which puffs of smoke still rose, often missing the targets by a half-mile. The aim of the air force was equally abysmal as civilians, journalists, ambu-lance drivers in well-marked Red Cross vehicles, and even the troops themselves, can substantiate. But pinpoint tar-geting was not the real object of the Mexican Air Force. "The bombardments are so the transgressors will under-stand and come to talk with the government," a sentry posted outside Rancho Nuevo told *La Jornada*.

Frustrated with being cooped up in San Cristóbal as reports of bombed-out villages filtered into the city along with the refugees fleeing the war zone in panic, human rights activists sought to reach outlying communities to assess the damage but were repeatedly turned back by the military. On Saturday, January 8th, one week after the

Zapatista occupation of the royal city, several hundred marchers trudged 28 kilometers up and down María Auxiliadora in defiance of the military. Led by CONPAZ, a network of progressive "coletos" that seeks to counter the conservative aristocracy, the line of march was packed with indígenas from San Cristóbal's Indian barrios, as well as members of international delegations that had hurried to Chiapas after an emergency call by Bishop Ruiz for foreign observers to bear witness to human rights abuses that appeared to accompany the massive military deployment. The day was cold and cloudy; intermittent rain— "chipichipi"—dripped on the participants as they slogged uphill. San Antonio was abandoned, the outlying forest blackened by rockets. Bombings were audible near Tenejapa where there was less cloud cover. Two Austrian activists, Elizabeth Turek and Helmet Santler, spoke to reporters, giving thanks for "God's Blessing" of the rain that had prevented the bombing of María Auxiliadora that afternoon.

Days earlier, 170 families from San Antonio, Corralitos, and other outlying hamlets had descended the mountain and found refuge at the diocese-run Don Bosco sanctuary at its base. All over the highlands, refugees—perhaps as many as 20,000 Indians—waving white flags, their few possessions trussed up on their backs, streamed out of the bombing zones and asked sanctuary in San Cristóbal, Las Margaritas, Comitán, and Altamirano. Many, like the wounded Augustín Lorenzo, told hair-raising tales of being bombed, interrogated, and tortured by their own government. The specter of Mexicans bombing Mexicans had deep scratch with civilians and military both—Roderic Camp told *El Financiero* of a distraught sergeant crying to his superiors that he had been trained to fight the "gringos," not his "own people."

REBELLION FROM THE ROOTS

* * *

The air war over Chiapas was waged with an expensive, volatile mix of imported high tech equipment. Leading the attack were the Pilatus P-7s that Marcos had pegged New Year's afternoon in San Cristóbal. The Swiss Pilatus-Werkes had sold the Mexican military 75 of the planes through 1992, a $20 million (USD) deal. Although the P-7 is listed as a trainer, it is easily converted into a fighter and the plane has made a record for mayhem in other Third World counter-insurgency campaigns: Guatemala, Myanmar, South Africa, and Angola. Swiss TV film of P-7 attacks by Angolan government forces on rebel Unitas positions in 1993 created a furor in the land of cuckoo clocks and official neutrality. A company rep countered criticism of the Mexican deal by insisting that Mexico's 20-year record of "internal peace" had prompted the Pilatus sale.

The helicopters in the military's fleet were the building blocks of the air campaign. Drug war largess had given Mexico the wherewithal to purchase over 100 HUEYs and Bell 212s. 82 choppers in the fleet are under military control and at least 22 more are leased to Mexico for a nominal fee and fall under the purview of the federal prosecutors' office (PGR) for exclusive use in anti-narcotics raids. There is little doubt that the U.S. aircraft was used by the Mexican military to wage war on the Indians of Chiapas. Interviews with civilians detained by the military in the war zone during the first two weeks of January confirm that at least three PGR-leased Bell 212s, usually parked in Villahermosa, Tabasco, were utilized by the military to ferry prisoners and the dead from Ocosingo, Rancho Nuevo, and other outlying areas to Tuxtla Gutiérrez—Interior Secretary spokesperson Eloy Cantu called such activity "logistical support." The problem with such support is that it is beyond the scope of the agreement with the U.S. State Department for the use of the choppers. According to a House Foreign Affairs committee staffer who pleads anonymity, the Mexican government had first to ask U.S. permission before deploying the Bells to Chiapas, a request that was never made.

"We ask if the U.S. Congress and the people of the United States approved this aid to combat the narco traffic or to kill Indians in the southeast of Mexico?" Marcos questioned U.S. President Bill Clinton in a letter posted January 13th but delivered to reporters days later.

On January 12th, a group of human rights investigators and reporters approached a PGR helicopter on the ground on the southern flank of Rancho Nuevo. The crew was reluctant to be filmed and refused to answer questions about their mission. In Washington that same morning, State Department spokes David Johnson admitted that the U.S. was concerned about the use of the helicopters but denied any improprieties in their deployment in the Chiapas theater. A chance meeting with a U.S. diplomat in San Cristóbal later that same day yielded the information that the Bell 212s had been returned to Villahermosa. Although a sharp diplomatic interchange was later reported by *El Financiero* columnist Carlos Ramírez, there has never been any public acknowledgment of disagreement between the Clinton and Salinas administrations on the use of the anti-drug whirlybirds against the Zapatistas.

Truth-in-reporting standards require that I note that the use of the Bell 212s only became news after the rebels put 12 bullets into the fuselage of #1140 in the hills above Ocotal—the chopper barely made it back to base at Rancho Nuevo. Despite its high-tech fighting capabilities, the Mexican Air Force was not invulnerable to ground fire—SEDENA bulletins reported at least six aircraft (three helicopters and three fixed-wing craft) were damaged during ten days of bombing in Los Altos, four of them on the slopes of Tzontehuitz January 7th. Children in the plazas of San Cristóbal, playing at war with wooden replicas of automatic weapons, trained them on the sky. As planes streaked in overhead, I watched one boy pull his slingshot from his pocket, fix it on a silver-winged Pilatus, and fire away.

The spread of the airwar over Chiapas was not healthy for children, former U.S. Attorney General Ramsey Clark cautioned at a Hotel Mazariegos press conference January 15th. After touring the war zone earlier that week, Clark, who has investigated U.S. culpability in war crimes in Panama and Iraq, called the Mexican military's aerial attacks upon civilian populations a violation of the Geneva Convention—a point made by *El Tiempo*'s Amado Avendaño, who had been running the protocols for days.

* * *

The aerial attacks on the Altos of Chiapas were not the only bombs aimed at civilian targets in Mexico on the heels of the Zapatista uprising. On January 6th, a Federal Electrical Commission (CFE) tower above Tehuacán, Puebla, 120 miles southwest of Mexico City, was sabotaged, blacking out sections of the Mixteca Indian Sierra. Although the tower was reported dynamited, witnesses say no explosives were used to bring down the lines. The same night, in an apparently coordinated action, persons unknown backed a stolen pick-up truck into a second CFE tower near Uruápan, Michoacán 300 miles to the northwest of Tehuacán and 1,200 miles from San Cristóbal. Both acts of sabotage remain unclaimed—the EZLN later protested that it had no hand in the assaults.

The January 6th attacks were the first in a wave that

would jangle nerves all over Mexico for weeks. Just before midnight on January 7th, a 1987 yellow Tsuru blew sky-high in the parking garage of Plaza Universidad, a shopping mall in southern Mexico City, near the Autonomous University, lightly injuring five civilians. Two days later, Mexico City police announced that the dynamite used in the car bomb attack had been stolen by the Zapatistas from the Pemex drilling station at Nazareth in the Sierra of Corralchén on December 29th, and arrested five suspects said to be affiliated with the PROCUP—the Revolutionary Party of Workers and Farmers-Popular Unity. PROCUP, which incorporates elements of Lucio Cabañas's Party of the Poor, had last been heard from in August 1991. After its ideological guru, an ex-university rector named Felipe Martínez Soriano, was jailed, accused of masterminding the killing of two *La Jornada* watchmen who had refused to accept a packet of PROCUP newspapers, the Sorrianistas blew up a McDonald's in Mexico City. The evidence supporting PROCUP's involvement in the Plaza University bombing was flimsy. Of the five suspects taken into custody for the shopping mall blast, one was a Guatemalan doctor—the proof of complicity being a copy of the critical weekly *Proceso* found in his apartment.

But if the PROCUP was bashful about the Mexico City sabotage, the Sorrianistas were quick to claim the bombing of an Army bank on the fringe of Acapulco's touristy Gold Coast the following night—the PROCUP has cadre in coastal Guerrero, the region from which Cabañas hailed. Closer to the capital, a dynamite charge took out a third CFE pylon near Cuautitlán, an industrial suburb where major transnationals like Ford have production operations—police reportedly deactivated a second charge at the Cuautitlán site that could have plunged the whole Valley of Mexico into darkness. Even nearer to the nerve center January 8th, a pick-up truck, reportedly attempting to lob mortars into Military Camp #1 on the western edge of the capital, blew up after a first launching went awry—the assailants apparently escaped. That same Saturday night, a massive explosion ripped up a PEMEX pipeline at the Miguel Hidalgo refinery in Tula, Hidalgo, 60 miles northeast of Mexico City—Petroleos Mexicanos officials called the incident "an accident."

The bombs were not confined to continental Mexico. The consulate in El Paso Texas on the northern border was firebombed January 5th. Mexico's embassy compound in Guatemala City was scorched January 8th. Subsequent blasts were recorded at embassies and consulates as far away as Berlin, Bilbao (the Basque ETA's bailiwick), and Sidney, Australia.

When the Mexican stock exchange opened for business Monday, January 10th, the capital was enmeshed in a paroxysm of bomb psychosis. 27,000 police were mobilized to detain suspicious motorists and track down bomb threats. Cops swarmed over Benito Juárez International Airport and set up security cordons around key PEMEX and TELMEX (the recently privatized phone company) and CFE installations. Police dogs bounded through the high gloss hallways of the spanking new glass-and-steel "Bolsa Mexicana de Valores" on Reforma—some reports suggest that a bomb was actually found on the Stock Market premises. But the real bomb blast victim of the day was the market itself. At the end of the panic-driven trading session, the Mexican Stock Market was down 6.2% of its total worth, the biggest crack since October 1987 when the Mexican exchange preceded Wall Street into the toilet. "This (the Zapatista rebellion) is evolving into a real crisis," the director of the national Confederation of Chambers of Commerce grumbled grimly to the business press.

* * *

The Zapatista pullback to the base area in the Cañadas of the Lacandón jungle was accomplished in silence. Indeed, the EZLN had made no statements since the occupation of San Cristóbal, when the rebels had proclaimed the Declaration of the Lacandón Jungle, copies of which, reprinted in a Zapatista magazine *El Despertador Mexicano* ("The Mexican Waker-Upper"), were sent, in plain brown wrappers, to a select handful of national and international correspondents during the first week in January.

The absence of EZLN response to President Carlos Salinas's January 6th "ceasefire" offer, conditioned on the Zapatistas laying down their arms and "identifying their leaders" was the most glaring item in the communications gap.

The identification of the EZLN leadership had become an obsession for the Mexican government. From day one of the rebellion, the message from the Mexican government and its colleagues at Televisa was that the uprising was led by Guatemalans and communistic priests, who, under the baton of Red Bishop Ruiz, had manipulated a bunch of disgruntled Indians into serving as cannon fodder in their subversive crusade to overthrow the institutions of Mexico. *El Sol*, a right-wing wildly-speculative newspaper chain owned by the Mexican supermillionaire Mario Vázquez Raña, reported that 3,000 Salvadorans, many veterans of the Farabundo Martí Liberation Front (FMLN) were massed on the Tapachula-Tecún Umán border on the Pacific coast of Chiapas.

Both Guatemalan and Salvadoran rebel commands were shaken by the Mexican government's allegations—the URNG, the unified leadership of four Guatemalan guerrilla armies, and the last active guerrilla force operating in

Central America, is headquartered in Mexico City where it was about to embark on a new round of torturous peace talks with the Carpio government. The FMLN, now a legitimate political party embroiled in a bruising election, denied any complicity in the Zapatista brush fire. The denials did not dampen *El Sol*'s fevered imagination: on January 6th, the scandal sheet reported the arrest of "Zapatista General" Jesús Sánchez Galicia on a bus to Villahermosa. "Galicia" was identified as a Guatemalan who had fought with the FMLN after having received basic training with the Peruvian Maoist "Sendero Luminoso" ("Shining Path"). In full color front-page photos, the poor man appeared half-naked, dazed and burnt by cigarettes, a popular police torture technique—the burns were described as "battle wounds." "Galicia" was later determined to be a native of Córdoba, Veracruz whose real name was Jesús Meza Yeladaqui.

The pursuit of the shadowy foreigners behind the Zapatista uprising was put into perspective by a colloquy involving a left opposition PRD federal deputy and a group of beleaguered refugees. Had they seen any foreigners among the rebel troops, Jesús Martín del Campo asked. "You mean like yourself?" the Indians reportedly asked back.

The arrest of "Subcomandante Marcos" also stirred up the press. From the first hours of the war, an all-points bulletin had been issued for a blonde, green-eyed foreigner, 1.7 meters in height, 160 pounds in weight, who was known to be fluent in four languages. On January 5th, soldiers stopped a likely suspect at a roadblock between Tuxtla and San Cristóbal. Peter Visher Garrido, a blonde, green-eyed Venezuelan ornithologist, tracking migratory birds in Ocosingo on a Smithsonian grant, was interrogated for eight hours at Rancho Nuevo. The confiscation of

Visher Garrido's computer files reportedly triggered a diplomatic interchange between the U.S. and Mexico with Washington demanding the return of its property.

While the military was busily interrogating foreign agitators, the real Zapatistas were stripping off their rubber boots and their red bandannas and melting back onto the ejidos from which they had emerged. "Do you want to go home?" *The New York Times*' Tim Golden asked a Zapatista sentry on the edge of Altamirano January 4th. "This is where I live," the young rebel quietly replied.

By the 3rd, the Zapatista fighters had bolted from Rancho Nuevo, Altamirano, Las Margaritas, and were fighting their way out of Ocosingo. On the route down from the highlands, they dug up swatches of the three roads that lead to their base territory in the jungle and mined other stretches, utilizing the dynamite they had indeed expropriated from PEMEX December 29th. Trenches were dug and trees felled to seal off the zone from ground attack.

The air force responded by spreading its aerial attacks southeast, hitting the Sierra of Patehuitz, San Quintín on the fringe of the United Nations-sponsored Montes Azules Biosphere, and San Miguel, the gateway to Zapatista territory. Bombing was particularly intense around Guadalupe Tepeyac, the site of the Solidarity Hospital Salinas and Colosio had visited in August, where the kidnapped General Castellanos was now being held. 18 truckloads of fighters had departed from Tepeyac December 30th for the New Year's Eve raids, and it was here at La Realidad, in the middle of the jungle, 20 kilometers from the Guatemalan border, from which the General Command reportedly directed EZLN destinies.

15,000 troops were now in Chiapas and *El Tiempo* reported January 12th that all of them were advancing on

Tepeyac. Long lines of armored vehicles, including 18 tanks, lumbered down the strewn dirt tracks that led into the rain forest, halting every hundred yards to remove obstacles and circumvent blown roads. Correspondent Thomas Long, who had often accompanied Salvadoran troops into the field, marveled at the carelessness of the soldiers as they slowly removed barriers in low-lying valleys where they could easily be ambushed by guerrillas positioned on higher ground in the trees. Long was equally astounded by the Zapatistas' failure to attack.

The silence of the Zapatista command was unnerving to the Salinas government which was being forced into a military option that could mire the Army for years in the swamps of the Lacandón jungle. Moreover, the troops were committing atrocities on the civilian population under the watchful gaze of the international press. Why was the EZLN so zealously guarding its tongue?

Then on Sunday morning, January 9th, a group of Tzotzil-speaking men approached independent international correspondent Epigmenio Ibarra in Larrainzar, thought to be the spiritual birthplace of the Zapatistas, and not 25 miles from San Cristóbal. The men asked Ibarra if he knew Amado Avendaño. The first communiqué in 10 days from the Zapatista Army of National Liberation was published the next day in Avendaño's *El Tiempo*. The epistle had been written collectively by the Clandestine Indigenous Revolutionary Committee under Subcomandante Marcos's signature and was dated January 6th, the day of the government's "ceasefire" offer, exposing a logistical lag in communication that would always be a problem between the two combatant armies.

The communiqué insisted there were no Guatemalans or Salvadorans or priests in the EZLN ranks, and denied that the Zapatistas had borrowed military strategies from

110

Central America—"Villa and Zapata are our teachers." The letter further elucidated that EZLN leaders wore ski masks as "a vaccination against Caudillismo (domination by one leader)." Arms had not been supplied by devious foreign backers—"we spent ten years accumulating these weapons." An inventory of Zapatista losses (nine confirmed dead, 20 wounded as of mid-day January 5th), prisoners taken and released, and weapons expropriated, was attached. The communiqué also made it perfectly clear that the EZLN was not laying down its arms or taking off its masks or identifying its leaders anytime soon—but the rebels did pledge to respect a ceasefire if the Zapatista Army of National Liberation was recognized as "a belligerent force" and the rules of war, as codified in the Geneva Convention, were applied to the hostilities.

This witty, defiant initial communiqué was the first of many from "the mountains of the southeast" under Marcos's florid signature. Also included in the letter was a contrite apology to the press and the 700 new pesos taken as a war tax from two *Excelsior* reporters and *El Tiempo*'s Gaspar Morquecho on the third morning of the conflict.

Bad Blood, Unquiet Bones

Of all the bones left to bleach under the mid-winter sun of Chiapas, the bones of the Ejido Morelia would rattle around the longest and the loudest.

Early on the morning of January 7th, troops stormed into this coffee and corn-growing community of 300 Tzeltal-speaking families an hour out of Altamirano on the track towards Belisario Domínguez and the Lacandón jungle. The Army, by its own admission, had reconnoitered the neighborhood the day before and there were unconfirmed reports that 14 reputed rebels had been taken prisoner. Villagers heard explosions and felt the impacts as the Mexican Air Force bombed and strafed fleeing Zapatistas in the nearby Sierra of Patihuitz. Then on Friday morning around 6:30 A.M., dozens of armored vehicles (Amnesty International reports 50) rolled onto the ejido and 400 soldiers charged from hovel to hovel, dragging the men out and herding them onto the basketball court at the center of the settlement, the military's customary m.o. in Chiapas Indian communities suspected of subversion.

The ejido Morelia is a former finca, once the property of the family of General Absalón Castellanos Domínguez. Despite being chartered by the PRI-run government, the Tzeltal "ejidatarios" of Morelia have resisted the advances of the ruling party's campesino federation, the CNC, an attitude that does not endear them to Altamirano's ladino cowboys. Although the ejido is less than an hour outside of Altamirano, it physically feels days away, a green and solitary space set below the blue mountains of the southeast—on whose heights the Zapatistas have trained for ten years.

113

Other than the attention focused upon this impoverished outpost this past January 7th, the abandonment of
Morelia by both government and non-governmental agencies, is spectacular. The ejido has a basketball court but no
net, a government clinic but no government doctor, a powerful thirst but no potable water, a full schoolhouse but
only one teacher (three days a week), even a church without a priest.

All morning long, the men were forced to lie face
down on the ground, their noses and mouths driven into
the dirt. Anyone who moved was kicked, their necks
stomped down upon by the jackboots of the troops.
"Today is the day we turn Morelia into an orphanage," a
soldier barked. The soldiers wanted most to know about a
mysterious woman doctor who sometimes visited Morelia,
Alejandra, a non-Indian, who was now alleged to be a
member of the rebels' high command. Three men were sin-
gled out, forced into the deserted hermitage of Jesus Christ
of Good Hope, a square, weather-beaten building fronting
the basketball court. For four hours, their compañeros listened to the screams of Sebastián Santis López, 60,
Severino Santis, 47, and Ermelindo Santis Gómez, 39.
Severino's head was repeatedly pushed into the filled bap-
tismal font and held there under water. Electric cables were
attached to the men's testicles and they were burnt. "The
soldiers brought them out bathed in blood," said one witness, "all we could do is listen to their lamentations." The
three prisoners were shoved into a military ambulance.
Then a list of 30 or 33 more names were read out and as
each man meekly signaled his presence, he was hog-tied
and thrown up in a military transport. Before they left the
ejido, soldiers are accused of sacking the town's sparse
stores and looting what valuables the villagers guarded.
"They were smoking marijuana," one elder told *La*

Jornada with disgust. "They even shit in my beans," angrily complained Felipa Luna, an old woman and one of the few ejido residents willing to give reporters her name. "The Army reads the newspapers and comes and gets you," another villager said to explain his reluctance to identify himself.

In their odyssey from prison to prison, the men of Morelia lost track of time. In Altamirano, the soldiers beat and burnt them with cigarette lighters. On the road to Comitán, Alejandro Muñoz, the greeneyed leader of the bricklayers' union incarcerated because the color of his eyes suggested he was Subcomandante Marcos, saw the men naked in a coffee warehouse where they were held for a day, amidst dozens of dead bodies. When the group was moved, gasoline was spread upon the bodies and they were burnt, another prisoner held with the men of Morelia, told Mexican human rights workers.

Taken to Tuxtla in helicopters, the men were blindfolded, their hands tied behind their backs with yellow thongs, and crammed, with over 100 other suspected "Zapatistas" into the maximum security section of Cerro Hueco. They were given no food for five to seven days. Two weeks later, all but eight of the prisoners taken from Morelia ejido were released. After bail was posted by the National Indigenous Institute, the men began to drift back to the jungle town. But three of those taken prisoner— Sebastián Santis, Severino Santis, and Ermelindo Santis, did not reappear. No one had seen them since they had disappeared into a military ambulance near noon on January 7th.

Then, weeks later, relatives out tracking the three men were told by a pigeon hunter about a pile of bones dumped in a ravine a few hundred meters off the road up to Altamirano. The site is described as a "zopilotera" into which dead animals were sometimes thrown to the carrion birds. Strewn among the bones were articles of clothing: a blue kerchief, rubber boots, a leather one, false teeth. One by one, the relatives identified the articles as belonging to the three men.

Fearful that the authorities would not let them remove their dead for burial in Morelia, the relatives summoned representatives of the Fray Bartolomé de las Casas Human Rights Center from San Cristóbal. "It's my father that died here—the other two are my relatives," Severino's son spoke into a camcorder, brought along to film the discovery. "Now I want to take them up. They've been here too long. They're suffering here. It's not fair—he's a person, a Christian. But now we've found them and even if it's just dirt, I'm going to bury them. It's my father. I've had a lot of pain for him..."

Upon hearing of the find, a public justice ministry officer and a National Human Rights Commission representative had rushed to the discovery site and would not let the villagers remove the remains without further determination of cause of death. A yellow rope was strung and a crime scene set up. After hours of bitter back and forth, the authorities were reluctantly allowed to carry the bones off to Tuxtla for further examination but were required to return them within 72 hours for burial in the ejido.

The bones got no farther than Altamirano just down the road. At the military checkpoint, a narrow gully crawling with troops, soldiers arbitrarily confiscated the remains because the public ministry pick-up truck did not have "the proper sanitary permits" to haul human bones. The remains of the three men were dumped into a box and deposited in the municipal president's offices under military protection. Two days later, military forensic experts were helicoptered into Altamirano to examine the find. *Irish Times* correspondent Michael McCaughan, tipped off

by a late night call from a drunken CNDH official, surprised the officers sifting through the remains in a patio of
the Presidencia. McCaughan asked the officers, each of
whom was wearing surgical gloves, what they were doing
with the bones. "They are accusing us," was all the Army
surgeons would say to the reporter. The military forensic
experts' conclusions: the bones were mixed animal and
human fragments—the human bones were those of a 28-
year-old male and they had been lying on the ground for
three years.

Human rights workers, who had gathered outside the
president's offices, were appalled at the Army's self-excul-
patory report and promptly faxed a demand to the CNDH
that a civil investigation be conducted. Members of the
Fray Barolomé Center, CONPAZ, and the Boston-based
Physicians for Human Rights (PHR) vigiled all night outside the municipal offices until they had extracted a pledge
from local authorities that the bones would be released
from custody.

Finally, on Friday, February 14th, the public ministry
returned the bones to the ejido. A solemn Mass was said in
Tzeltal in the dilapidated hermitage in which the men had
been tortured weeks before. The three widows watched
gravely, saying little as the cameras and the tape recorders
of the national and international press snapped and
hummed in the tropical heat. But the bones still did not
make it home to the ground. PHR emissary Tom Crane
was concerned that no independent tests had been performed and patiently convinced the elders that the fragments be left displayed on the altar until such time as
experts could be brought in. The world-renowned pathologist Clyde Collins Snow came to Morelia the next week
and won approval from the families to examine the
remains in order to independently determine the cause of

death.

Snow, a courtly Oklahoma country doctor, has pieced together skeletal remains at massacre sites in Argentina and El Salvador and was on his way to work common graves first in Ethiopia and then in Guatemala when the Chiapas call came in. Now he sat in the half light of the abandoned clinic, assembling the fragments while curious children stared through the broken window. "That's Sebastián's mouth," one whispered as Dr. Snow fitted the human jawbone together. Meanwhile, Tom Crane took blood samples from the mothers and sisters of the murdered men so DNA identification could be attempted.

The painstaking work was overseen by National Human Rights Commission ombudsman Jorge Madrazo. Pacing up and down impatiently, Madrazo seemed distrustful of the two interlopers, dubious that any cause of death could be determined by their efforts, worried too that the gringos would accuse the most likely suspects in the murder of the men of Moralia—the military, a conclusion that would make his job infinitely more difficult.

Because no bullet wounds could be detected, Dr. Snow received permission from the families to transport the skulls out to Ocosingo in order to x-ray them for metal fragments, a test that would determine if the men had been shot with military weapons.

The Army was not pleased to see the bones being trucked back through the Altamirano checkpoint.

Again the remains were seized by the military, this time because "a possible illicit act" may have been committed and again they were locked down for safekeeping in the municipal offices. Military forensic experts were again flown in from Tuxtla to determine if, indeed, these were the same bones the same team had identified on February 14th. Once the identification was made, the remains of

Bad Blood, Unquiet Bones

Sebastián Santis, Severino Santis, and Ermelindo Santis were swept into burlap bags and turned over to Madrazo to return to the ejido where a funeral feast was scheduled for Sunday.

By now, the bones of Morelia had acquired a magical aura in the Wild West atmosphere of Altamirano. Ranchers' wives stood in the street and refused to let Jorge Madrazo carry off the remains. "If we let the bones leave, the Army will leave, and the Zapatistas will come and kill us!" one woman screamed. The bones of Morelia had become the relics that would protect the landed gentry of Altamirano from the Indiada in the jungle just down the road. Madrazo argued that the National Human Rights Commission did not want the Army to abandon the town, that his agency defended the rights of everyone, ladinos and Indians alike. Then the police escort arrived and the good women saw that Madrazo was resolved to carry the bones back to Morelia by any means necessary. The Doñas of Altamirano returned to their kitchens. "These bones aren't even good for the soup of night anyway," hissed Hermelinda Culebra within earshot of *Ojarasca*'s Bellinghausen.

On the ejido, the villagers had slaughtered an ox to mark the return of the men and the end of their painful ordeal. When the bones came home in the late afternoon, the scent of barbecuing beef was on the sultry air to greet them, a rare aroma in Morelia where the Tzeltales eat meat only on the most festive occasions. The villagers seemed indifferent to the bitter dispute over whose bones were being returned. "For us, there was no doubt—they had the same clothes, the same teeth, Who else could the bones belong to?" one hungry villager asked Bellinghausen, wondering if the "barbacoa" was ready to eat yet.

REBELLION FROM THE ROOTS

* * *

The Zapatista uprising was terrible for business. On Monday, January 3rd, the first morning after the Zapatista uprising that the red-hot Mexican stock exchange was open for trading, the market lost 3.4% of its total value— some analysts think that investors used the troubles in Chiapas to skim profits that had piled in during the last weeks of December in joyous anticipation of NAFTA start-up. But the Mexican stock market is more than a monster moneymaker for the Salinas government—in this "formerly" third world nation the health of the "Bolsa Mexicana de Valores" is a leading indicator of the administration's self-esteem.

The initial reflex of the Salinas braintrust was to quash the insurrection as quickly and cleanly as possible to head off more precipitous sell-offs and the capital flight that could be just down the pike. When the Army was turned loose, its mission was to restore order and obedience to the institutions of the land—and cool the nervousness of investors.

For Carlos Salinas, calling upon the military was a tested impulse—within weeks of taking power in December 1988, the President had ordered the military to arrest "La Quina," the oilworkers' union czar. The Army followed orders and crushed strikes and muted post-electoral turmoil in explosive states like Michoacán and Guerrero. Now Salinas called upon his troops again to quell his political enemies and provide a quick-fix finish for what business bigwigs were already calling a "crisis."

The Army came out of its corner swinging on January 2nd, pissed off, "encabronado," literally like "a big bad goat" and figuratively, like "a furious cuckold." 1993 had not been a swell year for the military. Repeatedly accused of excesses in the drug war, the Army had become embroiled in an unpleasant tiff with human rights groups in the Indian Sierra of Chihuahua over several dead Tarahumaras. Then along came General José Francisco Gallardo, a career officer who had risen through the ranks and who was now incarcerated at Military Camp #1, for purportedly defaming the Brass after his doctoral thesis, calling for an ombudsman within the military justice system, was printed in an obscure University publication. From his cell at that notorious military base, Gallardo smuggled out tapes and gave interviews to the international press that blasphemed the name of the military, in a nation where the institution remains as untouchably sacrosanct as the Virgin of Guadalupe and the President of the Republic.

But, ultimately, what had most miffed the military was the 25th anniversary of the massacre of 337 (best count) students at the Tlatelolco housing complex in central Mexico City on October 2nd, 1968, the eve of the first Olympic Games ever to be staged in the Third World. Although there is no question that the massacre was perpetrated by Army troops, saying so in Mexico is frowned upon. But in October, a blue-ribbon commission of former student leaders—now influential opposition politicians, professors, and social advocates—had demanded that the military open its archives so that responsibility for the killing might publicly be affixed. Defense Secretary Antonio Reveillo Bazán had responded by slamming shut access until 1998.

But if the military high command was "bien encabronado," the grunts had to be whipped up to a murderous frenzy. The Mexican Army has always been a comfortable haven for poor mestizo and Indian rural youth. In the ranks, they prosper at distant, peaceful garrisons, growing soft and dependent upon the ample corruption that power brings in Mexico, particularly when it is backed up by big guns. To watchers like Camp, the troops, whose activities in recent years have been pretty much confined to giving haircuts and digging latrines, punctuated by an occasional firefight with the drug traffickers, were just not prepared for the war in Chiapas. Charged by Salinas with quickly clearing up this messy situation before foreign investors panicked, the Army responded with unabashed brutality.

Despite overwhelming evidence compiled by Mexican and international human rights observers on the ground in Chiapas in January 1994, the military assiduously denies any violations of individual guarantees during its aborted 12-day campaign to crush the Zapatistas. Military bulletins insist the Army did not visit Morelia ejido on January 7th (SEDENA claims troops were in the area on the 6th), and high-ranking officers categorically deny any involvement in the murder of the three Santises.

The military also denies any hand in the executions in the Ocosingo public market. "Our Army does not give the coup de grâce" General Godínez admonished Blanche Petrich. Military autopsies exonerate the Army because none of the bullets removed from the corpses of the dead men matched Army .38 and over calibers, a fallacious assumption thinks Dr. Tom Crane. Crane, Snow, and a Florida pathologist examined the autopsy reports and found that the size of the exit wounds were compatible with .9 mm military sidearm. The Army autopsy was "gibberish," Crane says, underscoring that the wrist burns displayed by the victims, indicating they had been bound behind their backs before being shot, were not even mentioned in the military report. Dr. Snow, who, at the request of the CNDH, reviewed photographs of the dead men, found the positions of the bodies conformed with other summary execution scenes he has reconstructed. Americas

Watch (now Human Rights Watch) and the PHR have asked the Attorney General's office to reopen the investigation but, by mid-summer, no action had been taken on the request.

Similarly, the military rejects complicity in the killings at the Ocosingo IMSS-Coplamar clinic. A perfunctory exhumation by the Attorney General's office tagged all 11 victims as Zapatista fighters, despite the fact that one of the corpses had a catheter still inserted, a hint that Caralampio Trujillo Santis was a hospital patient killed in his bed. Eyewitnesses, as reported by a Fellowship of Reconciliation observer team in Ocosingo the second week in January, say at least four people visiting patients were killed inside the hospital by the military.

The Generals are particularly sensitive about allegations of bombings of civilian populations, a Geneva Convention violation. "Not a single bomb was dropped," Air Force General Humberto Lucero Navárrez informed *El Financiero* January 25th. "It's untrue—its based on yellow journalism and rumors," General Godínez told *La Jornada*'s Petrich, emphasizing that the air force used only "rockets" and G-3 machine gun tracers when attacking supposed rebel positions.

"Does no one care for the rights of the poor policemen and soldiers who were murdered? We are the ones who have the widows and the orphans" General Godínez complained angrily. "These other people have killed, stolen cattle and vehicles, and committed an infinite number of crimes..."

"Human rights are just plain silliness," another general, Othón Calderón, a military commander with long roots in the region who had been hurriedly flown in from the state of Morelos to oversee field operations, told the hotshot *Los Angeles Times* freelancer Ruben Martínez at a military roadblock in January. "My job is to restore order and I'm going to do my job..."

* * *

The tall rawboned Texan listens attentively as Manuel Moshen Culej tells his part of the story. Both are seated on little wooden chairs set atop the knoll upon which Culej's adobe and wood compound is spread. The dateline is Chilil, the first village on the devious dirt track leading to the municipality of Chanal where there had been heavy fighting just the week before.

Don Manuel explains how he was installing an outhouse when the soldiers came charging over the top of the hill January 4th, ransacked his home, and found a single-shot .22 he uses to keep the coyotes off his chickens. That was enough to convict Culej of treason. The soldiers beat and kicked him repeatedly around the head and chest— "my children were right here, watching"—Culej flinches at the humiliation. Then his hands were lashed behind his back, his head covered with a canvas death hood, and he was thrown up in a truck with several dozen other men from Chilil, his neighbors.

The tall Texan crosses and uncrosses his bony legs like an uncomfortable stork, takes notes, asks the translator questions to ask Culej. As everywhere in Los Altos during the first days of the war, video cameras whir.

At Rancho Nuevo, there were more beatings. "They threw me in the ditch where the soldiers piss—I thought I would die right there." Then Culej, and the others, were slung into helicopters and transported to Tuxtla, first to the Judicial Police headquarters and then to Cerro Hueco, stripped and beaten and questioned for days he cannot count. Maybe a week later, long after midnight, Manuel Culej was rousted from his cell and released into the darkened streets of the state capital without a penny in his pocket to make his way home, 60 miles into the Sierra.

"Were the Zapatistas here in Chilil?" inquires the lanky Texas lawyer in the plaid shirt. Ramsey Clark is the former United States Attorney General, now an obsessed war crimes investigator. "In Chilil, we are all from the PRI," Don Manuel sobs in a singsong voice, his small, sun-burnt face warped with sorrow. "I am the representative of our communal lands, Señor. Why has our government done this to us?"

When, on January 4th, Samuel Ruiz issued an urgent call for human rights observers to come to Chiapas to wit-ness the unfolding Mexican government offensive, the Bishop found a ready-made audience in the U.S. and Canada. Human rights had been an up front item during the bruising battle to defeat the North American Free Trade Agreement. Activists opposed to "this NAFTA" had long advocated that the trade treaty incorporate a social charter that would guarantee linkage of improvement on human rights to the commercial issue, a demand that was pointedly ignored by both the Bush and the Clinton White Houses. Now, still smarting from the President's buy-out of Congress to insure start-up of the agreement by the first day of 1994, labor, environmental, and human rights advocates who had come together in the Citizens' Fair Trade Campaign to oppose NAFTA, found themselves at a crossroads as to what future tacts to take. The New Year's EZLN rising came on the very day this unique—and frag-ile—coalition had to grapple with North American "eco-nomic integration" as a fact of life.

The first groups to respond to the Bishop's call arrived in Mexico City January 6th, caught a few hours of shuteye, and were in San Cristóbal by 11 A.M. the next morning. The New York-based Center for Constitutional Rights was one of the first international delegations to touch down. A five-member Canadian Interfaith delegation drove in from the east, getting to Ocosingo soon after the fighting ended, on the same day. Americas Watch and Amnesty International had teams in the highlands during the first weeks of the conflict as did the pacifist Fellowship of Reconciliation, the Minnesota Human Rights Advocates, a delegation from southern California coordinated by Loyola University law school, an American Indian team sent by the International Treaty Council, and, later, an anti-NAFTA labor delegation

Ramsey Clark was joined by other luminaries in the international human rights orbit. Representative Joséph Kennedy and his sister Kathleen flew in to meet with Bishop Ruiz, to whom the Robert Kennedy Foundation has just given the annual Letelier-Moffitt Human Rights Award. Quiché Indian Nobelist Rigoberta Menchú led an "Indigenous Peace Initiative" into the region that included delegates from the nations of the Mapuches (Chile), the Miskitos (Atlantic Nicaragua), the Mam (Guatemala), the Nahua (Mexico), the Canadian Cree, New Zealand Maori and Lapland Sami.

The International Red Cross was another featured human rights player. The Swiss-based organization's arrival in Chiapas lent a stamp of seriousness to the war and the IRC's presence reminded combatants and observers alike that the rules of the battlefield, as codified in the Geneva Convention, were being systematically violated by the Mexican Armed Forces.

Rigoberta Menchú has long had links to Bishop Ruiz whose priests received 100,000 Guatemalans fleeing Huehuetenango during the Rios Montt-sponsored ethnocide of the early '80s. Moreover, the perilous existence of more than 40,000 refugees in the region—thousands in the war zone alone—made Menchú's mission to Chiapas particularly pertinent. In early January, under the guns of war, she had helped guide some 900 refugees home from Comitán, an agonizing exodus and return that has been slowly, quietly, developing for the past 18 months.

Rigoberta has other political allies in Mexico where she herself has lived in exile for 13 years, keeping her Nobel here at the National Anthropological and Historical Institute (INAH) rather than returning it to her homeland until Guatemala passes from the dark night of tyranny. A Mexico City resident, Menchú sometimes visits with President Salinas in Los Pinos and regularly hobnobs with the mavens of the State and of the PRI, a delicate balancing act for a woman whose outlook is much to the left. At the Foreign Press Association one January afternoon in the smogbound capital, Menchú was asked by reporters if her investigations of human rights abuses in Chiapas violated Article 33 of the Mexican Constitution, which prohibits intervention in domestic political affairs by "extranjeros" (foreigners). Menchú responded that she was not an "extranjera": "I'm a Mayan woman. These people in Chiapas are Mayans. It is not our fault that they have drawn the border where they have drawn it..."

The vagaries of that border engendered a bizarre turnaround in the flow of refugees during the weeks of fighting in Chiapas. After Zapatista forces camped near La Revancha, a tiny jungle clearing within a kilometer of the Guatemalan border January 3rd-7th, air attacks so spooked the locals that 73 villagers sought refuge at El Quetzal, a coffee finca just scant meters into Guatemala. For the first time since the Mexican revolution, Mexicans, who have often entertained fleeing Guatemalans, were now asking for refuge in Guatemala.

The international human rights delegations were met

on the ground in San Cristóbal by their Mexican counterparts—CONPAZ and the diocesan Fray Bartolomé de las Casas Center were there to set up interviews and itineraries. 33 non-governmental human rights watchdog groups from all over the Mexican landscape, under the rubric "All the Rights for Everyone" ("Todos los Derechos por Todos"), banded together to probe rumored military atrocities. Human rights work is a growth industry in this nation where such abuses are pandemic. Sergio Aguayo, who heads the long-lived, privately-endowed Mexican Academy for Human Rights, estimates that close to 300 non-government human rights groups have sprung up all over Mexico since the government announced creation of the National Human Rights Commission (CNDH) four years ago.

The CNDH is the first official organ of the Mexican government mandated to confront chronic human rights concerns here. Critics label the Commission an export item, designed to mellow out the nation's authoritarian image and make Mexico a more palatable partner in the new North American Economic Order. There is substance to this critique. The Commission was created in the wreckage of the 1988 elections in a nation where 550 citizens have disappeared into thin air after being taken into custody by security forces over the course of the past two decades. The CNDH drew its first breath in June 1990 just as opposition activists who had nearly put Cárdenas in power two years earlier, were beginning to disappear or turn up dead by the dozens.

Commission members and its director serve at the pleasure of the president. Among the Illuminati whose names are on the letterhead of this prestigious panel are the much-garlanded novelist Carlos Fuentes; Carlos Payán, the publisher of *La Jornada*; Hector Aguilar Camín, editor of

Nexos and the intellectual darling of the Salinas years; and old institutionalized warhorses like agrarian guru Arturo Warman and Rodolfo Stavenhagen, an apostle of indigenous rights. But the gut work of the CNDH is performed by a large legal staff, first under the baton of the present Secretary of the Interior, Jorge Carpizo, and more recently directed by his excellent friend and disciple, Jorge Madrazo, whose official title is The Ombudsman.

Since its creation, the CNDH has handled over 20,000 complaints but sustained only 4,000 of them for further investigation and resolution. Concluded Commission investigations result in "recommendations" to governors that are often resisted or complied with only cosmetically. For those who call the CNDH hotlines for help, there are dangers: investigators' phones were found to be tapped by an unstated government agency in April 1991.

The opposition on the left is particularly unhappy with the CNDH because the Commission has pursued only 60 of the more than 270 violent deaths of Cárdenas's militants that have been recorded since the formation of the Party of the Democratic Revolution (PRD) in 1988. As noted, the November 1991 Veracruz drug plane shootout, filmed by the DEA, is the only recommendation the CNDH has ever made to the military and even that determination deferred to the military code of justice.

"There are no sacred cows," Madrazo promised reporters after landing in Chiapas January 5th, pledging that the military would not be exempt from review of human rights abuses. In Ocosingo later that day, the Ombudsman pressured the federal Attorney General's office (PGR) into exhuming the 11 bodies buried in a common grave in the Coplamar cemetery. Later, Madrazo would accept the PGR conclusion that all of the dead were Zapatistas despite overwhelming eyewitness testimony to the contrary. Similarly,

Madrazo did not challenge the military's own autopsy of the five young men executed in the market. The Ombudsman also appeared to agree with General Godínez that bombings of civilian populations were a figment of Indian imagination, opting for the rocket theory of humanitarian attack—"rockets do less damage than bombs," the then-heavily mustached Madrazo told *La Jornada*.

Rather than attending to the dead, the CNDH's mission was to minister to the living. The Ombudsman inspected refugee facilities and hunted down the missing as he traveled through the war zone. He also agonized over the abuses committed by the Zapatistas—in particular, the kidnapping of General Absalón Castellanos. An analysis of 289 complaints of human rights abuses received by the 33-member "Todos" group reveals that 49.3% were registered against the military and barely 6% against the EZLN.

In a front page *La Jornada* editorial January 18th, Dr. Aguayo chastised the CNDH's "profound timidity" in confronting the military. The Ombudsman should have done much more, wrote Aguayo, but this would, no doubt, have caused frictions.

* * *

The human rights powerhouse Amnesty International has been looking hard at Chiapas for the past decade—Amnesty's first-ever special report on Mexico (1985) spotlighted the astonishing abuses committed during General Castellanos's years as governor and, as late as June of 1993, AI was issuing urgent alerts asking its members to take action on Chiapas cases. Amnesty was particularly concerned about the June 3rd violent arrests and jailing of 22 Tzeltales in El Carmen on the edge of the Zapatista zone soon after the Army's firefight with the EZLN. Many villagers were beaten and the arrested campesinos hauled off to Ocosingo. Among the detainees were three village grandfathers, one reportedly 103 years old.

The Argentina-born Amnesty chief investigator Morris Tidball-Binz, working out of London, and the ironically-named Carlos M. Salinas from AI's Washington office, were on the ground in Chiapas for four days January 18th-22nd. After the obligatory visit to the Bishop, the team moved speedily through the war zone, driving into Morelia and Chalam de Carmen ejidos and collecting testimony from aggrieved Tzeltales in the Altamirano refugee camps. Echoing Madrazo, the AI people critiqued the Zapatistas, condemning the rebels' deprivation of the General's liberty, despite Absalón Castellanos's crimes—many of them documented by Amnesty International itself.

The final stop on the AI tour was to be Cerro Hueco, the fortress-like penitentiary up above the Tuxtla zoo. Inside Cerro Hueco, the serene public patio in which ice cream vendors ply their product is belied by the stinking darknesses of the "bartolinas," the maximum security confinement cells where at least 70 suspected Zapatistas were still being held. Tidball-Binz and Salinas had arranged the visit through the CNDH, which exercised unusual dominion over who entered the prison and who did not—"jealously guarded access" is how Dr. Aguayo put it. But when the Amnesty honchos showed up at the front desk, no one had ever heard of them. A call to the local offices of the CNDH was reportedly met with insults and obscenities. Steamed, Tidball-Binz and Salinas stomped back to their hotel and began working the phones to Washington. It was Friday afternoon and the right folks might not be home.

The first call, so the story goes, went to Congressman Robert Torricelli's office. The New Jersey Democrat, the blunt-talking Chairman of the House Hemispheric Affairs Subcommittee, it is said, called the White House and the

REBELLION FROM THE ROOTS

White House contacted Los Pinos. President Carlos (no M.) Salinas de Gortari reportedly rang up Jorge Carpizo and the new Secretary of the Interior, under whose purview the nation's jails now fell, ordered state authorities to provide access. Finally, prison officials got back to Tidball-Binz and M. Salinas to inform them that the prisoners of war in Cerro Hueco were ready for viewing.

AI met with "Zapatista" prisoners on Friday afternoon January 21st: 71 dazed, hungry men who stood accused of crimes like "sedition," "riot," and "rebellion." Most had been blindfolded for days, their wrists rubbed to raw flesh by the yellow thongs that bound them. State prison director Gilberto Ocana had refused to feed the prisoners for five days after their arrests, arguing that he didn't have the budget to cook for the rebels and urging that their families, trapped in the war zone, come down to Tuxtla to make sure the men had food. Most of the "Zapatistas" were non-Zapatista Mayan farmers swept up by the military, as in Morelia. Many insisted they were actually supporters of the PRI—one group of town officials from Tenejapa was picked up during a holiday binge in San Cristóbal. Most had been forced to sign confessions under extreme duress—carbonated Tehuacán water laced with powdered "chile piquín," the time-honored "Tehuanazo," a cornerstone of the Mexican justice system, were sometimes applied. Others were nearly asphyxiated when a plastic bag was pulled down over their faces. These were two of the interrogation techniques listed by Salinas in his testimony before the Torricelli committee in February.

Also jailed in the maximum-security cells was "Jesús Sánchez Galicia," the supposed second-in-command of the EZLN so luridly portrayed on the front page of "El Sol." Fellow prisoners said Jesús Meza Yeladaqui (his real name) had been the most seriously beaten of the men. Yeladaqui denies that he is "a terrestrial guerrilla." "I'm a guerrilla yes, but a guerrilla for God," he told *La Jornada*'s Garduño.

＊　＊　＊

The eyeful that national and international human rights groups and their counterparts in the press were catching in Chiapas was not at all salubrious for the sunny image of stability and peaceful development—the new "Mexican Miracle"—that Salinas had spent so much time and good money cultivating for the past six years. The Zapatista uprising had put the kibosh on the advent of NAFTA and sullied Salinas's PR-purchased international reputation. Now, the U.S. Congress was suffering palpitations of recrimination about its rush to invite Mexico into North America. Those who had supported NAFTA ever since George Bush and Carlos Salinas had first cooked up this hemisphere-wide, multi-national marketing scheme, just wanted Chiapas and its creepy, ski-masked Zapatistas to crawl back into the box. Those who had fought the good fight to defeat the treaty clucked "we told you so" and wondered about the escape clause embedded in the arcane language at the back-end of the document. Those liberal Democrats who had backed Bill Clinton on NAFTA in defiance of their labor, environmental, and human rights-oriented constituencies, had now to mollify surly homefolks.

"As NAFTA supporters, we are concerned about reports that human rights abuses may have been committed by your government forces," hemmed and hawed a letter initiated by San Francisco's Nancy Pelosi and signed by 24 other Dems who had put their political future on the line November 17th by backing Bill Clinton on NAFTA.

Other old NAFTA foes took more direct action. Small Business Subcommittee Chair John LaFalce (R-Ohio) flew to Chiapas to catch the action first hand, then stopped off in Mexico City on the rebound where he was denied access to the imprisoned General Gallardo at Military Camp #1, igniting an international incident. Direct action caught up too with Sacramento Democrat Robert Matsui, Clinton's House pointman on NAFTA, whose California offices were invaded January 6th by a pro-Cárdenas group, "Americans for Democracy in Mexico." The protestors requested a halt to the bombing and the abrogation of the North American Free Trade Agreement.

From the Redwood Forest to New York Island during the first two weeks of January, anti-NAFTA activists joined with Chicano militants, exiled Mexicans, American Indians, and Central American Solidarity networkers at rallies outside Mexican consulates and fund-raisers in church basements. On San Francisco's Market Street January 5th, one older Mexican from a barrio homeless group, stood outside consular offices, tightly clutching a treasured portrait of Emiliano Zapata. "He has come again at last!" the old "bracero" (fieldworker) kept shouting, "Ya viene de nuevo!"

One Democratic Congressperson who had resisted the Clinton White House on NAFTA and who remained unrepentant, was the powerful 10-year House vet, Torricelli. As Chairman of the House committee that sets legislative policy and administration attitude on Latin America, the ambitious, publicity-prone politico from industrial New Jersey has used his unlikely committee chairmanship to build a small dynasty back home that one day, handlers hope, will springboard Torricelli into the governorship or at least a Senate seat. The Chairman's crowning legislative achievement, the aberrantly-named "Democracy for Cuba Act" that barred from U.S. ports ships that first put into Havana, was designed, in part, to service a district in which the venomous Cuban exile gang, Alpha 66, has a voice. Opposing NAFTA on job flight grounds earned the congressman more points back in Bergen County. Now the rebellion in Chiapas, and the brutal military counter-attack, was vindication for Torricelli's nay vote on the trade pact, and he was going to rub it in the Clinton administration's nose. Hearings were announced for early February—"U.S. investors need to know about the stability of their investments," Torricelli self-righteously declared to Dolia Estévez. What had the White House known about Chiapas and when had they known it, a Torricelli staffer asked rhetorically.

The news of the Torricelli probe into the explosion in Chiapas was deemed an "unfriendly gesture" by Mexico's foreign minister. Legislators on all sides of the Mexican aisle denounced the hearings as the usual gringo intervention into the nation's affairs. Sergio Aguayo and Jorge G. Castañeda, who had both been invited to testify in Washington, canceled out, reportedly distrusting Torricelli's motives.

The U.S. Congress was not the only extra-national body to reconsider Mexico's claim to first world membership as the result of the military onslaught in Chiapas. On January 9th, the European Parliament asked for an end to the bloodletting and suggested that continued violations by the Army could result in suspension of a 1991 European Community-Mexico trade pact.

The conflict in Chiapas was also brought to the attention of the InterAmerican Human Rights Commission (CIDH), meeting in Washington under the aegis of the Organization of American States. That august body was presented with a thousand pages documenting mostly-military-attributed abuses against civilian populations perpetrated during the weeks of war in southern Mexico. The valiantly independent human rights advocate MariClaire Acosta, who presented the documentation on behalf of the "Todos" coalition, was excoriated by PRI-sponsored lawyers' associations for appealing to a non-Mexican legal body for intervention. Responding to the NGOs' charges of military atrocities, the Mexican government, represented by Ambassador to Washington Jorge Montaño, labeled the accusations as being "inappropriately" lodged—the proper forum, the Ambassador stressed, was Mexico's own National Human Rights Commission. Montaño was sent out on a whirlwind tour of key U.S. cities in February to calm investor fears and accuse the Zapatistas of driving 20,000 refugees from their homes.

The East Coast Intellectual Cartel weighed in on Chiapas post-haste. By the end of the first week of the rebellion, Noam Chomsky was writing for *La Jornada*, calling the Zapatista rebellion just the tip of the NAFTA iceberg—"still worse disasters" were on line. While the left, buoyed by the joy of a new cause for solidarity in the too-long unfashionable South, mustered their experts at low-rent forums in drafty bookstores, the elegantly-appointed Brookings Institute summoned the Mexicologists to Washington to examine the causes of this oddball rebellion. Was NAFTA really the issue, the experts asked Mayan Indians imported from Chiapas for the session.

The public policy drumbeat was kicked up by editorials in the majors that lamented how Salinas's economic "miracle" had been subverted by the glaring social needs of the populace. The *Los Angeles Times* reassured its readers January 6th that, despite the rebels' daring boast that they would advance on Mexico City, the capital "was not the city it was when Emiliano Zapata occupied it. Only a major invasion could threaten (the capital) today..."

Across the page, in Column Left, the wily Robert

Scheer reminded his flock of the Gore-Perot NAFTA debate in which the Veep admitted Mexico was not "as democratic as we'd like to see it" but pledged that the benefits of the treaty would help the U.S. to influence its neophyte trading partner in that direction. Now Scheer was stunned by the "deafening silence" of the Clinton White House.

But if the Casa Blanca was culpably muted about events in southern Mexico, the striped pants set down at Foggy Bottom was publicly muttering. "Instability in Mexico does not make for a good commercial associate," Alexander Watson, Undersecretary of State for Latin American Affairs, explained to *El Financiero*, pointing to the Mexican government's "inability to resolve its social problems." John Shattuck of State's Human Rights section, who, like Watson, would testify before the Torricelli subcommittee, was worked up about reports of extra-judicial executions. State was conducting its own investigation, he told Congress.

Also on his way to Washington to calm Congressional clamorers and provide background on the conflict in Chiapas was Ambassador James Jones, a former Oklahoma congressman-turned-banker—he directed the American Stock Exchange until fingered by Clinton to head up the embassy on Reforma, replacing a career diplomat, John Negroponte. Jones, who has never held a diplomatic post, has no experience in Latin America, and does not speak Spanish, would go up to the Hill to disclose, behind locked doors, that a Cuban rifle had been captured from the rebels, a ploy thought leaked to *Proceso*'s Carlos Puig by four separate sources, in order to derail Castro-foe Torricelli's hearing. The alleged content of Jones's secret testimony was vigorously denied by a Mexico City embassy press officer.

As the war on the southern border entered its second week, observers on the northern border, like *El Financiero*'s Carlos Vigueras, across the line in Texas, noted increased Border Patrol ("Migra") air activity over El Paso-Juárez. At the Tijuana-San Ysidro crossing, the U.S. Army Corps of Engineers and the Migra soldered in new sections of the ten-foot-tall, jaggedly-tipped steel wall that now looms along this intensely-trafficked corner of the dividing line.

Anti-immigration hysteria is a hot button in recession-ridden California but politicians are riding its coat tails to electoral success all over the country too. What Chiapas, and the profound instability it represents for the United States' southern neighbor, would mean in terms of increased illegal immigration was a question to be quantified by INS accountants. Meanwhile, the politicians saw votes in hyping the Mexican menace and the Clinton administration was busily ratcheting up its proposed 1994 Immigration Control Act, a bill that would bar Mexican kids from U.S. health and educational benefits and greatly increase military and civilian vigilance all along the nearly 2,000-mile border with Mexico, just in case the craziness uncorked by the Zapatistas spread north.

* * *

Back on the Ejido Morelia this June, the unquiet bones of the three Santis men were still buried but not resting very comfortably. Just up the road was the military, bristling with guns and "prepotencia" (bullying arrogance). Every time the villagers came through the checkpoint in Altamirano, a crowded backdoor to the jungle, the soldiers would shake them down, order them around, the women most of all—three Tzeltal women from a settlement deeper in the forest charged that they were raped by soldiers here in early June—and there was palpable bitterness about the continuing hectoring presence of the troops and the humiliation to which the villagers and those who came to help them (CONPAZ is a key lifeline for the Morelia ejido) are constantly subjected.

At the military roadblock one afternoon in June, the soldiers, mostly Indians themselves, were vigorously shaking down Indians who might possibly be smuggling guns or gasoline or victuals to the Zapatistas—carrying too much bread through the checkpoint gets one tagged as a suspected subversive. The Sergeant, a burly man, had a copy of a right-wing tract called *Why Chiapas?* sticking out of his back pocket—the pamphlet's argument is that Bishop Samuel Ruiz is the Zapatistas' supreme commander. Now the Sergeant took time out from barking orders to impress a U.S. reporter with the military's good deeds. All of this vigilance was really just part of the "Permanent Campaign Against Narco-Traffic" (wags say "Marcos-Traffic"), he explained, pointing to a banner dangling limply between trees. "We are just trying to keep the young people of Chiapas off drugs," he insisted. The military performs humanitarian labors in this region. "We bring doctors and dentists to the people. We respect their rights," the Sergeant bragged.

But the ejidatarios of Morelia, I protested, say you are violating their rights.

"Pinche bola de Zapatistas." spat the officer, "fucking ball of Zapatistas, we're just waiting for orders to go in there and exterminate the subversives..."

"¡Alto Al Masacre!"

"What is at play in Chiapas is not just Chiapas but the TLC (NAFTA) and Salinas's whole neoliberal project," the Subcomandante warned the press up in San Cristóbal and ten days later, it did not take a Wall Street whizkid to fathom that the uprising and the bad press the military was getting in its painful aftermath, was poisoning the commercial environment.

As already noted, on the first trading morning after both the Zapatistas and NAFTA kicked in, Monday, January 3rd, the Mexican Stock market plummeted sharply. It continued to slump Tuesday the 4th, and rose for the final three days of the trading week, finishing up 14 points above where the market had begun. The expectations of NAFTA apparently had vanquished the Zapatista bummer.

Then, on Monday, January 10th—the day of the bomb scare at the dazzling Paseo de Reforma bubble, the "Bolsa" cracked badly, unloading 6.2% of its total value, the fifth largest loss in this hot-blooded young market's history. Market watchers suspect that Hacienda—the Finance Ministry—inserted what students of Mexican money call "la mano negra," the black hand, buying up generous amounts of TelMex stock with National Development Bank (Nafinsa) bonds in order to head off free fall. Stocks rallied slightly on Tuesday after Salinas announced a surprise cabinet shakeup. But on Wednesday and Thursday, the market was sliding fast—a purely Mexican phenomenon, isolated from world market malaise (Wall Street reached a new record high on January 14th). When trading ended Friday afternoon, the Mexican Stock Exchange was off 144 points, its worst week since the October 1987 crack.

Why was the market—which, more often than not, obeys its own inscrutable internal rhythms—so close to Carlos Salinas's heart? For starters, his vaunted "Mexican Miracle" was built on huge dollops of foreign investment, $50 billion (and perhaps $20 billion more than that) poured into Mexico from December 1988 through the same month 1993, according to Banco de México ledgers, fully 60% of which had been sunk in the stock market, not exactly the most stable subsoil upon which to found a new economic order. Capital flight has sunk Mexico before—the great 1982 debt crisis, from which Mexico has spent a decade never fully recovering, came about through an unfortunate collision of precipitous drops in petroleum prices, Mexico's unexpected inability to make steep foreign debt payments on money borrowed mainly to pump oil, and a hemorrhage of runaway capital that provoked near-fatal peso devaluation. This doomsday scenario must have given Carlos Salinas de Gortari the midnight sweats.

Despite self-serving optimism and strained assurances that the long-range forecast remained rosy, Salinas's Mexican Miracle was flying on low octane by the first month of 1994. The punch that had characterized the early years of the Salinas "sexenio" (six year term), seemed to have gone as flat as former super-welter champ Julio César Chávez's right hook. Perhaps it was the absence of challenges that caused Salinas to lose his sizzle: the major privatizations were history, the Constitution had been restated to allow for wide-open North American investment opportunities in every aspect of Mexican life, and NAFTA was a fait accompli whose implementation was still being sorted out. Inflation had been trimmed to just (barely) a single digit but the cost had been terrific. The cooling off, combined with deep recession in California, Mexico's leading trading partner, had limited 1993 growth to 0.4%—the last two quarters revealed negative growth, the classic signature of spreading recession. At Salinas's peak quarter, the fourth of 1990, growth had been just a shade under 7%. Other indicators were even more depressing: net income was declining and real unemployment ranged as high as 33% and climbing, estimated José Luis Calvo, a UNAM economist sharply critical of official labor stats— the Secretary of Labor was claiming 3% but such data is marred by tainted criteria and is easily disproved by counting the number of Mexicans, forced into the underground economy, who sell in the street to eek out enough to feed their families.

Moreover, the nation's commercial opening to the north has yielded a booming trade deficit ($5 billion in the first quarter of '94) when five years back, Mexico was running a surplus—albeit on only half the volume of trade. The government fiscal deficit was also on the rise after several years of surplus and January reserves were said to show a $4 billion drop from November—such figures are highly speculative as the real reserve totals are a state secret zealously protected by the palace guards.

But the President's real Achilles heel, some doctors of economics diagnosed, was an overvalued peso, worth less and less against the dollar day by day. The last three Mexican presidents have been forced to devalue the peso in the sixth year of their terms, a legacy that excites disdain among the masses and makes coronation of the PRI's hand-picked successor conflictive enough to threaten a smooth transmission of power. Carlos Salinas really did not have to be reminded that 1994 was the sixth year of his sexenio.

Mexico boasts that it has enjoyed 65 years of social peace through the rule of the monolithic PRI but investment analysts know that such social peace is built on sand. The Economist Intelligence Unit, a country risk service that provides quarterly ratings designed to guide international investors, rates Mexico below drug- and violence-ridden Colombia in investment security—one determining factor is the social explosion that is always percolating just beneath the thin-skinned surface of Mexico's authoritarian, rigidly-stratified society.

Chiapas added another dangerous asterisk to Mexico's portfolio. On June 10th, the more biblical invest-ment guides, Standard & Poor's and Moody's indexes, decided to postpone risk rating Mexico until Chiapas had simmered down and a new president was chosen. This is like international redlining, one astute business advisor poses; it means that no one in the neighborhood—namely Mexican corporations—can get their hands on internation-al paper.

The images of dead (presumed) Zapatistas, face down in the blood-splattered patio of Ocosingo's public market, run in front cover full color by *Newsweek*, and in more prosaic black and white by international wire services ranging from AP to Xinhua, certainly was not boosting Mexico's investment risk standing.

* * *

The electoral mode further complicated Carlos Salinas's plate. On January 10th, his political son, Luis Donaldo Colosio would hit the hustings and for ten straight days previous, the PRI's p.r. machine had been mired on the back pages as the nation focused on the rebel-lion of ski-masked Indian rebels in the southern jungle. Even on the very day Colosio kicked off his campaign, sig-nificantly in the all-Indian, PRI-ruled municipality of Huejutla in the Huasteca of Hidalgo, news of the crusade's inauguration was crushed by the fortunes of the uprising. Political memories could not recall the last time the debut of the PRI's anointed pretender to the throne did not gather banner headlines throughout the land.

To be fair, Colosio's January 10th campaign opener was pushed off the front page by his mentor Salinas's startling about-face in Chiapas. In a short address to the nation, the President observed that the upheaval in the south demonstrated that "something was not functioning" and that which was not functioning, had to be fixed.

When Patrocinio González was summoned that morning by his cousin to Los Pinos, the Secretary of the Interior must have known the fix was him. In Mexican power politics, the offering of "sacrificial lambs" ("chivos expiatorios") is how the "caciques" (bosses)—and the President is only the Boss of all Bosses—expiate sins. Patrocinio was obviously the goat in this drama: as Governor of Chiapas, he had allowed the Zapatista threat to ferment, and, as Secretary of the Interior, he had downplayed the reality of the guerrilla resurgence, deliberately misleading Salinas about a problem the President didn't really want to know about anyway.

One year and six days after he had assumed responsibility for the internal security of the nation, Cousin Patrocinio closed the doors of the President's office behind him, lit a long, unfiltered cigarette, and strode bravely to his waiting limousine. Accosted by the press pack, the domeheaded "Mano Dura" ("Hard Hand") waved a cheerful good-bye, rolled up the window behind him, cleared out his desk, and flew home to Chiapas where, a week later, his political godson, Elmar Setzer Marseille, would be deposed too. In Tuxtla, Patrocinio González Blanco Garrido Cannibál, the son of two governors of southeastern Mexican, reportedly sold off his 51% control

145

of the regional Aviacsa airline, put his BCH (now union) banking portfolio in the hands of trusted confederates, and flew off to Germany for a much-needed vacation. The political "chisme" (gossip) on the Mexico City cocktail party circuit that week was that Patrocinio had been ordered to stay away for a long time, maybe even six years, the next sexenio. Nonetheless, by spring, Patrocinio was spotted at a cuenavaca hideaway.

* * *

High echelon musical chairs is a benchmark of PRI rule. Assigned to fill Patrocinio's shoes was the nation's Attorney General, Jorge Carpizo. Doctor Carpizo's appointment as Secretary of the Interior was the key to Salinas's salvation, the sign that the President was about to sue for conciliation rather than pursue the Zapatistas into the jungle and risk long years of wasteful, winless war. The appointment of Carpizio, the founding director of the National Human Rights Commission, as Attorney General in early 1993 after the former AG was mysteriously shipped out to France as ambassador, was viewed by human rights advocates as the light at the end of a long, tortuous tunnel. The Attorney General or "Procurador General" of the Republic heads the eternally corrupt federal judicial police, the source of the most spectacular human rights violations, and it was fervently hoped that Carpizo would be able to weed out the bad cops and control the less vicious of his charges. Alas, the dream was not to be. The killing of Cardinal Posadas put Carpizo on the hot seat and his fantastical explanation that the Cardinal had been a victim of mistaken identity—detailed in an annotated video that cynics labeled the "nintendo"—soured his honeymoon with the public. Moreover, Carpizo never gained full control of his agency and abuses continued.

Now as Secretary of the Interior, he would oversee not only Mexico's internal security apparatus but also such areas as immigration, control of the media, and, most critically, the organization of the 1994 presidential election.

A balding, serious—if mercurial—bachelor whom gay activists proudly proclaim to be a closeted brother, Jorge Carpizo, although "a man of the system," is unique because he has no stated party affiliation. His curriculum spotlights a convoluted stint as Autonomous University rector during which he created conditions for a University congress election said to be one of very few fraud-free voting processes ever held in Mexico. The congress was the rector's concession to the largest student demonstrations since 1968, an outbreak of militancy directed at Carpizo's own efforts to limit open enrollment at the gigantic university.

The appointment of this highly respected jurist as Secretary of what is called "Gobernación," Salinas told the nation, would both "insure that tranquillity returned to Chiapas" and "guarantee the 1994 election." A tough-talking Mexico City D.A., Diego Valadés, later booted up to the Supreme Court in the wake of the Colosio killing in March, would substitute as Attorney General in Carpizo's place.

* * *

But the big bombshell dropped by the President on January 10th was the selection of Manuel Camacho Solís, former Mexico City regent (unelected mayor) as the government's unofficial "Commissioner of Peace and Reconciliation" in Chiapas—unofficial because, Salinas said, Camacho Solís had requested no salary and that no new government structures be created around his efforts to bring the Zapatistas to the bargaining table.

If there is a turning point to this story, Camacho's appointment was it. From the "Conciliator"'s appointment forward, the Mexican government's mission in Chiapas has been one of co-optation rather than coercion—it is the terms of that co-optation that are negotiated, not the terms of war. For the PRI government, turning towards peace was crucial in trying to regain lost international prestige. Salinas's abrupt, adroit veering of course also disoriented Zapatista strategies which, Marcos says, were geared to the certainty of protracted war.

The choice of Camacho as conciliator was an astonishing one. Just 43 days earlier, the former PRI president and Secretary of Urban Development and Environment had angrily resigned as the popular regent of the largest city in the world, after Salinas unveiled Colosio as his successor. Camacho, who thought he had been running neck and neck with the then-Secretary of Social Development for the "dedazo," fumed. At an unprecedented November 29th press conference, Camacho Solís, who has long been the PRI's conduit to the left, decried the lack of democracy within the ruling party structures he had served so long, and expressed frank disappointment at the President's failure to name him as his heir. Then the ex-regent went home to swank Lomas in a snit to consider quitting the PRI and declaring himself available for an independent candidacy, a course taken by dissident PRIista Cuauhtémoc Cárdenas in 1988 after Miguel de la Madrid had named Salinas as his successor.

For 48 hours, Camacho sat in council, weighing his political future and surrounded by loyal, clever lieutenants, and, on the third morning, the phone rang and Manuel Camacho Solís accepted appointment as Mexico's new foreign minister, the first stop-off, tongues wagged, on his way to golden exile as ambassador in some exotic foreign capital. Now 40 days later, Salinas had fingered this thoughtful, ambitious politico to rescue his regime from the deepest doodoo it had stepped in since the blatantly fraudulent 1988 election. To paraphrase the Subcomandante and John Haldeman together in one breath, the whole neoliberal enchilada was at stake

There are, of course, those who saw more sinister motives in Salinas's dispatch of El Camacho to Chiapas as his hand-picked conciliator of peace. The chances of getting the Zapatistas to the peace table after they had finally launched a war for which they had been training for ten years seemed so remote that some commentators like Carlos Ramírez (a "Camachista") feared the Conciliator's appointment signaled long-heralded exile. After all, Chiapas was as far away from the center of Mexican power as an ambassadorial posting to some sensitive Central American republic of bananas.

* * *

Given the high echelon switcheroo just 48 hours earlier, President Salinas's unilateral January 12th declaration of a ceasefire was an anticlimactic formality. After being informed by Secretary of Defense and General of Division Antonio Reveillo Bazán that the first stage of the military's mission in Chiapas had been achieved and that the four invaded municipalities were now secured by the Armed Forces, Salinas took to the airwaves. As Commander-in-Chief, the President ordered his troops to fire upon the "transgressors" only if they themselves were fired upon. From that point in time (10:09 A.M. January 12th, 1994), with rare exception, the Mexican Army has held its fire in Chiapas.

How the military, more "encabronado" than ever because of the goring it was taking in the international press for its atrocious behavior during the 12 days of fighting, would respond to the President's ceasefire order, was the story that day. León Lazaroff, an earnest, hustling freelancer, was covering it from the Nuevo Momón finca, another of Absalón Castellanos's former properties deep in the jungle, when the troops rolled by around 11:30, still advancing on Guadalupe Tepeyac where the General was thought to be held and where aerial attacks had been intense all morning. Lazaroff watched maybe 40 trucks and 18 armored vehicles push past the abandoned estate at which dozens of fleeing Tzeltales had gathered. Two and a half hours later, while the refugees at Momón agonized about whether there was really a ceasefire or not, Lazaroff watched the Army roll back up the same jungle track, turning away from Tepeyac. The turnaround, even with the General right at the end of the road from which they were now backing off, was a graphic illustration of the turn towards peace. Although the bombing in the sierras of the Cañadas would not tail off for days, the truce on the ground has lasted for months.

The final tally of 12 days of war in Chiapas remains clouded in claim and counter-claim. The CNDH, in its annual 1993-94 report issued this June, lists 159 dead, including 16 soldiers and 38 security agents. The Commission says 67 civilians were killed and another 38 bodies remain unidentified, putting the Zapatista death toll at, at least, 48. Of 427 civilians reported disappeared, 407 had been located by February—the June totals do not list the disappeared. According to the Human Rights Commission, 107 people were wounded during the fighting: 46 civilians, 41 soldiers, and 20 security agents. 149 arrests were officially recorded. The government count is considerably less than the diocese's first call of 400 deaths, an estimate that Don Samuel has never corrected. The uncounted corpses strewn about the war zone—such as the grinning bones we found behind Rancho Nuevo—or hidden away in rumored common graves or cremated in coffee warehouses on the road to Comitán, challenge the government's bottom line inventory of death and devastation in Chiapas.

* * *

As the troops trudged up from Nuevo Momón in the jungle dusk, another army was filling the Zócalo of Mexico City—the biggest outpouring in six years of Mexico's disenchanted "civil society," that unstated coalition of opposition rank and file, urban slumdwellers, independent campesino organizations and disaffected union sections, ultra-left students, liberal intellectuals, peaceniks, beatniks, rockeros, punks, streetgangs, and even a few turncoat PRIistas, all of whose red lights go on at once whenever there is serious mischief afoot in the land. Although estimating crowds is not a fine science in Mexico, veteran civil society watchers call "the March for Peace in Chiapas" the largest gathering since the huge protests following the stealing of the '88 election from Cárdenas. 80,000 to 100,000 participants seems within range and reason, depending on whether the estimate is based on four or five marchers to a square meter of the 48,000 square meter surface of this great stone esplanade where Mexico's national drama has been acted out since the Aztec-Mexicas wrenched the steaming hearts from their sacrificial victims at the twin temples of Tláloc (God of Rain) and Huitzilopochtli (the butterfly Sun God), the ruins of which still wall one side of this enormous public space.

Behind a great banner that urgently demanded "¡ALTO Al MASACRE!" ("Stop the Massacre!"), and chanting "Asesinos!" ("Murderers!") in thunderous unison at empty government offices, the marchers—many of them carrying flickering candles of peace—packed in around the jerry-rigged stage. Coordinated by CENCOS, a hive of activist liberation theologists, captained by the indomitable social agitator Pepe Alvarez de Icaza, the march culminated in the most ecumenical rally since Cárdenas put together his magical coalition in '88. On stage, along with Cuauhtémoc and Don Pepe, were PANistas and PTistas, PRTistas and Foristas. Ramón Danzos Palomino and Valentín Campa, the fragile old leaders of Mexico's communist workers and farmers, stood like bookends to the illustrious troublemakers gathered on stage. Rosario Ibarra, who has struggled for 20 years to find the Disappeared of Mexico ever since her own son, an urban guerrillero in Monterrey, vanished into police custody in 1975, followed to the microphone the son of the late Salvador Nava, a lifelong warrior against the ruling party from the right side of the political spectrum, up in San Luis Potosí. But it was the keynote orator who raised eyebrows: Father Miguel Concha, provincial of the Dominican order in Mexico and human rights crusader whose Fray Francisco de la Vittoria Center is a vigilant clearing house for the documentation of abuse in Mexico.

The choice of a priest to make this address was in itself an astounding measure of how much Mexico had changed since 1988 when the clergy was still banned from political participation, could not even vote or wear clerical garb in public, and was the traditional bogeyman of the Mexican Left. Now here was Father Concha first judiciously condemning the terrorist bombings that had everyone understandably jittery, then dissing Salinas's neo-liberal models and the damage they had wrought upon the poor. "We all want peace," the Dominican said simply, "but not at any price." Father Concha wrapped up his sermon with a homily from the Gospel of Saint Luke: the Hour of the Publican had come again, he said, when the rich man must return fourfold what he has stolen from the poor....

"This isn't just about Chiapas—it's about NAFTA and Salinas's whole neo-liberal project," Marcos had warned *L'Unitá* the first day of the war in San Cristóbal, the one on which the Zapatistas had promised they would advance on the center of the country. Now, on the perimeter of the enormous congregation, here and there, reporters spotted faces canceled by dark ski masks. The Zapatistas had made good on their promise. They—or at least their supporters—had arrived in the capital.

The Crimes of
Mi General

Even in his sunset years, General Absalón Castellanos Domínguez kept to the fastidious routine bred into him during 40 years in the barracks. Only now, his army was mostly a four-footed one: 66 Swiss Holsteins, grazing placidly on the verdant pastures of the General's beloved 300 acre spread, the Rancho San Joaquín, eight kilometers east of Las Margaritas, between the fincas "Bello Pasaje" and "La Libertad," land that remained part of the patrimony of his illustrious bloodlines.

The General and Elsy Herrerias, his devoted wife, had returned to San Joaquín on New Year's Day, spotted the Zapatistas congregated in front of the damaged government palace in Las Margaritas, fretted to his godson and driver, the Tojolabal Indian, René Ruiz, that the "bronca" (dispute) looked serious, and ordered him to drive on to the ranch just down the road. He seemed worried about the cows. The bovines—and, of course, his prized horses—were always on the General's mind these days. "I get 20 liters a day from each of my cows. You have to have good stock. Ranching is intensive not extensive these days," a bearded, blindfolded Absalón would instruct a Spanish reporter one month later, a prisoner of war "somewhere in the Lacandón jungle," dreaming of cows...

General Absalón Castellanos Domínguez is the scion of two families who are fabled, even in the feudal state of Chiapas, for their greed, rapine, brutality, and lust for power. His maternal grandfather, General Belisario Domínguez, a delegate to the post-revolutionary constitutional congress and a state and national icon, held vast estates in the seat of Chiapas independence, Comitán de Domínguez, in the rolling hills 60 kilometers from the Guatemalan border. Absalón's paternal grandfather, also named Absalón Castellanos, was notorious for the "mano dura" he displayed against the historically-tranquil Tojolabales of Comitán and Margaritas.

120 years ago, four out of the 10 surnames listed as "the Chiapas family" by the contemporary scholar Antonio García de León, were either Castellanos or Domínguez. The families took turns as titular rulers of Chiapas. A Domínguez was the governor of the state who crushed the doomed Chamula uprising of the talking stones in 1868.

After the revolution, the Castellanos and Domínguez clans were forced to make adjustments to maintain their great estates. Absalón's father, Matías, was a "mapache," donning the mask of Zapatismo to keep the federal government from dividing and distributing his landwealth among the serfs. Absalón's fondly-remembered cousin Rosario Castellanos grew up in Mexico City but, plagued by her family's lurid penchant for Indian killing, returned to Chiapas in the 1950s to work with the National Indigenous Institute and found redemption in "Indigenismo." Rosario Castellanos wrote many volumes of prose and poetry, most notably *Balum Canán* (1957), that bemoaned the lot of Chiapas Mayans. Doña Rosario, considered Mexico's founding feminist, died tragically, electrocuted while serving as ambassador to Israel in a freak 1975 accident. Another of Absalón's cousins, Jorge de la Vega Domínguez, found salvation through the PRI, serving in several cabinet posts and as president of the Institutional Party during the epic 1988 presidential electoral fraud.

Long before he was crowned governor in 1982, General Absalón had worked hard to earn a mystique for the hard hand. The massacre at Golonchán June 15th 1980 is perhaps the high point of Absalón's gore-splattered resumé. On that day, Tojolabal villagers, organized by a left splinter faction, who had occupied the heart of an abandoned finca 40 miles from Comitán, were assembled at Golonchán to receive the visit of then-Governor Juan Sabines, brother of the romantic poet Jaime Sabines. But instead of poetry or political bartering, the campesinos were dealt lead bullets. Troops, under the command of General Absalón, topdog of the Chiapas Military Zone, opened fire at point blank range, killing upwards of 50 Indians. "Many, many died, became cadavers, were eaten by the dogs and the buzzards," María Gómez Hernández, an eyewitness, told the veteran Chiapas journalist Juan Balboa. Today, it is impossible to find this name, "Golonchán," on any Chiapas map. On July 19th, 1983, the Agrarian Reform ministry removed it from the agency's lists of claimed parcels, explaining that there were no longer any living claimants to the finca.

General Absalón was summoned to rule his tormented home state in 1982. Although 40 years of distinguished military service, during which he had directed the National Military Academy in addition to commanding various military regions of the republic, had not much prepared the General for political battle, Absalón answered the call of then-PRI presidential shoo-in Miguel de la Madrid, to become the ruling party's gubernatorial candidate, the first military man in 30 years to run Chiapas—the state is unique for having had 17 military governors in the 170 years of its existence as a political entity. de la Madrid's choice of Absalón obeyed the tenseness of the times. Prompted by the massacres inflicted by "President" Efrain Ríos Montt, Guatemala's evangelical despot, refugees, guerrillas, and the Guatemalan army crashed the vulnerable southern border with impunity, threatening Mexican sovereignty and carrying with them the virus of resistance and insurgency. A disciple of General Marcelino Barragán, the Secretary of Defense who had ordered the 1968 slaughter of the students at Tlatelolco, Absalón Castellanos Domínguez could be trusted to quash any outcropping of subversion that might undermine national security and the security of the 19 Chiapaneco families (the contemporary "Family of Chiapas") that controlled seven million hectares of the state's richest farmland.

As Governor, Absalón had a spotty record—the spots are colored in blood. According to a petition for political condemnation submitted to the Mexican Chamber of Deputies by Unified Socialist Party (PSUM) delegates in 1987, General Castellanos was responsible for 153 political murders, 692 arbitrary detentions, 503 cases of torture, and 327 disappearances of activist campesinos. Among the political murders cited by Amnesty International in its landmark 1985 first-ever Mexico report, "Human Rights In Rural Areas" was that of CIOAC lawyer Andulio Gálvez in Comitán de Domínguez—witnesses testified that the Guardia Blanca ("White Guard") of Absalón and his brothers were the material assassins. In 1987, sociologist Araceli Burguete, researching 565 incidents of political violence during Absalón's years as governor, for the Mexican Academy of Human Rights—later published under the title of *A Chronicle of Recent Genocide*—was shot by Castellanos Domínguez's gunsels in San Cristóbal. Burguete, who was pregnant, recognized the would-be killers from her research.

Absalón's governance sowed terror all over the state. "Chiapas is on the verge of guerrilla war," Tuxtla's conservative Bishop Felipe Aguirre Franco told reporters in 1987, "and it is not because of the Guatemalans..." Under the direction of Secretaries of State Javier Coello Trejo, a 300-pound authentic "coleto," who later would become Mexico's ironfisted drug czar until his well-deserved fall from grace in 1990, and Eduardo Robledo, the PRI candidate for governor of Chiapas at this writing, bodies kept turning up all over the territory, mysteriously interred in shallow, unmarked graves. This reporter was in La Independencia, a municipality adjacent to Comitán, soon after the 1988 killing of five Tojolabales, members of a group that had seized the government palace there in a land and power dispute that had simmered for years. The killings were the work of Absalón's much-feared public security forces, who opened fire, Golonchán-style, on the group after first announcing that the Governor was on his way to negotiate. Days later, the bodies of the men were unearthed by dogs near Bellavista and Absalón, although denying complicity, sent the widows the equivalent of $500 USD for their troubles. "I don't want Absalón's dirty money. I want my husband back," one of the widows scowled when I spoke with her that day in La Independencia.

"The constitution is Absalón's whore," Manuel Hernández, a fellow journalist, jailed with six others and facing 40 years for having blocked a highway to demand higher corn prices, told me one noon in early 1988 on the yard in Cerro Hueco. The naked enrichment of the Castellanos Domínguez clan was another benchmark of the General's regime. Opponents decried Absalón's assignment of state funds to build roads between the family's 14 ranchos, encompassing more than 60,000 acres, according to a *Proceso* inventory published during the final year of his administration. Absalón opened the door of the Lacandón rainforest to his brothers—Ernesto Castellanos Domínguez's network of clandestine sawmills scandalized the jungle's protectors. Brother Ernesto finally caught his come-uppance after expanding into a second pristine forest, the Chimilapas, a million-acre reserve straddling Chiapas and Oaxaca, where Zoque Indian villagers captured and detained him and a wood cutting crew in December 1987. Ernesto's pick-up has been on display in front of the Santa María Chimilapas town hall ever since.

The list of particulars is lengthened by Absalón's treatment of his own Indians. Although, the General has long boasted of his closeness to the local Tojolabales—"they were my first friends as a child. I often gave them my old shoes" he once told journalist José Ortiz Pinchetti—the facts substantiate gross un-neighborliness. In 1961, the General sold the Momón finca to Tojolabal sharecroppers for a tribute of 10,000 sheaves of sugarcane, to be paid every year for ten years. By the 1970s, after payment had been completed, the ranch was back in the Castellanos Domínguez clan's hands because, the General argued, no land papers had ever been signed. In 1993, apparently to stay within personal landholding constraints embedded in the Mexican constitution, Absalón sold Momón to a son. On the eve of the Zapatista rebellion, crime continued to pay for the old man.

Despite the savage swath that detractors attribute to him, the General claims a clear conscience. "I have maintained social peace and tranquility during economic crisis," the outgoing governor told a graduating class of police cadets in Tuxtla, his last official act as the "elected" king of Chiapas in June 1988. Soon after, he went home to putter about the San Joaquín, supervising the daily milking of his mooing troops and exercising his sleek horses. René Ruiz tells reporters that even though Absalón's prized Andalusian stallion "Carbonero" had died earlier that fall, the General took daily pleasure in training a successor,

"Federal," a newly-acquired Alsatian.

A session astride "Federal" was one item on the General's agenda when he arose promptly at 5:30 A.M. on the morning of January 2nd. The 72-year-old military man's inflexible routine began with a brisk walk around the perimeter of the ranch, followed by a frugal breakfast. San Joaquín has no telephone and the General had not bothered to switch on the TV the night before, Ruiz says, explaining Absalón's innocence about events unfolding just down the road.

After supervising the milking of his generous herd, Absalón was reviewing house plans for a dream hideaway hacienda he intended to build on one corner of San Joaquín, when, just after 11:30 A.M., there was a loud banging on the front gate. "Just a minute!" Ruiz heard the General holler as the old man picked up his 50-key chain and marched the 75 yards from the main house to the entranceway where 40 men, waving "cuernos de chivos" (AK-47s), greeted him cordially. More were banging on the side gates to the compound. "Wait! Don't break anything!" Absalón barked, unlocking each entrance one by one, to admit the Zapatistas.

The interlopers were polite and anonymous, remembers Elsy Herrerias: "They were indígenas but I don't know from where—they could have come from anywhere in Latin America." While one group of Zapatistas dredged the ranch house and surrounding areas for weapons, another marched Absalón into his study and questioned him closely, under hand-tooled leather portraits and caoba plaques declaring him "Cattleman of the Year," the gifts of local ranching associations.

Finally, around 2:30 that afternoon, the rebels, satisfied that the only weapons on site were a hunting rifle and a souvenir pair of .45s, loaded up on bread, meat and soda pop, and packed Ruiz and the General into the ranch's new pick-up. Elsy was left behind, the rebels choosing two prize cows instead, which they carried off in one of the two three-ton trucks with which they fled towards Guadalupe Tepeyac, 80 kilometers southeast, deep within Zapatista-held territory.

* * *

The Commissioner for Peace and Reconciliation hit the ground running. "I've come to play!" Manuel Camacho Solís emphasized to the press corps jamming the fountained patio of the Hotel Mazariegos January 13th. The photo ops included the Conciliator embracing Bishop Ruiz and pumping the beefy mitt of General Godínez. "The presence of the military will guarantee peace," Camacho Solís beamed the day after the cease-fire was declared, a gesture of conciliation to a military whose esprit de corps had been indecorously assailed. On January 14th, Camacho formally proposed Don Samuel as mediator between the government and the EZLN, a motion which the Zapatistas had already made.

An EZLN communiqué dated January 11th but not received until January 17th had set stipulations for the choosing of a mediator. As a Mexican by birth, a seeker of solutions to social problems, and a member of no political party, the Bishop fit the Zapatista profile for the job.

The EZLN communiqué, only the third revealed since the New Year's Day offensive, also demanded the Army stop bombing civilian populations and again requested belligerent status for the Zapatistas. Finally, Communiqué #3 apologized for the delays in communication between the EZLN General Command and the general public and promised to speed up delivery. In San Cristóbal, Camacho evaded a response to the demand for belligerent status, a designation that would give the EZLN Geneva Convention standing: "I call them by their name," he reflected at a pandemonious press conference. "For me, they are a reality."

Manuel Camacho Solís was well-positioned for the role of conciliator. His family is peppered with military men (his father was Chief Army Surgeon), a pedigree that made him an acceptable choice to the military. His late wife, Lupita, was the daughter of a former Chiapas governor and the niece of Monterrey Bishop Adolfo Suárez Rivera, the reigning president of the CEM or Mexican Episcopal Conference, the maximum political expression of the nation's Church hierarchy. Bishop Suárez, unlike Bishop Ruiz—with whom he has occasionally had testy words, is an authentic "coleto."

On the other end of the social ladder, Camacho Solís had plenty of practice bargaining with the riffraff. As Secretary of SEDUE, whose purview included (the agency was disappeared in 1992) urban development and the environment, Camacho Solís day after day took on anguished mobs of housing solicitors, the displaced "damnificados" of the great 1985 Mexico City earthquake. His ability to think on his feet, appear to be listening carefully, find common ground with his adversaries, and neutralize the aspirations of poor people who, after all, only want to be heard by their government anyway, may have saved the PRI's skin after the 1988 electoral fiasco—the ruling party lost the capital handily to Cárdenas but remained in control of the city because the Mexican Constitution mandates the President to name the regent or mayor of the federal district. The "D.F" and suburban zones encompass almost a fifth of the nation's population, concentrated in 16 "delegations" or boroughs, 18 million people, the most overly-inhabited urb on the planet, and Camacho's challenge was to win the megalopolis back for the PRI. The Mayor responded with panache, sometimes strolling onto a zócalo seething with unhappy demonstrators to shake hands with recalcitrant "colonos" (squatters) and "ambulantes" (street venders) and encourage negotiation. Manuel Camacho Solís, a man of many connections, even had a peripheral tie to the EZLN, having himself once been associated with the purported political ancestors of the Zapatistas, the so-called "Popular Politics" movement, centered around the Autonomous University of Nuevo León.

Camacho came to San Cristóbal with an eager, honed staff, forged when he was still Mexico City mayor—the team's spin doctor was Juan Enríquez Cabot (of the Boston Cabots), a hotshot young pitchman who had been cleaning up in Mexico City real estate until his boss resigned as regent. Enríquez, who had attached his star to Carlos Salinas in 1988 only to be sacked as international press chief soon after the candidate took office, had switched to Camacho's corner post-haste, and, was a fervent advocate of the conciliator's ambitions to be the president of Mexico. Also included on the Camacho squad: Alejandra Moreno Toscano, former Mexico City cultural czarina, and a tough-talking manager with a savvy feel for the press. El Camacho's handlers put their product on the street right away.

Wearing slacks and, perhaps, a preppy sweater, rather than the Stetson and guayabera and chuj PRI honchos usually affect when they tour these zones, the Conciliator stepped briskly through the streets of the four invaded municipalities. The press corps thundered on his heels as Camacho, a black ribbon of mourning on his breast to lament all the dead of Chiapas regardless of political persuasion, stopped to pat small Tzeltal women on the shoulder and assure them that "everything will be better now." The Commissioner for Peace and Reconciliation went on state radio, the surest route to Zapatista ears, sending out a message asking pardon of Chiapas's indigenous peoples for a half millennium and more of their suffering. "Are you the Bishop?" an Indian woman asked in Ocosingo. "No, I am the Commissioner of Peace," Camacho reportedly responded, but the old woman was already kissing his hand.

During the first weeks of seeking to establish contact with the Zapatistas, Camacho practiced a shuttle diplomacy that had him often in the air between Chiapas and Mexico City, meeting with the President, Secretary of Defense Reveillo Bazán, and the new Secretary of the Interior, Jorge Carpizo, in lengthy, closed-door sessions. The press bulletins were upbeat. On January 15th, Salinas proposed an amnesty that would pardon all insurgents who had been "pressured" into participating in the Zapatista uprising, a futile gesture intended to lure in a few marginal rebels and maybe, as some cynics conjecture, to block prosecutions of troops guilty of human rights violations.

The Amnesty edict did not at all please the Zapatista high command. Fuming over his pipe "somewhere in the Lacandón Jungle," Subcomandante Marcos formulated a reply to Salinas's offer that has the flavor—and, perhaps the sustaining power—of Fidel Castro's 1954 "History will absolve me" speech to the Cuban court before being sentenced for the July 26th assault on the Moncada barracks.

"Why do we have to be pardoned?" the Sup asked, "what are we going to be pardoned for? Of not dying of hunger? Of not being silent in our misery? Of not humbly accepting our historical task of being the despised and outcast? Of having picked up arms, having found all other roads closed? Of not having paid attention to the Chiapas penal code, one of the most absurd and repressive in history? Of having demonstrated to the rest of the country and the entire world that human dignity still lives, even among some of the world's poorest peoples? Of having been well-prepared before we began our uprising? Of having carried guns into battle, rather than bows and arrows? Of being Mexicans? Of being primarily indigenous people? Of having called on the people of Mexico to struggle, in all possible ways, for that which belongs to them? Of having fought for liberty, democracy, and justice? Of not following the example of previous guerrilla armies? Of not giving up? Of not selling out? Of not betraying ourselves?

"Who must ask for pardon and who can grant it? Those who for years and years have satiated themselves at full tables, while death sat beside us so regularly that we finally stopped being afraid of it? Those who filled our pockets and our souls with promises and empty declarations?

"Or should we ask pardon from the dead, our dead, those who died 'natural' deaths of 'natural causes' like measles, whooping cough, breakbone fever, cholera, typhoid, mononucleosis, tetanus, pneumonia, malaria, and other lovely gastro-intestinal and lung diseases? Our dead, the majority dead, the democratically dead, dying from sorrow because no one did anything, because the dead, our dead, went just like that, without anyone ever counting them, without anyone saying 'ENOUGH ALREADY!' which would have, at least, given some meaning to their deaths, a meaning which no one ever sought for them, the forever dead, who are now dying again, but this time in order to live?

"Must we ask pardon from those who have denied us the right and ability to govern ourselves? From those who lack respect for our customs, our culture, and ask for papers and obedience to a law whose existence and moral basis we do not accept? Those who pressure us, torture us, assassinate us, disappear us for the serious 'crime' of wanting a piece of land, neither a big one nor a small one, but a simple piece of land from which we could grow something to fill our stomachs?

"Who must ask for pardon and who can grant it?

"The President of the Republic? State officials? Senators? Representatives or Governors? Mayors? The Police? The federal army? The great gentlemen of banking, industry, commerce, and land? Political parties? Intellectuals? The mass media? Students? Teachers? People in the neighborhoods? Workers? Farmworkers? Indigenous peoples? Those who died uselessly?

"Who must ask for pardon and who can grant it?

"Well, that is all for now.

"Good health and a hug, and, in this kind of cold weather, you should be thankful for both (I believe) even though they come from a 'professional of violence." (Translated by Frank Bardacke).

* * *

Despite his radio spots beaming reconciliation towards the jungle, three weeks after the war in Chiapas had exploded, Manuel Camacho Solís, a man gambling his political life on getting the defiant Zapatistas to the bargaining table, was telling reporters that he feared the dialogue had hit a wall.

What exactly were the political ambitions of Manuel Camacho Solís, a rejected heir of King Carlos Salinas who had unceremoniously dumped cold water on the ex-Regent's ardor to sit on the throne of Mexico? During ten straight days of optimistic press briefings, Camacho's staff hinted broadly that their man was still a presidential candidate, and even insinuated that this status would be helpful in bringing the Zapatistas in from the jungle. As the Commissioner of Peace and Reconciliation, Camacho had come to represent a third force in the conflict, one that sought a return to domestic tranquility, the price for which was still under discussion. "You are worth more than whatever president!" a worshiper shouted when the Conciliator attended Sunday Mass in Don Samuel's labyrinthine cathedral. In Ocosingo, eagle-eared *La Jornada* reporter Ricardo Alemán overheard Tzeltal-speaking bystanders discussing the Commissioner's presence in the city. "They say it is El Colosio!" "No, it is the other one, El Camacho..."

Since the desultory kick-off of his bluntnosed presidential campaign, Luis Donaldo Colosio had been in cold storage at the back of the book every day. The first rallies necessitated "the trucked-in ones" to pad out attendance, an antique PRI peccadillo. In Coatzacoalcos, the dying oil boom town in southern Veracruz, pissed-off unionists sat down in the middle of the highway to block the candidate's motorcade. In Guadalajara, an excited woman with razor-sharp fingernails accidentally slashed the PRI standard-bearer on the cheek, drawing blood. No one noticed. The Colosio campaign couldn't make it within 15 pages of the front one. Whatever Camacho did, whatever he said, wherever he went, was in eight-column headlines. One apocryphal tale (reported by *El Financiero*) has Colosio, who was a smiling man in public but known by his underlings as a boss with a nasty temper, turning beet-red and nearly putting his fist through the conference table at the mention of the hated Camacho's name.

Despite his irritation, Luis Donaldo Colosio bore a bit of the burden for the upheaval in Chiapas. As the reform-minded president of the PRI, he had failed to reform one of the most corrupt state political structures in an entity that regularly racked up nine out of ten votes for the ruling party. And, as Secretary of Social Development, the successor agency to Camacho's SEDUE, Colosio had pumped billions of new pesos into Chiapas via the "Solidarity" funnel, little of which had ever reached the "extreme poor," short-stopped, as always, on the way down the pipeline by PRI government bureaucrats. Some political sharpies began to consider that when Salinas spoke about "fixing what was not functioning," he might have been referring to Colosio. Pointed commentary began to appear to that effect: NEXOS, a PRI-influenced intellectual monthly, ran a Rafael Segovia spoof of García Márquez's *Chronicle of a Death Foretold* in which both the ruling party and its candidate appeared as trainee corpses. "CAMACHO FOR PRESIDENT" one *Financiero* op-ed piece declared January 19th, reasoning that only Manuel could save the nation.

Rumors of imminent substitution filled the press on both sides of the border. Led by the *Washington Post*, the international pack dismissed the Colosio campaign as hapless and dead-ended and shamelessly promoted Camacho's chances—Enriquez had done the same duty for Salinas in '88. Speculation of his imminent candidacy was rooted in the glaring detail that Camacho, having resigned as foreign minister and having refused to accept any salary or any "new government structure" to facilitate his mission, fitted the constitutional requirement by virtue of having separated himself from a government post six months before the presidential election. Moreover, Colosio himself remained unregistered—inscription of candidates would not take place until March 1st. But even that deadline did not close the door to a Camacho bid—any party could substitute its candidate up to 30 days before the election for reasons of incapacity.

94-year-old Fidel Velázquez, the boss of Mexican

labor for more than half a century (a Guinness Book record for such longevity, topping the old record set by the United Mineworkers' John L. Lewis), worried that his candidate, Luis Donaldo, might suddenly "take sick" and withdraw. The mummified Velázquez heartily opposed Camacho Solís's attempts to negotiate with the Zapatistas, who he wanted to personally "annihilate," a posture that earned the ancient labor boss the sobriquet of "The Terminator" at pro-Zapatista rallies in late January.

By the final week of the month, the political ambiance had been thoroughly poisoned. Some suspicious souls saw the imprint of the "dinosaurs," the highly-nationalistic, thoroughly-corrupt old guard of the PRI, upon the proceedings. Where had dirt-poor Indian farmers without even a centavo to buy a tortilla for their families, scored fancy new uniforms and "cuernos de chivos"? Acclimated to an authoritarian system where all power is imposed from above, the possibility that people could, for once, move on their own resolve, is foreign to many Mexicans. Now Salinas's enemies—perhaps ex-Interior Secretary Fernando Gutiérrez Barrios—had financed the Zapatistas in order to "chingar" his former master and his hand-picked heir apparent. H. Ross Perot was mentioned in the political "chisme" columns of *El Sol* as another likely suspect in the thickening plot.

Finally the gossip got so dicey that on January 27th, Carlos Salinas was forced to summon the cream of the PRI to a power breakfast at Los Pinos where he re-anointed Luis Donaldo Colosio as the one and only candidate of the Institutional Revolutionary Party. "We're not going to allow them to make 'bolas'" (translation: "Don't let them complicate things for us") was the pull quote of the day. 48 hours later, just to square accounts with Camacho Solís, the presidential press office issued a coolly phrased bulletin, praising the Conciliator for his loyalty to the president.

Throughout this spasm of political jockeying, the Zapatistas had been regrouping, watching their military advantage slip away as the Army encircled them, and considering their political options. Protracted war appeared to have been scratched from the agenda for the moment. Could this tiny, totally committed army, having trained for ten years to go to war with the Mexican military, survive the possibility of peace?

The communiqués had now begun to flow more easily from the jungle. Marcos's letters protested harassment on the fringes of the liberated zones but boasted of the EZLN's tactical advantage: "Not with all the federal soldiers can the army close off the roads we have followed in our misery and now in our rebellion," one early communiqué reads, a note that ends with a typical Marcosian twist, mentioning the Televisa "telenovela" (soap opera) "Savage Heart," its star-crossed villain "Juan del Diablo," and garnished by a fillip of English ("but of course"), slim clues to an identity the nation was already begging to discover. The defiant, playful tone found echo throughout Mexico as, one by one, *El Tiempo, La Jornada, El Financiero* and *Proceso* circulated the epistles for the guerrillas.

The Zapatistas first "welcomed" Camacho to the region (published January 18), then endorsed the principle of "dialogue" (January 20th), insisting that it was not their intention "to hold the country hostage" and promising not "to impede the coming electoral process." "Change will not come with just one current or caudillo," Marcos wrote in the name of the Clandestine Revolutionary Indigenous Committee, an apparent call to parallel action in other regions. All the communiqués rejected, flatly, the notion of laying down the arms they had so carefully accumulated over ten years, until the Zapatista demands were fulfilled.

By the end of January, the interchange between the Commissioner and the Subcomandante had a manic-depressive tilt to it. The two spokespersons would flirt ("coquetear" the headlines called it), then pull away from the table to listen to what their respective constituencies were telling them. Deep in the canyons of the Cañadas, the rebels strained to hear what the civil society was saying far away in the cities and sierras of deep Mexico. Curiously, through all the push and pull of those first weeks of dialogue, the name of General Absalón Castellanos Domínguez was rarely mentioned.

* * *

The watershed of support for the Zapatista cause that had inundated the zócalo on January 12th was building to tsunami proportions all over the land. Just on the other side of the military roadblocks, the Tzotzil, Tzeltal, Tojolabal, Chol, and Mam campesinos of Chiapas made it clear that they backed their armed cousins down in the jungle. At a ten-hour January 12th meeting in a sweltering San Cristóbal coffee warehouse, representatives of 140 state farmers and indigenous organizations rose one after another to let yet another presidentially appointed commission know that they emphatically supported the EZLN's just demands. The "Special Chiapas Panel," which came to be known as "Los Reyes" ("The Three Kings") because they promised many gifts, featured Eraclio Zepeda, the master storyteller and leftist raconteur, once Fidel Castro's bodyguard; Eduardo Robledo, Absalón's former Secretary of Government and soon-to-be candidate for governor himself; and anthropologist Andrés Fábregas Puig whose position it was that the Zapatistas were outside agitators. The

172

January 12th meeting marked the birth of the CEOIC, The State Council of Campesino and Indigenous Organizations. With veteran social fighters like Domingo López Angel, Antonio Hernández, and Margarito Ruiz at the helm—the organizers of the 1992 500 Years of Indigenous Resistance outburst—the CEOIC quickly became a powerful voice in the feverish hurlyburly of 1994 Chiapas politics.

The Zapatistas' cry for justice had startling range and resonance in indigenous sierras all over Mexico in January. As far away as Sonora, on the northern border, Mayo Indians encamped in front of the Hermosillo state capital, joining their land demands upon the government with those of the Zapatistas. Usually quiescent Otomí women went to see the governor of Querétaro to demand justice and endorse the EZLN program. In Felipe Carrillo Puerto, Quintana Roo, local police grabbed Mayan ejido leader Marcelo Canoen Mundo and accused him of stockpiling weapons for the Zapatistas.

As the Zapatista phantom galloped through Indian Mexico, masked guerrillas were spotted up at Palmar del Rio in the Sierra Negra of Puebla. In the Mixtec Sierra of this key central Mexican state (400,000 indígenas), 25 villages banded together behind an old troublemaker named Gaudencio Ruiz and raised the banner of the Zapatista Movement of the South. In the state of Puebla, where electric lines were sabotaged in the wake of the EZLN offensive and bomb threats were emptying out factories on the industrial strip every day, military authorities suddenly got nervous about handing out permits for five tons of gunpowder, the crucial ingredient of the wild Nahua Carnival recreation of the Battle of Puebla up in Huejotzingo. Real-life armed uprising was threatened.

The adjoining impoverished states of Oaxaca and Guerrero were of even more immediate concern to the government. If the virus of armed rebellion were to spread out-wards, these threadbare, deeply Indian entities were fertil-ized with enough unjust killing and third degree malnutri-tion to make Chiapas look like a vacation paradise. Oaxaca alone is a basket of 18 distinct "etnias," 1.2 mil-lion Indians, a third of the state's population, who live in seven highly indigenous sierras coasted by luxury resorts like Huatulco, a guerrilla delight.

On January 22nd, Zapotecs in San Juan Yagalá in the Sierra of Juárez seized 15 state officials in frustration because Governor Deodorio Carrasco had failed to show for a meeting of bi-lingual maestros. "GOVERNOR OF OAXACA KIDNAPPED!" jumped jittery headlines in the state dailies. Other Oaxacan Indians were active: Mixtecs marched to the moribund National Indigenous Institute in Mexico City, raised a pro-EZLN banner, and sat down on the concrete in a hunger strike to protest the agency's inat-tention. In Juxtlahuaca, a popular killing ground, seven armed Triquis were taken into custody—the militant MULT organization expressed support for the Zapatistas.

And on the Isthmus of Tehuántepec, in Juchitán, where the COCEI, the long-lived, left-wing alliance of workers, farmers, and students from five Isthmian "etnias," holds power, assemblies were convened just to discuss the Zapatista Declaration of the Lacandón Jungle and decisions were made, says Leopoldo DeGyves, a COCEI founding father. 4,500 activists were mobilized and occupied state and federal offices in 11 cities and towns on the isthmus and, by the third day of the takeovers, Carlos Rojas, Colosio's successor as Secretary of Social Development and mayordomo of the "Solidarity" funds, was flying to Juchitán to meet with DeGyves and his com-pañeros.

Proclaiming support for the Zapatistas became a

weapon of pressure for Indian leaders. "There will be Zapatistas everywhere in Mexico if our demands aren't listened to," Genaro Domínguez, veteran "advisor" to the National Coordinating Body of Indian Peoples (CNPI), declared after a surprise hour-long meeting with Carlos Salinas February 2nd. "The lesson for us here is that if you pick up the gun, the government will listen to you," Domínguez later told me.

Michoacán, Cuauhtémoc Cárdenas's home turf, which, despite the opposition leader's denials, has plenty of armed Party of the Democratic Revolution cadre out in the hills of the Purépecha meseta, was another likely suspect. EZLN wall writings began appearing around Lake Pátzcuaro the second week in January. In the meseta, old revolutionaries tried on ski masks, gifts from a longtime companion. "You should have been here the day before yesterday, Juanito," Ermelinda Baltazár laughed, slapping tortillas onto the hot "comal," "the PRI tried to seize the sawmill and we went up there with what we had"—in this very Indian, very Cardenista hamlet, "cuernos de chivos" (AK-47s) have long been a staple of the environment. "We just opened up on them—bip! bip! bip!" chortled Ermelinda's brother, Miguel. "Sounds like Chiapas to me," interjected a big city reporter. "Ay Chiapas!" bellowed the compañera, "that's where the real wild Indians ("indios salvajes") live..."

Sandwiched between Michoacán and Oaxaca, the state of Guerrero has a colorful history of guerrilla warfare, dating back at least to the 1814-1821 war of liberation from Spain when Vicente Guerrero, the state's namesake, and the black renegade priest, José María Morelos, roamed the hotlands. From 1910 through 1919, Emiliano Zapata periodically paid visits to the state. The rural schoolteachers, Genaro Vázquez and Lucio Cabañas, rose separately in the central sierra in late 1960s.

If the Zapatista disease was going to break out again somewhere soon, Guerrero was the place. This is a state where every home is an arsenal and homicidal violence is endemic—in one recent outbreak of bloodshed, 28 members of one rural family were slaughtered by members of a smaller family from the same town so, the killers explained, they wouldn't be rubbed out first themselves. In Tierra Caliente, where the poppies bloom, 140 drug murders have been recorded in the past four seasons. Along the Costa Grande, 55 armed kidnappings were noted between April 1993 and March '94, according to an *El Financiero* investigation. In early June, the paper reported it had been tipped by U.S. military intelligence sources in Washington that 20,000 AK-47s were en route to private collectors in the state.

Conditions have not gotten much better in Guerrero than when Cabañas rode the Sierra around Atoyac—even the Governor's name is the same: Rubén Figueroa, the son of the similarly-named millionaire politico once kidnapped by Cabañas. In early January, Cabañas' errant heirs, the PROCUP, had bombed Acapulco in "solidarity" with the EZLN. Zapatista leaflets were reportedly plastered all over Atoyac de Alvarez, Lucio's hometown. In the Sierra, the "enmascarados" (masked ones) were said to be moving again. Rubén Figueroa Jr. acted swiftly. "Judiciales" with military back-up, and the dread Motorized Police were unleashed, set up roadblocks on both the Costa Grande and the Costa Chica, north and south of Acapulco. Heavily-armed security forces combed the Montaña.

A remote confluence of Mixtecos, Amuzgos, Tlapanecos, and Nahuas, La Montaña is the poorest region on the Mexican map—its social indices, literacy, health care, income. and nutrition are all on the bottom of the national economic charts. Political consciousness remains surprisingly high—one town, Alcazauca, was ruled for a decade by the Mexican Communist Party and during the 1992 500 Years of Indigenous Resistance campaign, delegations from La Montaña led the march on Mexico City. Now the Guerrero Council of 500 Years of Indigenous Resistance marched again. This time on Chilpancingo, the state capital, where, on January 25th, thousands of indigenous Guerrerans proclaimed solidarity with the EZLN. The march was led down the twisting switchbacks of the Montaña by a ski-masked tyke, "Subcomandante Marquesito." The message from the Montaña to the distant Zapatistas was loud and clear: "In the name of our rivers and our mountains, our birds and our butterflies. In the name of our grandparents and all the generations that were sacrificed before them," the Indians of Guerrero proclaimed their support "for the men and women without faces."

The torrent of support for the Zapatistas was not limited to the Indigenous. In Puruarán, Michoacán, 1,100 sugar workers, whose three-century-old sugar mill had been shuttered and cannibalized by a millionaire crony of the Salinas family to whom the plant had been "privatized," voted unanimously to join the EZLN and a commission was dispatched to Chiapas to make arrangements. Democratic farmers in Chihuahua took over land and blamed it on the inspiration of the EZLN. "El Barzón," an association of prosperous small producers who have run out of bank credits just as North American grain is poised to pour across the border, endorsed the Zapatista Army of National Liberation and blocked highways in central Mexico with their tractors. Leader Maximiliano Barbosa flew south to meet with Marcos.

In provincial cities, school children drew pictures of

the military beating up on Indians and peace rallies were held in the central plazas of Morelia, Puebla, Cuernavaca, Acapulco, Chihuahua, Durango—more rock concerts than militant demonstrations, where—canned food and sacks of rice and old clothes and money for medicines were collected and caravans organized to drive south and deliver the goods. The civil society was on the move.

In Mexico City, small groups had begun to meet each day on the zócalo to hail the Zapatistas in songs and speeches. Every demonstration in the capital, for whatever reason—from students protesting the admission fee at the annual downtown bookfair to striking police officers' marches—carried some emblem of the Zapatistas. On January 25th, thousands gathered in front of the Chapultepec Avenue studios of the hated Televisa Corporation and painted the blank facade with EZLN slogans. "Salinas for Absalón!" a ski-masked chorus chanted at a Cárdenas rally at the Monument of the Revolution in early February—the rally was designed to show off the left center option's broad base of support. Since the uprising, Cárdenas had sought to distance himself from the EZLN—while espousing their goals—and the appearance of Marcos clones on the campaign trail reportedly unnerved him.

As might have been foretold, the Zapatistas quickly invaded Mexico City's left cultural salons—a scent the crabby Nobel laureate Octavio Paz caught a whiff of right away. A January 24th Paz commentary in *La Jornada* charged that left elites were manipulating the Indians and criticized the "civil society" for demanding an end to the massacre in Chiapas on the very day that Carlos Salinas declared a cease-fire. Carlos Fuentes, a writer who resists being embalmed by accolades from the state, replied that the shots fired in Chiapas had "hit their mark. They had awakened the national conscience..."

Now, as January ticked away, the first reporters were already working their way back into the canyons of Las Cañadas, invited by the Subcomandante to the first interviews, where they would tell the compañeros how true a chord the Zapatistas had struck out there, in deep Mexico.

* * *

As the days and the weeks wore on, the name of Absalón Castellanos Domínguez dropped out of common usage. One wants to think that the kidnapping of a high-ranking general and former governor would arouse compassion among his powerful caste but the Mexican government does not like to discuss the kidnapping of the aristocracy in public—such shared concern tends to give the rabble bad ideas.

Where was the General? René Ruiz, Absalón's Tojolabal aide-de-camp, had been driven back up to La Soledad by the Zapatistas and cut loose January 3rd. He had to walk six hours back up to Rancho San Joaquín but was more worried about his General—Absalón had eaten little that first day, "María" cookies and a few gulps of water. 10 days later, medical personnel, released by the Zapatistas after the takeover of the Solidarity hospital at Guadalupe Tepeyac, staggered into Las Margaritas and reported that the ex-governor was being held in a hut right behind the clinic and appeared to be in good health.

Talk of a prisoner exchange was in the wind by the third week of the month. A January 20th communiqué from the CCRI hinted broadly that the time was ripe for such an exchange. On January 20th, 71 accused Zapatistas remained locked down in Cerro Hueco.

Reporters who got within a few miles of Tepeyac on January 27th and were shooed off by three gun-toting rebels, asked the young men where the General was being held. "We haven't seen Absalón around here lately—we really don't have the time to go visit him," one faceless Zapatista quipped, "he's probably out cutting firewood in some Indian village. At his age, my papa carried 30 kilos. We are proving to Absalón how we suffer here..."

Spanish reporters were the first to find the General. In a January 30th *La Jornada* interview, Maribel Herruzo described the hostage as being blindfolded 24 hours a day, unshaven, and disoriented. He had not been beaten, the white-bearded, hawk-faced Absalón thought, because he was a prisoner of war. He had been moved 15 times by his count but was well-fed—beans and sometimes chicken, the General said, "very delicious." Then he began babbling about his cows. He had not bathed in a month. "They kidnapped me because they think I have ranches," the old soldier cackled.

On January 31st, 38 alleged Zapatista prisoners were released from Cerro Hueco under bond posted by the National Indigenous Institute and encouraged to return to the homes from which they had been abducted in the first days of January. 31 more presumed rebels were still not free.

On February 3rd, the Conciliator unilaterally announced the creation of two "free zones"—"zonas francas"—one at San Miguel and the other encompassing Guadalupe Tepeyac, into which the two militaries could not venture and where only the International Red Cross would patrol, bringing humanitarian aid to the communities trapped by the war. The "zonas francas" institutionalized military encirclement of the Zapatistas and, ironically, guaranteed them a liberated chunk of national territory.

The creation of the zones also defined a space in which prisoners could be released to the International Red Cross—indeed, such a presentation would give the Zapatistas international standing and bolster their demand to be recognized as a belligerent force, figured *El Financiero*'s unusually informed Carlos Ramírez.

It was at this stage of the bargaining that word came from the Zapatista side of the barricades that General Absalón Castellanos Domínguez had been sentenced to a life of hard labor "in some Indian community" for his many crimes against the indigenous peoples of Chiapas, felonies that included homicide and torture and kidnapping and theft of property. The good news—or bad news, depending on how you stand on Absalón's guilt—was that the General's sentence had been commuted.

Reporters who finally reached Guadalupe Tepeyac February 4th went looking for Absalón but could not find him. He was not in back of the clinic, had not been there for weeks. Instead of chatting the General up, the press corps was addressed by nine local speakers who expressed their inconformity with the government's trickery, and offered testimony that the local "Solidarity" hospital was a fraud. Then the townspeople sat the reporters down and served them transparent soup, two tiny strips of cow meat floating on the surface. "This is the soup we are saving for Manuel Camacho," one Zapatista supporter told *La Jornada*.

Handing over the General now clearly implied that peace talks would follow and the coquetry on both sides of the barricade grew intense. Absalón's people were restless for his release. Absalón Castellanos Herrerias, a Tuxtla blues club owner, "understood" the Zapatista struggle and "agreed" with their demands but could not understand why the rebels had taken his father. Javier Coello Trejo, the corpulent "Iron D.A." and disgraced drug czar, who had served Absalón as Secretary of Government, reportedly offered his 300 pounds of flesh in exchange for the General's release.

San Cristóbal photographer Antonio Turok and

videographer Carlos Martínez caught up with a much happier Absalón in an interview published February 10th. The General was no longer blindfolded, was allowed to walk around the camp on his own. He confirmed the "pardon" the rebels had granted him—"I hadn't done anything anyway. I'm not a 'terrateniente' (large landowner). I only have one ranch, the San Joaquín—it's a matter of record." The General refused to believe the reports of Army atrocities—"this is not the military I know." He wondered if he might have his pistols back when he went home because they had sentimental value. His imminent release left Absalón strangely wistful: "Sometimes I feel like I am in my old "cuartel" (military headquarters) here. I hear the decisions being made, the orders given, I've relived my most active days here."

Finally, on February 14th, after a month of uneasy interchange, the Conciliator and Bishop Ruiz jointly announced that the General would be freed 48 hours hence at Guadalupe Tepeyac on Ash Wednesday. Elsy waited impatiently up at San Joaquín. The General's sons had gathered at Nuevo Momón.

* * *

It had been five years since Don Samuel—J'Tatik in Tzeltal—had set foot in Guadalupe Tepeyac, a distant and forgotten corner of the diocese. Now the Red Bishop was planted in the middle of a jungle track in the broiling heat, clad in glistening white robes and a Bishop's surplice. He had brought with him the ashes that symbolized the Lenten season with which to mark the faithful.

The Commissioner for Peace and Reconciliation and his team were also in place, Alejandra Moreno Toscano, a supremely urban woman, directing press traffic in the steaming maw of the Lacandón jungle.

300 members of the working press had been trucked in for the historic interchange but their movements were confined to a white circle, chalked like some magic ring, in a clearing at the bottom of the road to La Realidad around the bend from Tepeyac. For hours, the media jockeyed for position, elbows slamming into ribcages, swatting at weird winged insects, and subsisting on mushy bananas. Then, abruptly, one of the villagers got on the microphone set up behind an old desk at the foot of the rise, and ordered all cameras to be turned off. Absalón's release was off because Televisa, after having been disinvited by Marcos ("Televisa doesn't have to be there because they invent the news anyway"), had shown up in Tepeyac anyway. After several tense minutes, the Conciliator was able to assure the speaker that the cameras belonged to Channel 11, the National Polytechnic Institute, and Televisa was not on the scene— the truth is that Televisa was renting the Channel 11 picture and cutting off the sound whenever a Zapatista supporter launched an anti-government harangue.

The endless, sweltering wait was interrupted at 17:25 Jungle Time when General Castellanos, escorted by five small, masked Zapatistas, two of them women, appeared at the top of the hill and briskly marched down the road, which, by now, was lined on one side by men and on the other by women and children, all of them sporting freshly-laundered duds for the occasion. "Viva El EZLN!" they cheered, "We Want Peace!" "That All the Landowners Should Die!" and "Death to the Corrupt Ones!" rang in the stoic, Quixote-bearded Absalón's ears as he passed through this last gauntlet of shame.

Don Absalón Castellanos Domínguez had been declared guilty by the Justice Tribunal of the Zapatista Army of National Liberation of "having obliged the Indians of Chiapas to rise up in arms," and he had been sentenced to "perform manual labor in some indigenous community for the rest of his life," but, in a message "to the people of Mexico and the people and governments of the world" the EZLN had commuted the sentence, "condemning (Absalón) to live until the end of his days with the pain and shame of having received the pardon and the good will of those he had killed, robbed, kidnapped, and plundered." The EZLN insisted that Absalón was being handed over to the Conciliator in exchange for "all Zapatista combatants and civilians unjustly imprisoned since the war began January 1st."

Then, the stubby Major Moïsés, the engineer of the January 2nd kidnapping and the only rebel in ski mask in the sultry heat, nudged the General in the direction of Camacho and Don Samuel. "Señores Periodistas (Mister Journalists) from Mexico and other countries in the world, we have given our word and you are witnesses that we speak with honor."

Now everyone was embracing everyone else, first El Camacho and Absalón, then Absalón and Don Samuel, two old enemies who, ironically, had never met, then Absalón and Elsy and the middle-aged sons, Don Samuel daubing and crossing the ashes on the forehead of each tearful family member. The Conciliator and the five Zapatistas shook hands, formally, the first peaceful physical contact between the government and the rebels. Franz Meyer walked Absalón to the International Red Cross ambulance to check his vital signs and determine whether or not he had been released in good health, in accordance with international protocols. The Zapatistas took the opportunity to take a powder.

When the General's health status had been determined, Aaron, a small, dark-skinned man in a beautifully pressed short-sleeved shirt, walked up to the microphone and read a lengthy document entitled "The Popular Clamor of the Chiapas Jungle." Addressed to Licenciado Manuel Camacho Solís, the Envoy of the Peace, the "Popular Clamor" attacked the "PRI-gobierno" without mercy and brought life to the Zapatistas' 11 points—the document is, in essence, a rough draft of the "pliego petitorio," the formal petition of demands—the Zapatistas would present at the forthcoming peace talks. "The Clamor" also accused General Absalón of having embezzled state funds to build mansions in Tuxtla and of being a cruel thief of 60,000 acres of good Indian land. Absalón, amazed at this last minute outburst of impertinence, kept shaking his head, no, this is a lie. At last, he could no longer contain himself. "What you have heard here is totally false!" he shouted into the mike and then profusely thanked Camacho Solís and J'Tatik for obtaining his freedom.

The nation watched these astonishing events with its mouth open. Such withering criticism of the PRI-run government as Aaron had just delivered was just not permitted on Mexican television. The exotic setting intrigued viewers. But what made the most lasting impression on a public that had already seen a lot since January 1st, was how small were the rebels. So magnified by the press and national aspirations had the Zapatistas become that their actual size had been forgotten. Now Camacho had to bend to shake the small hands of these men and women without faces whose weapons almost seemed longer than they were. For the first time since January 1st, the Zapatistas had shown themselves to the world and they were short.

The ceremony was finished and dusk, with a zillion frisky bugs, was settling in over the jungle. Truckloads of journalists lumbered back up to Ciudad Real. The release of General Absalón had not been an exchange—the 31 remaining presumed Zapatistas in Cerro Hueco had not been released simultaneously. We wondered what the "enmascarados" had gotten for letting this torturer of the Indian peoples go home alive, after 45 days in captivity. Months later, Major Rolando would tell me "saving the life of just one compañero was worth letting that 'puto' (whore) go." By mid-summer, all of the so-called Zapatistas in Cerro Hueco had been released, in batches, on one legal pretext or another—the last five to go home included poor Jesús Meza Yeladaqui, pulled off a bus in Villahermosa January 5th and accused of being a Sendero Luminoso-trained, Guatemalan-born Zapatista commandante.

But, says Rolando, seated in a schoolyard "somewhere in the Lacandón jungle" as the first rains of the season massed in the east, the Zapatistas won another concession from the government in letting Absalón go, that was never much publicized. As late as June, anonymous trucks were still plying Zapatista villages, delivering sacks of rice and sugar to the campesinos, the real price of the General's ransom.

"The wars here are always brutal but they have their own logic and that logic leads to dialogue," Walter "Chip" Morris, the author of the superb volume, *Living Maya*, told Hermann Bellinghausen, as they observed Carnival up in San Andrés Larrainzar, the Tzotzil village with Zapatista antecedents. Morris's analysis of the war is laced with cultural understandings that ideologues like myself often miss: "The declaration of war is a way of saying 'I am'. When the other military replies with a strong attack, they too are saying 'I am'. With the Maya, you cannot talk until you know with whom you are talking. So the release of Absalón is their way of saying 'now, we can talk'.

"But you must be patient. The EZLN has entered into a slow period of conversation in accordance with its own times and needs..."

The Conquistador Mazariegos falls—and the Zapatistas are born.
500 years of resistance march October 12, 1992. (Photo: Antonio
Turok)

The Zapatista Army of National Liberation in their natural habitat, January 1994. (Photo: Antonio Turok)

188

First air casualties of the war in Chiapas. Dead youths gunned down January 2nd en route to Rancho Nuevo. (Photo: Marco Antonio Cruz)

Marcos dialogues with the public from the balcony of the San Cristóbal Government Palace. New Year's Day 1994. (Photo: Guadalupe Mendoza)

U.S helicopters being used to transport corpses, Tuxtla Gutiérrez, January 4th. (Photo: Marco Antonio Cruz)

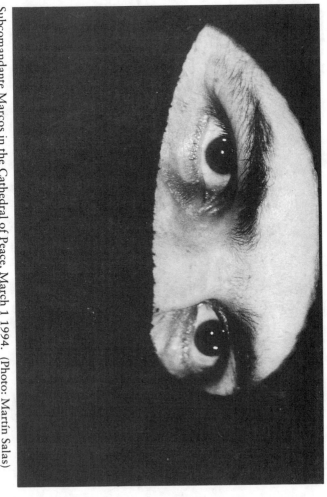

Subcomandante Marcos in the Cathedral of Peace, March 1 1994. (Photo: Martín Salas)

Caravan for peace and human rights, San Cristóbal, January 8th. (Photo: Marco Antonio Cruz)

193

Civilians killed at military roadblock near Rancho Nuevo, January 4th. (Photo: Marco Antonio Cruz)

Zapatista crossing bridge "somewhere in the Lacandón jungle." (Photo: Antonio Turok)

The takeover of San Cristóbal: the archives in the street. (Photo: Antonio Turok)

The takeover of San Cristóbal: sleeping Zapatistas under a "pinta" that mocks General Godínez. (Photo: Antonio Turok)

The Red Bishop and the Conciliator; Samuel Ruiz and Manuel Camacho Solís in the Cathedral of Peace, San Cristóbal. (Photo: Martín Salas)

Cuauhtémoc Cárdenas visits the Zapatistas near Guadalupe Tepeyac, May. (Photo: Marco Antonio Cruz)

The Specter of Chinameca

By the ninth year of the revolution, Emiliano Zapata was tired. Since 1910, the Caudillo of the South had commanded an army of campesino-guerrillas against one Mexican government after another and, still, there was no end in sight to the war. Presidents and dictators kept reneging on their pledges to return the communal lands of Anenecuilco, Zapata's home town in the Cuautla Valley of Morelos state, to its rightful owners. First Porfirio Díaz had refused to honor the Nahua villagers' ancestral claims, then Madero had convinced Zapata to bury his arms and still the titles were not forthcoming and the Caudillo was obligated to dig them up again and resume the war. Then the bloodthirsty Huerta had Madero killed and Zapata's army had been forced to retaliate in kind. In the middle of the war, he had struck a deal with Francisco Villa, the Centaur of the North, to keep the authoritarian Carranza from consolidating power. In December 1914, after their Aguascalientes convention had resolved the question of how they would govern, the two legendary revolutionaries together took the capital and then met under an ahuehuete tree in Xochimilco, the famed Aztec floating gardens in the south of Mexico City and Zapata had, at last, thanked Villa but said he didn't want to be president, no, he was going home to Morelos and await title to the lands of Anenecuilco. Pancho Villa shrugged. He couldn't wait around much longer either. He was already overextended in the north and had to split town to regroup his troops, leaving the radical politicians of the Convention in charge. Meanwhile, Carranza and his ally, the one-armed Obregón smashed south from Sonora, taking Veracruz and crushing the Villistas at Celaya and León in Guanajuato three times in the spring of 1915, finally capturing Mexico City in July. A constitutional congress was called the next year to let the world know that the Mexican revolution was officially over and done with.

Up in Morelos, Zapata waited for government confirmation that the haciendas belonged to the Nahua villagers from whom they had been stolen by the Church and the Crown and the criollo upper crust. Even after Carranza signed the most radical agrarian reform law ever enacted in Latin America (but a pale shadow of Zapata's own Plan of Ayala), Zapata's people did not gain control of the great haciendas. The campesinos of Anenecuilco and dozens more small Nahua towns in the south of this tiny state dug up their arms. This was a war that never ended.

By 1919, Emiliano Zapata and his campesino army had, once again, become a pounding headache for the sensitive Carranza, a patrician landowner who affected a long, white, 19th-century beard and smoked glasses. "Zapata is beyond amnesty," he told the *New York Times* in March of that year. "The peace of Morelos and all central Mexico depends on the utter downfall, the permanent absence, or the extinction of Emiliano Zapata..."

Carranza's wish list was duly noted by General Pablo González, military chief in Morelos and an ambitious young officer who had sworn to bring Zapata to justice. Cleverly reading the Caudillo's increasing desperation, González staged a fake feud with his acolyte, Colónel Jesús Guajardo, who commanded the 50th regiment. News of the falling-out awakened Zapata's interest. The Caudillo was short on ammunition and armed men and he calculated that Guajardo might be ripe for defection. Such things had happened before in this unending war.

The Specter of Chinameca

Guajardo's regiment—over 600 men—were encamped at the Chinameca hacienda at the far end of the Cuautla Valley. Zapata sent messengers with notes and communication was established. Guajardo even volunteered to attack Zapata foes in Jonacatepec as proof of his intention to mutiny against Carranza's federal army. A dozen civilians were killed in the attack. When Zapata, guarded by 30 faithful men, met up with Guajardo and his legions (they were hauling a prize machine gun) late on the afternoon of April 9th, 1919, the two men embraced and the Colónel, in a gesture of undying friendship, presented the Caudillo with a sorrel, the Golden Ace. Emiliano Zapata was, above all, a lover of horseflesh. The two agreed to meet again in the morning to seal their deal.

Even if he was Carlos Salinas's master teacher at Harvard, let's hear how Zapata's definitive biographer, John Womack, (*Zapata and the Mexican Revolution*, Vintage 1968) tells what happened next:

"Shortly after dawn on April 10th, Zapata and his escort were up and riding. This was Zapata's home ground. Chinameca hacienda lay along the Cuautla river barely 35 miles below Villa de Ayala. It was one of the first places he had seized after joining Madero in 1911. And, as he recalled later in the day, he had almost been trapped and killed there in that summer's crisis. Many times, he had ridden these same country roads—as a young man, headed for markets or stock auctions, then for the last nine years as a rebel, revolutionary, and outlaw, hiding and hunting. He knew every path, creek, and fence. The countryside was cool and fresh in the early April morning. The rains and planting had already begun. In August, he would be forty. Of his children, he knew only the eldest, Nicolás, now thirteen; and he had hardly reared him. There was no omen about the day, a plain Thursday: dealing with

Guajardo heightened the tension, but the basic strain of trust, fear, and hope was old and familiar. At almost 8:30 in the morning, he and his men came down out of the hills to Chinameca.

"Outside the hacienda and backed against its front walls, stood various shops, and in one Zapata and Guajardo conferred. Inside the walls, Zapata's escort rested. But the talk of ammunition and attacks was soon interrupted by reports that nationals were in the area. Zapata quickly directed Guajardo to guard the hacienda, and then organized patrols from his own men and sent them out on reconnaissance. He himself led one patrol. Although there was no sign of the enemy, Zapata posted sentries and returned to the hacienda environs. It was 1:30 in the afternoon. Only Guajardo's troops were inside the walls now, except for the aide Palacios, who was in conference with Guajardo about collecting 12,000 rounds from his cache of ammunition. Zapata waited. Invited in to join Guajardo for dinner and close the deal, Zapata chose to keep waiting. But as Guajardo's officers went on repeating the invitation, tacos and beer sounded better. The day had started early, and there had been a lot of rough riding. By two o'clock, Zapata was growing impatient; finally, at 2:19, he accepted. Mounting the sorrel Guajardo had given him the day before, he ordered ten men to come with him inside the hacienda gate.

"'Ten of us followed him just as he ordered,' a young aide at the scene reported...that evening. 'The rest of the people stayed outside the walls under the trees, confidently resting in the shade with their carbines stacked. Having formed ranks, Guajardo's guard looked ready to do (Zapata) the honors. Three times the bugle sounded the honor call; and, as the last note died away, as the General in Chief reached the threshold of the gate...at point blank, without giving him time even to draw his pistols, the soldiers who were presenting arms fired two volleys, and our unforgettable General Zapata fell, never to rise again."

Emiliano Zapata was a fiery, handsome master horseman, who fought valiantly for the most cherished cause—the land of his people. To Mexicans, all Latin Americans, indeed, the whole world, he is the symbol of the incorruptible revolutionary, a powerful voice for revolutionary morality. But what his countrymen and women most remember about the legend of Emiliano Zapata is not so much his nobility but how the Caudillo of the South was betrayed and assassinated by the government. With Zapata's death April 10th, 1919 inside the walls of the Chinameca hacienda, many students of history are convinced that the Mexican revolution died too.

* * *

At the end of January, Epigmenio Ibarra, the correspondent and news producer who had been handed the first communiqué from the EZLN January 10th in San Andrews Larrainzar, got an intriguing phone call at his Mexico City office: the Zapatistas had concluded they needed more than Marcos's quirky, slow-arriving communiqués to get their message out. Now they wanted to tell the story of their revolution—in person. Would Ibarra be interested in being part of a team that would go into the jungle and meet with and film the General Command?

Around the same time, Elio Henríquez, Amado Avendaño's son-in-law and the Jornada San Cristóbal stringer, had received feelers from the Zapatistas. A telephone call would soon be made. Blanche Petrich, one of the most diligent reporters in Mexico, took the call up in the capital, packed her bags, and caught the first plane to Chiapas. Epigmenio and his French cameraman, Philippe, hooked up with Petrich and Henríquez in San Cristóbal and the local art photographer Antonio Turok, whose work has become synonymous with the Zapatista uprising, was added to the crew. On the appointed night, the intrepid quintet was loaded into an appropriately anonymous automobile, told to go to sleep, driven to the end of the paved road, blindfolded and loaded into a cargo truck, and when that dirt track ran out, the reporters were hauled up on mules—a slight problem for Petrich whose mobility is challenged. No one seems to be able to calculate how long they rode—watches were confiscated at the beginning of the trek. Four masked Zapatistas kept Blanche steady on the mule. In the dark, along the canyon track, she lost her cane. At last, the team reached the base camp of the Clandestine Revolutionary Indigenous Committee "somewhere in the Lacandón jungle." Petrich was assigned to a tiny stick and mud hovel. A miserable pallet was laid on the dirt floor. "I can't sleep here," she told herself. She fell asleep immediately. The next morning, the interviews began.

Petrich's interview with Comandantes Ramóna, David, Felipe, Javier, Isac, Moïsés, and, most of all, Marcos, Turok's stills and Ibarra's video, put the first human face(mask) on the Zapatistas since the struggle had ignited January 1st. In this initial—if truncated—guerrilla campaign of the 21st Century, in which images were as vital as bullets, the five-part Petrich interview may ultimately prove as significant as Herbert Matthews' *New York Times* interview with the reportedly dead Fidel Castro in the Sierra Maestra circa 1956.

Marcos's responses to Petrich's probing were devoured by a public hungry to meet the witty, heroic guerrilla, already a legend in his own time. Some samples:

Petrich: "Generationally, are you from '68 (the year of

the student massacre that altered Mexicans' relationship with their government)?"

Marcos: "Definitely from after '68. It's so stylish these days to be from '68—but what do we know here in the mountain? Nah, I'm not. I was just a kid. I come from a little later. Sure it affected me but what principally influenced me was the electoral fraud—the most scandalous being in 1988..."

Petrich: "It must be pretty hard out here..."

Marcos: "The Lacandón jungle, for a Ladino, it's the worst thing that can happen to you. Worse than a program on *24 Hours*. We came here in a process of learning and teaching. The compañeros showed me what they knew of the mountain and I showed them what I knew. And that's how I began to acquire rank, sub-lieutenant, lieutenant, first captain, second, subcomandante. That's where they gave me the examination to be the press spokesperson. But I failed and they left me as a subcommander..."

Petrich: "Will you sit at the negotiating table?"

Marcos: "The committee is still deciding this. If they say they will, I have to support that. But I tell you, all the compañeros and the committee too, we see the ghost of Chinameca and the image of Carranza standing right behind Salinas..."

On January 12th, when Carlos Salinas had announced the unilateral cease-fire in Chiapas, the President had excercised the poor judgement to allow himself to be photographed before a somber portrait of Venustiano Carranza, an image not designed to instill confidence among Zapata's children. Now the Zapatistas would go to the negotiating table with the phantasm of Chinameca flashing before their eyes.

* * *

The CCRI reached consensus on attending the peace talks in early February, after the first interviews were published and Ibarra's videoed hour-long interview with the Subcomandante aired at primetime on the nation's leading cable system. The selection of delegates commenced. Couriers crisscrossed the "mountains of the southeast" on foot, carrying the decision of the General Command to Zapatista communities and assemblies were convened to pick delegates. "We are not going to send any pigeons—the delegates will be our best fighting cocks," Marcos boasted to Vicente Leñero in a lengthy *Proceso* interview conducted four days before the talks were scheduled to be initiated.

The selection process was lengthy and complicated. Communities that had prepared ten years for the protracted war now had to be convinced in five languages that talking to a government that had never listened to them before was the EZLN's best option, that a "civil society" that had paid little more than lip service to Indian misery for 500 years, now would defend Indian lives with their own. The decision to go to San Cristóbal was not taken lightly. It required much discussion. The days whittled down and the nation nibbled on its nails. 350 "news gatherers" had been registered on the accreditation rolls kept by Don Samuel's diocese for the still-homeless peace talks. Now "the Third Army" was poised in Mexico City, waiting for a time and a destination to which it could jet its crews.

Where these historic talks would be held was not confirmed until the very last minute. Early scuttlebutt featured Tapachula, Comitán, or even Huehuetenango, the first Guatemalan provincial capital to the south. Marcos joked that he'd go anywhere except Mexico City for the "dialogue," because General Godínez would use the capital's venomous pollution as a weapon against his country-born delegates. Manuel Camacho would only say talks would be held "somewhere in the state of Chiapas" but not in the Zapatista Lacandón or the free zone because those locations presented too many security and logistical problems. Ultimately, on February 19th, the Conciliator leaked word to the press of what it had already known for weeks: that the "Jornadas (Workdays) For Peace and Reconciliation" would begin that Monday morning, February 21st in Don Samuel's sprawling Cathedral of San Cristóbal.

The doors of the Cathedral were only a hundred miles northwest as the crow flies from General Command headquarters at La Realidad around the bend from Guadalupe Tepeyac and a little less from the "gate" to Zapatista territory at San Miguel—but the distance between the Zapatista base camps "somewhere in the Lacandón jungle" and the great oak portals of Don Samuel's sanctuary was mined with all the treachery that festooned the road to Chinameca.

"Chinameca's in this whole process" Marcos, hunkered down in a dirt floor hut, told Leñero, *El Financiero*'s Oscar Hinojosa, and the *New York Times*' Tim Golden February 17th. "Our enemies know that the direction of our movement is going up there—not just some commission. They can ambush us in a minute and then bullfight with the protesters." Under the cry of "No Nos Deja Solos!" ("Do Not Leave Us Alone!") the Zapatistas summoned compañeros and compañeras of good will to interpose their bodies between the bullets of the enemy and the EZLN delegates, in a non-government "Belt of Security" around the Cathedral. In the high-octane enthusiasm of the moment, hundreds of volunteers poured into San Cristóbal to take up the task.

But getting into the Cathedral through three of the municipalities they had blasted New Year's Day—Las Margaritas, Altamirano, and Ocosingo—remained a serious logistical consideration.

* * *

No quadrant of the Mexican geography had responded to the EZLN's cry not to be left alone more vigorously than the Chiapas just on the other side of the military roadblocks. "After a long night that seemed to have no end, it was necessary for the Zapatista thunderbolt to part the shadows. The poor of Chiapas and all of Mexico are with you!" resolved the CEOIC at the end of January—by now, this broadly-based indigenous-campesino coalition had grown to 280 organizations—with 14 groups, bitter rivals, including PRI farmers confederations and independent left formations like the OCEZ and the CIOAC, controlling the votes at marathon sessions where each of the 700 delegates in turn rose to participate in a hothouse atmosphere of democracy in motion.

On January 25th, President Salinas was flown into Tuxtla under the highest military security—his first visit to the war zone—and met with CEOIC delegates for several hours. The tongue-lashing administered by the irate campesinos left Salinas wincing and his aides staring off into deep space just waiting for the session to end.

Nonetheless, Salinas did not learn the lesson of the rebellion very well during this flash fact-finding mission to Chiapas. Four days later, at the World Economic Forum in Davos, Switzerland, before 400 of the globe's most influential bankers and 30 of its heads of state, Carlos Salinas swore that his nation was thoroughly at peace and, indeed, there had never been an Indian uprising in Chiapas at all.

While the President snowed the bankers upon Alpine slopes, Chiapas was fast coming unglued. A political insurrection was sweeping through the state's 111 (out of 112) PRI-controlled municipalities, only 82 of which actually had municipal presidents still in office. In many towns in Los Altos, the citizenry questioned the whereabouts of

"Solidarity" moneys—another million (USD) of which was supposed to be in the pipeline. In Mastapac, coffee country in the west of the state and Amado Avendaño's hometown, city hall was burnt to the ground and the Pan-American Highway blocked for half a day on February 9th. By February 12th, 26 town halls in the Altos across the state had been occupied by irritated residents, including four government palaces to which the Zapatistas had done significant damage January 1st. Municipal offices seized in this latest civic insurgency included Simojovel, a north Chiapas town with an enormous legacy of civil strife; Chanal, where the blood feud between Catholics and Evangelical Presbyterians poisons the air; and Teopisca, 32 kilometers east of San Cristóbal and a burg with little track record for public disobedience. "This hasn't happened here since the revolution," one elderly witness told *La Jornada* as 2,000 citizens stormed city hall and ran the PRI mayor out of town.

The response of the "Pelón" (or "Baldheaded One" as Salinas is commonly called) was to invite 13 Chiapas mayors to Los Pinos to "dialogue" about their needs and their dreams. After the meeting, to which the mayors, some adorned in ceremonial sombreros, were flown in a chartered jet, two of the invitees could not go home to the communities they purportedly represented for fear of being tarred and feathered.

"The spontaneous municipal uprisings, the rebellions of maestros and municipal workers, the blocking of banks (by campesinos), the takeovers of land, and the general climate of civil disobedience is making Chiapas ungovernable," the sage Chiapas historian Antonio García de León wrote in *La Jornada* February 26th.

The always combative rural teachers of Chiapas had seized upon the climate of conflict cresting across the state to make their claims for a better deal. So had city workers in Tuxtla. So had the farmers. A wave of land occupations by independent campesino groups—most integrated into the CEOIC—complicated the maintenance of public peace. On February 9th, the Mam Supreme Council took over 11 fincas in the Soconusco. Far to the east, in Chilón, near Palenque, Choles took 38 separate properties. In Ocosingo, a municipality that accounts for 17% of the Chiapas land-mass, 27 ranches were overrun in the first valley alone. The nation's then-new (now ex-) Attorney General, Diego Valadés, flew into Chiapas to investigate the robbery of 20,000 hectares (50,000 acres) of private land and the organization of 100 illegal land takeovers—plus the report-ed abstraction of 10,000 head of cattle. Since the 1992 Salinas-engineered revision of Article 27 of the Mexican Constitution that ended land distribution to the land-poor, any brave individual who occupies private land is subject to a maximum 40 years in prison.

The revision of Article 27 was one of the matters the Zapatistas planned to discuss with Manuel Camacho Solís up in San Cristóbal.

As might have been anticipated in so radical a climate, the cattle ranching elite responded in kind to the percola-tions of rebellion and change sweeping Chiapas. The gnarly, archly-conservative chief of the National Small Property Owners Confederation flew into Tuxtla to warn ranchers that Don Samuel and the Church of Rome, German environmental groups, certain international financiers, and other not yet named co-conspirators wanted to convert Chiapas into an Indian reserve that would be beyond the reach of Mexican laws. Such food for thought intoxicated the ranchers' associations of Ocosingo, Las Margaritas, Comitán, and Altamirano. Public marches were organized to demand continued military presence in the region and the immediate advance of the troops on Guadalupe Tepeyac. The maddest dogs were in Altamirano, a cowtown bursting at its seams with 9,000 refugees from the war zone. Captained by hunky Jorge Constantino Kanter, a "natural leader" as such demagogic types are known on the Mexican political tongue, the Stetsoned, fancy-mustached white ranchers of the region zealously witch-hunted Zapatistas.

One popular Constantino target: the eight Saint Vincent de Paul nuns who have maintained their threadbare, ramshackle San Carlos Hospital on an Altamirano sidestreet for the past 18 years, with little fanfare. To the "natural leader" and his cohorts the hospital was a Zapatista hotbed, "a guerrilla encampment"—in the first days of the conflict, three Zapatistas and two policemen had been treated at the hospital and one, a police officer shot through the jugular, did not survive, explains Sister Patricia Muyrán, a root of the ranchers' venom, she thinks. Now, every day, Constantino Kanter and his klan were at the front gate, threatening to burn the nuns out. The Sisters of Saint Vincent de Paul rushed to the hospital chapel to pray.

It was into this lynch mob environment that a truckload of relief goods, collected by Autonomous University students in Mexico City, had the misfortune to venture on the afternoon of February 19th. A mob of several hundred surly ranchers, their wives, and their Indians, surrounded the "Ricardo Pozas Caravan for Peace"—Pozas, a UNAM dean of anthropology, whose studies of Chamula life are required reading for students of highland Mayan culture, had died of old age during the first days of the war. The Caravan was headed for the notorious Morelia ejido, considered by the Altamirano mob and the soldiers who backed them up, to be a "bola" of Zapatistas. The furious crowd stripped the truck, spat on the students, confiscated film from the photographers, and matters got so unruly that the Conciliator had to be called and the judicial police dispatched, to rescue the "Ricardo Pozas Caravan for Peace" from Constantino Kanter's pistoleros.

At this writing, Jorge Constantino has just resigned as a candidate of the Institutional Revolutionary Party for the Chiapas state congress, running on the lower half of a ticket with Lázaro Hernández, the indigenous leader of the ARIC ("Rural Association of Collective Interest"), a campesino organization furious at the Zapatistas for stealing its base. ARIC and other campesino formations that have organized the more than 300 ejidos in and around Zapatista turf, were resentful that the EZLN should have exclusive rights to the government's ear up in San Cristóbal. Such jealous rivals constituted one further danger for "the men and women without faces" to circumvent on the road up to the royal city.

On the eve of the peace conference, Chiapas was electric with rumors that the "White Guards" of the ranchers, the bands of gunsels traditionally hired by the ranchers' associations to protect the herds, were re-arming. In Ocosingo, the Citizens' Defense Group (UDCO) had received Army counter-insurgency training, Marcos charged, and Guatemalan-style civil patrols were being organized. The grapevine chimed with the chisme that a Chiapas "Contra" was training in the hills of Comitán de Domínguez, the Juarista National Army.

The threats to his personal safety notwithstanding, the "Sup," as the youth of Mexico were now affectionately calling him, packed to go up to San Cristóbal, ironizing over which of his rags to wear and wondering what price his "pestilent" ski mask might bring at auction and whether or not the appearance of a certain soft drink on the conference table would enhance EZLN coffers.

Despite the specter of Chinameca darkening their vision, the Zapatistas were coming in from the cold. What the hell, reasoned Marcos, we're already living "de prestado," on borrowed time, having fully expected to be blown away in the daring takeovers of the four municipalities. Now the Zapatistas were returning to San Cristóbal but "not to beg anyone's pardon or supplicate...

"We don't go to mendicate alms or recover the leftovers of the full tables of the powerful. We go to demand what is the right and reason of all the people: liberty, justice, democracy. For everyone, everything. For us, nothing...

"For the indígenas, everything. For the farmers, everything. For the workers, everything. For the students and the teachers, everything. For the children and the old people, everything. For everybody, everything. For us, nothing...

"For us, the smallest of these lands, those without faces and without histories, those armed with truth and fire, those who came from the night and the mountain, the true men and the true women, the dead of yesterday, today, and forever—for us, nothing, For everyone, everything!"

That the children of Zapata could overcome their fears of government treachery, so indelibly manifested by Zapata's assassination at Chinameca, long enough to come in from their jungle to hear what the Man had to offer, signals just how closely the Zapatistas were tuned to the popular sentiment palpable that winter on the streets and in the sierras that are at the heart of deep Mexico.

Conversations in the Cathedral

Don Samuel's house had just been splashed with a fresh coat of canary yellow paint, not so much in anticipation of "The Jornadas for Peace and Reconciliation" but to signal the completion of yet another restoration of the Cathedral of San Cristóbal.

There is no figure of San Cristóbal in the Cathedral of San Cristóbal. Although this vast house of worship features a variety of gaudy plaster saints, there is no statue of the probably fictitious martyr on the premises. This is because San Cristóbal was considered too much of a peacenik for Ciudad Real's warrior merchants, advises the church's designated historian, Andrés Aubry.

The block-wide fortress-like edifice, rechristened the "Cathedral of Paz" for the encounter with the Comandantes, is a labyrinth of church offices, living quarters, social service agencies (the Fray Bartolomé Center occupies one wing), archives, chapels, a courtyard with Mayan stelae, and, of course, the magnificent cathedral itself, with its expansive, gilded altar, a semblance of Sevilla, framed by burnished "retablos" of floating martyrs, painted not by itinerant Spaniards but by indigenous artisans taking a crack at Christian iconography. In its many layers of decor, Aubry suggests that the Cathedral is like an Indian "huipil," an embroidered dress that is worked on by many hands over many years. Personally, I have always found the cathedral floor a chilling space, the sightlines interrupted by cold alabaster columns, the pews cramped, and the bleeding saints frozen in the cathedral's baroque niches give me the willies.

Begun in 1539, the structure, like most of these sorts of public works projects, has never quite been completed—the only remnants of the original church building are two eroded stone gargoyles over the great oak lintel. The church's first occupant, Bishop Bartolomé de las Casas, did not stay here long. De las Casas, upon whose crusade to protect the Indians from genocide the current occupant of the cathedral models his mission, was, like his modern-day avatar, reviled and denigrated for his efforts on behalf of the "originals." The "authentic coletos" of mid-16th century Ciudad Real made life so unpleasant for the Bishop that he was obliged to take final leave in 1546, just six years after being appointed to the sinecure. Don Samuel has absorbed almost six times that amount of abuse in the 34 years ago he has served the diocese of San Cristóbal since his arrival from the fanatically Catholic ghetto of Guanajuato, via a stint in Rome, to assume command of this distant outpost of the One True Church.

Liberation theology caught fire from the radical encyclicals of Pope John XXIII, the roly-poly preacher of social change who electrified the Church in the early 1960s. The message of "accompanying" the poor and the powerless took particular root in the blood-drenched soil of Latin America—the Colombian guerrilla-priest Camilo Torres embodied this gospel of vindication until his death in 1966 in a military ambush. The 1969 Medellin Council of Latin American Bishops took up Camilo's cudgels, deeming it the Church's obligation to stand up to "institutional violence," a bold declaration in a time when the institutions were all run by the "gorillas," the military dictatorships. The Peruvian Gustavo Gutiérrez and the Brazilian Boff brothers, Leónardo and Cleodoves, were the theologists of liberation, but theology is never the strong point of the Church of the Poor, with its Maoist insistence on practice. The stars in the liberation church firmament still touch nerves: the Salvadoran martyrs Oscar Romero, Rutilio Grande, Ignacio Ellacuria and Ignacio Martín Barro, the Nicaraguan Ernesto Cardenal, and Sergio Méndez Arceo, the excellent compañero of Fidel Castro, who preceded Samuel Ruiz as Mexico's officially-designated "Red Bishop."

Never a very popular strain in a national church that was persecuted by revolutionaries for being the sanctuary of the rich and the reactionary, Méndez Arceo's brand of liberation theology was a continuing offense to the sensibilities of the Mexican hierarchy. Headquartered in the Cathedral of Cuernavaca, the imposingly bald-pated Bishop lured in a motley crew of experimental educators, cutting-edge psychotherapists, religious mystics, and not a few mountebanks, welcomed revolutionaries and fellow travelers to town, and built Christian base communities throughout Zapata's home turf of Morelos. Finally forced to resign in 1984, when he reached the mandatory 75 year retirement age—the Cuernavaca diocese was cleaned up by the late Cardinal Juan Jesús Posadas—Méndez Arceo was a galvanizing figure at rallies and forums protesting everything from the U.S. invasion of Panama to the fraudulent 1988 Mexican elections until his death in 1992.

Don Sergio's passing and the death of Don Pepe Llaguno, liberation Bishop of the Tarahumara, left Samuel Ruiz as the dean of the Mexican Church's martyred and maligned liberationists: Bishop Arturo Lona of Tehuántepec on the Oaxacan Isthmus; Bishop Carlos Talavera of Coatzacoalcos; and emeritus Bishop Bernabé Carrasco are the only other survivors on the left in this long-standing ecclesiastical dispute over what the real mission of the Church should be here in the New World.

When Don Samuel came to De las Casas's cold cathedral in 1960, the diocese's social structure was in as much a state of disrepair as the gargoyles over the front door—the diocese served the rich in the cities, the authentic "coletos" and the ranching elites and there was little contact, let alone an "accompaniment" of the indigenous peoples of Los Altos and the jungle. Don Samuel set about building outreach, signing on foreign nuns and priests—often Europeans, who shared his liberation vista. The number of religious workers in the diocese grew from 13 to 130. 7,000 Tzotzil, Tzeltal, Tojolabal, Chol, Zoque, and Mam speaking lay catechists and deacons were trained to serve the spiritual—and the social—needs of their communities. The October 12th-15th 1974 "Fray Bartolomé de las Casas Congress of Indigenous Peoples," a rare government-church conclave, celebrating the 500th birthday of San Cristóbal's first bishop, was a demarcation point for the diocese's social mission. Don Samuel was said to be shaken when speaker after speaker rose in the cathedral to denounce the oppression of the Mayans in a language reminiscent of today's young Zapatistas: "In Chiapas, we, the Indians, live in the mountain and the ladinos live in the cities and the fincas and the ranches, Our government has abandoned us. Who is going to defend us? Only we ourselves can do this by organizing everyone," reads the transcription of one Tzeltal farmer's contribution to the congress.

The 1974 congress inspired Don Samuel to create social structures through which his indigenous parishioners could channel their egalitarian energies. Young social agitators were invited into the diocese to organize "ejidatarios" (communal farmers) under the banners of the Union Quiptic, the Union of Unions, and ARIC, the organizational sea from which the Zapatistas eventually emerged. Within the spiritual realm, the demand for greater participation in diocesan affairs by indigenous communities sometimes led to acrimony. "The Ladinos think they own the Holy Spirit," Don Samuel once was told by a Tzeltal catechist, recalls the Jesuit Mardonio Morales, a white-bearded, 30-year veteran of the jungle. The local churches, particularly in the Tzeltal zone, became increasingly autonomous. Today, in Zapatista towns, catechists, their faces masked by bright red "paliacates," say Mass and, elsewhere in the diocese, nuns deliver the Host.

Don Samuel's social message—his homilies are often so dense as to be indecipherable—sometimes obfuscates his ulterior mission, which is to win heathen souls to the Church of Rome. In Chiapas, this is serious business—although Mexico is nominally 90% Roman Catholic, in this southernmost state, only 67% are devotees of the True Faith. Indeed, the National Geography and Statistical Institute indicates that Chiapas has the highest number of professed atheists in the Mexican union (345,000). But the real heretics are the "Protestantes." In 1914, U.S. Protestants divided Mexico up into sectors (the Cincinnati Plan) and the southeast was awarded to the Presbyterians. Nonetheless, in this year of Our Lord 1994, the Presbyterians are far outnumbered by Evangelicals, often home-churched across the border in heavily hallelujah'd Guatemala where U.S. missionaries have a deep foothold. Half a million Presbyterians and Evangelicals are said to be loose in Chiapas, winning souls every minute of the day and night for their God. One recruitment pitch has been to badmouth Don Samuel as the Great Beast, the 666, the Satan of San Cristóbal. Don Samuel has responded in kind by implying that the born-agains are agents of Yanqui imperialism, infiltrated by CIA operatives.

One of the most critical conflicts between Christians has been localized in San Juan Chamula, 20 minutes from downtown San Cristóbal. Addled by drink and starving from land hunger, the Chamula "tushones" (PRI bosses) have expelled 25,000 mostly-Protestant Indians from their communal lands, for violating traditional beliefs—i.e. not drinking "posh," the sugar cane "trago" that fuels Chamula's syncretic spiritual life, the sale of which is controlled by the tushones. Down the years, the "expulsados" have become a force for social change in the highlands and Don Samuel has often spoken up on their behalf. Bishop Ruiz is, himself, a Chamula "expulsado"—in 1985, the tushones threatened diocesan workers with death and Don Samuel withdrew his priests from the town. Today, services are performed in the "Chamula Ceremonial Center," once the local Catholic church, by a Greek Orthodox swami brought in from Tuxtla.

But Don Samuel has more formidable foes than the heretics. The ranchers and the landed elites have been on his case for decades. State authorities arrest and deport his priests, nuns are harassed by the Guardia Blanca, the "Red Bishop" is regularly accused in big, scrawled wall-writings of being "the King of the Guerrilla." Ten years back, the state of Chiapas was trying to lock him up for treason—in 1983, Genaro Domínguez, the wiley leader of the CNPI, was threatened by Absalón's police with being cast into the Sumidero from a helicopter if he didn't sign a confession to the effect that Samuel Ruiz was inciting revolution in Chiapas. One "corrido" (ballad) collected in Comitán by *Proceso* in the spring of '93, begins: "On the 25th of January, in San Cristóbal did arrive/ A goddamn guerrillero/ dressed up like a Bishop/ He called himself a Communist/ with a machine-gun in his hand/ Preaching like an artist/ and convincing the Cristianos..."

With this kind of jacket, it was not unexpected that Samuel Ruiz would be fingered for fomenting the Zapatista uprising. On January 2nd, the detestable Zabludovsky informed the nation that Pablo Romo, Ruiz's disciple who heads the Fray Bartolomé center, and Father Joel Padrón from Simojoval, once jailed by Patrocinio as an agitator, were the EZLN's supreme commanders. Patrocinio González himself, never a fan, accused Don Samuel of confusing religious work with social struggle and blamed the rebellion on the catechists. The military claimed the rebels were utilizing radio transmitters paid for by the diocese. Up in Mexico City, Luis Pazos, a small man in a polyester suit, who runs the fabulously successful "Free Enterprise Study Center," labeled Samuel Ruiz "Comandante Sammy" and charged, in his best-selling broadside "Why Chiapas?" that the Red Bishop was financing the Zapatistas through his European Catholic backers.

In Ocosingo, the Army took more direct action—machine-gun fire raked the roof of San Jacinto Church and the adjoining convent and fragmentation grenades were tossed into the bell tower. Four separate searches ("they broke down the door every time" reports Father Trejo) were made for rebels the good fathers and nuns of Ocosingo were said to be hiding in the church's 16th-century crypt.

Lest the confusion persist, the Zapatistas had tried to make their lack of religious affiliation crystal-clear from the get-go. The January 11th communiqué insisted "we have no ties to Catholic religious authorities or any other creed. We have not received orientation, direction, or support from any church structure, not from any diocese in any state, not from the Papal Nuncio, not from the Vatican, not from anyone..."

"We want liberation—but without the theology" insists the Sup.

REBELLION FROM THE ROOTS

* * *

Even without the guerrilla tag, Don Samuel was in hot water with Rome where the Holy Father had seemed to suggest that liberation theolgists better repent or they were going to fry in Hell. "Samuel Ruiz has become a great source of trouble for the Pope" comments churchwatcher Dr. Soledad Loaza, director of the Colegio de Mexico research institute, observing that J'Tatik's De las Casas-like thesis collides with Karol Wojtyla's Eurocentric version of the Gospel.

Don Samuel and John Paul had an opportunity to discuss their differences on August 6th, 1993 when they met on the Yucatán at Ixamal. A Mayan Mass was being pronounced and the Red Bishop took the opportunity to slip El Papa a copy of a recently-issued pastoral letter "In This Hour of Grace," an epistle decrying the continuing suffering of the Mayan peoples, blasting Carlos Salinas's neo-liberal economic blueprint, the revision of Constitutional Article 27, and implicating the PRI in upcoming electoral fraud. Papal Nuncio Giralamo Prigione was scandalized.

Prigione has feuded with Ruiz for years, much as he did with Méndez Arceo, vetoing the visas of prominent liberation theologists and endorsing the expulsion of troublemaking priests like the Belgian Marcel Rotsaert. During a visit to the Holy See in September 1993, Prigione, reportedly egged on by Patrocinio, persuaded the Sacred Congregation of Bishops, under the pen of African prelate Bernard Gantin, to draft a letter chastising Don Samuel for failing to follow the rules.

The Red Bishop was in São Paulo, hobnobbing with the silenced Boffs and Bishop Pedro Casaldáliga when, on October 26th, a fax arrived signed by Prigione, ordering Don Samuel to return to Mexico to face the music. The São Paulo retreat, which Don Sergio had often attended, was labeled as "unauthorized" by the Vatican.

At the Mexico City nunciatory, Prigione read the Bishops' riot act, alleging mismanagement of the San Cristóbal diocese and "Marxist interpretations of the Gospel." The nuncio, avowing to be only a messenger, refused to give Don Samuel a copy of the charges. "I am still the Bishop of San Cristóbal," Samuel Ruiz defiantly told reporters who had been waiting outside in the street,

As word spread of the nuncio's treachery, so many faxes supporting Don Samuel showed up at Prigione's palatial offices in Guadalupe Inn that he had to have his fax number changed. On November 24th, it is estimated that more than 10,000 Indians jammed the Cathedral of San Cristóbal and the neighboring Plaza of the 31st of March to protest the Vatican's intentions to remove J'Tatik from his diocese.

After the New Year's Day Zapatista declaration of war, Carlos Salinas's first inclination was to finish off the Red Bishop, first by permanently isolating him from the rest of the hierarchy and then setting him up for eternal exile to the Siberia of the Vatican's choosing. José María Córdoba Montoya, the house Svengali and conduit to the High Clergy, worked the phones to the nuncio—a prelate so close to the Institutional Party that his name is sometimes written PRIgione—and to the nuncio's crosstown rival, Ernesto Corripio Ahumada, Mexico's surviving Cardinal. According to La Jornada religious writer José Antonio Román, Córdoba wanted Corripio to issue a forceful condemnation of the EZLN and Don Samuel's purported sympathies towards the rebels. A similar letter was being circulated among Chiapas's two other Bishops, Tuxtla's Aguirre Franco, an Opus Dei member, and Tapachula's Felipe Arizmendi. In the spirit of ecclesiastical unity, both Bishops felt Don Samuel should be consulted before the letter was made public. Faxes were exchanged and a rewrite, citing the social causes of the rebellion, added to the document, before the three Chiapas Bishops signed on the dotted line, the first point of agreement between them since Patrocinio rammed through his abortion-on-demand law in 1989.

Then, on January 10th at a Mexico City junta of the CEM, Cardinal Corripio publicly embraced Bishop Ruiz and endorsed his "accompaniment" of the poor of Chiapas, taking a rude slap at the despised Prigione and torpedoing Córdoba's nefarious scheme. Despite owing their ecclesiastical appointments to the nuncio, many members of the CEM have become disillusioned with Prigione, who had grown so thick with Salinas, Córdoba, and Patrocinio that he now bypassed the Bishops' Conference in his dealings with temporal authorities. Now, by backing Don Samuel, the movers and shakers of the Mexican Church suggested that Giralamo Prigione's 16 year stay on these shores, was over. There were public calls, later retracted, for the nuncio's removal by the Vatican.

It was, indeed, the Miracle of Miracles! Within a few short weeks, the Zapatista uprising had propelled the once-vilified Ruiz from the margins of his church to its very center. Indeed, many members of the hierarchy suddenly saw Don Samuel as the Catholic Church's last best hope for social credibility. "Bishops who would never speak of us except badly, now come here and find a space—the hierarchy has an opportunity for conversion," Father Romo exulted. Similarly, the Salinas regime, which initially had sought to pin the rebellion upon the Red Bishop, now saw Don Samuel as its political salvation. Federal bodyguards were assigned to protect J'Tatik. Church attendance boomed: Bianca Jagger, Robert Kennedy Jr., Rigoberta Menchú came to converse in the Cathedral and TV crews jostled for the best shot every Sunday at Mass. In February, just before the talks between the rebels and the government were to get underway, Don Samuel's Brazilian supporters nominated him for the Nobel Peace Prize.

Despite his multiple defenders, Samuel Ruiz's innocence is not quite as white as the driven snow in this matter of fomenting rebellion. In 1976, the Bishop of Torreón, Fernando Romo, invited Samuel to that Coahuila city to take a look at the organizational skills of young radicals in the "Tierra y Libertad" workers' colony. The Red Bishop was impressed by the work being done by the group, whose political handle was "Línea Proletaria"— "Proletarian Line"—and whose ideological orientation was unquestionably Maoist. Ruiz invited them to come to Chiapas and help create independent social structures in the jungle. "Don Samuel saw the mask but he never looked behind it," explained the Jesuit, Mardonio Morales, to *Proceso* in September '93—before he was silenced by the diocese. Father Mardonio saw the Torreonistas arrive year after year to work on outlying ejidos with the Bishop's blessing. One of those eager young men who came to "the mountains of the southeast" in 1983, the one who now took the name of "Marcos" but concealed his face under a "pestilent" ski mask, was even right now on his way up to the "Cathedral of Paz" to "dialogue" with Don Samuel.

*　*　*

Unlike New Year's Eve, San Cristóbal was properly prepared for the Zapatistas' return. Three concentric circles of security—Military Police (400) and civilian volunteers from the Mexican Red Cross (300) and a dozen national and local NGOs (400), saturated the central plaza, its feeder streets, and the freshly-painted Cathedral, not so much to protect the people of San Cristóbal from the dread insurgents but more to safeguard the EZLN delegates from the wrath of the ranchers and the authentic "coletos" and other dark forces of reaction bent on teaching these upstart Indians a lesson.

To commemorate the Zapatistas' return, San Cristóbal de las Casas had draped itself all in white—white clothes, white flags flying from private homes, white doves released in the dawn to petition the gods for a successful conclusion to the "Workdays (Jornadas) for Peace & Reconciliation."

Don Samuel finished up Sunday morning Mass just after 9 A.M. It was Saint Eleuterio's feast day, February 20th, but the Tatik had made no mention of the "Martyr of Persia" when he counseled the usual full house of worshipers and reporters. Instead, the Bishop instructed the faithful to seek spiritual solace at Santo Domingo or any other of the dozens of baroque churches in the city because the Cathedral was going to be closed to the public indefinitely. This cavernous house of worship now had a higher mission: in his homily, the Bishop, a prelate who resembles a thickset Yoda, the neckless, Lucasland space guru, rebaptized the elephantine edifice "the Cathedral of Peace" and San Cristóbal de las Casas "The City of Peace." "We are the Living Gospel bringing the Good News of Peace to our city," Don Samuel cooed from the pulpit.

Afterwards, the Bishop changed robes, prayed quickly. Pablo Romo knocked timidly at the door to tell him that the Conciliator was waiting outside in the car. "Mother of God," Don Samuel muttered, took a deep breath, and put his fate in the hands of the Creator.

At 9:30, on a gray, streaked February Sunday morning, Bishop Ruiz and Licenciado Camacho Solís left San Cristóbal, driving north. They were being followed, in fact, escorted, by the Highway Patrol, two International Red

Cross ambulances, two other unmarked civilian vehicles, and a rattling busload of reporters. The convoy was the last to leave—two others had departed in the dawn to pick up EZLN delegates at the gates in Guadalupe Tepeyac and San Miguel. Civilian vehicles had been added because the Zapatistas were coming in armed and the IRC cannot transport armed combatants.

The convoy navigated out of town over the Puente Blanco, hugging the road to Chamula. The press bus was halted at the Chamula-Zinacantán turn-off and told to wait. The fork is called "La Ventana"; someone said it was in Tenejapa community lands. The turn-off was marked by a tarnished old statue of Emiliano Zapata, placed there years before by the local chapter of the PRI's National Farmers' Confederation. Don Samuel and the Conciliator had continued northeast through Chamula and into the winding hills beyond. Reporters guessed San Andrés Larrainzar, 25 kilometers to the north, was their destination.

90 minutes later, Camacho and the Bishop were back, loaded with Zapatistas, nine of them in three unmarked cars, Marcos said to be among them. That Marcos and the EZLN leadership had come as far as Larrainzar in the highlands to be picked up, skirting military barricades down in the jungle, indicated a capacity for mobility not noted since the first days of January.

The vanguard convoy sped down Insurgentes into the treelined plaza and screeched to a halt in front of the Cathedral of Peace at precisely 11:58 on *La Jornada*'s watch. Camacho and Ruiz bailed out first. Two small Indians, their faces masked by paliacates, emerged from the back seat, carrying enormous suitcases. Three armed Zapatista women popped out of the second car, then a ski-masked man hauling a bulky pack. Two heavily-armed rebels, also ski-masked—one of them wearing a ribboned Chamula ceremonial hat—jumped from the third vehicle to cover the backs of their comrades.

The Zapatistas arrival was greeted by "Vivas!" and applause from the several hundred onlookers—many of them Indians and mestizos from San Cristóbal. None were more eager than the hordes of paparazzi who surged towards the guerrilleros to get a closer shot. The NGOs linked arms and held off the determined press pack. "Yoohoo, you're Marcos! We know you!" yodeled one photographer at a Zapatista soldier nearly bent double under a pack that hinted he had come to stay awhile. The Subcomandante hesitated, then continued towards the open cathedral door where Don Samuel and Manuel Camacho Solís were now stationed to greet the insurgents. Decked out in black ski mask, bandaleros of red-tipped shotgun shells crossed over his olive fatigue jacket and cradling his pet shotgun, Marcos started up the steps. "Yoohoo, Marcos!" the paparazzi persisted. Then, ever so coyly, the Sup reached down and pulled up his pants leg to display a muddy boot and a slice of hairy white flesh before he evaporated into the cathedral. "Enseñando pierna," the maneuver is called in Mexican cheesecake argot, "showing some leg," a gimmick usually employed by starlets at major motion picture premieres.

It was going to be that kind of week.

* * *

The "Jornadas for Peace and Reconciliation" were not programmed to begin until Monday morning but the Zapatistas got right down to business. In all, 19 delegates had been chosen by the assemblies and the Clandestine Revolutionary Indigenous Committee, 12 members of the political leadership and seven from the military structure.

Over the course of the next ten days, the press came to know many of their names if not much more—Ramóna, the monolingual Tzotzil comandante and Ana María, who had commanded the first takeover of San Cristóbal, Victor Manuel, Raúl, Eduardo (also a ladino), Humberto, Adán, "Jelipe" (who had read the Declaration of the Lacandón Jungle from the municipal palace balcony here January 1st), David, Oscar, Moïsés—Absalón's keeper, and, of course, Marcos. The EZLN plan was to present a 34-point "pliego petitorio," a formal "petition of pleas"—the presentation of such petitions is often how independent campesino groups negotiate grievances with the government. Now the text of the petition had to be ironed out in five languages and the Zapatista delegates lapsed into caucus mode.

The hours ticked by. For 30 hours there was no news, a complete black-out from Sunday noon until Monday dusk. Just what was going on behind the fat walls of the yellow Cathedral? The Third Army grew antsy. María de la Luz Ruiz, Don Samuel's sister, who had volunteered to cook for the insurgents, was located and queried. The Zapatistas go to bed late and get up very early, she told Ricardo Alemán. For lunch, they had chowed down on spaghetti and meatballs, a Caesar salad, and peaches in their own syrup.

Word hit the pressroom at the Mazariegos that a 6:30 press conference had been called in the Cathedral and the troops scrambled. Metal detectors and pat-down searches hardly dampened the ardor of the "communicators" (Mexican governmentese) to go to church. Inside the Cathedral, the news gatherers were segregated between cold Corinthian columns by the tools they used: cameras and electronic media in the center, notepads, pens, and mini-recorders to the sides and everyone separated by a good 15 feet from the ornate speakers table. The Cathedral had been only minimally modified for the "Jornadas," a plywood wall thrown up to cover the base of the alter so that the martyrs in the retablos seemed unanchored, floating off towards the vault of the roof, on their way, at last, to heaven. Upon the impromptu wall, Manuel Camacho, the government's unpaid, unofficial negotiator, had hung a small Mexican flag—not a common sight in a country where Church and State endlessly bite each other's back.

Soon after 18:30, Don Samuel, followed by 19 masked and armed Zapatistas, filed in from off-stage left and took their stations around and behind the table. The Conciliator, looking especially preppy in a dark sweater he would not remove for days, chose to enter from the right. "This is an historic occasion," Don Samuel intoned, modestly. Indeed, the Grand Guignol spectacle of masked guerrilleros bringing large caliber automatic weapons to the peace table in a Cathedral filled with sailing martyrs, has already earned a perverse niche in the recent history of Mexican surrealism.

Don Samuel greeted the Conciliator, greeted the Zapatistas. The cameras zoomed to Subcomandante Marcos, hunched over to speak into the microphone to the Bishop's right. "Through my voice speaks the voice of the Clandestine Revolutionary Indigenous Committee," he breathed, establishing his identity as the spokesperson. The Subcommander then asked each of the delegates to introduce themselves, which at least 11 Zapatistas did, some in Chol, others in Tzotzil and Tzeltal and Tojolabal—no Zoque or Mam speakers had made the trip. As the delegates offered their greetings, Don Samuel felt obligated to inform the uninitiated that the delegates were speaking in their own tongues.

Marcos had quietly hand signaled Comandante

Ramóna, the diminutive leader of the Zapatista women. Now she produced a sensationally folded Mexican flag from her "moral" (woven shoulder bag), handed a corner to the Sup and struggled to drape it across the table but her size subverted her stretch. Gallantly, El Camacho stepped into the breech, grabbing a corner of the patriotic cloth. The cameras rattled like a thousand Gatling guns, the flash bulbs blasted as if war had just been declared all over again. For 38 seconds, Camacho Solís and Subcomandante Marcos stood together, exhibiting the tri-colored, snake-and-eagle insignia'd flag to the nation. When the shooters seemed satiated, the Conciliator dropped his end of the banner and delivered his own greeting: "This shows that we are meeting here under one flag..." The symbolism seemed propitious for the success of the negotiations.

The 6:30 P.M. press call became the mechanism for getting the news out. During the day, the press corps chased hollow rumors of phantom press conferences or covered the ugliness down in Altamirano where the ranchers were determined to burn the nuns out—a hospital shed had been torched—and the bones of Ejido Morelia were trying to get home. Or else reporters hung around San Cristóbal's multiple artsy-fartsy coffeehouses, buying up souvenirs from the Chamula women, who, displaying marketing talents that Mattel would envy, had, overnight, stitched together a million ski-masked Zapatista dolls that quickly became the hottest item on the street.

By Tuesday evening, the nation was on the edge of its seat, ready for the next installment of the political "tele-novela" (soap opera) unfolding inside the Cathedral of Peace—Don Samuel now even referred to the participants as "actors." Marcos-mania was sweeping across Mexico— by the third week of February, the Subcomandante was observing the general public from every magazine cover and daily paper in the land. Saturday night at Mexico City's Bellas Artes, the maximum house of institutionalized culture in the nation, during a performance of "Nabucco," the stirring Verdi opera featuring the exodus of the Israelites from Babylonia, a young man had risen in the second balcony to shout "Que Vivan los Indígenas! Que Viva los Zapatistas!" and the impeccably-coiffed gentry on the floor had responded with "Que Vivan!"

"Buenos noches, compañeros. I'm going to speak for a long time so you better change your cassettes now," the Subcomandante warned the press. "Say no to piracy!" Marcos urged the "communicators," thumbing his nose at Televisa, which of course, had cameras on the premises despite Zapatista warnings. Then the Sup got serious, his voice world-weary but quick-tongued, at first soft but then deepening, swooping, sometimes cracking: "When we came down from the mountains, carrying our packs and our dead, we came to the city to find the patria (the father-land).

"We came to the cities armed with truth and fire," Marcos continued, sounding a little like the Indian prophet-warriors of 1712 and 1868. "We came to ask the patria why you have left us alone for so many many years..." The Subcomandante's slow oratory, replete with repetitions and cadences that make a San Francisco poet salivate with delight, was building towards a climax as he probed the reasons for the war. "Why do we have to sleep with our boots on and our souls upon a string?" he asked. "We have become soldiers so that we do not have to become soldiers," he explained. "Now we have decided to give peace a chance." Marcos sounded a Lennonist note. When the guerrilla-poet was done a half hour down the pike, there wasn't a dry eye in the house. Apparently moved by the Subcomandante's expostulation, Manuel

Camacho Solís rose to his feet to conclude: "There are many of us in Mexico who want more democracy, more liberties, who want more justice!"—a cry against PRI politics as usual that Carlos Salinas was surely auditing in Los Pinos.

Later that night, long after midnight in fact, the oft-mini-skirted PRD deputy, Patricia Ruiz Anchondo, carried away by Marcos's message, went and hired a roving band of troubadours to serenade the Subcomandante, presumably asleep deep within the bowels of the Cathedral of Peace.

* * *

On Wednesday, the third official day of the Jornadas, showbiz was shelved. The Zapatistas presented their "pliego petitorio" and Camacho, in constant touch with his President, had begun to respond—Salinas told reporters he had instructed the Conciliator to be "generous." At the evening press conference that night, Marcos startled the newshounds by announcing that 25% of the "pliego" had been "resolved." The press seemed to think this meant that 25% of the Zapatista demands had been met by the government but what the Subcomandante apparently intended to communicate was that the government had made "responses" to a quarter of the Zapatistas' 34 points, and that those "responses" having been made, the delegates could move on to discussion of the next point in the "pliego petitorio," pending approbation by the Zapatista base assemblies. The misunderstanding was to dog the results of the peace talks for months.

Bubbling with reconciliation fever, Marcos then told the press that the EZLN's national demands were off the table—"the table of San Cristóbal is too small to resolve these issues." Zapatista national demands included

235

Salinas's resignation, the appointment of a transitional government, the separation of the government from the electoral apparatus, the re-negotiation of the NAFTA-TLC to protect Mexico's poorest farmers, and the reinstatement of Constitutional Article 27. 'We do not have the moral authority to speak for the rest of the nation," the Sup pleaded, urging the "civil society" and the political parties to take up these issues. "We will join them."

A smiling, optimistic Camacho, who had made it clear before the talks opened that such EZLN demands as Salinas's ouster would not be a proper issue for negotiation, took the microphone to remark that the "Jornadas were bringing their first results..."

Although live broadcasts were banned from the Cathedral, a Tabasco station, XECA, had bootlegged out the signal anyway. In Villahermosa, the capital of that neighboring state, PRI presidential candidate Luis Donaldo Colosio had just arrived in the XECA studios and the station cut away from San Cristóbal. After a brief spasm of political palaver, Colosio took listeners' phone calls. The first caller groused grumpily that the station had cut Marcos off in the middle of a press conference just for the "pinche PRI."

On Thursday, the spirit of reconciliation soared to new heights. Now Marcos advised his followers that 50% of the EZLN petitions had been "resolved," including a demand that the NAFTA-TLC be renegotiated. "The Zapatistas have lowered their tone," *Ojarasca*'s Bellinghausen observed. Others, like UNAM jurist Luis Javier Garrido openly worried about co-optation. Like so many militant independent campesino groups before them, the EZLN had gone behind locked doors to negotiate with the government and cutting deals under such conditions is how the PRI has traditionally stolen the thunder from the left. Marcos's now daily announcements of percentages of "resolution," an old PRI-government ploy, were also baffling. ""When the government says 50% of the problem is resolved that usually means the two sides are very far apart," warned a colleague. "It's just a way of saying that nothing very much has been accomplished...."

In between the negotiating sessions and the nightly press briefing, the Zapatistas met incessantly with the "communicators," in layers, two hours for national radio, two hours with international print. Marcos did most of the talking, sucking thoughtfully on his pipe and offering sage witticisms that worked as sound bites. At one session, with international radio reporters, the correspondents cajoled the Sup into responding in English. Where had he learned to speak the language of the oppressor? By reading "Hoostler" and "Magnum," he joked—previously, Marcos had told Leñero that his teachers were "Playboy" and "Penthouse." The "machismo" (male chauvinist piggism) implied in the answer dismayed admiring distaff reporters. "Maybe I should read some other magazines," the Sup apologized to Monitor radio's Sandina Robbins.

But there were also signs that the Subcomandante was getting weary of all the chitchat and jumping through of hoops at the media circus that the "Jornadas" had become and just wanted to go home to the peace and quiet of his jungle. "We have been out in the mountain a long time" he reflected, confessing that he and his comrades didn't have much feel for how things worked out here in cosmopolitan, commercial Mexico anymore. "For a lot of people, we have become commodious heroes"—Marcos was suddenly deadly serious—"but it is we who suffer the deaths..."

The Zapatistas were plainly offended by the merchandising that accompanied their visit to San Cristóbal. The dolls, pens, tee-shirts flooded the streets—and now there were these maldita condoms, "Los Hombres Alzados," "the men who have risen up," whipped together by a local AIDS education project, Marcos's ski-masked image on the packet, which lied, "I recommend them. I love them."

"Marcos! Marcos, look what I have to show you!" trilled a young Mexican reportera, rushing the table with a packet of "Alzados." The Sup recoiled in horror, rose up, reputedly muttered that "I have become a masked man of latex," and stomped out of the Cathedral interviewing room with several Zapatistas right behind him. After a confused ten-minute hiatus, the "hombres alzados" returned and Juan asked for the word to deliver a stern denunciation: "We have risen up in arms because our dignity was not respected yet you keep looking at us like animals in a zoo...

"People of our own blood, our own death, are selling us like merchandise. They are selling the heroic blood of our martyrs right here, in the streets of San Cristóbal..."

* * *

Now there were no more 6:30 press conferences in the Cathedral. Sometimes, a frayed and distracted Don Samuel would appear after nine P.M., announce that there had been "advances," that the final documents were being drawn up, excuse himself, and pad back into the dark warren of offices clustered around the Cathedral floor. Marcos would emerge in the mornings, accompanied by a handful of "enmascarados" and hint at progress or lack thereof. Yes, it was true that the EZLN's national demands would not be answered in the document presently under consideration but that would not prevent the rebels from "pronouncing" them. Only the "civil society" could resolve these issues—the Zapatistas were not sidestepping their responsibilities but they "just wanted to give the country the chance it never gave us" to rectify itself. "Be clear," Marcos warned, "we are not for sale!"

A week after the talks had been initiated, the actors were permanently lodged in the Cathedral, never once venturing beyond its stout walls, Camacho apparently closeted amongst them. Negotiations were head to head in five languages and the translations slowed the proceedings to the pace of molasses. Although they had discussed disrobing in the privacy of the Cathedral's inner sanctum, the Zapatistas decided to continue the talks behind ski masks and kerchiefs. As a concession to the Conciliator, the rebels did not carry automatic weapons to the peace table.

In the first days, Camacho impressed the delegates by saying little and listening intently but, gradually, the Conciliator had begun to assert his voice, joking with the Zapatistas that he was awaiting their "destape"—a reference to the unveiling of the PRI presidential candidate and a rite that Camacho himself had been denied. At week's end, Marcos was kvetching that The Conciliator had belittled the EZLN's national pretensions by emphasizing how small an area in Mexico the Zapatistas actually controlled—four municipalities out of the more than 2,000 into which the nation was divided. This was precisely the strategy Camacho had been mandated to pursue by the President—limiting any settlement to state and municipal concessions had been Salinas's condition for joining the negotiations. Judging from Marcos's daily agonizing before the press, the tactic had struck a nerve.

Two of the stickier items on the table were indigenous autonomy and reinstatement of the original language of Constitutional Article 27. The EZLN had urged that co-governors be elected in indigenous regions so that Indian peoples could administer their own affairs, particularly judicial ones. Greater indigenous representation in state and national elected bodies was demanded. Respect for Indian identity and an end to discrimination against native peoples, were also enfolded in the "pliego petitorio."

The government responded by promising to summon a special session of the legislature at which the outgoing Salinas administration would introduce a series of reforms strengthening Article Four of the Constitution—Article Four defines the rights of Indian communities but makes no mention of autonomy, an issue viewed with trepidation by the PRI government.

Similarly, the federal government sought to resolve the deadlock over Article 27 by altering Article Four—under the revisions of 27, ejido land and Indian communal lands, the two forms of land tenancy available to poor campesinos, were deemed open to "mercantile speculation" by foreign and national Agribusiness. The government's offer seemingly exempted Indian communal lands, a concession that came much too late to help Zapatista-based ejidos that are generally composed of families already removed from their original communal lands in the highlands. Moreover, as UNAM agrarian economist José Luis Calva quickly pointed out, the reform would pit two constitutional articles against each other with no clear definition of which one held sway.

Other agrarian demands were answered by the Conciliator and the government he represented, in typically cavalier fashion: a commission would be established within 90 days to review the campesinos' difficulties in obtaining bank credits to buy seed and fertilizer. The government's "ProCampo" subsidy program, an agrarian sibling of the "Solidarity" public works giveaway, would be extended throughout the Zapatista zone. Still another commission, appointed by the governor, would be immediately convened to formulate a census of all Chiapas land that could be distributed to poor farmers—Camacho made it clear that no expropriation of finca land was contemplated. Giving carte blanche powers to interim Governor Javier López Moreno to distribute land to the landless was akin to appointing a fox custodian of the henhouse. In Chiapas, the PRI governor is the permanent creature of the landowning class.

Marcos had insisted to Petrich at the beginning of February that the 1992 revision of Article 27 was the "detonating" factor in the Zapatista decision to go to war. Now the Zapatista demand was to return Article 27 not just to its original 1917 Constitutional language but to the language of Emiliano Zapata's much tougher 1915 agrarian reform law ratified at the long-ago Aguascalientes "Sovereign Revolutionary Convention" and based on the Caudillo's Plan of Ayala. Anticipating Zapatista demands during the run-up to the talks, Agribiz tycoons, the soon-to-be-phased-out Agrarian Reform bureaucracy, and the powerful old PRI dinosaur, Carlos Hank González, Secretary of Agriculture and Hydraulic Resources, jointly attacked any return to the original language as "absurd and archaic" and a signal to investors that Mexican agriculture was too troublesome a venture to dabble in.

In reviewing the federal government's responses to the Zapatistas' agrarian demands as published in the 32 "Pledges for Peace and Reconciliation," Calva reasons that EZLN acceptance of the options Camacho offered, would have left Carlos Salinas's neo-liberal schema for Mexican agriculture wholly in tact.

The fox and chicken house simile was operative in the Salinas-Camacho proposed resolution of NAFTA-TLC impacts on indigenous campesinos. The dramatic challenge Marcos had made to the treaty on the very first day of its life was met by an offer to turn this knotty matter over to

Secretary of Commerce Jaime Serra Puche for a study offering relief, said study to be completed within, you guessed it, 90 days. As Mexico's chief negotiator on the North American Free Trade Agreement for the past three years, Serra Puche had consistently argued that the NAFTA-TLC would benefit small farmers in Mexico, rather than—as more sober heads counseled—remove them from the land as inept competitors in a dog-eat-dog free market.

Other responses promised still more commissions or the succor of already existing social programs. The demand for electrification in a state that produces half the nation's electricity and where two-thirds of indigenous homes are unlit, would be studied by the usual commission reporting back in the usual 90 days. The promise that new roads would be cut into the Zapatista region, embedded in Point #11 of the "pliego," alarmed environmentalists committed to conserving the Lacandón jungle. The so-called "women's demands," presented by Comandante Ramóna, which contained health, education, nutrition, and housing petitions—including a demand for "stoves, refrigerators, and washing machines" would be assigned by Sedesol—the Secretary of Social Development—to "Solidarity" largess.

Several of the Zapatista demands clustered around reforms to state laws. Camacho pledged that an emergency session of the state legislature would be called to draw up a new Chiapas penal code—the present one allows for confessions to be obtained by torture. General elections would be held for all state and municipal offices under a new state election code. Ocosingo, the largest municipality in Mexico, would be divided in half to allow indigenous representation on state and federal bodies—a reform the state legislature later refused to even consider.

The release of all political prisoners would occur under the recently concocted Amnesty statute once a final peace agreement was inked by both parties. No belligerent status was conferred upon the EZLN. Nothing in the proposed document obligated the Zapatistas to lay down their arms now or in the future.

The political demands embedded in the Zapatista petition did not ask state power. Unlike previous Latin guerrilla models, the Zapatistas had never made any pretensions to the taking of same. Rather, political demands were either retributive or reformist. Salinas chose not to respond to such ticklish matters as his own resignation and the installation of a transitional government. The demand for political condemnation of Patrocinio and Setzer was dismissed as being out of sync with the conciliatory nature of the "Pledges for Peace and Reconciliation."

The demand for separation of the PRI government from the electoral mechanism was answered with a two point declaration, with no "resolutive" content, that defined the desire for "democratic options" and referred to "the road to reform" the 1994 presidential election was supposed to be taking. The calling of a special session of the Mexican congress to further tinker with the COFIPE electoral law, presumably with the end of removing the government from control of the Federal Electoral Institute (IFE), was announced by Camacho—it should be noted that this special session was not called to assuage Zapatista thirst for democracy but rather was agreed upon by nine political parties in entirely independent negotiations conducted over three months by the Secretary of the Interior, When finally convened in April, the legislators tampered with the COFIPE but left the government playing the decisive role in the 1994 presidential elections.

* * *

Sensing that the negotiations would not reach an early conclusion, the Third Army had deserted in droves, an exodus that greatly pained local tourism entrepreneurs. The Zapatista uprising had cost San Cristóbal $6 million by March in canceled reservations and empty rooms and restaurants and the arrival of mobs of media reps, armed with open-ended expense accounts, had revived flagging spirits in a town where a third of the populace depends on tourism to stay economically alive. But the press is a fickle carrion bird to pin your nest egg on, winging in to momentarily feed where the action is and flying on to the next story in the morning. With the media having flown the coop, "Insurrection In Chiapas," an eight-day "Reality Tour" through the war zone, booked by the trendy San Francisco-based Global Exchange, was the only tourist game in town.

As the negotiations wound down behind locked Cathedral doors, those reporters who had stuck it out were often down in Altamirano, covering the Constantino Kanter klan's racist tantrums. The grapevine had the Juarista National Army advancing on Ciudad Real. On Saturday night February 26th, a young member of the NGO security cordon burst into the press room at the Mazariegos, pale with fright—100 armed ranchers were marching down Insurgentes towards the Cathedral! The depleted press corps rushed to cover the confrontation but the purported malefactors proved to be a troupe of Triqui Indians from Oaxaca, the MULT, come to San Cristóbal to offer the Zapatistas their unconditional support.

The Cathedral remained draped in silence. Rumors floated that the Zapatistas had left town secretly—and, in fact, five delegates had, sometime on Saturday night, melted back into the mountains. It was said Marcos himself had slipped out of town Sunday, after dark, with the Chamulas returning from San Cristóbal market. It was said, too, that El Camacho had escaped but a "graphic reporter" was introduced into the premises to show otherwise, snapping the Conciliator in a small church office where he apparently slept, gabbing on the phone, apparently with the President.

Finally, Don Samuel let it be known that, after ten days of intense dialogue, "The Jornadas for Peace and Reconciliation" had concluded and final documents would be presented Wednesday morning, March 2nd, in the Cathedral of Paz.

Only 70 reporters remained in town for the magnum event. They joined the principal actors in this drama, now dubbed by T.S. Eliot aficionados "Conversations In The Cathedral," at a few minutes before 10 on a foggy San Cristóbal A.M. under the spiring vaults. Don Samuel underscored the religious context:"Peace is a gift of God but it is also a conquest—to announce Peace, you must also be a constructor of Peace..."

The use of the word came to the Zapatista side of the table next. Marcos, unaccountably, had removed himself from the front lines and now hunkered over in the back row, quietly chewing on the pipestem inserted in the mouthslot of his well-worn pasamontaña (ski mask). Comandantes Ramóna, Juan, and Humberto sat to the Bishop's right and it fell to Humberto, who had scant public exposure until this moment, to summarize the "pliego petitorio." Given the rubric of reconciliation that graced the spectacle, the Comandante's words were surprisingly hard-edge: "We want the great quantities of land that are in the hands of the finqueros and the national terratenientes and the foreigners and other persons who own a lot of land but are not farmers, we want these lands to pass

245

into the hands of those villagers that have no land at all...we want the federal government to return the Swiss, the Pilatus airplanes used to bomb our villages and that the money accumulated by that exchange be applied to programs to better the life of workers in the city and the country...we want the government of the United States to retire its helicopters because they are being used to repress the Mexican people..." These last two demands had not been included in the Zapatista petition. "For everybody, everything!" Humberto echoed the Zapatista refrain, "for us, nothing..." In the back row, Subcomandante Marcos puffed away energetically on his pipe.

The Conciliator would now respond with a 35-page document, the government response to 32 out of 34 demands listed in the "pliego." The document, "The Pledges for Peace and Reconciliation," was read, page after page, by Camacho aide Robert Salcedo, another ex-member of his Mexico City Hall team, When he was at last done, The Commissioner for Peace and Reconciliation summed up the Labors, offering dates and steps and the roster of potential signators to the final accord—once, of course, the Zapatista communities had ratified acceptance of the government's 32 pledges. "There are no winners or losers in this process," the Camacho riffed—but, of course, he himself was the big winner: sent to do an impossible job, the ex-presidential hopeful had not only lured the rebels to the peace table but also aced their national demands with promises of commissions and regional improvements. Camacho was "contented...very contented." Peace was at hand and the shortest guerrilla war "since World War II" (sic) was virtually over and, best of all, the solutions had been achieved by Mexicans!

The previous week, the *Wall Street Journal* had run an interview with Manuel Camacho Solís—approved by Juan

Henríquez—announcing that he was still very much a candidate for the presidency of Mexico.

The formalities were winding down. Now the voice returned to the Zapatista, to Juan, to whom fell the responsibility of thanking the hosts for their honesty and hospitality, a gracious tradition that still prevails in Indian communities across the land. "We have encountered attentive ears here, prepared to listen to the truths that issued from our lips. The dialogue of San Cristóbal was a true one. There was no duplicity or lies. Nothing was hidden between our hearts and those of the people of reason and authority. We have the obligation to reflect well on what these words say. Now we must speak to the collective heart that orders us."

At center stage, Don Samuel signed three copies of the Pledges, one for the Cathedral archives, and one each for the respective actors to be approved by their respective constituencies. Don Samuel and Manuel Camacho embraced yet again. Everyone was contented...very contented. "This has been a kind of kairos, a great step forward in the construction of God's Kingdom," Don Samuel hosanna'd, predicting the final accords could be signed "before the end of the month."

The Zapatistas sat coolly in their seats. the smoke billowing up around Marcos's masked ears. The loquacious, outspoken voice of the rebels had said nothing, absolutely nothing, during the ceremony. Perhaps he was wondering if, after all the pomp and puffery, he was really going to get out of the Cathedral of Peace alive. This was also a concern of Camacho's—he had warned against provocateurs in his remarks. Now, before some nut took a potshot at the commandantes and blew their coup right there on the spot, the Conciliator and the Bishop hustled the 14 remaining long-packed-and-ready-to-go Zapatistas out of the Cathedral and into the waiting IRC and civilian vehicles. Camacho and Ruiz escorted Marcos and his companions in the direction of San Andrés Larrainzar, from whence they had appeared out of nowhere, ten days previous.

What remained of the press corps went back to the Mazariegos to pound out the wrap-ups. The government had already begun to dismantle the press room and, although it has remained opened for many months, the space has hardly ever been the same since. Virtually every story filed that day from San Cristóbal had a similar spin: the Zapatistas had won unprecedented concessions from their government and peace was at hand. It was only a matter of days, or, at most, weeks, before the definitive peace treaty would be signed. "What the Zapatistas have achieved in a few short weeks is extraordinary," wrote blue-ribbon historian Enrique Krauze, editor—with Octavio Paz—of the glossy, high-brow monthly *Vuelta*. The U.S. press was equally as observant. Under an editorial, entitled "Rebels With A Difference," Will Hearst's *San Francisco Examiner* extolled the Salinas government for its generous handling of a difficult situation: the Zapatistas had won many unprecedented concessions, "not a bad score for a naive, ragtag insurgency in the backwoods..." The leftist savant Alexander Cockburn pontificated on the venerable pages of *The Nation* that the Zapatistas' "victory" had been one for all the Americas.

The Zapatistas themselves had a slightly different take on the conversations in the Cathedral. "Until now, the only solution to our problem has been pure promises and a mountain of paper," one unidentified delegate told *La Jornada*, upon taking hurried leave of the Cathedral of Peace. In an unguarded moment, Marcos had told the same paper that the government hasn't "resolved even one percent of our problems"—again drawing a fine line between "response" and "resolution." Since the opening salvo of the Jornadas, the Subcomandante had insisted that no decision would be made without the consent of the communal assemblies and he had warned that there had been opposition in those assemblies to even sending delegates to the dialogue in San Cristóbal. In the Zapatista structure, the assembly is the crucial building block—no decision is taken without extended consultation. This has been true for years—there would be no EZLN today if the total immersion of the communities in the decision-making process was not a visceral reality. But this concept of communal participation is foreign to a world and its pundits accustomed to top-down leadership in which the approval of the "pueblos"—the people and their villages—is a mere formality that their leaders are charged with guaranteeing.

The Zapatistas knew better. Now, as they stuffed their belongings into the waiting cars, preparing to leave town still armed and masked, with their dignity in tact, they knew the next step would be even more dicey: to take home this offer to their fathers and sisters, brothers and mothers and cousins and uncles, this piece of paper upon which, like so many others, the forked-tongue promises of the bad government had been inscribed. With this task heavy upon their hearts, the Zapatistas began their descent into the canyons and the jungle of the Lacandón to begin the consultations that could bring a measure of peace to Chiapas.

Back to the Jungle

"The greater the growth of the tree, the deeper are its roots" the Mayan Indian prisoner who, one day, would lead the insurrection in the jungle logging camp, was warned when he first came to the "montería." The story is told in Bruno Traven's classic saga of uprising in the Lacandón, "The Rebellion of The Hanged." For the prisoners, gangpressed in their native villages or shanghai'd while sleeping off drunks in Ocosingo jail, the depth of the roots were a life or death concern. Under the whips of the "capatazes" (foremen), the men were required to cut a daily quota of mahogany and the iron hard roots of these enormous trees took hours to hack apart. Those who could not take down the required number of trees each day, were hung from the stout branches of the "caobas" until their skin pulled back and white bone shown through. The roots of the Zapatista Army of National Liberation are inescapably entwined with the roots of the great mahogany groves of the Lacandón jungle.

When the Europeans first stumbled into this jungle in 1530, they literally could not tell the forest from the trees. The Lacandón began but did not end, part of one contiguous rainforest extending all the way from Campeche and the Yucatán to the Gran Petén of Guatemala, across the Usumacinta—a swatch of green biomass second only in the New World to the Amazon basin. What early map makers defined as the Lacandón totaled 3,000,000 acres of pristine lakes and rushing rivers, priceless forests of mahogany and cedar, uncounted plant species never seen before, a blazing green wilderness populated by jaguar and ocelot and herds of tapirs, crocodiles and wild boar and howler monkeys. Quetzals and Guacamayas and clouds of brilliantly pat-terned butterflies leapt through the braided canopy over-head.

The jungle was not unpeopled. The population of the Lacandón vacillated with the Mayan civilization that sur-rounded and pervaded the tropical forest but the Lacandón has been inhabited since man's memory began. When the imperious Spanish explorer Bernal del Díaz sent in his sur-veyors, the intruders were greeted rudely by irritated Indians whom the foreigners named for the river by which they dwelt—the Lacan-Tum or "big rock." The "Lacan-Tum" knew the forest and battled long and arduously to keep the Spanish out. The guerrilla war of the first jungle Mayans was protracted. In 1563, priests, dispatched by the new Bishop of Ciudad Real, corralled a group of Lacan-Tums and Christianized them on the spot and the previous-ly unconquered Indians divided into two camps in the for-est, the resisters moving to Sac-Balan ("white jaguar") at the headwaters of the Ixcán. A century more of hit-and-run warfare elapsed but time was running out for the Lacan-Tum. In 1659, the Crown's troops, operating out of the Capitanía of Guatemala, cornered and decimated the last of their warriors at the Usumacinta. By 1769, only five elderly Lacan-Tums were left, encamped around a jungle mission on the Guatemalan side of the river.

The disappearance of the last "Lacandónes" coincided with the arrival of the first new ones, anthropologically designated as "Caribes," migrating Mayan rebels from Campeche and the Gran Péten whose first settlements were in the eastern sections of the forest and who now advanced south from the magnificent jungle city of Palenque. As defi-ant and feisty as their predecessors—and, ultimately, their Mayan Zapatista successors—the new Lacandónes fought off marauding Christians for three centuries.

In 1994, most contemporary Lacandón centers have

been evangelized. But today's Lacandónes, championed and preserved by the late San Cristóbal anthropologists, Franz Blom and Trude Duby and their Na'Bolom Institute, have had to make accommodations with a modern world that seeks to conquer not them so much as their forests, tree by tree.

The history of the Lacandón is etched in the massacre of both trees and people, as the forest's historian, Jan De Voss, never tires of communicating. Both were always lurking in the bush, but how to get them out of the jungle was a knotty logistical problem. In 1822, the year Chiapas declared its independence from Spain and Guatemala, Capitán Cayetano Román Robles was awarded the contract by the government of the incipient republic of Chiapas, established at Comitán de Domínguez, to explore the wealth of the forest all the way to the juncture of the Jacaté and the Usumacinta—or what is now the municipality of Ocosingo, a sector of the forest called, by its denizens, "the Desert of Ocosingo" or, more poignantly, the "Desert of Solitude."

As De Voss vividly tells in his *20 Journeys to the Desert of Solitude* (Secretary of Public Education 1988), the forest did not really begin to fall until one day in 1859 when Felipe Marín, an itinerant merchant logger from the Tabasco side of the jungle, felled 72 great caobas and cedros and rolled them into the river. A week later, Marín recovered 70 logs downriver at Tenosique and the rush for the green gold was on. By 1880, there were 15 booming "monterías" operating around the confluence of the Jacaté and the Usumacinta. The logs rolled out of the jungle to the ports of Tabasco and the Yucatán and were landed in Liverpool and Calais and New York City, sold as "Tabasco Wood" to build the polished mansions of the moneyed classes of the north.

REBELLION FROM THE ROOTS

Porfirio Díaz's free market overtures to outside investors—so reminiscent of Salinas's six years in office (Díaz dictated for 30)—was great for business but bad for the Lacandón. At the turn to the 20th Century, the forest was so hot a property that international entrepreneurs were scrambling to get in. Four freewheeling speculators, three operating out of Mexico City along with a Spanish nobleman, the Marquis of Comillas (for whom the southern lateral tier of the forest is still named) bought the entire three million acre jungle for their own profit, divided it into monterías and went after the wood. It is the horrors of those logging camps—and the resistance of the Mayans chained to their axes and saws—that Bruno Traven wrote of in *The Rebellion of the Hanged* and five other jungle novels, albeit ten years later, after the revolution had visited this distant corner of Mexico. Traven's thickly moralistic tales revealed the abuses and exploitation of the monterías to the world—the camps persisted into the 1920s—and their exposure established this reclusive German anarchist exile, as one of Mexico's most popular and prolific writers. Traven spent several years working on the post-revolutionary government's anti-locust projects in Ocosingo and when he died, in 1969, his ashes were scattered along the Jacaté river.

The Mexican revolution reached the Southeast in 1914, straining relations between the owners of the logging camps and their ill-treated employees. Revolutionary troops rode from one montería to another, freeing the Mayan serfs from capitalist bondage. In other camps, such as Traven describes in *The General from the Jungle*, the Mayans took matters into their own hands, forming their own armies, slaughtering their bosses, and marching upon the cities. Because it so disrupted the massacre of the trees, the revolution gave the ecology of the Lacandón a brief respite from the murderous designs of the logging industry

By the mid-20th century, the industrial North was running out of resource reserves and the forests of southeastern Mexico looked more and more inviting. With the post World War II housing boom cresting in 1949, U.S. giant Vancouver Plywood put together a combine fronted by Mexican "prestanombres" ("lend-a-names") to conform with Mexican law and bought 1.5 million acres of the forest outright from President Miguel Alemán, a head of state known to be prone to such under-the-table privatizations. Now flying the flag of "Maderas Mayas" and tied into dozens of subcontractors with long and lurid histories in the Lacandón, Vancouver began mowing down the choicest groves. Fortunately for the rainforest, Alemán's successor—Adolfo Ruiz Cortines—had second thoughts about handing over control of large hunks of national lands to the gringos, and refused to grant permits for a projected downriver mill complex. The Lacandón had been saved again.

* * *

The poor began to stream into the Lacandón in 1954. The first wave of settlers were, like the "new" Lacandónes before them, Chol refugees pushed out of Palenque. They were soon joined by highland Tzotziles, squeezed off the undernourished soils of Chamula, expelled, the Tushones mandated, because they interpreted Holy Writ to proscribe the consumption of sugar cane alcohol. The "expulsados" came to the jungle as if it were the promised land, threw up their huts, carved their cornfields from the trees, and named their settlements appropriately: "Palestina" and "Nazareth" and other stations of biblical renown.

So the exodus to the jungle began, a "spontaneous" colonization, the sociologists describe it—but one which had its roots in the despotic rule of Caciques and Tushones, land hunger and religious feuds and family arguments and the dreams for a better future where the grass was much greener. The pain and hope of exodus has deep resonance in the jungle—in the late 1970s, Don Samuel commissioned Padre Mardonio and his brother Ignacio to translate the Book of Exodus into Tzeltal and, even today, the story is read in village churches in the Zapatista-controlled zone.

Two decrees, in 1957 and 1961, deeming the jungle open for colonization further doomed the trees. The declaration of the southern agrarian frontier threw open the doors of the Lacandón to the displaced campesinos of tropical Mexico: Non-Mayan Indians from Oaxaca, forced off their communal lands by government dams arrived in the Desert of Ocosingo; indígenas dislodged by the White Guards of southern Veracruz's murderous cattle kings, a regional industry sustained by World Bank credits; landless mestizo farmers from as far away as Guerrero and Michoacán joined the flow in pursuit of a patch on which to grow a little corn. In 1960, the municipality of Ocosingo had a population of just 12,000. By 1990, at least 250,000 lived in what had once been "the Desert of Solitude."

The new settlers traveled the beaten tracks through Ocosingo and Comitán, Las Margaritas and Altamirano, pushing their way down the canyons, "Las Cañadas," into the Lacandón basin and the heart of what was left of the jungle. Some groups got tired and stopped along the way, saw a spot and decided it was home. Other more mercenary adventurers enlisted in the private armies of the ranchers, became their advance guard, slashing and burning into an area, planting a crop or two, and then giving way to the cattlemen right behind them who sold off what remained of the "monte" (the trees) and ran their cattle on the cleared land that was left behind—with or without title to it.

The mix of exile, hope, hard work, and frustration was a heady one in the jungle. Highland and lowland cultures clashed and blended. In the 1980s, the babble of tongues was intensified when Zoques, thrown from their lands by the Chichonál volcano, and Guatemalan Kanajobales and Mames, driven north by an army that took delight in bayoneting babies, added to the brew of Tzeltal, Tzotzil, Tojolabal, and Chol speakers that bubbled in the jungle.

For the Mexican government, the Lacandón frontier was a social safety valve, a region far from the center of power, where the potentially-explosive indígena and campesino masses of deep Mexico could be put to work, a natural reserve, if you will, for the poorest of the poor.

The settlers were not kind to the forest. They saw the jungle as an enemy and hated it and hacked it down with righteous indignation. They were pioneers on the southern agrarian frontier and they had God and justice and the Government on their side as they extended their fields and claimed the cleared land as part of the ejidos each settlement strove to certify. "We destroyed the forest out of necessity," Humberto Moreno, the director of the Union of Ejidos would declare years later.

For the pilgrims, the promise of paradise lasted but a cruel minute. By the time a campesino would put in his third crop of maiz, the fragile jungle soil, denuded of treecover and nutrients, would burn up. The rains changed because the trees were gone. Corn stood stunted and scorched in the "milpas." "When we came to Rizo de Oro ("curl of gold") 30 years ago, we thought this was a pretty place," Caralampio Aguilar told Tim Golden in January. But the soil dried up and chemical fertilizers did even more damage and where the Tzeltales of Rizo de Oro used to get 30 sacks of coffee from a hectare, now they got five. Today, the settlers have to sell their labor to the "finqueros" in order to feed their families. The ejido's petitions for an extension to its lands remains adrift in a desk drawer at the Agrarian Reform bureaucracy on the Calzado de Huesos ("Avenue of the Bones") up in Mexico City. In early January 1994, Caralampio Aguilar had turned his attentions from subsistence farming and peacefully petitioning his government to the fortunes of war. Now he is the Zapatista communal representative in this canyon hamlet.

Las Cañadas, the Canyons, form the western-most sector of the Lacandón. Other geographical quadrants are the Marquis de Comillas, the Lacandón communities clustered around Lacanja on the east, and "La Selva," the 400,000 hectare historical heart of the jungle. The Cañadas funnel down the steep ravines from 2,500 meters above sea level to just 200 close to the Lacandón floor, a broken-in parts still-jungly terrain, the kind of landscape guerrillas who have gone to cover, find comforting.

"30 years ago, when I was young, we came out here from Altamirano with my father. This was all mountain then but the people who were here before us cut it all down and moved on. We were new people and now we're some of the oldest..." Carlos, a white-haired Tzeltal spoke. His rail-thin wife, Joséfa, a Tojolabal, listened carefully.

"The land they gave us is in the mountain and the ranchers had taken the valley. We have asked for a little piece down there for a long time. I started fighting for it 30 years ago but we have no papers here yet..." Carlos and Joséfa have given three sons to the Zapatistas, first one went and then the next. "Now my sons are suffering for us..."

There are 1,056 settlements in the Cañadas, 117 of them ejidos, a population of 65,000, 60% of whom are younger than 20. All are indigenous peoples whose odyssey stopped here. Many of the original settlers have crossed bloodlines, like Carlos and Joséfa, Tzeltal and Tojolabal, Ladinos and Choles and Tzeltales. "Everything was new when they came here," Bellinghausen wrote recently in *Ojarasca*. The newness and the cultural mix has had an oddly modernizing effect. The peoples of Las Cañadas are hardly the most backward settlers in this former jungle. But they may be the most litigious.

According to Agrarian Reform stats, the Cañadas have the highest percentage of land solicitors in the nation—15 out of every 100 heads of families. Here, there is a kind of permanent war with the ranchers, with rival ejidos, with a government that sometimes gives the same land to two ejidos (a deliberate confusion called "tierras sobretitulados" or "over-titled lands") and sits back to watch the campesinos kill each other over ownership. The governors of Chiapas and the PRI Party they represent, have been more than Machiavellian in pitting one group of angry Indians against another, of singling out "natural leaders" and corrupting them with crumbs or killing them when they resist a buy-out. The fermentation in the Cañadas has always been palpably combustible. "Here, violence has been the mother of colonization," observes Na'Bolom's Andrew Mutter. "This war didn't just begin January 1st..."

* * *

Those curious parties thumbing through history for a date upon which to hang the commencement of the current hostilities in the Lacandón should turn back the page to 1972. That was the year that President Luis Echeverría, whose instincts were demagogic, sought to stem the by-now out-of-control stampede into the forest, by handing over 645,000 hectares of the Lacandón jungle to 66 Lacandón Indian heads of families, its supposed original owners (defined as "originales" in the edict). The presidential decree converted the forest from "national terrain" to Indian communal land ("bienes comunales") and ordered all but 1,100 longtime Chol and Tzeltal settlers ("neoselváticos") to evacuate the Lacandón at once.

Ironically, Echeverría's order transformed each impoverished Lacandón male into one of the largest "latifundistas" (great landowners) in Mexico, holding the equivalent of 25,000 acres of priceless hardwoods. Lumber companies moved in with alacrity, bribed the Lacandón "latifundistas" with drink and television satellite dishes, and the bible, and walked away with long-term concessions to cut what was left of the forest.

In a fruitless gesture to right a bit of the immeasurable havoc his edict had set in motion, Echeverría later created a federal-state logging corporation initialed COFALASA and canceled all private contracts. Over the course of the next decade, each year for the next ten years, COFALASA took 10,000 trees—35,000 cubic meters—of top-grade cedar and mahogany out of the heart of the jungle, fattening the fortunes of such Chiapas wood barons as Ernesto Castellanos, the General's sibling. During Absalón's reign, the whole family shared the boodle—a nephew ran a state entity, CORFU, which reportedly swindled indigenous settler communities such as Benemérito de las Américas out of their forest rights, and then refused to pay up, claiming the communities owed the Castellanos Domínguez family old debts.

Given the volatile colonization of the jungle, the tragedies and the dreams the settlers had brought with them, Echeverría's orders to vacate bred immediate resistance. Alarm spread as the first villagers in Palestina and Corrozal were kicked off the land they had won from the jungle. Inspired by the 1974 Fray Bartolomé de las Casas Indigenous Congress, Don Samuel sent his priests and volunteers—the "Torreonistas" among them—into the Lacandón to act as "catalysts" in creating settler organizations to resist forced removal. Out of this struggle to remain in the jungle grew Quiptic and the Union of Unions and ARIC, independent formations that challenged the PRI's CNC and its hegemony over the region's farmers. Like the Catholics, the Marxist Leninist left sought to capitalize on the discontent in the jungle. Brigades of "Socialist Workers" and "Proletarian Liners" made a beeline for the Lacandón. Armed struggle was an option even then—"the Popular Forces of National Liberation," a guerrilla unit in Ocosingo municipality was crushed by the military in 1974 and the Guatemalan guerrilla leader Yon Sosa was killed in a confrontation with the Mexican Army in the forest two years earlier.

Institutional irresponsibility continued to fan the flames of rebellion. On January 12th, 1978, Echeverría's equally demagogic successor, José López Portillo, declared the creation of the UNESCO-sponsored "Montes Azules Biosphere," Mexico's first international ecological reserve—380,000 hectares encircling the heart of the jungle. The designation, like Echeverría's before him, had been dreamt up without any prior study, any consultation with those who lived inside its announced boundaries, any management plan, or even any budget to draw one up. Indeed, the clearest aspect of the declaration were the boundaries, and, like his predecessor's orders six years previous—which had been largely disobeyed—everyone who lived inside the first Mexican, UN-blessed biosphere and reserve

261

had to pack up and go home.

Why López Portillo, a politician with international pretensions, chose to pour oil on the Lacandón fire, is subject to review. In 1978, there was no substantial environmental movement in Mexico and, of the handful of groups that had begun to act, few were focused on saving the Lacandón. Rather, recalls Miguel Vázquez-Sánchez, chief researcher at the Southeast Investigation and Study Center (CIES), international lobbying for the creation of the reserve was much more intense—the biosphere program was a new UNESCO concept and it is speculated that the Mexican president was buttering his bread for a U.N. post once his one-time term in office was done.

Whatever López Portillo's ulterior motives were, the declaration of the Montes Azules Biosphere and Ecological Reserve turned up the tone of the turmoil. 40 communities and ejidos, 23 of them in the Cañadas bordering the reserve, were directly affected—the "Biosphere" declaration quashed their dreams of expanding ejido lands into the forest. It is not just anecdotal to notice that the bulk of the Zapatista fighting force are 16 to 24 years old—children born into their parents' struggle to stay in the forest following the 1972 and 1978 presidential edicts.

Standing sentry at a Zapatista roadblock "somewhere in the Lacandón jungle" in January, Major Sergio remembered his family's battle to stay on their land within the Montes Azules reserve, and the refusal of the government to heed their petitions: "the only way left for us was to take up arms..."

"The first experience the young colonos of Las Cañadas had with a factor external to their lives, was the pressure brought by environmentalists to preserve the forest," writes Xochital Leyva, a sociologist and CIES fellow, in *Ojarasca* magazine (January 1994). Seen in this light, the

EZLN, an army nurtured in the Cañadas between 1984 and 1994, may be the first force for revolutionary change in Latin America that is rooted in the conflict between preservation of the planet's diminishing biomass and the gut desire of the poorest of the poor, for what passes as progress under the banner of development. The Zapatista rebellion represents an initial skirmish in the coming resource wars of the 21st century.

Since its designation in 1978, Montes Azules has proven as unmanageable as many of the 280 UNESCO-sponsored reserves, almost all of them in the Third World where development vs. conservation controversies flourish. CIES studies indicate that 10% of the Montes Azules reserve has already disappeared in the years since López Portillo's edict. A doctor friend in a clinic bordering Montes Azules saw the sign demarcating the biosphere's boundaries moved three times in the year he did his rural internship there. Ejidos with nothing to lose took a last whack at the forest and those who refused to leave continued to live where they were.

Nor was the exploitation of forest resources by outside interests diminished. Big time species dealers moved into the Lacandón and ransacked its animal and plant wealth. Jorge Hank Rhon, son of the present Secretary of Agriculture and veteran PRI "dino" Carlos Hank, reportedly plucked tens of thousands of parrots and tropical mammals, including big cats, from the Lacandón before application of CITES international sanctions put him (purportedly) out of business. $20 million worth of Camador palm, an ornamental plant used extensively in U.S. office building decor, was shipped yearly from the Lacandón to Continental Wholesale Florists in San Antonio, Texas via refrigerated trucks, owned by none other than Jorge's pop, Carlos Hank, according to a 1988 report in *Ambar*, Juan

Balboa's Chiapas-based investigative monthly.

"We came to populate the southern frontier of this nation. We endured suffering and illness. We received the lashes of the social conflict in Central America. We suffered invasions and aggressions and it is shameless that the transnational corporations continue to exploit the region and we, the original settlers, are not allowed the development of such a strategic zone" ejido leader Julio Sabines Pérez explained to Balboa.

But the government was, in fact, shutting the door to such development pretensions. In 1989, Governor Patrocinio González, backed up by federal orders a year later, imposed a complete ban on logging throughout the state. "Not one log or plank more will be cut in Chiapas," Patrocinio warned. As if Chiapas needed a new police agency, the state forestry patrol was created to enforce the ban. Although the cut wood that the ejidos already had stacked on the ground before the edict, was considered legal under the governor's decree, the Judicial Police and the newly-uniformed Forestry Patrol, confiscated the farmers' trucks at stops in Ocosingo and Margaritas and Altamirano—90% of all cut wood in Chiapas travels these roads. Indeed, the March 1993 killings of two uniformed military officers in San Isidro Ocotal—the first Zapatista confrontation with the Mexican Army—may respond to the wood-cutting ban—the army men were said to have been confused with forestry patrol officers and their burnt, dismembered bodies were found on the site of a clandestine sawmill.

Today, reporting from "somewhere in the Lacandón jungle" is a rank misnomer. The jungle is around here somewhere but you'd have to walk three days to San Quintín to find out where. Moreover, it is a jungle to which the Zapatistas are not particularly keen on returning. The EZLN is thoroughly committed to modernizing the lives of its constituents—although the rebels take pains to insist they do not want such progress at the expense of what is left of the Lacandón.

Demands for "stoves, refrigerators, and washing machines," roads, farm equipment, and, most of all, land, alarm those who defend the integrity of the forest. CIES director Ignacio March worries that the government will "subdivide" the jungle in an effort to come up with enough fresh land to sate the landhunger of the landless. Poet-ecologist Homero Aridjis, vicar of the very literary "Group of 100" (Gabriel García Márquez, Paz, Fuentes) cries out (in the *New York Times*) that cutting one more road into the jungle "will be the death of the Lacandón," a jeremiad the bard has wailed before...

"Ecologists? Who needs them? What we want here is land, work, and shelter," Major Mario told *La Jornada* in January. "All they tell us is not to cut the trees, not to burn the land—but how can we not do so when we have to eat?" a Zapatista woman argued with *Los Angeles Times'* correspondent Juanita Darling soon after the conflict detonated.

Nonetheless, the EZLN has been kinder to the Lacandón in its more official stances: the sixth point of the Declaration of the Lacandón Jungle calls for the end to the plunder of "our natural wealth" in zones controlled by the Zapatistas, a point amplified in the "pliego petitorio." The rebels' Revolutionary Agrarian Law calls for an end to contamination of water sources in the jungle, the preservation of virgin forest zones, and reforestation of logged-out areas. The lands they demand, say the rebels, should not be carved out of what's left of the Lacandón, but, rather, confiscated from the finqueros. "Few armed groups have ever included such demands in their manifestos" observes

Vázquez-Sánchez.

"This is a revolution that sprang from the ashes of a dead forest," Na'Bolom's Andrew Mutter says darkly. What environmentalists most fear is a military solution to the Zapatista rebellion. A full-scale Army invasion of the jungle would signal apocalyptic desolation for the Lacandón, a doomsday scenario complete with aerial bombings, land mine explosions, forest fires, and the sort of defoliation practiced by the Guatemalan military chasing URNG guerrillas in their half of the jungle. In the vision of S. Jeffrey Wilkerson, director of the Veracruz-based Institute for Cultural Ecology, roads would be bulldozed to move armored vehicles, dumping sediments into crystalline rivers, uprooting wildlife, and disrupting migration patterns. Even worse, oil wells could be blown.

No one—outside of PEMEX—knows with any certainty just what kind of mischief the national petroleum consortium is up to in the Lacandón. Mutter thinks there are over a hundred wells, dead or alive, in the region but PEMEX considers such information, a national security secret. The mammoth state enterprise has an unprecedented record for destroying southern Mexico with impunity as attested to by the poisoning of the Coatzacoalcos river and the wanton devastation of vast stretches of Tabasco state. In the Lacandón, from the air, the bald patches around Pico de Oro on the eastern flank of the jungle and the sprawling network of roads cut between drilling stations, palpitate like raw, painful scars against the land.

The Zapatistas' most significant contribution to the ecological integrity of the Lacandón may have come when they forced 1,400 employees of PEMEX, the U.S.-owned Western Oil, and the French Geofísica Corporation to abandon test drilling operations in the jungle and flee for their lives during the initial days of the conflict.

The EZLN seeks to balance developmental needs against environmental concerns because, above all, the Zapatistas grew up in this forest and live in its remnants. Their parents and the communities they fight for are here and, after all the years of struggle to stay in the Lacandón, they are not going anywhere else. It was to this jungle of conflicts, its combative communities, mud and wattle homesteads, scrawny cattle and stubbly cornfields and coffee patches, abandoned schoohouses, empty clinics, makeshift churches, and town basketball courts, to which the Zapatista leadership returned in early March, to bring back the bad government's 32 responses to their long-standing grievances, to the assemblies upon which their army is founded.

Into the Zapatista Zone

"Before, in my civil life, I was just a regular kid, mischievous, illiterate, unprepared for what life brings one," Major Rolando reflected upon his youth, leaning into the rough hewn wall in the sultry darkness. A silent compañera hovered in the doorway, half listening to the give and take of the conversation, her carbine ever at the ready. The hut was dark enough to obscure the features of the two young Zapatistas but both were masked, she with a paliacate and Rolando in his pasamontaña.

"I am the son of campesinos from here who migrated to the city to put more food in our mouths. We were six in all. When I went with my family, I was 11, just turning 12. I never went to school after that. I couldn't. My father put me into the construction. This was in Tuxtla, there was much building going on. I worked seven, eight years, seven days a week, busting my balls without learning anything else. This is how the Patrón works—he wants to keep you from learning new things just to keep you nailed to a lousy job..."

The Major, a slender young man of 25, seemed pleased with the way he was telling his story. He was becoming a regular Marcos, talking to these gringo reporters every night on the Garrucha front. Now he fished a crumpled cigarette from his uniform breast pocket, a match flared. Although alcohol and drugs are outlawed in the Zapatista zones, the young rebels are always puffing away on storebought cigarettes. Rolando continued:

"On one occasion, I returned home to the Cañadas to visit my grandfathers and I heard about the struggle and

269

that there were the men up in the caves. It really didn't take much to convince me that this was the way. My analysis was the same as theirs. That was eight years ago and it hasn't changed. I didn't have to go to the city to know racism but I did and it helped me to see it The schools in those cities are so elegant for those who have the possibilities. For us here, the Indians, the true men and women, they build cages...

"So I went to the mountain and accepted the life of a guerrillero. I am glad. I learned to read from the compañeros and how to do my sums and how to handle a weapon. I give my thanks to the organization for the pride it has given me but, even more, for the privilege to serve my people.

"No," Rolando laughed, a boyish amiable laugh under his blue mask, "no, no I don't feel like I'm a part of history. We're not gods or anything like that. One feels small but a part of something big. I may have changed in the 'EZ' but I am still the same in many ways. I feel like any man or woman here. My dream? I guess to stay alive long enough to see the end of this change we are bringing..."

* * *

All Mexican wars since the Conquest have been, at one stage or another, "wars of the flea" the resistance to the European invasion was waged by small "focos" of determined indigenous fighters who perennially emerged from the forest to commit mayhem upon the "caxtlán" ("white" in Tojolabal). The war of liberation against Spain and the defeat of Napoleon II's invading troops 40 years later, were fought by standing armies of Indians and mestizo farmers that quickly melted back into the rural populous, the sea in which clandestine insurgency classically swims. The 1910-1919 revolution of the landless that toppled the criollo oligarchy often turned on the damage a few well-placed fighters could do to the advancing columns of the federal army—Zapata's demolition teams repeatedly blew up troop trains, narrowing the odds between the two armies. Similarly, the Cristiada (1925-30) was waged by guerrilla bands of Catholic zealot campesinos who inflicted impressive damage upon the newly-consolidated Revolutionary Army. In short, the "guerra de la pulga" is a Mexican tradition.

Mapped into a vast national terrain seamed by inaccessible mountain ranges and defined by vividly distinct regions, rebellion and revolution in Mexico have often grown from disparate nuclei tightly clustered around charismatic local leaders and the success of these individualized uprisings has mostly depended on the strategic and logistical alliances struck between these "focos"—the word made au courant by Regis Debray's post-Cuban Revolution nomenclature for the eruption of multiple armed insurrectionary bands up and down the spine of Latin America, in the turbulent 1960s.

Mexico, being the skull of this lacerated continent's skeletal remains, was not immune from the epidemic of revolution fever that swept the Americas in that decade. The first outcropping was in the north—the attack led by Arturo Gamíz on a military barracks in Chihuahua City, 300 miles from the U.S. border, on September 23rd 1965. The Liga Comunista 23rd de Septiembre, which took its name from the date of Gamíz's suicide act, established focos throughout northern Mexico. In 1967 and '68, Genaro Vázquez and Lucio Cabañas, rural Guerrero schoolteachers, rose separately and declared war upon the government of Gustavo Díaz Ordaz, spreading insurrection to rural central Mexico.

REBELLION FROM THE ROOTS

From Paris to Prague to Chicago, 1968 was a watershed year for the Revolution. In Mexico, the student unrest erupted, predictably, on the anniversary of the Cuban revolution, July 26th. Police occupied preparatory schools within the UNAM system, a flagrant violation of university autonomy. The battle was joined. For months, the young people skirmished with the Díaz Ordaz government, convening the biggest marches in remembered Mexico City history after the military invaded the UNAM itself and the more working-class National Polytechnic Institute. The demands of the young people was mostly defensive: free the swelling number of political prisoners and get the Army off campus. Díaz Ordaz, who had plotted 1968 to be the crowning achievement of his regime with Mexico playing host to the Olympic Games in October, the first Third World nation ever so honored, saw the International Communist Conspiracy manipulating the students. In October, long after the leaders of the revolt had been jailed, at a not very well-attended rally in the Plaza of Three Cultures in the downtown Tlatelolco housing complex, the order was given to troops on the perimeter of the meeting, to open fire upon the students and their families, many of them residents of the mostly middle-class complex. There was no escape from the withering crossfire of troops under the command of General Marcelino Barragán—Absalón's patron—and hundreds (some say thousands) were killed. Their deaths were hardly recorded—not one Mexico City newspaper reported the terrible bloodletting the next morning. In the 25 years since the Tlatelolco massacre, the Mexican government has never varied from its preposterous claim that "about 30" students were killed—the best count of the dead was supplied by a conscientious Reuters reporter who visited morgues, hospitals, and police lock-ups in the hours following the mass killings and totaled 337 dead.

The bloodbath that stained the Plaza de las Tres Culturas on October 2nd, 1968 closed down peaceful options for change. Those student activists that did not drift off to the U.S. or Europe or into the pipedreams of drugs, dropped deep into the underground, joining the 15 urban and rural guerrilla focos that flowered in the wake of '68. For the next six years, self-declared Marxist-Leninist guerrilla factions, most notably the Liga Comunista 23rd de Septiembre and the Party of the Poor, kidnapped bankers and U.S. Consuls and governors, blew up state offices, robbed banks, and offed the pig, with abandon. By 1974, the military—said to be advised by the Central Intelligence Agency—had gained the upper hand, finally snuffing Cabañas—but not his party—in December. Another victory over the guerrilla also registered in 1974: the liquidation of the "Armed Forces of National Liberation" (FALN) in Ocosingo, Chiapas. The government proudly announced the death of one "Comandante Pedro" at El Diamante "somewhere in the Lacandón jungle."

"We have no one with us now from that time," Major Mario reflected at an EZLN roadblock this winter, "but they are our examples..."

Díaz Ordaz's successor as PRI president of Mexico was the bluff populist, Luis Echeverría, a politician who cultivated a leftist patina and maintained cordial relations with Socialist Cuba in a period when this stance was even less popular in Washington than it is today. Echeverría, who, as Díaz Ordaz's Secretary of the Interior, was the highest-placed link in the chain of command that give the military orders to open fire at Tlatelolco, treated students and rebels to the back of his hand—political prisoners begged for the same sympathy Echeverría showered on his favored Cuban revolutionaries. During his six year reign,

Luis Echeverría is held responsible for over 300 disappear-ances of campesinos and activists in the state of Guerrero, Cabañas' home turf, according to a registry held by the Eureka group, a gathering of relatives of the disappeared, headed by the valiant Doña Rosario Ibarra de Piedra, whose own urban guerrilla son, was taken by authorities in 1975 and never head from again.

On his other hand, Echeverría wore the velvet glove of co-optation, buying up, by the bunch, rebels who couldn't take it anymore and incorporating them into his adminis-tration. When it served his purposes, the President, a con-summate political animal, did not hesitate to invent mili-tant farmers organizations and stage takeovers of private land, such as the great Mayo and Yaqui valley mobiliza-tions in Sonora in 1976.

In Mexico City, radical energies invariably are con-centrated around and emanate from the UNAM, the swarming (90,000 students) and dilapidated university complex in the south of the City. The circle gyrating around a young economics professor named Adolfo Orive, the son of a cabinet minister in the Alemán regime and a top-level manager for Echeverría, was particularly active during 1967-68. Orive happened to be in France in the midst of the Paris spring, studying with the Maoist guru Charles Bettelheim, and he returned to University City with his batteries charged for the Mexican summer. The Emiliano Zapata allied brigades, organized by Orive to resist the military occupation of the campus, were pat-terned on his personal blueprint of control from the bot-tom up—in which all decision-making was made by "pop-ular" (in the sense of "proletarian") assemblies of students, workers, and campesinos. The assemblies later became the cornerstone of Orive's "Política Popular" movement.

After Tlatelolco, Mexico City became too hot for

274

those UNAM radicals who had somehow managed to avoid the Díaz Ordaz dragnet. Even the son of a future Echeverría functionary found the climate sticky. The provinces looked inviting: a struggle over increases in student fees at the Autonomous University of Nuevo León made Monterrey particularly so. Orive's brigadistas chugged into town, dug in around the university, began organizing house by house, block by block, colony by colony, particularly in the improvised, impoverished squatter settlements on the edge of this rapidly modernizing industrial giant of the north. Massive, violent landtakers resulted in the creation of the Tierra y Libertad (an old Zapatista cry) encampment in Monterrey and, by the early 1970s, similarly-named encampments had blossomed throughout the north, in Durango and Torreón and Saltillo in the Laguna region straddling Durango and Coahuila, an area where President Lázaro Cárdenas had chartered a series of always-militant ejidos. In some cities, like Saltillo and Torreón, Orive's "Polítca Popular" movement impressed priests, who, in the spirit of Medellin '69, were immersed in parallel organizing efforts among the newly-urbanized poor. The Bishop of Torreón was so enthusiastic about the work of the "Pepes" that he even urged a visitor from Chiapas, Samuel Ruiz, to invite a brigade to the jungles of the Lacandón.

Politíca Popular's fortunes boomed after a 1976 confrontation with Monterrey police in which six "Red Guards" were martyred by gunfire—Hector Camero, a leader of the Tierra y Libertad encampment, recently told *Proceso* that he blamed Orive for sending the Red Guards to their death. "The revolution costs lives," Orive reportedly responded to Camero's criticisms, at the time. The martyrdom of the "Red Guards" spread the "Pepes'" "line of masses" ("línea de masas") throughout northern industrial cities. But the growth of "The Organization" (as initiates referred to it) strained relations between local Pepe leaders, the base assemblies, and the direction—a group that operated under the initials of the OID ("Organization of Ideological Direction") and was headed by Hugo Andrés Araujo, a "natural leader" from the Laguna. By 1978, relations between Orive and Araujo had reached a point of no return and the latter took his brigades and moved operations to the San Luis Potosí Huasteca where a campesino-White Guard war was then raging. During his stint in the conflictive Huasteca, Araujo was protected by Raúl Salinas de Gortari, then Sub-secretary of Rural Roads and the outgoing Mexican president's brother. Historians of that era in Mexican radical history maintain that both Salinases were active in the Pepe structure. Today, Hugo Andrés Araujo is director of the Institutional Revolutionary Party's farmers confederation, the CNC. Orive, after a reconciliation with his old nemesis, heads CNC training programs.

But back in 1978, Orive was on the left flank, about to embark on his long march to Chiapas—before the first brigade left in December of that year, Camero remembers being taken by Orive to a fund-raising dinner at the Mexico City home of Manuel Camacho Solís, one further clue that influence in Mexico is concentrated in very, very few hands. 16 years later, El Camacho would welcome the lineal descendants of Politíca Popular to the Cathedral of San Cristóbal to talk peace.

* * *

The first 12 brigadistas came to the mountains of the southeast carrying the banner of "Proletarian Line" ("Línea Proletaria"). According to the Jesuit Mardonio Morales, the interlopers' arrogance disaffected local priests. "Orive told us we should attend to the pastoral work and they would provide the organization," Morales told *Proceso* last September before the diocese ordered him not to speak with the press. "They wanted us to give up the communities to them." For the Jesuits and the Dominicans who preached libertarian in the lowland half of Don Samuel's diocese, the conflict was an ethical one—the padres' commitment was to "accompany" the poor, the big city radicals wanted to "direct" them.

Don Samuel, who had originally extended an invitation to the Pepes to help organize the jungle, was suspicious about the brigades' motives, says Father Mardonio, but did not force them to leave. The Bishop noticed the organizational advancements made by the leftists and figured they served the Church's purposes which Ruiz had defined as dismantling "the structures of domination."

Línea Proletaria appeared in the Cañadas at a propitious moment: the fall-out from Echeverría's 1972 edict to evacuate the forest was already drawing blood and the newly-issued Montes Azules order was further fodder for the flames. The leftists rapidly formulated a series of Tzeltal campesino alliances, "Quiptic Ta Lezubtesel" ("United for Our Future"), the Union of Ejidos, and the Union of Unions—ARIC. These formations followed basic PP principles: the assemblies made all the decisions and there were ostensibly no leaders—nonetheless, Mardonio accuses the "Torreonistas" of manipulating the assemblies and of utilizing the Church to enforce assembly decisions. In some communities, Mardonio insists, priests, under the leftists' spell, refused sacraments to those opposed to "The Organization," paving the way for Protestant conversions. The Jesuit also charges that it was the Pepes who first raised the banner of the indigenous church, demanding more autonomy from the diocese, an effort that produced the designation of hundreds of Tzeltal deacons who displaced local priests and were permitted to conduct Mass. Mardonio's list of grievances bears a word of caution— competition between Jesuits and Dominicans for Don Samuel's favor has always been rigorous within the San Cristóbal diocese.

By his own account, the man we know as "Marcos" came to the Cañadas in 1983, as part of a brigade of 12, the same number as the survivors of the "Granma," the old tub that had transported Fidel Castro from Veracruz to Cuban shores in 1956. Was this brigade organized by Política Popular? One historian consulted says the Pepes sent no brigades after 1981 under their own banner— Pedro Moctezuma conjectures Marcos's brigade was recruited from a successor formation, possibly in Monterrey.

We know precious little about the fate of the other 11 disciples of revolution—seven "went to work in another area," Marcos relates. Several others could not take the rough and tumble of the Mountain and went home to the cities. Three stayed, one of whom—a one-time confederate of Arturo Gamíz and perhaps the group's leader—was gunned down at an Ocosingo police stop the year after this newest band of "Torreonistas" arrived in the jungle. He is still recalled by the Zapatistas as "a great scientist—one who knew all the guerrilleros and the mistakes they had made. He died in combat valiantly," Major Sergio told La Jornada. The contemporary "Marcos" honored his old compañero by taking his name.

The brigadistas of 1983 plunged into the ferment of the Cañadas, the pioneer spirit of its peoples, their collective memory of exodus and their sense of being chosen, with untypical dedication. The new outlanders had not come so much to do good works as to organize an army. The three survivors of this metaphorical "Granma" made for their Sierra Maestra right away, the caves in the mountains in the Sierra of Corralchén, where the May 1993 firefight with the Army would take place, and the deeper jungle in the hills above Guadalupe Tepeyac, up against the Guatemalan border. Year in and year out, the Men of the Caves trained vigorously up in the Mountain for the coming war. Their only contact with the villages was as medical volunteers, promoting vaccination campaigns throughout the Cañadas. Children died in their arms—but many lived. By the dawn of the '90s, the Cañadas' young population knew all about the Men of the Caves. There was hardly a young adult—girls very definitely included—who had not gone up to the Mountain to take target practice.

There seem to be four distinct stages in the Zapatistas' decade-long gestation, analyzes Julio Moguel in an insightful *La Jornada* piece (June 19th, 1994) The first stage, "The Installation of the Foco," takes in the early years in the caves—"we had to learn if the Mountain would accept us," Marcos tells, "the Indians taught us how to walk..." "Indian Appropriation" came next, a process in which the foco yielded to the Tzeltal vanguard—much as Don Samuel's church had to yield to the indigenous one. In the Cañadas, the force of culture inevitably transforms missionaries into followers.

The construction of an army was the next task. First self-defense squads were organized to repel the assaults of the ranchers' White Guards. "The compañeros came to see that it was not just one ejido that was being attacked and so alliances were made," Marcos describes this period of building. The fourth stage of development, the construction of a base to provide the logistical support that is so vital to the success of the "guerra of the pulga," is pegged, among other factors, to the price of coffee. Before 1989, the Zapatistas had to compete for the sympathies of the villages with the "organizations of hope," the "Quiptics" and the "ARIC"s built by the brigades that had preceded Marcos to the jungle. Nourished by the church, such groups promoted the illusion that "self-sufficiency" and peaceful redress of grievances was still possible. But after the International Coffee Organization floated the price of its product on world markets, a ruinous gesture, this equation changed radically for 64,000 Chiapas coffee-growing families, many of them with influence in the social organization of Las Cañadas. Besieged by the precipitous drop in prices, Patrocinio's wood-cutting ban, and Salinas's cutback of agricultural subsidies in favor of free market "solutions" to Mexico's agrarian crisis, the organizations of hope hemorrhaged left—at least 40% of the ARIC defected to Zapatista formations, estimates its leader, Lázaro Hernández—others claims the percentage of defection was far higher. The Independent Alliance of Campesinos—Emiliano Zapata" (ACIEZ), a Zapatista mass organization, was constructed to receive the formerly hopeful. ACIEZ went national ("ANCIEZ") in 1991, joining with other radical farmers groups that advocated the armed option at a secret congress in the Sierra Negra of Puebla, indicates a leaked government report obtained by then-*El Financiero* columnist Raimundo Riva Palacios.

The growth of the Zapatista Army of National Liberation was complicated by the death of communism. Maoist in their historical underpinnings, the Zapatistas appeared to have embraced early on the socialist models nearest to them—but the defeat of the Sandinistas in the 1990 Nicaraguan elections did not bode well for the future. When the FSLN gave up the ghost, the EZLN learned "not to trust the parliamentary model," Marcos explains. The Cuban experience seems more a symbol these days than a model to emulate. The stacking of guns by

Salvador's Farabundo Martí Liberation Front (FMLN) was truly alarming. Marcos confesses that he thought the monumental turn-away from the armed struggle to build socialism, as symbolized by the tearing down of the Berlin Wall, had cooked the EZLN's goose.

"When the whole world was saying no to armed struggle because communism had disappeared, we thought the people here were going to say no to the Change, much less the armed struggle. This was logical—the ideological bombardment was strong. But in the communities, the reverse happened. This was the time when more people came over to incorporate themselves in the militias of the Zapatista Army. Things had gotten so bad that the towns declared they were left with no other road to take. When, on the international level, everyone was saying no to armed struggle, the indigenous farmers of Chiapas were saying oh yes, oh yes, oh yes..." (Leñero, *Proceso*, February 21st 1994).

By the end of 1992, the assemblies had given the Zapatista military wing one year in which to prepare the war. The war itself was voted and the vote taken in classic Zapatista fashion, family by family and settlement by settlement. "How could we go to war without first asking those who would fight?" recalls Isaac, a young member of the Clandestine Indigenous Revolutionary Committee. "Yes," agrees Marcos, puffing away on his ever-present pipe "somewhere in the Lacandón jungle," "the great scandal of this war was that it was democratically voted upon—we still have the voting certificates around here some place..."

* * *

"When we first came here, we felt invincible. We felt that with our convictions we would defeat any army. Then,

281

we began to speak with the communities and they had a very important lesson for us. The democratic organization, the social life of the indígena is very honest, very clear. It's very difficult to turn them into patsies or corrupt them. Moreover, we saw a lot of people die. Many kids. They died in our hands while we dedicated ourselves to the health campaigns that the government doesn't bring here so we had to do them ourselves. We didn't do this to be do-gooders. These were our people. Our combatants carried out these vaccination campaigns for a long time. And the people died anyway. There were kids, four or five years old, that played they were going to be Zapatistas. They would say 'when I'm big, I am going to go and vaccinate the people,' but the next day they would be dead, of diarrhea and fevers..."

The three ace reporters squatted uncomfortably upon the rough-hewn beam. They had many questions but this quiet, driven man who called himself "Marcos" gave them no space in which to interpose them. Outside in the forest, dawn was straining to break through the darkness. There was not much time left to discover what they had come for.

"Before the war, the girls played about what they were going to be when they grew up—and now even more. That instead of getting married, they are going to the mountain to make their lives, to learn Spanish. This is almost impossible for an indigenous woman, to learn Spanish, and how to use a weapon—that's a big jump..."

Leñero, the others, tried to break into the monologue but Marcos would not quit.

"When they decided to fix a date for the war, the women argued with us: 'What's the problem? Our death is our own. Now you're going to tell us how to die? Are you coming or do we have to leave you behind?' How could we answer? 'Wait another five years to see if the new government will change things? No, we didn't have the right to say that...too many people died all the time. We had to follow and declare the war..."

* * *

"The Zapatista Army was not born democratic," the Subcomandante challenges the illusions of those who come to see him. The EZLN is and has always been, a political-military organization insists its chief military strategist. When he speaks with reporters his shotgun is never very far from his hands. Marcos seems to subscribe to the theory that if you have a gun at the ready, you can kill those who have come to kill you before they get the drop, a dubious truth at best but one which shapes his death-riddled, military posture: "It's not AIDS or cancer that's going to kill us. Bullets will. They're trying to murder us..."

When one enters Zapatista territory, one is always talking with men and women tightly gripping or lovingly stroking their weapons. At fiestas, the Zapatistas sing an updated version of the old Villista corrido "Carabina .30-.30." The title is one measure of the modernity of the EZLN arsenal. Jean Francoise Boyer, correspondent for the French "Libération" and a veteran of Salvadoran skirmishes, scoffs at Zapatista firepower—World War II M-1s and M-2s, a handful of automatic weapons, and a lot of single-shot .22s, much inferior to anything he's ever seen in Central America. Nonetheless, the Zapatistas have used their antiquated weapons of war to blast their way onto the front page of Boyer's paper.

Each Zapatista fighter must buy his or her own weapon from a common stockpile and this creates a bond between combatants and their guns that state armies have a hard time matching. According to Marcos, the EZLN filled in its armory through various routes—mostly the "hormiga" (ant) run south, one "cuerno de chivo" picked up here, another there. Most automatic weapons in Mexico descend from the northern border, from cities like El Paso where hundreds are sold to individual buyers each day and then smuggled south for re-sale at $500 USD each, a few months' pay for a low-wage construction worker or half the coffee harvest for an angry-enough farmer.

Another source of weaponry were the anti-narcotics police and military troops engaged in coordinated drug campaigns. As Marcos explains the skam, the anti-narcos would bust the narcos, confiscate their weaponry, and wholesale them out to dealers who, in turn, sold them back to the next smuggling gang who, of course, had them confiscated when they too fell to the law. Reselling these guns over and over again is a lucrative business for anti-narcos: "They sold them to us because they thought we were selling them to the traffickers..." Still another source were the White Guards, who periodically upgraded their killing tools—having just been issued UZIs, their M-16s (gifts from the Mexican military) were up for sale.

And, lastly, says the chief military strategist of the rebel army. the troops armed themselves the way the farmers of Mexico usually arm themselves—with their single-shot .22s and rusty shotguns and even their machetes and slingshots. The EZLN has been criticized for sending its combatants into battle hopelessly unarmed, some with only a wooden replica of a rifle to defend themselves from the armed-to-the-teeth Mexican military—one such hand-carved weapon was found next to the five young men executed in Ocosingo market on the second day of the war (although insiders suggest the flamboyant, Ninja-clad L.A. photogapher Les Stone dropped the prop next to the bodies to up the drama quotient of his *Newsweek* shot). Marcos's response to the charge is soldierly: a combatant who doesn't yet have a weapon has to learn to carry its weight, to move in battle with one...

Despite the Subcomandante's testimony that the EZLN arsenal was acquired ad hoc, there are those such as Luis Pazos who argue that the weaponry and the uniform are proof that the Zapatistas must have a clandestine backer: "La Quina," the imprisoned oilworkers union boss Joaquín Hernández Galicia, jailed by Salinas on charges of stockpiling weapons in early 1989, is sometimes mentioned as a Zapatistia angel. But Marcos denies access to such upper echelons of the armament game. "If we had met up with one of those famous arms traffickers, you and I would be talking in the Ajusco (above Mexico City) right now" the Sup boasted to Leñero.

Charges by Pazos and *Excelsior*'s José Pérez Stuart charge that the EZLN's uniforms are evidence of outside financing borders on the absurd. The uniforms are not always uniform, they are home-stitched and not very fashionable—*Vanity Fair* called them "shabby." With their red plastic stars and bars to denote rank, their bright green plastic fanny packs, and high orange plastic canteens, the Zapatistas look a little like kids playing soldier—an impression quickly debunked by the troops' surly crowd control techniques.

How many men and women fill the Zapatista Army of National Liberation uniforms? The low-end estimate following the January 1st takeovers was 1,200—2,500 at the outside—but, as Marcos underscores, it is just not good strategy for an army to reveal its full strength. In February, the military estimated Zapatista strength at 12,800 but the figure made no distinction between armed fighters, "milicianos" who have not yet earned their guns, and the civilian base, the "ejidatarios" and their families that kept the EZLN troops "alive in the mountains." The Zapatista

Army is an army of farmers and provisions are made for its troops to rotate between the fields and military duty.

The Subcomandante claims one hundred Mexican soldiers deserted to the EZLN in January (none has ever been interviewed), a number that, if true, adds fighting capacity, and that there are other armed groups throughout the country, prepared to act out of stated alliance or in synchronisity if a general offense is warranted, assets that up Zapatista range and firepower considerably. Whatever the gross numbers, 2,500 Zapatistas, as poorly armed as they are, can potentially defeat ten times that number of Army regulars on their own turf: "We are inside our terrain. They have to come here and get us..." (Marcos).

Was the original Zapatista master plan to suck the maximum Mexican military force into the jungle and wage a prolonged war upon them, the political terms to be dictated by long-term government losses? If so, the Mexican government's early turn towards peace must have been a serious strategic blow.

Marcos is the most visible military honcho in the EZLN hierarchy but some experts, such as 1970s guerrillero Jaime Velver Payán now of the Center for the Study of Armed Movements, suggest that there is a general above the Subcomandante who remains veiled. Rumors have floated for months that a Ladina woman holds that post— the mysterious Dr. Alejandra, formerly of the Ejido Morelia, is advanced as one candidate for the command.

Ironically, despite their gun-happy bravado, these post-Cold War guerrilleros are not at all wedded to an armed takeover of the state. In fact, the Zapatistas do not train their sights on any kind of taking of state power, a task Marcos delegated to the unarmed Civil Society at the now-legendary National Convention in August—an odd strophe for a revolutionary army. Is the Zapatista Army of

National Revolution a revolutionary force? The argument can be made that the EZLN differs from the campesino organizations from which its soldiers bloomed mostly in the fact that they carry weapons when they go to make their demands. Some call what the Zapatistas do armed propaganda rather than armed struggle—the political theater of the Colombian M-19 stealing the sword of Simón Bolívar and the Black Panthers, shotguns in hand, posing on the steps of the Sacramento California state capital is recalled. Jorge G. Castañeda, a student of Latin revolutionaries, disdainfully labels the "EZs" "armed reformists."

* * *

The EZLN was not born democratic but "the form and organization of the indigenous communities permeated and dominated our movement and we had to democratize in the Indian way." In reality, the Zapatista Army is much more dedicated to doing politics than fighting wars. All fundamental decision-making power seems weighted to the EZLN political committees. As in predecessor structures dating back to the Tierra y Libertad encampments in Monterrey and Torreón on one hand and a millennium of indigenous social organization on the other, the communal assembly is the supreme and ultimate arbiter of EZLN direction. Each communal assembly selects its own officers: a "responsible" to secure the communal safe house, education and health commissioners who meet regionally, and delegates to one of four Clandestine Revolutionary Indigenous Committees or CCRIs, each of the four Zapatista language groups having their own—each CCRI has 16 to 40 members depending on regional population. 11 delegates are chosen to sit on the ruling CCRI-General Command under which Marcos, a subcommander, emphasizes that he serves. The Subcomandante himself serves on the CCRI as the leader of the EZLN's military wing.

"We are not a classic guerrilla," the Sup says in a spurt of understatement. Within the Zapatista game plan, war is not considered the sole pathway to liberation—nor is being a combatant the only way to Heaven. "Many came to the mountain and couldn't take it here and so we sent them back to work on another level," Marcos explains. "If your tendency is to become a mass-based army, then you can't put so much emphasis on the old traditional guerrilla discipline—the you're-with-us-or-you-are-dead school of thought. You can't raise the step so high that nobody can climb it; you have to make room for all the people to participate to the best of their abilities and so you are always in the process of looking for what unites people," the Sup told longtime Latin American correspondent Alma Guillermoprieta on assignment for Tina Brown's *New Yorker* in April—the *New Yorker* and Brown's former employer, *Vanity Fair*, waged a dingdong battle to get Marcos interviews into print.

* * *

"Before, my work was like that of every other woman here, take care of the kids—in my case, it was my little brothers and sisters. Go for the firewood, make the food. Help the husband. But what if the husband comes home and scolds you, he's drunk and he says bad things to you and hits you. It's not fair because the woman can't move. She has to stay with him, that's her work. It's like she is his property....

"That is one reason why I went up to mountain. I did not want this to happen to me. My parents were really opposed but I went anyway. Now they have come to understand how jodido we are and how we do not have any choice but to declare the war. They have become proud of me..."

Captain Irma is squeezed into a child's desk outside of the abandoned schoolhouse at La Garrucha, her polished carbine across her lap. Azucena and Graciela, two teenage lieutenants, flank her on either side. All are wearing ski masks or paliacates but under their disguises, the three seem scarcely older than the kids who normally fill the schoolhouse, their older sisters perhaps. In the Zapatista zone, a graying reporter sometimes gets the sense that he is interviewing an army of very convinced children.

"Things have changed around here a great deal since we declared the war. The woman is not just her husband's slave now. Her parents just can't sell her to a man. Now the women have grown more equal. They have the opportunity to learn. They read books and speak Spanish. The old ways are over with around here

"In the war, its all equal. Now we cook the food and wash the clothes together. We fight the war together..."

The appearance of women combatants in the EZLN ranks—about a third of the fighters are women and women comprise 55% of the Zapatista logistical support base—is not unique in the history of recent Latin American wars of the pulga. Women were and are on the frontlines and incorporated into the direction of the Sandinista National Liberation Front, Peru's Shining Path, the M-19 in Colombia, the Salvadoran FMLN and the Guatemalan URNG. Women have been combatants in every Mexican war dating back to the skirmishes between the Aztec island-states of Tenochtitlán and Tlatelolco, battles that featured brigades of nearly naked women warriors. During the Mexican revolution, Zapata's Southern Army of Liberation included battalions of women—in Puente de Ixtla, Morelos, the mothers and sisters and daughters of slain Zapatista soldiers fought fiercely "to avenge our deaths" under the command of the blue-clad tortilla maker known as "La China."

But despite the antecedents, the incorporation of women into the ranks and the leadership of the EZLN is a revolutionizing step for the Tzeltales, Tzotziles, Tojolabales, and Choles of the Lacandón. In Las Cañadas, women have an average of seven children each (2.8 is the Chiapas state average). With 60% of the population below the age of 20, many adolescent girls are sold into marriage before they are 15. 117 women out of each 100,000 die in childbirth in this region—the highest maternal mortality rates in Mexico, and infant mortality is twice the national norm. 30 to 40% of the women are monolingual and 60% do not read or write.

"Why have the women suddenly demanded to participate?" Comandante Ramóna, a leader of the CCRI-General Command, asked Blanche Petrich in rapid-fire Tzotzil. "Because women have been the most exploited since when? 500 years? And they are still oppressed...before the revolutionary laws were approved, they didn't have the right to speak out or participate in an assembly. They couldn't take office. We still get up at three in the morning to prepare the corn for our husband's breakfast and we don't rest until it is late at night. If there is not enough food we give it to our children and our husbands first. So the women sense they are being exploited and not taken into account and now they have decided to take up arms and become Zapatistas..."

The Revolutionary Law of Women, promulgated January 1st in the Declaration of the Lacandón Jungle gives women the right to participate in revolutionary struggle and receive military rank; guarantees the right of employment and a just salary; the right to decide the number of children a woman wants and can take care of; the right to participate and take office in the community; the first rights of women and children to health care and nutrition; the right to education and to study ("to even drive a truck if she wants"—Captain Susana); a ban on forced marriages; and severe penalties for the physical mistreatment of women.

Passage of the Revolutionary Law by the communal assemblies led to what Marcos tags the first Zapatista uprising. In March 1993. Susana, a young Tzotzil, traveled from Zapatista community to Zapatista community soliciting the opinions of the women and testing the ideas contained in the revolutionary law. "We want to have the number of children we decide to have," "we want that we are not forced to marry someone we don't want to marry," "we want our voices to be heard and respected." The demands were translated from Spanish into the four Zapatista languages and the process was slow but, as the women began to understand, they applauded the law. "It's good my woman doesn't understand all this castilla (Spanish)," one young Zapatista male was overheard to remark. "Well, compañero, then you're screwed," Susana shot back "because they're translating the law into all the languages..."

Despite this incipient battle of the sexes, there appears to be plenty of romance within the Zapatistas' tender ranks. Combatants are permitted to couple up upon notification of the command and Zapatista weddings are held. "But there are no children," Captain Irma explains a little wistfully. "How are we going to care for them? Where would we put them? How can we feed them if there is hardly enough food for us now?" The use of contraceptives is encouraged—"Los Hombres Alzados" have a place in this war after all—but are in short supply, given the ardor of liberated youth—or were before the August convention when the Sup claimed his troops had confiscated 6,000 condoms from convention-goers.

"Things have changed here a great deal since we declared the war," Irma says, the dark eyes framed in her ski mask brimming with seriousness. One hand is nervously caressing the carbine across her lap.

* * *

In what do the Zapatistas believe now that socialism is in a state of cryogenic repose? Big time gringo correspondents are always trying to shake the "S" word out of Zapatista mouths. "We're building socialism" one callow young rebel told Tim Golden on the fourth day of the war and, in true troglodytic redbaiting fashion, the *New York Times* headlined this confession the next morning. One noonday in June, I sat, appalled, as a clean-cut *San Francisco Chronicle* correspondent interrogated a young Zapatista officer, asking him repeatedly: "What is your ideology? Tell me what your ideology is..."

Despite the suspicions of the *Times* and the *Chron* and the aspirations of such U.S. Marxist-Leninist cadre as Workers World, the Revolutionary Communist Party, the Sparticists, the Fourth International, Socialist Action, Covert Action, or whatever's left on the ultra-edge, the Zapatistas have not embraced socialism. Arnaldo Martínez Verdugo, onetime director of the Mexican Communist Party, scratches his head at the absence of traditional Marxist bluster—the Zapatistas do not even refer to the machinations of the Clinton White House as "Yanqui Imperialism." To the politilogue, the EZLN is located much closer to Antonio Gramsci than Karl Marx (with a dash of John Lennonism blended in)—economics are not always the whole story. The Zapatista vision is not one of clearly demarcated divisions between social classes with the industrial proletariat being the motor of revolution. For the EZLN, the guiding philosophy may be as simple as "justice for the campesinos and the indigenous peoples" and "Basta Ya!"—"Enough Already!," not all that removed from the ideology of the rebels' namesake.

"Zapata's life and struggle mean everything to us. How he was betrayed by the government. We say here that Emiliano Zapata never died, that he still rides through our towns. He is present here, in all our meetings, even if it is only in a photograph. To us, he is the bringer of the great hope. When the government canceled Article 27, they put another bullet in Zapata's heart and in our heart too. This is why we declared the war..." Major Rolando's cigarette glows in the Zapatista dark. In EZLN territory, the words of the old revolutionary are studied and discussed like scripture. It took Angel three years to read Womack's *Zapata and the Mexican Revolution* from cover to cover, the first book he has ever finished. "It cost me a lot of work," the young Zapatista admits.

On the 75th anniversary of Zapata's death at Chinameca this past April 10th, Marcos stood upon a rough-hewn platform at La Garrucha and deified the Caudillo of the South as Votán, the Mayan "Guardian of the Heart of the People." "Votán Zapata, light that came from far away and was born here in our lands! Votán Zapata, name that changes, man without face, tender light that saves us," the ski-masked Subcomandante incanted, like the priest some insist he really is. Marcos's melding of the Caudillo of the South with the deity that guards the people's innermost secrets is yet another reminder that the Mayan past is quite alive in the Zapatista zone.

Zapata is the centerpiece icon in the EZLN pantheon but other Mexican heroes and martyrs are always present—the "Mexican Waker-Upper" ("El Despertador

Mexicano") is the reincarnation of a tract published by the founding father of the Patria, Padre Miguel Hidalgo on the eve of Mexico's war of liberation from Spain. Marcos himself exudes a keen enthusiasm for Mexican history and a patriotism that borders on the maniacal, e.g., the unfurling of the flag in the Cathedral of Peace and a dramatic presentation of the "tri-color" at the National Convention.

There remains one other thread in the Zapatista fabric that, if pulled, might unravel this eclectic ideological web. One has only to attend the simple churches that have functioned without priests in Zapatista territory for years to find it. On a Sunday morning in Garrucha, a well-traveled guitar strikes up a hymn and the paliacate-covered catechist named Sergio intones Mass to a houseful of men and women, summoned to the long cool building in their Sunday best. Afterwards, the women follow Sergio to catechism and the men stand around the basketball court with bibles in their hands to discuss the Ten Commandments and what they mean on Zapatista turf. The discussion technique is called "tehuané," to agitate or stir up, in Tzeltal. I catch words like "participation" and "production," "coffee," and "corn," Judas and JesuCristo, and, of course, "la lucha."

"We have read the Bible and it tells us that Jesus Christ fought for the poor" Rolando advises, "like us, he was a subversive...."

* * *

Who is Marcos? I thought you would never ask. With his bandaleros zigzagged across his powerful chest, his weapon ever at the ready to blast the forces of the evil government, and his penetrating gaze darting rays at interviewers from inside his black ski mask, he is the carefully calculated image of the compleat guerrillero, sent from the recent past to remind his people of the revolution that never went away. Is this myth-drenched masked man just a typecast illusion slapped together with the smoke and mirrors of a made-for-TV movie or is he the real deal? Will the true Marcos please stand up?

Who is Marcos? Listen:

"I lived in the bus terminal in Monterrey and sold used clothing. In the afternoon, it would rain and I went and watched pornographic movies. I traveled to San Diego. I was a taxi driver in Santa Barbara. I worked in a restaurant in San Francisco until I got fired for being gay. Then I worked in a sex shop. I gave demonstrations to the clients on plastic blow-up dolls. I lived below the Golden Gate Bridge. Then I went to New Orleans and worked at Preservation Hall [author's note—a personal dream. Marcos loves Sidney Bechet]. I was a security guard for a massage parlor. I was a runner for the stock market on Wall Street. I came here by accident in 1983. I was drunk. I got on the bus to go to Acapulco but I made a mistake and wound up in Ocosingo. There is a lake near here called Miramar. I asked which way the sea ("mar") was and they told me 'that way' so I started walking and pretty soon I realized I was in the mountains and I never left. The Indians made fun of me because I read *Don Quixote* and the poems of Pablo Neruda [he still does] but they were glad when I could tell them stories at night..." The dawn was just breaking over the encampment at Garrucha. Marcos had been gabbling on for hours in this vein and Trina Kleist, who had recently picked up the *San Francisco Chronicle* string, had to get back to civilization to modem off her wild scoop, a tale that heightened Marcos' stature considerably in Sodom-by-the-Bay.

Is Marcos really gay, the Queer Nation had to know. Weeks later, Marcos would add mystery to the mystery.

"Yes. Marcos is gay in San Francisco, black in South Africa, an Asian in Europe, Chicano in San Ysidro, a 'rockero' at the University City, an anarchist in Spain, a Palestinian in Israel, a Jew in Germany, an Indígena in the streets of San Cristóbal...in short, Marcos is a part of all the oppressed minorities that say enough already, Basta Ya!" The words are similar to a Joaquín Sabina ballad.

Who is Marcos? Who is not? For starters, Marcos is not the Dominican priest Pablo Romo, the ornithologist Peter Visher Garrido, the unfortunately green-eyed Alejandro Muñoz, the *Irish Times* correspondent Michael McCaughan, all of whom have been accused, interrogated, and sometimes jailed for being Marcos. Marcos is not the half brother of Patrocinio González Garrido, as reported by the Tabasco-based *Southeast Daily*—"at least I have a mother," Marcos laughed maliciously when informed that he'd been id'd. Marcos isn't Marcos Rojas, a Sandinista on the Southern Front, as reported by *La Prensa*, and he is not Gonzallo Rojas, a Mexican volunteer in Nicaragua and PRD leader with whom Televisa deliberatley confused him. Marcos isn't Walter Meade Treviño, either, a minor government bureaucrat, unveiled by the national daily *Excelsior* as the Subcomandante himself. Meade Treviño, who skies 6'9," is suing. Nor is Marcos Jerónimo Hernández López, "the Monk of Altamirano," who allegedly "dropped from sight" in 1990, only to be dug up by Zabludowsky's low-life scandal-sheet "Summa." The Jesuits too, are suing.

In late May, the *Miami Herald* reported that the Secretary of the Interior was working on two solid leads, based on fingerprints lifted from the San Cristóbal Cathedral of Peace—one a seminarian, the other an ex-guerrillero with a long criminal record. I ask Major Rolando what would be the repercussions for the "EZ" if the true Marcos was unmasked? "We are all Marcos," the young officer laughs gently, tugging lightly on his pasamontaña.

Who is Marcos? He is not an Indian. By his own count, he is one of three ladinos who remain in the EZLN. He is approximately 5'8" tall, around 160 pounds under the layers of clothing he always wears, light-skinned and powerfully built with broad shoulders. He has the long lean hands of a pianist. His eyes are amber and not green. The pores that map what one sees of his face are large and discernible. He has what he invariably describes as "a pronounced nose," only the bridge of which is open for public viewing. He seems to have a short, tightly-cropped graying beard under the lower half of his ski mask—although he insists that he is smooth-shaven, the bristles peek through the woof of his pasamontaña and children complain about the "picas" when they are asked for a kiss. Marcos appears to be straddling 40, born between 1954 and 1956 if coordinating his many dropped hints is a credible test of detection. He seems to have been born to an upper crust family—he told *Vanity Fair*'s Ann Louise Barbach that he had nine brothers and sisters, that he traveled often in the U.S. as a child, that his parents were both dead, that his family's belief system was "humanist." But then Marcos tells many reporters many different stories—one indication that the Sup has been to the States more recently than his childhood: he recognized Barbach's "Realistic" tape recorder as being exclusively marketed by the Radio Shack chain.

Some auditors, like Amado Avendaño, whom Marcos addressed by name on January 1st in San Cristóbal, place his accent in "Chilangolandia" (Mexico City), others detect the sharply defined dentals as being "norteño," from the north of the nation. My hunch is Uruápan, Michoacán. Marcos himself tells us he was born in "a provincial city" in "central Mexico" in an era when the only culture in town were the leftist cartoon books of "Rius" (Eduardo Del Rio), such as *Los Super Machos* and *Cuba For Beginners*—Rius, whose distribution came mainly through street sales by itinerant Mexico City hippies, was a key relay station in spreading the culture of the Revolution throughout the country in the 1960s. We are told by the Sup that he attended the UNAM (we do not know which faculty but his facility with words indicates a language art), that he took a post-graduate degree, that he dabbled for a while in journalism (this may just be to tease reporters).

Who is Marcos? Marcos is obsessed with hiding his face and his past, a kind of perverse self-absorption, perhaps a fatal flaw in his complex make-up. Marcos is a caudillo upon whose moods rest the precarious fate of his comrades He also appears to be a quiet, kind man with a talent for talking to kids, immensely serene, displaying a calmness that some say is eerily priestly. Marcos says the last time he was in a church was when he was eight years old and a candidate for communion. He says he is "a guerrilla without criminal antecedents," never having been fingered by the law for even so much as a traffic ticket. He is a lifelong insomniac, prowling the camp late at night. He has a sense of humor and a playful gift of gab that sparkles most in the dead of night. He is, by his own confession, "anti-solemne," against solemnity. For a revolutionary, he is a striking deviation from the usual rules of Stalinist Puritanism that stereotypes his vocation.

Marcos came to Chiapas with 11 other brigadistas, having been recruited by "The Organization" or a líneal descendant thereof, in a northern city of the republic. Once in place, Marcos "bet everything on the mountain" Marcos wears two watches, one on either wrist. One tells the War time, the other the time we live. When the two times are the same, then there will be peace. Marcos is a soldier but he is also a poet, his formal poetic lines mostly reserved for "el sexo feminino" (what we have seen of it is pretty florid). His real poetry is embedded in his prose, his deft use of colloquialisms and dramatically-charged refrains. He is a lover of literature who trundled books in his pack until the compas' taunts got to weigh too much. He chats up interviewers with booktalk: Cortázar, Vallejo, Borges, Cardenal, García Márquez, the writers of the Latin Boom. Carlos Fuentes says Marcos has read more Carlos Monsivais than Carlos Marx—and the chubby, elegant Monsi's *Days To Remember (Dias de Guardar)* is on the Sup's recommended reading list. During the build-up to the Convention in August, Marcos's interchanges with Fuentes, Monsivais, and other star literateurs were the hottest items on the literary front.

Marcos is single, says he has no steady lover although the yentas of San Cristóbal have tried to link him romantically with Comandantes Ramóna and Ana María. Judging by his intense flirtations with female interviewers, Marcos is deeply heterosexual but his bravery in staking out such dangerous turf as homosexuality in super macho Mexico must be as much admired as his audacity under fire.

Since January 1st, Marcos has attained a sex symbol status that could net him a major motion picture contract if he ever decided to cash in on the revolution and become the Mexican Stallone. While his Zapatista compañeras look at him as just another combatant (Captain Laura), his fans feel differently. "What a hunk!" trills the office manager of the Mexico City foreign correspondents association. The ex-wife of ex-President José López Portillo writes him gushy poetry in the staid pages of (gulp!) *Proceso* magazine and *Vanity Fair*'s Barbach (who was eventually beaten into print by the *New Yorker*'s Guillermoprieta) breathlessly calls him "this unique creature." "Why does this man motivate an almost irrational sexuality?" reporter Eva Bodenstadt asks herself on the pages of *La Jornada*.

Perhaps it is the mask. Mexicans have traditionally been daffy over men in masks. In ancient Mixteca cultures, men put on masks and became beasts, the shape-shifting "nahual" who channel nature's magic. Octavio Paz writes of the Mexican countenance as being itself a mask ("...even his smile"), shielding the viewer from seeing the pain of being Mexican." The Emperor-President of Mexico designates his heir through the "destape" (the unveiling) and for months before, the choice is pictured by political cartoonists as two eye holes under a mask. On the silver screen, "Zorro" and "El Santo" never revealed their true features—"El Santo," a masked superhero of the 1940s, earned his real living as a wrestler and set the style for generations of masked wrestlers like "The Blue Demon" and "Mil Mascaras" ("A Thousand Masks"), whose powers reside in never allowing their masks to be removed by opponents. The urban social activist known as "Superbarrio Gómez" today strides the streets of Mexico City, righting wrongs and halting evictions in a gold lamé cape and a scarlet and yellow ski mask—at the Aguascalientes Convention, Superbarrio gifted the Subcomandante with one of his unique masks. Marcos keeps the tradition of the masked myth alive—"it is his magic halo," remarks PRD deputy Liliana Flores, an admirer. "Hombres sin rostros"—"men without faces"— Marcos calls his compañeros." "What do we look like?" he asks, "just look in the mirror..." Will Marcos ever remove his mask and reveal his true identity? "I'm prepared to take off my mask when Mexico takes off its mask..." At one point during the Convention, the Sup asked thousands of his followers if he should take off his mask. "No-o-o" nayed the crowd high up in the "gradas."

As Marcosmania has grabbed the land, pasamontaña sales have taken off. Deputies wear them into the Mexican legislature to underscore obscure political points. Rock bands don them to be politically correct. The press corps slips on ski masks to burlesque its own obsession with the "enmasacarados." Every demonstration is guaranteed to produce a gang of pseudo-Marcosites. Underground sweat-shops churn out the pasamontañas by the tens of thousands but there never seem to be enough to satisfy demand. Does this mean that Mexico is getting ready for a mass revolution—or a masquerade? At various moments, Marcos informs that the Zapatistas put their ski masks on (a) because they could be identified by the authorities if they didn't, (b) because it is cold, (c) because the Zapatistas are too handsome to walk around unprotected, and (d) because being masked promotes egalitarianism among the EZLN leaders, and thwarts the germination of a "caudil-lo," a strong central figure around which revolutionary cells too often uncritically cluster—but, of course, the mystique of the masque has the potential of transforming Marcos into precisely this kind of caudillo.

The Zapatistas explain that Marcos became the EZLN's mouthpiece only because of his "facility with the castilla," that he is gifted in Spanish—and also speaks middling English too for the international press—but clearly, even without such linguistic talents, this charismatic, pipe-puffing masked man would still attract maximum attention.

The specter of a light-eyed white man, nearly twice the weight of the Indians he professes to serve under, and speaking for the Indígenas of Chiapas and the nation, has wrinkled up several noses. What the myth of Marcos tells us, writes '68 student leader Luis González de Alba (now a

301

Mexico City gay bar proprietor) is that "the Indians can't have a revolution unless the white guys bring the flashlights." Don Samuel is even more out of sorts with the masked idol: "People extol the name of Marcos as if the Indians can't think for themselves..."

Who is Marcos? A man seemingly fixated on death, not an uncommon strand in the Mexican collective consciousness. The man who took the name of his dead companion never tires of telling reporters that he himself is living "de prestado"—"when you get to Day 2, everything is extra." Convinced he would be killed in the first moments of the war, he is now obsessed with telling everything, writing it all down, spitting it all out "Once you have looked death in the eye, you cannot kid yourself anymore." "Death for us is life, a joy..." Death and Marcos walk together day and night and with ample reason, given the soup this Sup has stirred up—who knows that in the time it takes for this book to reach the remainder bins, we will not have long been speaking of the Subcomandante in the past tense? Asked one day to comment on the terrible coincidence in the fact that Che Guevara, Augusto Sandino, Malcolm X and Emiliano Zapata all breathed their last in their 39th year, the perhaps 39-year-old Subcomandante slyly shot back "well, I guess at my 63 years of age, I've survived the danger."

Who is Marcos?

A Bullet From Within

The candidate was not looking forward to the next stop. Tijuana is a grimy, crime-ridden whiskey-brown border boomtown where, in the best of seasons, the mesh of politics, cops, and drugs can erupt in spectacular violence. Moreover, Colosio had had perilous problems with the Tijuana section of his party ever since his boss, Carlos Salinas had summarily fired the good old boy Governor Xicoténcatl Leyva just a month into his presidency in January 1989—Leyva was said to have opened the Tijuana corridor to a Sinaloa cartel, under the direction of the four Arellano Félix brothers, and the bodies were (and still are) falling everywhere on the Baja peninsula. So careless had been Xico's style of governance that the state of Baja California Norte had fallen to Cárdenas in 1988, a cardinal sin in Salinas's book. As National President of the PRI, the unpleasant task of purging the Baja PRI—and particularly, its strident Tijuana section—fell to Luis Donaldo.

It was Colosio who had hand-picked Margarita Ortega as the 1989 Institutional Party gubernatorial candidate, beating back the exiled Leyva's proxies. And it was Colosio who, on the evening of July 4th 1989, went on national television to announce from Mexico City—without consulting with the local party hierarchy—that the PRI was conceding the governorship of Baja to the PAN's Ernesto Ruffo, the first time in the ruling party's 65 year domination of Mexican politics that the PRI had ever given up a state to the opposition.

The decision to cede Baja California Norte to the PAN cemented a much-needed political alliance with that right-of-center party but incited dangerous ire on the Pacific corner of the border. In 1988, the PRI controlled both the electoral college and the state legislature and could have successfully beaten off a PAN challenge if it wasn't for the order to cease and desist issued from Mexico City. The slogan "Do Something For Your Fatherland— Kill A Chilango!" proliferated on the walls of Tijuana. When Colosio came to town to make peace with his party after the PAN victory, PRI gangs followed him through the streets howling "Que se muera Colosio!," that Colosio should die...

Now, as the candidate flew up the Gulf of California from La Paz where the rallies were small but the air clean, he considered his campaign's bumpy fortunes. Buffeted by the Zapatista uprising, Colosio was heartened by Camacho's announcement just yesterday that the Conciliator was out of the race for good—"when it comes to choosing between a candidacy and peace, I choose peace," El Camacho had nobly volunteered. Maybe Luis Donaldo could put the Zapatista aberration behind him now. If he could just get through TJ unscathed, the sailing might get smoother now.

There were a lot of people waiting for him on the ground, an aide reported. Colosio frowned. This was his first visit to Baja as a candidate and *La Jornada* just that morning had noted that anti-Colosio PRI sectors were preparing demonstrations to protest his arrival. The candidate braced himself for the landing.

The Colosio entourage put into Abelardo Rodríguez International Airport at 3:51 P.M. on the afternoon of March 23rd. The skies above the Otay Mesa were smudged with industrial effluvia. The candidate sent his tall, slim, neurasthenic wife, Diana Laura, ahead to the hotel under military escort, to dress for dinner. Luis Donaldo would work his way into the city, touching bases in the hillside squatter colonies near the airport. Now his security wanted him out of the terminal quickly—airports had become nightmare allies for bodyguards since Cardinal Posadas was gunned down in Guadalajara. Indeed, the Cardinal's accused killers were supposed to have gotten on an Aeroméxico flight in the confusing aftermath of the hit and flown right into Tijuana, to this very terminal, where they were greeted by their longtime protectors at the Baja California State Judicial Police. Despite the proliferation of tens of thousands of wanted posters bearing their likenesses and offering a $5 million USD reward, the Arellano Félix brothers have been rarely seen since—only Papal Nuncio Giralamo Prigione and Tijuana priest Gerardo Montaña are known to have interviewed the most wanted drug lords in the land since the Posadas killing. But that's another story—or is it?

The Narcos own most of the police in TJ. Chapo Guzmán drills football field-length tunnels under the border just up the road from the airport and funnels uncounted tons of cocaine into California without anyone ever noticing. Not three weeks previous to Colosio's visit, the state judicial police had rescued a reputed Arellano Félix lieutenant from the federal judicial police on a downtown Tijuana street. Five people, including bystanders, were killed in the crossfire.

The crowd outside the airport doors was reluctant to move, recalls German Castillo, Colosio's longtime bodyguard. Castillo worked as a team with General Domiro García of the High Military Command ("Estado Mayor")—that was all the protection the candidate wanted. The two bodyguards allowed Colosio maximum contact with the public, a signature of his revived campaign. It also limited the number of people responsible for the candidate's personal security to but two trusted colleagues—the rule of the game is that if they want to get to you, they infiltrate your security apparatus, so keep security to a lean, mean minimum. Castillo put his shoulder into the crowd like a crack NFL blocking back and opened a path to the candidate's waiting car.

The first stop was a "Solidarity" rally—Colosio was heavily identified with the Pronosol funds he had dispensed for the past two years as director of that electoral clientele giveaway program and the PRI was counting on its Solidarity committees in the impoverished urban colonies of Mexico to be its electoral shock troops come August 21st. Moreover, since the Zapatista uprising, the PRI had developed a sudden concern for the nation's underclass and every campaign stop featured a photo op in which Colosio immersed himself in poor people to illustrate the ruling party's new-found compassion.

The first meeting was set for the Lomas Taurinas colony, a gully that years before had been bought up by a pair of Tijuana bullfighters and sold off in lots by unscrupulous speculators to the poor of Michoacán and Oaxaca and Guerrero who arrived in Tijuana by the dozens everyday to make their fortunes in the "maquiladoras" (U.S. and Japanese-owned border-based assembly plants) or pick garbage in the celebrated TJ dump or slide across the line, in the dead of night, to the first world glitz of the Golden State. The Lomas Taurinas had a nasty reputation for trafficking in guns and drugs and human beings, due mostly to logistics—the 10-foot-tall, jaggedly-tipped, rusting steel wall that now separates California from Mexico is just a five minute drive uphill from the colony down in the ravine.

But other than the unsavory scent of contraband, the Lomas Taurinas is much like any of the nearly 400 "popular" colonies that map the dry, suncracked hills above Tijuana, drawing the Third World within a quick breath of gleaming downtown San Diego.

What had given the Lomas Taurinas cachet with the Colosio campaign was its truculent Solidarity committee, under the thumb of the local "lideresa" Yolanda Lázaro. The folks from Lomas Taurinas were always marching on the Tijuana Palace of Government, demanding that the PAN mayor of the city release funds they accused him of squandering on middle-class PANista colonies. The mayor's car windows were sometimes punched out. The PRI liked that—anytime poor people get pissed at the PAN, the ruling party considers it a meritorious deed. The Lomas Taurinas was awarded the Colosio rally. Besides, the colony was only five minutes west of the airport.

The meeting began just after four and was much bigger than expected, 3,000 to 3,500 participants. The local PRI had padded the crowd with a lot of police. Colosio, who always drove himself, parked the rented blue Blazer a hundred yards uphill from the meeting site, a confluence of the colony's two unpaved streets. Castillo and the General moved him gingerly across a makeshift wooden bridge towards the pick-up from which the candidate would offi-ciate. The stench of "aguas negras" (raw sewage) drifted up into their nostrils—one demand of the colonos was to hook up the drainage system. Once again, the crowd was dense and immovable but security teams opened a breach for Colosio. The meeting was literally crawling with cops—besides the Estado Mayor which General García oversaw, National Security agents from the top-secret CISEN ("Center for Investigation and National Security") were on hand. So was the Highway Patrol, and state judicial police agents from the nearby La Mesa delegation prowled the crowd. The Colosio campaign's national security coordina-tor had contracted 160 young men to control the crowds and run off hecklers. The Tijuana PRI fielded its own team,

45 mostly fired cops who worked such details under the rubric of the TUCAN group (its initials stand for "Todos Unidos Contra Acción Nacional" or "Everybody United Against the PAN"), some of whose operatives were assigned to push paleta (fruit popsicles) carts around the perimeter of the gathering.

The only local police force not present at the rally was the Tijuana municipal police, under the direction of PANista Federico Benítez. Benítez, whose agents ultimately stationed themselves close by, had been asked three times the previous day, by the local PRI security director, Rodolfo Rivapalacios, not to patrol the rally because the presence of the municipal police might upset the embattled colonos.

The Lomas Taurinas meeting was billed as "a neighborly dialogue" ("dialogos vecinales"). The format of these seances is routine: representatives of the colony get up and read their demands and the candidate writes them all down and promises to fix everything once he is elected to high office. This "Neighborly Dialogue" was momentarily interrupted while plainclothes cops chased off five young men, perched on the hillside and waving a big hand lettered sign that read: "Colosio! Camacho and Subcomandante Marcos Are Watching You!" Then a scuffle broke out in front of the truck because Yolanda Lázaro had been denied an opportunity to harangue her people. Colosio smoothed tempers. The candidate gazed up at the littered, foreboding hillside above him, the cardboard shacks and undone cinder block hovels, the bruised walls upon which his name had been scratched in enormous letters. He responded to the neighbors' demands as he always did, smiling, assured, enthusiastic. No one seems to have taken down his exact words. "We are going to win here!" Colosio shouted triumphantly and stepped from the pick-up bed into what his bodyguards had come to call "the public bath." A traditional "banda de guerra" struck up blaring martial music. The sound system kicked in with the rollicking "La Culebra"—"the Culebra (snake) is going to get you—you better move your feet." Castillo put his shoulder into the mob and started to push his way uphill, his boss right on his side as always, and General Domiro covering the candidate's back. Then what he thought was a "cohete" (rocket) went off somewhere behind Castillo, to his right. "The Culebra's going to get you"—the sound system was deafening. The bodyguard felt Colosio go limp against him. Then Colosio wasn't there at all.

Castillo whirled around to see a hand emerge from the crowd closing around him and fire into Colosio's belly. By the time he reached his friend, Luis Donaldo Colosio, the heir apparent to the presidency of Mexico, lay face down in a pool of blood, his brains and guts splattered all over a garbage-strewn gully a hairsbreadth from the U.S. border. It looked to Castillo like a classic hit. "This was a professional job," he later told *La Jornada* at Colosio's funeral.

The time was 5:08 P.M. Pacific Standard Time, Wednesday, March 23rd, approaching the maximum news hour on both sides of the border. Millions of citizens of these two contiguous countries hunkered down to witness the drama live, the first post-NAFTA, bi-lingual presidential assassination ever broadcast, and one which stirred long painful memories on the northern side of the rusting border fence.

The first slug, fired centimeters from Colosio's right temple, had done the damage. Colosio was braindead but his heart was still pumping. The dying candidate was slung into the rented Blazer for a wild ride to Tijuana General Hospital. World-famous surgeons were summoned, helicopters chartered to lift the sinking candidate to the Scripps

Medical Center in La Jolla. A Televisa crew bribed its way into the hospital and plied the antiseptic floors, snooping for vital signs. Outside, a frightened mob had gathered, cursing and screaming on the esplanade in the dark. A little after 8 P.M., the death watch was over. The President would make the announcement.

Carlos Salinas learned immediately of the shooting, interrupted during a tête-a-tête with his new NAFTA associate Jean Chrétien. Córdoba Montoya brought the bad news. Now the long black limousines and armored Grand Marquises were arriving at Los Pinos—business leaders, the bankers, the directors of the Institutional party's sectors, its labor czars and legislative leaders, the military. "The situation is grave," General Ramón Mota Sánchez muttered clenchjawed to the press. Finally, at 10 P.M., an ashen-faced Carlos Salinas went on national—and international—television to put the official seal on the tragedy: "Luis Donaldo Colosio is dead. Mexico has lost a great friend and I have lost a great friend," the President gulped, declaring Thursday, March 24th a national day of mourning. The stock market would be shut down to hold off massive capital flight.

Three men had been taken into custody at the murder scene in connection with what the commentators were already calling the "magnicide." One, the suspected shooter, had been beaten bloody by the mob. He was identified as Mario Aburto Martínez, a 23 year-old mechanic and native of La Rinconada, Michoacán. In his first statement released to the press, Aburto claimed to be "a pacifist." Aburto had been immediately pounced upon by the crowd and pinned down by an ex-state judicial cop and member of the TUCAN team, Vicente Mayoral. Mayoral had kept shouting, "He's the killer!" Others thought they heard Aburto yell, "He did it!" at Mayoral after the second shot was fired. Mayoral was taken into custody as a material witness and released within 24 hours.

The third individual captured at the scene, José Antonio Sánchez Ortega, was described as a CISEN operative, a top-secret agency operating under the aegis of the Secretary of the Interior. Sánchez Ortega, who may have been photographed next to Colosio as he left the pick-up truck (positive identity remains in doubt), was nabbed running uphill towards his car, by members of the Tijuana Municipal Police, who had been hovering three minutes away—despite requests by the PRI to steer clear of Lomas Taurinas. When Sánchez Ortega fell into their arms, his shirt was splattered with Colosio's blood and he subsequently tested paraffin-positive as having recently fired a gun. The agent reportedly also tested positive for marijuana use. Federal judicial police snatched the CISEN agent away from the "municipales" late on the night of the assassination. Sánchez Ortega has not been seen publicly since.

* * *

Marcos was near La Garrucha on the afternoon of March 23rd, giving reporters a sour earful about how the press and the government were distorting the role of the consultations on the 32 points. He was furious that the government had misrepresented the EZLN promise to bring the 32 responses back to the communal assemblies for a yes or no decision as agreement to sign a peace treaty. "Peace isn't just a signature away," he told *Proceso* reporters. If he had reservations about the accords why had he not spoken up during the final ceremonies in the cathedral? "We were in enemy territory," the Subcomandante responded. Just then, Major Mario brought the news of the Colosio shooting, far away at the opposite end of the country in Tijuana. The two hurried off together.

311

The reporters caught up with the distraught Sup an hour after Salinas's mournful announcement: "It wasn't us," he blurted. "We might have attempted to take out Salinas or Córdoba but not Colosio. This hurts us. This hurts Camacho," He called the killing an "ajuste de cuentas," "an adjustment of accounts." "I never thought they would be so stupid as to stage a self-assassination to recover their lost prestige." Although he was panicked by the prospect of imminent army attack, Marcos did not see a military coup on the horizon. "It will be more like Fujimori in Peru—Salinas will stay in power until the year 2000," the Subcomandante predicted and begged leave to huddle with the General Command.

* * *

The throng assembled Thursday morning outside the stout iron gates at the National PRI Headquarters on Insurgentes Norte was surly early. When Colosio's coffin was trundled in after 8 A.M., the ambiance grew ominous. One by one, the PRI honchos, kingmakers, fixers, bagmen, alchemists, governors, legislators and lackies filed into the Plutarco Elias Calles Auditorium in the centerpiece mausoleum structure of the PRI compound. Outside the gates on the sidewalk, the rabble howled "Justice!" and "Quien Fue?" ("Who Was It?") and "Kill Camacho!"

The competition to fill Colosio's shorts had begun with the death of the candidate's brain. The hopefuls were gathering their power groups around them, preparing to argue their case before Salinas. Colosio's funeral was the place to cajole friends, collect old debts, and neutralize enemies. King Carlos would get a double "destape" this year, a first-ever for the PRI.

The last successful assassination of a presidential sure thing—General Alvaro Obregón—had taken place in 1928, the year before the party's founding. Nonetheless, the Obregón hit was probably ordered by the Institutional Party's founding father, General Plutarco Elias Calles, the same Plutarco Elias Calles whose name was on the marquee of the auditorium in which Luis Donaldo Colosio had been laid out. The PRI is nothing if not timeless.

The Obregón assassination had purportedly been perpetrated by José Torral, a "deranged Catholic fanatic," while he was sketching the President-elect's portrait in a San Angel café in southern Mexico City—but Torral died mysteriously in prison before he could reveal the identity of the "intellectual assassin." Similarly, three other less-successful presidential assassins had died in prison since the hit on Obregón.

The wheeling and dealing between power groups was said to be tense inside the Calles auditorium. Major Mexican political funerals traditionally revolve around "the standing of guard," in which teams of the departed solon's associates compete to demonstrate their loyalties and test their possibilities of succession. President Salinas, the widow, several of Luis Donaldo's closest aides and boyhood friends, stood the first guard. Also included in this first group was Ernesto Zedillo, another Salinas protégé and Colosio's campaign manager. A Baja California native, Zedillo was already being criticized for not having made the fatal tour with the candidate. As campaign manager, Zedillo bore the ultimate responsibility for scheduling the Lomas Taurinas meeting.

One wave of distinguished PRIistas after another took their grimfaced stance before their slain comrade's bier: the most mentioned possible "destapados" included finance minister Pedro Aspe, ex-education secretary Zedillo, the brittle president of the PRI Fernando Ortiz Arana, even ex-Interior Secretary Gutiérrez Barrios and Camacho. All of the above, save for Manuel Camacho Solís, took their place before Colosio's coffin. So did Carlos Hank González, agricultural secretary and padrino of the Institutional Party's old guard, who after several years of biding his time in innocuous cabinet posts, was about to take the PRI back.

After noon, Colosio's remains were moved to the Gayoso funeral digs off Sullivan Park for public viewing before cremation—next day, Diana Laura would fly Luis Donaldo's ashes to his hometown of Magdalina de Kino, in the Sonora desert, 60 miles from Arizona. The mob outside of Gayoso's was even more heated than at the PRI, swearing and hissing whenever an opposition politician appeared to pay their respects. Cuauhtémoc Cárdenas and his wife Celeste Batel had to fight their way into the modernistic funerary tower. Cárdenas had suspended his campaign upon news of Colosio's death—the Holy Week break was coming up. Leaders of the PAN were greeted with chants of "hypocrites!"

Inside the swarming chapel, Rigoberta Menchú draped a Mayan huipil over the slain candidate. Ex-presidents spoke darkly to the press. Miguel de la Madrid was worried that "the state of law has been broken...the leaders are masked and the political struggle is not in the open..." The participation of the Church in politics troubled both De la Madrid and Luis Echeverría, a preoccupation suggesting that the Colosio hit had been payback for Cardinal Posadas. Ex-president José López Portillo saw the shadowy hand of unspecified foreign powers who wanted "to kill Mexico."

Tensions swelled around 2 P.M. with the tardy arrival of Manuel Camacho. "You're not wanted here!" One man blocked the Conciliator's path and, as the crowd crushed menacingly in around him, another threw a long loping

314

punch at Camacho.

Camacho Solís had been in San Cristóbal when the foul deed came down. Reporters saw him pacing the patio at the pricey Casa Vieja hotel for hours that evening. The military had granted him immediate protection, had driven him the three blocks to the cathedral (in a white Grand Marquis no less) to see Don Samuel. "What will happen to us?" a sobbing woman bleated to the Commissioner for Peace and Reconciliation outside the church. The Bishop, who had just wrapped up a Mass to commemorate the 24th anniversary of the murder of Oscar Arnulfo Romero, was nervous: "Everything that alters the peace in the country, alters the peace here..."

Camacho had grabbed the first flight back to the capital and now he was surrounded by what amounted to a PRI lynch mob that was stridently blaming him for Colosio's killing. "Kill Camacho!" the lumpens howled, "Colosio Si! Camacho No!" "Before the eyes of the nation, I want to reiterate that I don't aspire to be president of the country," a shaken Conciliator stammered to Televisa, reaffirming the pledge that had warmed the cockles of Colosio's now-dead heart two days previous.

* * *

A thousand miles south of these moving scenes, the EZLN watched with trepidation as the PRI government tore itself apart. 24 hours ago, the Zapatistas had known the enemy. Now they had no feel for who was in charge. A communiqué from the CCRI-General Command, issued on the 24th, denies EZLN participation in "this cowardly assassination" and "profoundly laments that the governing group is not able to resolve its internal differences without covering the country in blood." "Colosio treated us with prudence and respect," the communiqué continued; whoever had killed him had done so "to destroy hope." Now the EZLN feared attack was imminent—an Army bombing had been reported at La Mendoza, near Altamirano on the 19th. "Now they will crown this despicable act of assassination with invasion." Consultations on the peace accord were suspended forthwith. The Zapatista Army of National Liberation was now on "Red Alert." Only "war correspondents" would be admitted into the zone. "Our steps will continue towards truth even if the path leads us to death," the General Command warned darkly.

The EZLN statement received but one line at the bottom of that day's front page *New York Times* dispatch, a harbinger of great inattention to come.

Death was more on Marcos's mind than ever. "The end of our cycle is near," he wrote on the 24th to his "beloved fellow moles." "We are the dark side of the moon," he noted in uncadenced poetry, "but we have helped you to see the whole moon." "Farewell," the Sup bade his avid public.

Two days later, Ann Louise Barbach and Medea Benjamin found the Subcomandante parked, Buddha-style, under a tree near Garrucha. He was fixated on the sky. "I can't talk. You have to leave. The Army will kill you both and blame it on the Zapatistas." 50 planes had overflown EZLN territory already today. The military was preparing "a surgical strike" that would have "low political cost" and "avoid killing large numbers of people." Despite his vow of silence, Marcos talked for four hours.

"They've arrested a pacifist for murder—it's JFK Mexican-style and they have their own Oswald. It can't be a lone, crazy person. Look, he put his gun to Colosio's head. The bullet that killed Colosio came from somewhere within the government..." Marcos jumped up to pose Major Mario as a Colosio stand-in, his finger jammed to the ski-masked aide's temple. "No one could have gotten that close to him. Only someone of confidence, someone from within. Look, Colosio had the best bodyguards in the country. They should have let the Zapatistas protect the candidates. We'd do a better job..."

* * *

The presumed triggerman, Mario Aburto, had a number of explanations for assassinating the presumed next president of Mexico: he really only wanted to wound Colosio to demonstrate his pacifist convictions to the world—but someone shoved his arm; he shot Colosio because he wanted to appear on a Telemundo talk show, *Ocurrió Así* (*It Happens Like This*); he did it for Mexico— "We have saved Mexico!" former Baja California Norte human rights ombudsman José Pérez Canchola, a witness to the federal judicial police's first interrogation of Aburto, reports the accused assassin told the cops. Depending on which of four separate transcripts of interrogations and interviews one peruses, the accused had either plotted the crime for a long time (he claims to have first tracked Salinas) or else just acted out of impulse; he was carrying his pistol to the rally to try and sell it and had became infuriated at what he perceived to be Colosio's slight of a woman petitioner, Aburto told the hard-hitting Tijuana weekly *Zeta* late in April.

During the initial interrogation, Mario Aburto insists that he was closely questioned about ties to the EZLN and Cárdenas's PRD—he is a native of Michoacán, Cuauhtémoc territory. Indeed, back home in La Rinconada, just outside the church-filled city of Zamora, Aburto's 87-year-old great-grandmother was picked up and held incommunicado while judicial police questioned her for 12 hours. The suspect's assertion that "we did it for

Mexico" suggests accomplices. Aburto is alleged to have told the federal judiciales on the night of the assassination that he belonged to a group with thousands of members—a neighborhood association membership card found in his wallet might have answered that description. Aburto has been variously linked to the Jehovah's Witnesses; an unspecified Los Angeles-based leftist organization or youth gang; a fictitious warrior cult in which he held the rank of "Caballero Aguila," the eagle clan warrior of the Aztecs. He has also been questioned about ties to the Union America party (PUA), a lunatic fringe Tijuana circle revolving around Enrique Messina that advocates annexation to the United States to escape PRI dictatorship and which labeled Aburto "a real patriot" for gunning down Colosio, and to the "Provisional President" of Mexico, a discontented architect named Rodolfo Macías, given to extravagant acts of civil disobedience, who was reported to be his distant cousin. In no published reports has Mario Aburto Martínez ever been questioned about his ties to the PRI.

"Mario was always poor and from the wrong side of the tracks. Maybe this was his way of saving Mexico," a cousin, Tony Canchola of San Pedro, California speculated to the *Los Angeles Times*. Aburto had spent a lot of time in San Pedro where his father, a fugitive from Mexican justice (a reported double homicide) has lived for years. Mario Aburto apparently became so attached to California that he even registered to vote—illegally—in Los Angeles County.

Doubts about Aburto's identity and motives arose immediately. On March 24th, then-Attorney General Diego Valadés announced that Mario Aburto had confessed to being the shooter. Pérez Canchola, who was invited to witness the interrogation as a gesture of openness on the part of the PRI government in a PAN-run city and state, says he never heard Aburto confess. All Aburto says is that his interrogators gave him a glass of colorless liquid, perhaps some drug, that sent him on an out-of-body experience which made him feel as if "I wasn't present."

The skepticism reached epic proportions upon the presentation of "Mario Aburto" at Almoloya maximum security prison in Mexico State to where the accused assassin was moved on March 25th. Almoloya, a high tech lock-up modeled on U.S. "super-maxis" like California's Pelican Bay and the federal Marían Illinois penitentiary, houses Mexico's most notorious narcolords and desperados. A young man purported to be "Mario Aburto" was presented framed in a glass window at a prison press conference March 26th. This "Mario Aburto" looked remarkably unlike the "Mario Aburto" all Mexico had seen being led from the murder scene—his mustache was gone and his hair clipped military-style. This "Mario Aburto" looked a lot huskier as he stared stonily through the glass at reporters. Pérez Canchola said he wasn't sure it was the same man whose interrogation he witnessed on the night of March 23rd. Comparison photos were displayed side by side in the press. Attorney General Valadés had to take out full-page newspaper ads arguing that fingerprint evidence established beyond a shadow of a doubt that this "Mario Aburto" "is exactly the same person."

Writer Richard Rodríguez notes that "chisme"—the rumor mill—is a great engine of social movement here. Conditioned to live under authoritarian rule that masks every gesture and brazenly lies to its citizenry day and night via the PRI-packaged media, a Mexican's only access to a few grains of truth is to glean them from public gossip. "Quien fue?"—"Who was it?," the question raised on the morning after outside the National PRI, turned up the usual suspects: Camacho, Zedillo, the elusive Gutíerrez

Barrios, La Quina, the Arellano Félix boys, the Church, Ross Perot, and the Zapatistas. Jorge Constantino Kanter was a gung-ho advocate for the latter hypothesis, urging the military to immediately clean out the EZLN snakepit that was poisoning the nation. Other intellectual giants worked the "contagion" theory—that the Zapatista uprising had unleashed the violence always seething like bad gas just below the surface of Mexico's highly unequal society. Among the subscribers to this perverse theory of culpability were Octavio Paz, Homero Aridjis, Hector Aguilar Camín, and *El Financiero*'s twin conservative columnists Luis Pazos and Sergio Sarmiento.

Other commentators—Carlos Ramírez (*El Financiero*) and Miguel Angel Granados Chapa (*Reforma*) were two—suspected more internecine plots. Utilizing Marcos's "ajuste de cuentos" postulate as a model, these hypotheses gravitated in two directions—down, i.e., payback to Colosio for having sold the Baja California PRI down the river, exacted by the Tijuana section's TUCAN team or up, i.e., a much graver conspiracy, hatched in the highest circles of power, to alter the course of presidential succession and involving National Security agents (the Sánchez Ortega premise). Who killed Colosio? "The squirrel," went the response to a riddle floating around La Merced market. "The squirrel?" "Si, he lives in Los Pinos (the Mexican White house, literally, the pinetrees).

In such an atmosphere of festering suspicion and generalized disbelief, the long-ruling (65 years) Institutional Revolutionary Party (PRI) was charged with selecting a replacement for Colosio.

* * *

Postponement or cancellation of the August election was one Institutional Party option. This proposition was nixed immediately by the new Secretary of the Interior Jorge Carpizo. Moreover, the opposition—in particular, the PAN—whose votes the PRI would need to accumulate the two-thirds majority required for constitutional revision, refused to come on board. The PRI selection was bedeviled by constitutional restriction—a presidential candidate must have resigned from high government office six months before the election, a legal restraint that eliminated from contention all sitting cabinet secretaries, notably Finance minister Pedro Aspe, otherwise the frontrunner. Only Zedillo, who had quit in time to become Colosio's campaign chief, the reviled Camacho, and the acid-tongued Party president Fernando Ortiz Arana, were eligible for the destape. The cry of such notables as Carlos Fuentes for a party convention to select Colosio's replacement, as mandated by PRI by-laws, fell on deaf ears.

Speed dictated the designation. The choice had to be made sooner than later to camouflage the dangerous vacuum of succession that was developing, one which was bound to have devastating repercussions on the stock market if it continued much longer. Mercifully, not 24 hours after Colosio's murder, the Clinton administration had extended Salinas a $6.5 billion line of credit, three times what the U.S. was committing to the ex-Soviet Union, to stave off its NAFTA neighbor's threatened collapse.

Now, the PRI braintrust was meeting night and day up in the windowless buildings on Insurgentes. Manlio Fabio Beltrones, Sonora governor, ex-National Security subsecretary, and Colosio confidante, stage-managed the putsch for Zedillo. The go-ahead came at last from the Carlos Hank group, after significant commitments were said to have been extracted in exchange, from Salinas. The green light was a huge mysteriously paid-for announcement run in every national newspaper and signed by 57 of the

PRI's hoariest dinosaurs—including ex-Baja California Norte Governor Xicoténcatl Leyva, who had not been heard from for many moons—endorsing Ernesto Zedillo as the best man for the presidency. One quid pro quo required by the Hank group was the immediate exile of José María Córdoba Montoya to Washington D.C.—the old guard of the PRI wanted Salinas's Svengali out of the President's ear in order to impose its own considerable weight upon what remained of his last days in office, the impending Zedillo campaign, and the coming electoral process.

On March 29th, six days after Colosio bit the bitter dust of the Lomas Taurinas, the white puff of smoke burst from the PRI's inner sanctum. The "acarreados" were trucked in from the Chalco misery belt plantation of poor people in the wastelands east of the capital, and taught to chant the name of the new candidate. Ernesto Zedillo, a Salinas protégé at Budget and (bumbling) ex-Secretary of Education, who had never run for any public office in his life, mentioned the very dead Colosio's name 39 times in his acceptance speech.

* * *

Salinas's appointment of Miguel Montes as special prosecutor with full powers to affix blame for the assassination, was guaranteed to handcuff the investigation. As a veteran PRI legislative leader, Montes had chaired the electoral college that confirmed Carlos Salinas's fraudulent taking of power in 1988. Awarded a seat on Mexico's Supreme Court—a judicial body that is not synonymous with integrity—Montes had reportedly confirmed the sentence of one José Antonio Zorrilla Pérez, the convicted "intellectual author" of the 1984 killing of flamboyant investigative reporter Manuel Buendía. Many of those close to the case have always considered that authorship went higher than Zorrilla, then head of CISEN's predecessor, the Direction of Federal Security. Indeed, Zorrilla Pérez had been personally appointed to investigate Buendía's death by then-President Miguel de la Madrid, whose involvement in the hit has been rumored. In sentencing Zorrilla Pérez and closing the lid on this Pandora's Box of recriminations, Montes performed invaluable damage control services for his party. Now charged with cleaning up the Colosio killing, he could be expected to run a similar operation.

That is why the nation was shocked out of its shoes when, on April 3rd, all TV channels were suddenly synchronized on the roly-poly Montes. Posed against a legal backdrop of leather-bound lawbooks, Montes—who looks like everyone's favorite Mexican uncle—described, in his supercilious singsong voice, the "concerted action" that had cost Luis Donaldo Colosio his life. Montes was visually aided and abetted by a previously unknown video recording of the hit, slipped to an Argentinean news agency on a Mexico City street, and which, purportedly, demonstrated complicated, coordinated gymnastics designed to cut Colosio off from his bodyguards and open a path for Aburto. Apprehension orders were issued for the previously detained Vicente Mayoral, his son Rodolfo, and an ex-municipal security cop named Tranquilino Sánchez, alleged to have taken General Domiro out of the picture—all three of them members of the local PRI's TUCAN team. Also arrested: the group's organizer and PRI security chief, Rodolfo Rivapalacios. Two other suspects, a mysterious man in a white hat and dark glasses, and "the Diver," who threw himself in front of Colosio to prevent his forward motion (or who simply slipped in the crush) remained unidentified. The accused shooter, Mario Aburto, was, claimed the Attorney General, already in Almoloya

Significantly, the video displayed and analyzed over and over again by Montes, shows only an arm elevating from the crowd and plugging Colosio pointblank in the right temple. There exists no footage of Mario Aburto actually shooting the candidate.

Not among those fingered by Montes was the CISEN man, José Antonio Sánchez Ortega, who has disappeared since being handed over to the federal judicial police by the Tijuana "municipales" on the night of March 23rd. The biggest catch in Montes's dragnet was Rodolfo Rivapalacios, a former state judicial chief investigator at the La Mesa delegation, up on Otay, not far from the airport. Rivapalacios is described as a "well-known torturer" by Tijuana-based Bi-National Human Rights Commission director Victor Clark Alfaro, who has long catalogued such abuses at La Mesa. In 1990, the newly-created National Human Rights Commission, in one of its first acts, recommended to PANista Governor Ernesto Ruffo that Rivapalacios be separated from duty. CNDH investigators had substantiated that the state cop had chained a Peruvian national to his desk for four days, forced chile piquín and bubbly water—the famed "Tehuanazo"—up his nasal cavities, attached electric wires to his genitals, and turned on the juice. A 30-year veteran of the Baja California Norte state judicial police structure, Rivapalacios was reluctant to give up his position—and he would not have had to do so if the governor had been a member of his own party and not a pinche PANista, thanks, in great part, to the treasonous efforts of Luis Donaldo Colosio.

Rivapalacios finally opted for private business, an offer he couldn't refuse, as chief of security for the Tijuana PRI. When he cleaned out his desk at La Mesa, Rivapalacios took with him his faithful lieutenant, Vicente Mayoral, and Mayoral's son, Rodolfo, a so-called "madrina" or freelance cop contracted by the "judiciales" to serve warrants.

By several accounts, Rodolfo Rivapalacios is not a pleasant man. His ex-wife says he once sent thugs to stab her 17 times in the neck with an icepick, after a dispute over communal property in San Diego. His children say he is capable of murder. "If anyone knows who killed Luis Donaldo Colosio, it is him," said the ex-wife to the *San Diego Union.*

Rivapalacios is the highest-placed Institutional Party official linked to the Colosio assassination. He organized the TUCAN team from a pool of ex-police cronies, several, like himself, ex-bodyguards for former governor Xicoténcatl Leyva. Leyva's connection to the Colosio killing has been repeatedly suggested. One unsubstantiated story floating around Tijuana since the killing has Rodolfo Rivapalacios trying to cash a 10 million new peso check ($3.2 million USD) at a Banamex branch near his luxury home in Playas de Tijuana between 10 and 11 A.M. on the morning of the Colosio assassination. The check was reportedly drawn on an account controlled by Xicoténcatl. The check's existence was being tracked by Tijuana municipal sub-prosecutor Sergio Ortiz Lara, a bearded, boyhood chum of Ruffo, when the former was surrounded by federal agents May 2nd on a Tijuana street, arrested, and stripped of his job for allegedly releasing a famous narco from custody during the March 3rd downtown shoot-out. Federal Judicial agents were spotted at the Ortiz Lara arrest scene driving a Cherokee, later reported by San Diego police as having been stolen in that city.

Independent investigation of the Colosio killing is both difficult and dangerous. A special tri-partisan legislative commission, appointed by Salinas to pursue an independent investigation of the assassination, resigned because

Montes refused to permit access to his investigation. Tijuana municipal police chief Federico Benítez was conducting his own investigation until it was rudely curtailed April 29th. Despite being pulled off the Lomas Taurinas rally by Rivapalacios, Benítez's men were on the scene like white on rice March 23rd, corralling Sánchez Ortega within minutes of the shooting. Municipal police investigators had recovered the only shell casing found in the Lomas Taurinas after the killing, an indication that three—not two—shots had been fired at Colosio. On the night of the assassination, sent back into the colonia to hunt a second weapon, Benítez's Special Group Officers had witnessed the military come up with a .38 very much like the one Aburto was, at that very hour (7:30-8:30 P.M.), identifying as his weapon at federal offices across town. Despite the high profile issue, Benitez was the only cop in town pursuing the two gun theory.

The possibility that two weapons had been used in the hit was first suggested while Colosio was still on the operating table. Heart specialist María Aubanel examined the two exit wounds and confessed to the press that she thought they came from two different bullets. The hypothesis is sustained by the impossibility of Aburto firing both shots—the second in the left abdomen could only have been accomplished if Colosio had made a complete 180 degree turn, a gyration judicial police replays have not been able to recreate.

Chief Benítez, a bookish, accidental cop, did not limit his detective work to the second gun. On the morning of April 28th, the Chief offered to show *Washington Post* correspondent Tod Robberson his dossier on Rodolfo Rivapalacios. When he unlocked his desk drawer and reached for the document, it was gone, apparently not an isolated event around the Chief's office, he let it be known.

A Bullet From Within

36 hours later, Chief Benítez was photographed slumped against a shattered windshield up on the Otay Mesa, having been lured to Abelardo Rodríguez International Airport by a bomb threat and then gunned down, gangland-style, just a few dozen yards from the steel fence designed to separate the third world from the first and five minutes from the Lomas Taurinas.

Like the slaying of John Kennedy 30 years before, the Colosio assassination is beginning to generate new assassinations. And like JFK, the killing remains deeply opaqued. In mid-April, Rivapalacios was released from Almoloya by a local judge because there was no physical evidence placing him at the assassination site—his release effectively immunized the PRI from charges of killing its own. Such cannibalistic tendencies were not good reasons for voting up the official party August 21st.

On June 3rd, Uncle Miguel Montes returned to the "pantalla chica" (TV screen), posed in front of those same leather-bound volumes, to disclose that Mario Aburto Martínez, 23, had acted alone, a sole, crazed (much psychological "evidence" was bandied about) gunman. No motive was advanced nor any explanation as to why Salinas's special prosecutor had suddenly flip-flopped from his previous assertions of a conspiracy. And on July 14th, after faxing pages of Aburto's spurious diary to foreign correspondences, Montes went back on the tube to wrap the case up: Aburto had indeed acted alone, his motives were "political" but unexplained. Then, Montes closed down the investigation and resigned on the spot. Thank you and goodnight. The outcry was so intense that Salinas was forced to appoint a fresh special prosecutor within 24 hours. There are a lot of switchbacks on the rocky road to justice in Mexico.

Three months after the killing, one had the distinct

327

sensation that the Colosio case was winding down. His name was off the walls now, Zedillo's painted over in even zippier letters. The old guard candidate had even stopped banging on Luis Donaldo's name at every rally out on the campaign trail. The decision had been made to slide the case out of the public spotlight. Every time you mentioned Colosio's name, it made people ask questions, one campaign aide told a U.S. reporter. Quien fue? Who was it? Who wants to know?

* * *

The bullets that cut Colosio down, also cut the Zapatistas down—at least to size, if not in terms of their mortality. For months, the EZLN had been flying high on its press ratings, stealing space every day from the traditional centers of influence where political power is jealously concentrated. Yet by March 24th, what remained of the press corps packed up for good—some were off to the capital to restart their lives and some to Tijuana to sift the clues. The Zapatistas disappeared from view under the hundreds of black-bordered squares the friends and admirers of the late Luis Donaldo Colosio were buying up in memoriam—in death, Colosio exacted his revenge upon the Zapatistas for seizing so much space for Camacho in what now seemed the distant past. Whatever happened to Marcos, *El Financiero*'s Sarmiento wondered in April? Now an army that had been living on its press notices since January 1st had finally been victimized by a moving news front. The Zapatistas suddenly seemed old and irrelevant. "We didn't declare this war to be in the newspaper or on the television," philosophized Major Rolando, trying to make the best of a bad thing by June.

The Colosio assassination also wounded the EZLN's pretensions of moral leadership. A civil society, shaken by

328

the killing (and rocked by the high-profile kidnapping of the nation's number one banker days before), how had second thoughts about the reasonableness of revolutionary violence. The prayers for peace resounded throughout Holy Week—there weren't many paeans for armed struggle. Poor Manuel Camacho warned that there had been a turn to the right in the national mood, a conservative backlash: "if the Zapatistas fail to realize things changed in this country with Colosio's assassination and think they can retain their popularity by not returning to the peace table, they will lose a great deal of prestige," the Conciliator told the *New Yorker*.

But, for the Zapatistas, the crucial meaning of the killing of Luis Donaldo Colosio was that the nation's focus had gravitated back to its natural center, the Capital, where all power in Mexico has been harbored since long before the European Conquest. One of the Zapatistas' greatest good deeds was to turn national attention, for a few short months, on the misfortunes of the faceless and the forgotten, the campesinos and indígenas, who are always the first to be dismissed in modern Mexico. Now the Zapatistas, who had been around so long they were practically neighbors, suddenly seemed far away, almost quaint, a distant dream lodged "somewhere in the Lacandón jungle." Who were those masked men? With Colosio's memory moldering and the EZLN slipping into leafy oblivion, all eyes fixed on the August 21st presidential elections—and the World Cup Football Matches about to kick off in the U.S.

Ballots or Bullets?

The Zapatista uprising, exploding as it did in the first hours of a presidential election year, made a profound and immediate impression upon the political parties. Caught napping on New Year's morning, the nine parties and their candidates slated to appear on the August 21st ballot were left in the starting gate, trying to figure out how to catch up.

From the opening gun, the PRI party line mimicked the government that it runs: the Zapatistas were "transgressors" who must pay the full penalty of the law. 10 days later, Salinas was suing for peace and Candidate Colosio's rhetoric melted from stern to tolerant to solicitous, even promising, prior to his unexpected retirement from politics, that he would meet with Marcos once the peace pact was inked. From January 10th onwards, the Colosio campaign obsessed on poor people, social troubles, Indians and farmers. For the Institutional Party, the pendulum appeared to have swung from neo-liberal rampage to healing the wounds that wholesale privatization and foreign investment-oriented "reforms" had inflicted upon "those who have the least." Much like Bill Clinton, Luis Donaldo Colosio, the next president of Mexico, would ride to high office promising to repair the lives of those who had been blown away by the free market fiesta of the Reagan-Bush-Salinas years.

The hostile posturing by the Indians of Chiapas had less scratch with the right-of-center National Action Party, the 54-year-old, pro-Catholic, pro-Capitalist PAN, founded by conservative banker Manuel Gómez Morín in 1939 to hex the red despotism with which President Lazaro Cárdenas menaced the land. Chiapas was a distant republic

331

to the PAN whose upwardly-mobile, middle-class base had little contact with indigenous issues other than how much to pay their maids each week.

During the Salinas years, the PAN had become the nation's second electoral force, favored by the PRI as a bulwark against the astounding penetration Cárdenas had made in ruling party bastions. Awarded the governorships of Guanajuato, Chihuahua, and Baja California Norte as political recompense for having consistently voted the PRI line against the PRD in the national legislature, by 1994, the PAN had been elevated to the niche of loyal opposition, whose economic outlook and offer of limited and negotiated democratic reform coincided quite comfortably with that of the PRI.

Now PAN candidate Diego Fernández de Cevallos, a blustery, bristle-bearded Mexico City criminal lawyer with aristocratic bloodlines, simply sidestepped the wild Indians of Chiapas, dismissing the rebels as a bunch of badly-dressed "enmascarados." "Politics is the work of people with names, faces, and addresses," snapped Carlos Castillo Perraza, the PAN's prissy prexy.

The pundits calculated the political cost of the Zapatista rebellion and issued Solomonic judgments: there were some who saw a silver lining for the PRI. Times of crisis made "the evil with which one is familiar more inviting than the good one doesn't yet know," wrote Miguel Angel Rivera in his daily "Clase Política" column in *La Jornada*. But most of Mexico City's house oracles considered that all three major parties had been severely damaged by the blow-up in Chiapas. *El Financiero's* Ramírez wrote one column, tasteless in retrospect, in which Colosio's corpse is found. The repeated false unveilings of Camacho, as substitute for Colosio, did not help the ruling party to heal. In Ramírez's vista, the least dented of the major contestants in the race for Los Pinos was the PRD's venerable warhorse, Cuauhtémoc Cárdenas.

* * *

Cuauhtémoc Cárdenas was the only candidate whose vision of the country coincided, at least in part, with the Zapatistas', particularly on issues like the reinstatement of Article 27 and the separation of the government from the electoral process. On the other hand, the "Engineer," as he is universally called by his colleagues, is an assiduously legalistic and by-the-book soul, who does not at all cotton to picking up the gun. On January 4th, Cuauhtémoc endorsed the EZLN's demands but condemned their violent means of achieving same. He objected to the use of the military in a civil conflict. He accused Carlos Salinas of provoking the rebellion by bludgeoning the poor with the tools of the free market. He condemned the sordid governments mercilessly imposed by the PRI upon the citizens of Chiapas. As the Army laid waste to indigenous communities, Cárdenas, whose father was a general and who won the troops' vote in 1988, advised the members of the armed forces that they had no obligation "to commit excesses against the civilian population." On January 12th, Cuauhtémoc joined notables of the civil society upon the stage at the massive Zocolo rally "to end the massacre," an event organized by PRD integrants—local PRD chapters had organized the first marches in support of the EZLN in Monterrey and Mexico City on the 6th and the 8th of January. Despite the resoluteness of his positions, Cuauhtémoc Cárdenas came under attack from a reawakened left, its embers stirred by the Zapatista example. The "Ingeniero" (engineer) was seen as straddling the fence by supporters of the EZLN and roundly critiqued for his perceived tepidness toward the rebellion.

The Party of the Democratic Revolution (PRD) is a snakepit of three left currents (15 tendencies, my count), and a closely-woven nest of ex-PRIistas (Cárdenas, Party President Porfirio Muñoz Ledo, once president of the PRI!). The PRD was chartered soon after the '88 elections were iced by the PRI, utilizing the registration of the Mexican Socialist Party (itself a confluence of many socialist rivers, including the long defunct Mexican Communist Party) to legalize the new party's electoral status. In 1988, buffeted by generations of defeat at the polls and in the street, the left leapt on the Cárdenas bandwagon en masse, without much questioning the Engineer's austere nationalist and statist political philosophy that is social democratic at best. Despite the migration of one-time Marxists to its ranks, the geopolitical fall of the Wall—and the prospect of obtaining a prized political post—has blurred socialist visions in the PRD to an amorphous demand for "democracy."

The Party of the Democratic Revolution is not a left party. Nor is the PRD even a very forceful proponent of party democracy. Cuauhtémoc Cárdenas appointed himself presidential candidate in November of 1987 and has never stopped running for the office. Party positions and PRD candidates are designated by deals brokered between currents that have been formed more around personality than ethics. Although the bases of the PRD—campesinos, the urban poor, social activists—have unselfishly volunteered over 270 dead, fallen in political violence since 1988, almost exclusively with the PRI, the masses of Cárdenas supporters have little participation in PRD decision-making except to shed their blood and attend the candidate's rallies.

The revolutionary general, Lázaro Cárdenas, the "Tata" ("father in Purépecha, the Indian language of his homestate of Michoacán), is a permanent fixture in Mexican plazas and schoolbooks. During his six years as President of Mexico (1934-40), he handed out ten times as much land as all his predecessors put together and traveled the land relentlessly, to consult with the farmers and the indígenas, the brigades of "maestros" (rural school teachers) and old revolutionaries that were his constituency. Tata Lázaro's expropriation of the Anglo-Gringo oil monopolies in 1938 earned him the undying admiration of his people for having stood up to the Northern Colossi. But Lázaro Cárdenas also created the structures for the incorporation of the most organized sectors of Mexican society into the state party, the Party of the Mexican Revolution, the papa of the PRI (it is commonly suggested the PRI has no mother).

Much as he avoids the pigeonhole, Cuauhtémoc ("the descending eagle") is his father's son and nostalgia for the revolution his father helped make won him a lot of votes in 1988—a contest he probably won with 39% of the popular vote to Carlos Salinas's 37% (both the PRI-Gobierno and Cárdenas's count are incomplete). Now that the ballots have been incinerated by the military under 1992 orders from the PRI-dominated legislature, we will never really know what the final tally was, will we?

At several ticks past 9:00 P.M. on election night, July 6th, 1988, a team of PAN technicians was conducted into the windowless Barranca del Muerto ("Ravine of Death") offices of the Federal Voters Registry (RFE) to view a computer screen on which were to be displayed incoming results. "We knew there were two systems—the real data and one displaying data designed to show that the PRI was winning. We had some ideas about passwords and we tried them and one of them got us in to the real system," details José Gómez Urquiza, one of the "técnicos" and a former

PAN deputy. To the amazement of the PANistas, the screen showed Cárdenas sweeping ten Mexico City and state districts from the PRI and their own party. A hurried meeting of RFE officials was noticed in the rear of the computer room. Then the screens went dead. The RFE officials declared the PANistas personae non gratae and they were escorted to the door. "The system has crashed," announced Secretary of the Interior Manuel Bartlett, under whose purview responsibility for the election fell, offering thunderstorms in Michoacán (where Cárdenas was winning big), blocked phones, and general overheating, as an explanation. The system remained "crashed" for a week while tens of thousands of ballots marked for Cárdenas, were found smoldering in garbage dumps or floating down central Mexican rivers. When the count resumed, Salinas was declared winner with a few scant decimal points over 50%, the smallest margin of victory ever accorded a PRI president-elect.

In addition to massive vandalism at the ballot box, cybernetic manipulation of incoming district results to the RFE Unisys mainframe was suspected—details were revealed in an *El Financiero* investigation. As in every election ever run by the PRI government, fraud was pervasive at every level of the 1988 election—but was more noticed because of the Institutional Party's oafish, heavy-handed efforts to steal the vote. Caught by surprise by Cárdenas's vast penetration, all the ruling party's vaunted "alchemists" could think to do was burn the ballots.

The tumultuous protests that followed came closer to toppling the Ancien Régime than any social thrust since the revolution. On one Saturday afternoon, ten days after the fraud was consummated, Cárdenas filled the Zócalo and all its feeder streets so tightly people could not raise their arms, a half million, it is conservatively estimated. There are those who insist that Cuauhtémoc could have taken the power that was legitimately his if he had called upon the military to support him that afternoon. Cárdenas, who had reason to believe the army would have massacred the people under orders from its commanders, retired to piece together the PRD.

The Engineer has been campaigning ever since, obsessively crossing and recrossing the geography of his country, touching millions of hands and not a few hearts, carrying his not very radical message, delivered in the same wooden monotone, from village to village and sierra to sierra. One sees an enormous terrain, most of it deep Mexico, when one travels with the "Ingeniero," a political leader whose tunnel vision crusade to save the Mexican Revolution does not allow him much luxury of charisma. Nonetheless, despite his deadly delivery, the lean and leathery Cárdenas has won the adoration of a considerable quotient of the Mexican masses.

The ex-PRI governor of Michoacán, Cárdenas left the ruling party soon after Carlos Salinas was unveiled as the presidential candidate by his political father, Miguel de la Madrid. Cuauhtémoc took with him from the PRI some close confidantes and a lot of votes. In the relative privacy of the polling place, the PRI faithful hemorrhaged left in '88 and formed the bloc of votes that put Cárdenas over the top. In '94, with the official party torn apart by Colosio's assassination, Zedillo's hastily-brokered candidacy, and Camacho's rebellion, the scenario seemed once again operative.

For the left, though, the Cárdenas honeymoon seemed finally over. The Zapatistas' New Year's Day rebellion had rekindled radical animation, gifted the revolution with new martyrs and heroes, and made armed struggle a successful form of redressing grievances, achieving concessions that five years of electoral turmoil had not produced. Suddenly, Cárdenas found himself accused of supporting the military in Chiapas, backtracking on his opposition to the "TLC" (NAFTA), and softening his line on free market economics. Although Cuauhtémoc's politics have hardly budged right since 1988, his handlers made efforts to portray him as the "candidate of stability and consensus" (international press chief Andrea Dabrowski) to combat the bomb thrower label the PRI-PAN try to hang on him. Some supporters have been disaffected by the image of Cárdenas addressing bankers' luncheons and Chamber of Commerce smokers. The Zapatista uprising breathed new oomph into this polemic.

Reduced to the prism of one-on-one combat, one intriguing subtext of the Zapatista revolution was the mano a mano (hand to hand) between Cuauhtémoc Cárdenas and Subcomandante Marcos for what was left of the Mexican left.

* * *

Mexican elections are like siccing a tiger on a tied-down burro writes García de León (*La Jornada*, April 10th). The PRI is not just a party—it is the government and has been so for six and a half decades, a vast malignant octopus in as absolute control of the state's apparatus of repression as it is of the nation's treasury. At best, Institutional Party rule resembles a semi-tropical Mayor Daley-run Chicago. At its worst, the PRI dictatorship massacres its own young. The PRI doesn't just think it owns Mexico—it thinks it is Mexico. No other party is permitted to use the three colors of the flag—the "tri-color" of the PRI is the "tri-color" of the country. The PRI is offended that anyone dares have an alternative vision of the nation and particularly one promulgated by a traitor to the

Institutional party like Cárdenas. The PRI hates Cuauhtémoc Cárdenas and seeks to crush him just as passionately as Carranza wanted Zapata's head served up on presidential flatware.

During the 1994 presidential election campaign, the PRI would pump in countless millions to bury Cárdenas alive. The ruling party would so dominate the electronic media that Cárdenas could not get a word in edgewise. When, in early June, the Engineer assembled 30,000 supporters at the UNAM (a shade under his '88 totals at the school), the appallingly-biased Zabludowsky ignored the gathering and interviewed Zedillo for 25 minutes instead. The government would throw open its coffers and Salinas would roam the land, freely dispensing checks to farmers and colonos—to make them forget Cárdenas's name. The PRI would forge a pact with the PAN to gang up on Cárdenas in all public utterances. The PRI government-would finance a handful of "satellite" parties, designed to eat away at Cárdenas's natural constituencies—an environmental party, a so-called "party of labor," even a "Cárdenist Front"...

It was, in fact, the candidate of this last-named ersatz entity, officially, "the Party of the Cárdenist Front for National Reconstruction," led by Rafael Aguilár Talamontes, a turncoat leftist whose initials best synthesize how his colleagues feel about him, who on January 12th first offered himself to the EZLN as their own personalized presidential candidate. Under their ski masks, deep within the leafy canopy of the Lacandón Jungle, the Zapatistas blanched in amazement at RAT's presumptions.

The Zapatista electoral posture reeks of cognitive dissonance. The many pronouncements of Marcos and the CCRI on this subject make mind boggling swings. The EZLN first seemed to be saying that the presidential candidates are all anti-democratic duds and the parties compromised and corrupted by political expediency—but, nonetheless, the Zapatista Army of National Liberation pledges armed upheaval in the land if the election is tainted by fraud. The Zapatistas would not "impede" the election and are "indifferent to who wins as long as the election is fair." If not "the country will rise up, whether we still exist or not" (Marcos to Petrich). In San Cristóbal, the Subcomandante remarked that if the August election proved fraudulent "there would not be enough cathedrals in all Mexico in which to negotiate with the Zapatistas and Villistas and Flores Magonistas who will rise up in arms!" By election day, however, the EZLN had grown less truculent, willing to try peaceful protest first if the PRI wasn't defeated at the polls.

Zapatista candidates' nights have a perverse edge— first invite the political parties to interchange views and then lambaste their candidates as opportunists. On February 15th, the CCRI, under Marcos's imprint, sent an extraordinarily formal invitation to all nine parties to meet with them in San Cristóbal: "From your ranks will rise the next president...it will be a great honor if you would attend..." RSVP.

The responses were uneven: Colosio never considered the invite (Camacho, after all, was Salinas's man in the cathedral); the PAN deemed it absurd to discuss the political future of the nation with a bunch of masked men ("I'm not negotiating with anyone who wears a sock on his head" riposted "El Jefe Diego"); the anti-clerical Popular Socialists (PPS), the Jacobins of Mexican politics, would not sit at a table "just to listen to priests," the Party of the Authentic Mexican Revolution (PARM) apparently could not dig up the air freight to ship its monstrously obese candidate south. Nonetheless, on the third morning of the

"Jornadas for Peace and Reconciliation," the Zapatistas took time out to exchange pleasantries with representatives of five parties to be represented on the August 21st ballot at an early morning huddle in the Cathedral of Peace. Like every event staged in that sacred space, the meeting was charged with dramatic potential.

The Zapatistas ensconced themselves up in the sacristy, Marcos conscientiously displaying his shotguns on the table before him. Like supplicants, the representatives of the parties stationed themselves humbly below. Amongst the guests was Jorge Gonzales Torres, the well-born cacique of the Mexican Green Environmental Party (PVEM) who brought his own entourage of Indians, contracted up in Zinacantan—being trailed around by authentic indígenas was a trademark of his campaign. The Frente Cardenista extolled RAT's qualities to be the official EZLN-endorsed candidate and presented the greetings of "their Indians." The Party of Labor (PT), a well-heeled "leftist" formation whose origins are shrouded in mystery, promoted the fortunes of the demure Cecilia Soto, once Lyndon Larouche's minion at the mendaciously-named "Mexican Laboral Party." Ironically, the PT is thought to have been chartered by the PRI, operating through old-time Política Popular agents in Durango and the Laguna. The very right-wing UNO-Mexican Democratic Party (PDM), a PRI-made "satellite" conjured up to drain votes from the PAN, pushed its man Pablo Emilio Madero, the elderly grand-nephew of the Father of the Mexican Revolution, Francisco Madero himself. An underground PRIista, a member of a dissident strain within the diseased ruling party, presented Marcos with documents that he was advised to study "once he had re-incorporated himself into civilian life." "First, we have to get out of here alive," the Sup cracked.

Was the PRI making overtures to Marcos? "This Marcos is very savvy, very smart. God knows what we could do with someone like that. We could really change things," an unidentified PRI government official confessed to Barbach.

The PRD had sent an all-star aggregation to converse in the Cathedral: Cuauhtémoc's two sons, Lázaro and Cuauhtémoc; Amalia García, the party's top-ranking woman; Mario Saucedo, himself an ex-1970s urban guerrilla who heads a PRD current that includes the party's most radical elements; and Herberto Castillo, the tall, stooped earnest engineering prof who had been a particular hero during the '68 student uprising. Marcos was moved by the white-haired Castillo's appearance, descending from the sacristy to embrace him. "It is a great honor to meet you," he mumbled, uncharacteristically silenced by the PRD leader's presence. The PRD appeared to have privileged access to the declaredly-non-partisan CCRI delegates, meeting with them privately the next day. Saucedo reportedly rented a room and stayed on for weeks.

Generally, Marcos was unsatisfied by the performance of the parties. He lectured their representatives: they had been asked to come in the spirit of "no nos dejan solos" and all they seemed to want to do was flap their chops about the virtues of their candidates. They just came for the photo op, the Sup popped off to the press. The PRD, which had sent its best horses, took justified umbrage. "We did not come to proselytize but to dialogue," the national committee responded in a tart note to the CCRI. Marcos apologized in the next mail, his note lamely explaining that the CCRI was firmly non-partisan and so when he criticized the parties' venial behavior, he was obligated to include all the parties and not single one out for commendation.

Ballots or Bullets?

* * *

The Colosio assassination did not level the playing field but it narrowed the angle upon which the three leading candidates competed. What was on its way to being the usual PRI coronation turned into a contest, albeit an apparently lopsided one, a 12-round decision rather than a first-round k.o. Not only the *New York Times* proclaimed Ernesto Zedillo the winner long in advance of election day. The party apparatus, bankrolled by the bottomless pockets of those whom Salinas had gifted with the phone company or an airline or a string of sugar mills, went into overkill for Colosio's stand-in. Despite a wobbly start, the rallies, stocked with "acarreados," soon resembled old-time PRI hokum, save for the metal detectors through which one had to pass to get into the plaza or the stadium.

On April 21st, Zedillo helicoptered into Rancho Nuevo, photogenically hugged Don Samuel in the cathedral, and took a turn, under an intense security blanket, around the Plaza of March 31st, even vaulting onto a park bench to reiterate Colosio's promise that he would meet with Marcos once the peace pact was signed.

Marcos was not unreceptive to the offer of a meeting with Zedillo—"I could teach him something about printing textbooks," he quipped, a reference to the ex-Education Secretary's revision of grade school history texts in which he downgraded such patriotic icons as Zapata and the "Heroic Children of Chapultepec," the teenage cadets slain by the Yanqui invaders in 1848. Nonetheless, Zedillo would have to cool his heels for an interview—"if he came here now a plane might fall on him and you know who would get blamed..."

One person with whom Zedillo did not meet during his two hour stopover in the royal city was Manuel Camacho—the Conciliator, worried about the languishing

343

peace talks still on hold because of the Colosio assassination, refused to be stigmatized by PRI politics at so delicate
a moment in Zapatista sensitivities.

* * *

Mexicans had been treated to some unusual spectacles
during the first months of 1994—the Grand Guignol in the
Cathedral of Peace, the bloodsplattered Colosio debacle in
Tijuana—but one of the most unlikely images of this fate-
ful year was surely that of the three presidential candidates
frozen behind their podiums at the historic May 12th U.S.-
style presidential debate, a first for the nation in many
ways. Never before in modern Mexican political memory
had opposition candidates been allowed on the same stage
as the PRI's exalted heir to the throne. Now here, before
the 130 million eyes of the nation's TV-accessed population, were the PAN's Diego Fernández de Cevallos and the
PRD's Cuauhtémoc Cárdenas boxing Ernesto Zedillo's
ears from the right and from the left.

Why had the PRI agreed to debate? Some pundits
thought the ruling party needed a national stage upon
which to display its brand-new replacement product. With
the polls—never an accurate measure of the public pulse in
Mexican politics—prognosticating a three-way race (a 30-
30-30 split), a boffo performance by Zedillo would vali-
date the victory the PRI was going to try and steal in
August anyway. If the youthful nerdish Zedillo flopped,
there was still a hundred days to election day to paper over
the "fracaso." On the other sides of the aisles, the opposition candidates, generally banned from appearing on
national television, had little to lose just by showing up at
the hermetic studios in the Technological Museum, deep
within Chapultepec Park.

There would be no live audience but giant screens—

the same used later in the summer to bring the World Cup to Mexico City's street people—were hung at public monuments throughout the capital. All eyes were fixed on the three frozen figures behind their podiums out there in the park. Cuauhtémoc led off in a punchless monotone, a riff about how the debate had been a long time coming. Zedillo invoked Colosio's name. Then Diego Fernández de Cevallos went berserk, lancing his two opponents with elegant invective schooled in Mexico City criminal courtrooms and the nation's equally felonious Chamber of Deputies. "I have come to debate!" the bearded, biblical Diego challenged the docile, what-me-worry smiling Zedillo and the frowning Cárdenas. Zedillo was here only because of two tragedies: the assassination of Luis Donaldo Colosio and the President's undemocratic "destape." Cárdenas did not get off lightly either. Energetically waving dossiers—what did they say?—El Jefe Diego accused Cárdenas of having been the very undemocratic PRI governor of Michoacán, trampling the rights of students and abrogating universal suffrage. Cárdenas, a dour, scowling man even on the brightest of days, seemed stunned by the attack—he had met with El Jefe the week previous and thought they had struck a non-aggression pact. "I've never hidden who I am," he responded gravely and then, ignoring Diego, went after the real villain: Zedillo and the PRI dictatorship. But the PRI standard-bearer ignored Cuauhtémoc's low-flame fire, kept his eyes pinned on the prompter cards in front of him, repeated the rags to riches story of his climb from shoeshine boy to Yale scholar that his trainers had hocus-pocused up to distinguish him from his highborn competitors, and read, by rote, his pledges to the nation. Only once did Zedillo seem ruffled—when he blasted his opponents for political profiteering ("lucrando") with Colosio's good name—Zedillo mentioned his predecessor ten times during the debate, his two opponents once between them.

90 minutes later, this political pillow fight was over. El Jefe Diego, whose performance had encapsulated the enormous "coraje" (anger, courage) the Mexican man and woman in the street feel towards the PRI-gobierno, was the clear winner of this muted bloodletting—snap telephone polls brought him in at 53% to Zedillo's 24% with Cárdenas bottoming out with a measly 7.9% perception of victory—although it must be pointed out that a good many Cárdenas supporters don't have telephones upon which they can be polled. Whatever the accuracy of such poll-taking in a land where the average citizen has good reason not to reveal how he or she really feels, Cárdenas had been flattened by the PAN, a turning point in the campaign from which he would have difficulty recovering.

There was another loser at this historic encounter—the Zapatista Army of National Liberation. Far away from the center of influence, deep in the heart of the Lacandón rainforest, the Zapatistas too were watching the Great Debate, listening in vain for some mention of their presence. There was none—one vague accusation by Cárdenas that the PRI-Gobierno had fomented the insurrection in Chiapas and then onto issues of vital national import like the decaying educational system. Just 132 days after the Zapatistas had electrified the nation and seemingly altered the course of the August election, the three chief candidates for the presidency of the republic had nothing at all to say about their revolution. The Zapatistas had indeed dropped clear out of the national picture.

* * *

It was a bleak morning after around Cuauhtémoc's nifty Colónia Condesa headquarters. The Ingeniero was about to leave for Chiapas, his first barnstorming tour of that wartorn entity since the EZLN had risen—ironically, Cárdenas had been through Ocosingo in mid-December. Now, the PRD advance guard in Chiapas had succeeded in wangling an invitation from the rebels to visit them in their natural habitat. "We have the understanding that you are a candidate for the presidency," the communiqué read cooly; the Clandestine Revolutionary Indigenous Committee was interested in hearing his views on their movement.

The prospect of an endorsement from Marcos both thrilled and chilled Cuauhtémoc's people. For months, Cárdenas had been desperately trying to deconstruct the bomb thrower's image the PRI and the PAN had hung upon him, making a point of addressing bankers and shaking hands with industrialists. Now he was about to meet with the #1 masked outlaw in the land. On the other hand, one handshake with Marcos could restore the animation of activist youth who had, in recent months, increasingly picked up the ski mask—everywhere Cuauhtémoc stopped on the campaign trail, there were always kids in pasamontañas, banners draped in the trees promoting the EZLN. The *New York Times*' "chismoso" (gossipy) Golden said the Engineer was obsessed by Marcos. There had been that ugliness when he had sent his sons to converse with the Subcomandante in the Cathedral and there were those who counseled against the meeting, who feared Marcos was laying an ambush from the left for the Ingeniero. In the end, recounts left historian Adolfo Gilly, who accompanied Cárdenas into Zapatista territory, it was decided to take up the EZLN on its invitation if just to clear the air.

Early on Sunday morning May 15th, a caravan of 27 vehicles (five containing Cárdenas and his committee, the rest conveying the press) drove convoy-style down from San Cristóbal, disembarking at military roadblocks, and proceeding through the gate to the Lacandón region at Las

Margaritas, hugging the 78 kilometer, up-and-down track that ends at Guadalupe Tepeyac. By noon, the caravan, in which 75 people traveled (reporters outnumbering politicos three to one), was lined up outside that jungle hamlet, arguing with the Zapatistas about who got into EZLN territory and who had to go home. The Engineer's 21 person "comitiva" was passed through without a hitch but the arbitrary selection of the press pool enraged the third army, many members of which spent the rest of the day swatting flies and fuming far from the action, so irritated at both the Zapatistas and the Cardenistas that their stories made the meet appear a much more sordid affair than the actuality.

Whatever goes on 20 minutes down the road from Guadalupe Tepeyac prior to a major EZLN "espectaculo" (show), it takes a long time to prepare. Cárdenas and his colleagues cooled their heels for four hours, penned in and around their sweltering cars in what Gilly describes as the "vestibule" to the main event site. Those of his fellow travelers who were not kvetching about the wait, fancied themselves on African Safari, Gilly says. At length, Cárdenas and his party were permitted to advance, escorted by heavily armed Zapatistas down a dirt path, lined, as during Absalón's release, by freshly-scrubbed men and women, each on their own sides of the street. Some were holding banners that said "If You Win Your Candidacy, Don't Forget Your Country!" and "Don't Change The Bread of The Poor for Junk and Plastic!" The chants were not all that friendly either: "Viva El EZLN!," "In Zapatista Tierras, We Don't Want Egoists!," "Cárdenas! Cárdenas! Get to Work or The War Will Catch Up With You!," and the ever-popular, if overly optimistic, "¡El Pueblo Unido Jamás Será Vencido!" (The People United, Will Never be Defeated!) Assailed from all sides by the militant cadences of the Zapatista bases, Cárdenas's normally stony face turned positively petroglyphic, the deep furrows grew deeper, his skin tone darker, Gilly recalls. At the end of the gauntlet, the path opened into a huge clearing—it was then called "La Realidad"—fronted by twin humps of treed hillocks. A stage had been set up and Cárdenas and his party conducted to it. "La Realidad" was filled with folks, perhaps 1,500 in fiesta mode—some of the partygoers, it was said, had walked three days from San Quintín adjacent to Montes Azules, to see, with their own eyes, this first meeting of the giants.

A trumpet heralded the military display: five horsemen galloped out of the cleft between the hills, one undulating a great Mexican flag, another puffing on his pipe as he urged his steed forward. The horsemen were followed by a detachment of 500 Zapatista troop pouring out of the hills in synchronized formation. Led by Marcos and Major Mario, "The 3rd Regiment Guardian and Heart of the People" circled the bandstand twice and then marched back off into the bush. Up on the platform, Cuauhtémoc, young Lázaro, left venerables Rosario Ibarra and Herberto Castillo, the sweating Porfirio Muñoz Ledo, Amado Avendaño—now the PRD candidate for governor of Chiapas—stood bug-eyed in wonder at the pageant.

At first, Marcos seemed the perfect host. He graciously welcomed Cuauhtémoc Cárdenas and his people, sounding a little awed to be sharing a platform with so many distinguished social agitators. Cárdenas was the only candidate to have had the valor to enter Zapatista turf—Pablo Emilio Madero had shown up in San Miguel one day before his appointment on May 9th and had been refused admittance, thereby nullifying the possibility of a new Madero-Zapata alliance.

The Subcomandante commended Cuauhtémoc's bravery in venturing into the zone because getting his picture taken and "dancing with" masked desperados would not win him a lot of votes—in the Cañadas, there have never been any polling places anyway. The EZLN was impressed, Marcos said, that the Engineer had come with his son. "We are trying to build a little ante-room of democracy here," he explained. "We are preparing for the democratic transition..."

Four Zapatistas then took the mike in rapid-fire order: "El Saqueo," "Mister," "Bruce Lee"—who warned, "Mister Cárdenas, if you win, pay a lot of attention to what you are seeing, or we will have many January lsts..." Comandante Tacho recited the Zapatistas' 11 points. This was the first time that a candidate has ever come to the Lacandón, he marveled, and then issued a chilling challenge: "If those who govern us do not do us justice, there are our troops—and they will!" The Zapatista harangues had tensed the air. The audience awaited a response from the Candidate. Instead, Major Moisés called for music. The Zapatista trio cranked up and, all of a sudden, Cárdenistas and Zapatistas were hoofing it up—Cuauhtémoc even shaking his boody with Rosario Ibarra, a rare sight.

The CCRI and not Marcos had invited Cárdenas to the jungle pow-wow and now the Ingeniero and his closest advisers met with the Clandestine Committee in a breezy cabin atop one of the hillocks overlooking "La Realidad," the first Zapatista "Casa de Seguridad" (safehouse). Those who were privileged to sit in on this high level huddle of the Mexican left describe it as an honest interchange of the similarities and differences of two distinct political projects. Marcos seemed warm, even emotional, offering tips to the Cárdenas campaign and suggesting that the debate had been a trap. Cárdenas said he thought fraud in the upcoming election would be much more sophisticated than in 1988. The meeting between Marcos and Cuauhtémoc and

Cuauhtémoc's son Lázaro continued under a tree outside. "They sat on the grass and we watched them from afar," Gilly recalls with a dash of awe—the encounter conjures up the sacred imagery of Villa and Zapata lolling under a ahuehuete tree in Xochimilco one day in December 1914.

The cow had been cooking all day and, as dusk descended, was declared fit to eat. Zapatistas and Cárdenistas broke bread together in a jungle clearing called La Realidad far from where the power had gone. A generator was switched on, a single light bulb illuminated the stage. It was time for the closing ceremonies. The Engineer took the microphone to thank his hosts and then delivered what turned out to be a standard campaign speech. There were coincidences in the goals of the EZLN and PRD, he began dryly. But the PRD has taken the electoral path, the path of legality—"the vote is the fundamental instrument of change." The nation was on the brink of democratic transition. His victory August 21st would be "the breaking point" with the PRI past. He invited the Zapatistas to accompany him on his long and wearying crusade to bring the Mexican Revolution back to Mexico. It was the usual no-frills Cárdenas pitch and those poor souls who had walked three days from Montes Azules to witness this miracle meeting of myths must have wondered what all the fuss was about in the first place. Applause from the Zapatistas bunched in the dark was scattered.

Marcos responded gracefully: should the fraud repeat itself August 21st, those who prepare it calculate badly if they think the Zapatistas are only concerned about Chiapas. "We still have hope in Cuauhtémoc Cárdenas," the Sup sucker punched, "but we don't have confidence in the PRD." Then, borrowing a page from El Jefe Diego, Marcos began to list the PRD's anti-democratic sins, Cárdenas's self-selection as candidate, the collusion between the party's currents to select candidates and PRD officials, the deals PRD honchos brokered behind closed doors with the PAN and the PRI Gobierno. The Sup trashed the PRD as a house of "palace intrigues, agreements between cupolas, lies, and the worse 'ajuste de cuentas." "Show us what is the difference between the PRD and the PAN or the PRI!" the Subcomandante cruelly demanded, pointedly adding "if you can't handle the post-electoral struggle, the men and women without faces will..."

Gilly calls Marcos's performances "a cry of intense anger" ("rabia"); Carlos Ramírez surmises the Sup was suffering from an attack of "Mal de Montana" ("mountain fever"). One anonymous Cárdenista who predicted the "ambush" argues that Marcos had a premeditated agenda—"the PRI and Diego couldn't have done it any better." Washing dirty linen in public is a political no-no in a land where revealing that the emperor wears no clothes wins few investigative journalism awards.

"This was hard, very hard—but it was real," is all Cárdenas himself would say to Blanche Petrich as he hopped up on the truck to head back to Guadalupe Tepeyac.

The rumble in the jungle sparked op-ed comment for weeks. PRD (ex-Communist Party) Mexico City bigwig Pablo Gómez wrote in *La Jornada* that Marcos had been insensitive to a party that has given the nation 250 martyrs in its brief combative existence, many more, he noted, than the EZLN. Others counseled that Marcos's contacts with the PRD come in a state where two guys named Jack Demosthenes Muñoz and Cherubim Mayorga ran the local party—the PRD's 1994 Chiapas senatorial candidate Irma "La Tigresa" Serrano has been the public mistress of PRI presidents. Still others counseled that Marcos's criticisms ought to be listened to closely.

Ballots or Bullets?

Gilly conjectures that Marcos was directing his remarks not so much at Cuauhtémoc's candidacy or even the futility of electoral struggle but rather at the PRD's growing base of the disenfranchised and landless, the lost citizens of the lost cities of the megalopolises, those who even if they do not put on the pasamontaña have lost their faces and their history to the PRI dictatorship, the forgotten ones who come to the Party of the Democratic Revolution to make change and then discover that they have no voice at all in what their party says. This army has been marching diligently behind the Ingeniero for six years now but their allegiances on August 22nd, the day after Armageddon, could be crucial to the transformation of the EZLN from a regional foco into a national army.

* * *

The Colosio assassination shoved the peace process in Chiapas to the back of the back burner. Suspension of the consultations in the villages and the imposition of the Zapatista Red Alert kept it there. Meanwhile, tensions between the ranching class and the peasantry continued to escalate with CEOIC launching new land invasions every day. On April 8th, "Francisco," a Zapatista committeeman from La Malinche, was killed in a confusing confrontation with "small property owners" in Altamirano. The Zapatista was the tenth indigenous farmer to fall since February—the March 9th slaying of Simojovel CNPA leader Maríano Pérez Díaz having particularly exacerbated tempers.

For the embattled campesinos of Mexico, April 10th—the anniversary of the betrayal and murder of Emiliano Zapata at Chinameca—is the high point of the protest year. To mark the annihilation of the Caudillo of the South up in Mexico City on April 10th, 1994, the

CEOIC was honored with leading 75,000 marchers from all corners of the republic, into the Zócalo, the largest out-pouring on this sacred date in years.

But the confluence of campesino groups who comprise the non—(read anti)—government independent agrarian movement in Mexico is not an easy one. Torn by ideological hairsplitting, Caudillismo, PRI-gobierno buy-outs, and sometimes bloody land feuds, the most important national formations—an alphabet soup of configurations (CEOIC, CIOAC, UNORCA, UNTA, CNPA, UGOCP—Jacinto López etc)—compete for moral high ground and government concessions, and each claims its own distinct deification of Emiliano Zapata—as, of course, does the Institutional Party, which has incorporated Zapata's home, history, and children into its personal pantheon of the revolution. The Neo-Zapatistas of the Lacandón are upstarts in the race to claim the mantle of Zapata as their own.

Given this loaded dynamic, it is understandable that the bearers of Marcos's message to the huge gathering in the Zócalo, a mysterious entity initialed CONAC-LN, encountered resistance from the organizers of the march (the CIOAC). Benito Mirón, who describes himself as "the legal advisor to the Zapatistas," finally had to snatch the mike away to pronounce the greetings of the CCRI-General Command. Mirón is active in the shadowy Independent Proleterian Movement (MPI), a violently anti-electoral grouping—in addition to being a longtime (17 years) government labor official. Despite such suspect antecedents, the Zapatistas had early on delegated Mirón as their conduit to the outside world and CONAC-LN set up operations in plazas around the nation, bringing the EZLN doctrine to the masses. Now Mirón was encouraged to read the Zapatistas' message by the visceral approval of the marchers whose numbers included many ski-masked

Marcositos.

75 years after Zapata's vile assassination and 18 days after Colosio's, the message from "the mountains of the southeast" was dusted with death and destiny. After giving the "usurper" Salinas the standard bird, (his treason could only be compared to Carranzas's), Marcos (the message is not under his name) speaks of those "who have covered their faces, erased their past, left behind their names and their land, and followed the footsteps of the war. None of us, men and women who walk by night, have a tomorrow..."

The Zapatistas, besieged, encircled, and ignored all at the same time, were still defiant. Underscoring that their message was being read before the National Palace, which borders the Zócalo, ("the House where the Lie Rules"), the CCRI said simply that their war "was for you, our brothers, the campesinos...we can't be with you today, brothers, our steps continue in the mountains—but our hearts are glad because, today, Emiliano Zapata has come again to the Zócalo."

In the Zapatista numerology, April 10th was also the 100th day of the war. Marcos invited national and international press to celebrate the date at La Garrucha. Trina Kleist was there: "300 guerrillas wearing the Zapatista Army of National Liberation trademark ski masks, and carrying a motley variety of weapons, stomped in double file from the dry brush. Behind a black and red banner reading '3rd Regiment Guardian of the Heart of the people,' they strode through a wide spot on a curving dirt road that serves as the village plaza, followed by 36 horse-mounted troops..." Later, "a homespun band led the singing of the Mexican National Anthem and the Zapatista Anthem on poorly-tuned guitars, a thumping bass, and an accordion..." Marcos delivered his hellfire and brimstone

Votán sermon: "Never again will Zapata-Votán die in our lifetime!" In post-performance conversations with the press, the Subcomandante justified all the war talk—the conditions were not conducive to peace. "Francisco" had just been killed. There was a lot of troop movement out there. The Red Alert could not be relaxed. The consultations would not be renewed.

Tensions between the armies were ratcheted up April 15th when persons unknown opened fire at a Mexican military roadblock east of Tuxtla. The troops were pinned down by incoming fire for an hour, a lieutenant had been killed. The "incident" occurred far north of the Zapatista zone but raised the possibility that other armed campesino focos had formed. The Army chose to write off the firefight to "narcos," explicitly exculpating the EZLN, a gesture the rebels noticed. On April 20th, Marcos told reporters that the Red Alert was winding down and on April 23rd, the one month anniversary of the Colosio assassination, the CCRI stood down, returned its troops to regular duty. The Red Alert was called off. To compound the sudden re-turn towards peace, the CEOIC, which had been camped out in DF since April 10th, reached agreement with the Salinas government over land rights to the ranches that their members had invaded since February.

* * *

Since the ugliness at Colosio's funeral, Manuel Camacho had been house bound, hovering in San Cristóbal, pluckily trying to restart the negotiations upon which his career depended. There were rumors that Salinas would soon dispatch him as ambassador to Fiji (Luis Echeverría once occupied the post). Don Samuel kept hinting that a new "spectacular" meeting with the rebels was only days away.

Ballots or Bullets?

On May 4th, under cover of early morning darkness, the Bishop, his Vicar, Gonzalo Ituarte, Camacho Solís, Alejandra Toscono, and Roberto Salcedo slipped out of San Cristóbal. No reporters were asked along. Six hours later, the Camacho-Ruiz party was seated in the same cabin above La Realidad that Cuauhtémoc and his entourage would enter ten days hence, the first safehouse. The Bishop and the Conciliator met with 10 members of the CCRI for eight hours. They returned very late to San Cristóbal and their pronouncements were eminently discreet, hopeful that the lingering consulations on the peace accords would soon be resumed.

The suspension of the consultations had produced a curious charade—the Bishop and the Conciliator and the interest blocs behind them invariably conveyed the impression that if only the consultations could be jump-started, a peace accord could be consummated before the elections. Now time was running out: the peace agreement needed to be signed now if the August 21st vote was not going to be conducted under threat of war.

What actually transpired during the May 4th session at La Realidad has never been publicly aired. No resumption of peace talks would take place as a result of the meeting. In mid-June, Marcos gave an interview to *Proceso*, published in August, in which the Subcomandante maintains that Camacho had offered to allow the Zapatistas to remain armed if they would sign a public peace agreement and say they had disarmed. Don Samuel was presumably a witness to this offer. Camacho would break a self-imposed vow of silence to deny such duplicity.

Before their suspension, the Zapatistas had made few bones about where the consultations were heading. The communal assemblies were convened March 14th and Marcos was already communicating negative tendencies to

Golden by the 18th—the story ran under the headline "Rebel Leaders Reject Peace Accord" and its text describes the Zapatista leadership as being "flush with power" and the consultative assemblies composed of "uniformly poor and uneducated farmers." "The government says in 30 or 60 or 90 days, it will produce a plan to make a study to make a law—it's not credible," Marcos argued. "These people have been tricked for a long time." Witnesses to the consultation sessions in March reported general dissatisfaction that the national demands were not on the table.

Resumption of the consultations in mid-May, after a nearly two month hiatus in which the power equation between the Zapatistas and the surviving rulers of the nation had been dramatically altered, did not anticipate a happy conclusion. Confidence that the government would or could fulfill its promises was at a low ebb, both in the communities and amongst EZLN leadership. Clearly, the only card the Zapatistas could play was to hold, hold out for a fresh dialogue, hold out for a new government, hold out to see what August 21st would shake out of the trees.

Marcos began issuing reams of amusing statistics. The surveys being conducted by CONAC-LN in public plazas around the nation, had produced 64,712 respondents, 87.56% of whom thought the government would sell the Zapatistas out. "We take our surveys as seriously as Doctor Zedillo takes his," quipped the Sup.

On May 20th, Camacho, sensing the mood in the Zapatista camp, sent urgent for-your-eyes-only communiqués to both Salinas and the EZLN, a last ditch effort, one surmises, to arm twist the rebels into signing. The rebels' popular support had been seriously undermined by the Colosio assassination, the Conciliator argued. But time was running out for the Camacho.

Given the delicate nature of the Camacho-Ruiz-

Zapatista-Salinas dialogue, the EZLN had a would-be visitor it definitely could have done without on the last weekend in May: U.S. Representative (Dem. NJ) Robert Torricelli, accompanied by his constant companion, the aging Bianca Jagger, and a carful of congressional clunkheads who had come to the Lacandón to offer Marcos an audience. Torricelli's petition for an interview, carried to the Subcomandante's lair by *El Tiempo* reporters, was burnt upon reception.

On June 3rd, Marcos announced the consultations had concluded, men had outvoted women 49% to 42%. Photos appeared in *La Jornada* of ski-masked rebels hand-tallying the votes. The June 11th "NO!" was resounding—newspapers just headlined the story with a big, inky N-O. "We looked for the word 'to surrender' ("rendir") in the Tzeltal language and did not find it, nor in the Tojolabal or the Tzotzil or the Chol," wrote Marcos. "The government has tried in vain to reduce our struggle to a regional one." The results were overwhelming: 97.8% against acceptance of the government proposals, 3.26% wanting to begin the war again, 96.74% voting to continue the dialogue.

The dismay on the part of the government was calculated. Columnists like Sarmiento and Pazos expressed mock shock and wrote lamentations against the barbarian Zapatistas for turning away from peace. No one, of course, was more disappointed than Manuel Camacho Solís—who must have known since the conclusion of the conversations in the Cathedral that the agreement was a no-sale down below. Now Camacho had been publicly humiliated by these ski-masked scumbags. Sure, he had gotten them to the table but he had not been able to make them bite. Even more embarrassing was the Conciliator's failure to wrap peace up in a pretty little package and hand it to the President prior to the August elections, an omission Salinas was not going to forgive. But Camacho Solís, always the diplomat, put the best face on the fracaso, inviting both sides to respect the cease-fire (resumption of hostilities was never an issue) and calling upon both parties to entable new talks.

Other observers, like the increasingly truculent PRI candidate Ernesto Zedillo, were more willing to call a fracaso, a fracaso—doing so immediately before maximum audiences of "acarreados" in Mexico City and Veracruz port. Camacho's response was programmed: on June 16th, taking a few desultory swipes at Zedillo, the Conciliator utterly and irrevocably retired yet again from all political involvement—or at least until the Salinas administration gave up the ship of state. Witnesses to this long-running drama doubted that the final curtain had really dropped on the now-ex Conciliator.

The EZLN rejection of the government's 32 points was meticulous, analyzing the reasons for each no thanks. Once again, the CCRI reiterated the eternal Zapatista demands for belligerent status, Salinas's resignation, the appointment of a transitional government, and fraud-free elections. But the explanation of the No vote was overshadowed by a second EZLN document published June 11th, The Second Declaration of the Lacandón Jungle. The new manifesto reaffirmed the Zapatista commitment to armed struggle but conceded picking up the gun wasn't the only road to democratic transition. The second declaration lionized the role of the civil society in leading social change. Indeed, in turning away from a government solution to their problems, the Zapatistas put their fate in the hands of the "Sociedad Civil."

The Second Declaration of the Lacandón Jungle also looked ahead to the elections and decided the Zapatistas had a role to play. To this end, the CCRI-General

Command was summoning the Civil Society to a "National Democratic Convention" prior to August 21st inside rebel territory. The goals of the convention would be "to organize the civil expression and the defense of popular will" (read "organize the post-electoral struggle if the PRI should win again")—and draft a new Mexican constitution. Some wags wondered if the Zapatistas were trying to start their own republic. Cárdenas told me he thought the EZLN had "an isolated view," that the geography in which they moved only let them see part of the picture.

The convention was to be modeled upon the October 1914 "Revolutionary Sovereign Convention," joined by Zapata and Villa in Aguascalientes, then rebel-held territory in an effort to outflank Carranza and establish a unified revolutionary government. Some students of history, like the hirsute PRD deputy Marco Rascón, point out that while the representatives of the two revolutionary generals debated day after day in Aguascalientes, Obregón took Veracruz, a victory that eventually boxed Villa into the Battle of Celaya, the waterloo for the revolutionary armies of the north and the south.

To the criticism of historians that Aguascalientes wasn't all that the Zapatistas claimed it to be, the CCRI-General Command initiated the Second Declaration of the Lacandón jungle with the words of Paulino Martínez, speaking for Emiliano Zapata at the 1914 Convention: "it is not just launching projectiles on the battlefield but launching new ideas and words of liberation that overthrows empires," Zapata's man emphasized: "The revolution is the wedding of the sword and the idea..."

¡Locura!

Surveying the caravan of 240 buses, mini-buses, pick-ups, ambulances, and miscellaneous vehicles nose to tail like a herd of motorized pachyderms lined up from the summit of the steep jungle switchback, around two hairpin turns, downslope, stretching several miles south onto the muddy valley floor below, my seatmate—a hardnosed, soft-hearted reporter for a leading Mexican financial daily—was impressed. "This is true locura (craziness)!" Paco Gómez Maza whistled softly.

Assembling 6,000 Mexican leftists and seeking to achieve agreement on anything beyond the death of the PRI, is, in itself, a kind of supreme craziness but then transporting those 6,000 delegates, invitees, observers, and national and international "journalists" deep into the jungles of the Southeast to celebrate such agreements with their Zapatista comrades, was a locura that only the poet-guerrilla Marcos, with his "Fitzcarraldic" vision, good humor, and immense powers of convocation, could have pulled off.

Contrary to the gleeful predictions of the rulers of Mexico and their purchased press, the "No!" vote breathed new life into the Zapatistas. The convocation of the "National Democratic Convention" seized the initiative back from the government whose "generous" offer the Zapatistas had so rotundly turned down. When the Salinas administration maliciously announced that the rejected 32 responses to the Zapatista demands would be applied to surrounding communities still dominated by the EZ's local rivals, the ARIC, because the responses were "just," the rebels opted for another road. In the Land of No, the Zapatistas were loudly saying yes to the civil society.

363

The call for the Convention was accompanied by a cry to the Zapatistas' developing national constituency to "romper el cerco"—break the encirclement of the Mexican troops. The Army's "cerco" or "fence" choked off incoming supplies and narrowed the Zapatista outreach. The Convention "would break the cerco" and consolidate the EZLN's national base, but, first, the devilish logistics of bringing thousands of supporters to their jungly lair had to be tested.

On June 12th, the day after the Zapatista "No!" and the first call for the Convention, 360 "Caravan of Caravans" volunteers, hauling 180 tons of food and clothing in 27 vehicles, became the first civilian convoy to successfully penetrate Zapatista territory with material aid. The "Caravan of Caravans" had left Mexico City's Zócalo two days previous at the conclusion of a demonstration of 10,000 EZLN supporters, each of whom had brought a few cans, a kilo of rice, beans, to the march. The Caravan was really a confluence of four separate caravans—the "Ricardo Pozas" of the UNAM's "historic CEU ("University Student Council"); the "Arturo Albores" caravan, sponsored by Mirón's CONAC-LN; "Corazón a Corazón" and "Ecumenia," associated with Christian base communities and civil associations that had PRD sympathies. The battle for control of the National Democratic Convention gestated within these strains.

The arrival of "the Mother of all Caravans," which had to negotiate four military checkpoints to complete its mission, overjoyed Marcos, who journeyed out to San Miguel to greet the visitors. Later, at La Garrucha, the Sup sprawled on the grass and exchanged jokes with the Caravaners, each of whom got two minutes with the ski-masked myth. Marcos was in high good humor. "These Caravaners tell worse jokes than even I do so there's a certain professional jealousy—my bad jokes are Nobel Prize quality." An ox was roasted and the "baile" (dance) declared. For the Zapatistas, the arrival of the "Caravan of Caravans" meant that the Convention was do-able "locura."

The National Democratic Convention—CND from here on out—had been immediately endorsed by the CEOIC, CONPAZ, CHILTAK, and other Chiapas-based activist formations. Around the rest of the nation, would-be Convention participants divided up along predictable electoral and non-electoral themes—with the MPI, the PROCUP, and their allies, queued up behind the armed struggle line, and the more civil society arguing to give the August 21st vote one more chance. Given this context, Marcos's July 2nd Convocation to the CND must have broken the "Ultras'" collective heart. The communiqué stated in bold type that "those who think armed struggle" is the only way to separate the PRI from state power, are "NOT convoked" to the Convention. Similarly, "those who are not willing" to try ("probar") the electoral path are "NOT convoked." At a hectic CND junta at the UNAM's philosophy faculty, the Ultras, led by the dagger-tongued ex-student leader "Pita" Carrasco, chanted that "the proletarian struggle is not a parliamentary one!" and sought to storm the podium. But Marcos's endorsement of the electoral mode carried the moment.

News of the polemic stirred up by his convocation reached the Subcommander in the jungle just beyond Guadalupe Tepeyac, where he was already drawing up plans for "Aguascalientes" and the construction of an enormous amphitheater to accommodate the convention-goers. World Cup fever gripped Mexico throughout the end of June and the first weeks of July and the rebel zone was not unaffected. Farmers in Zapatista communities went to their cornfields with radios plugged into their ears. Zapatista troops gathered around flickering TV screens to focus on the "Mundiales." Outside, in the nation, Mexico stood still for the matches. Football-field-sized screens were set up in public plazas and homicidal rallies followed a victory over Ireland and a tie with Italy. Even the three leading candidates for public office—Cuauhtémoc Cárdenas, Ernesto Zedillo, and "El Jefe Diego"—had to halt their onrushing campaigns to pay homage to the Mexican selection's performances in the great stadia of Gringolandia.

Marcos was not running for public office and did not need to pretend to be a fan. The Sup utilized the interval to transform the CND from a pipedream to a real one. "The difference between a handful of locos in January and a handful of locos in June is that now we are everywhere in the national territory," Marcos told his old friend, Epigmenio Ibarra. The Convention would not be the property of the EZLN, Subcomandante explained to Gaspar Morquecho in a *La Jornada* interview in which he railed against electoral abstentionism. The Convention could endorse a candidate, Marcos hinted, but it certainly would not be the ruling party one: "the permanence of the PRI in power is the condition that caused us to rise up."

Now Marcos was spending long hours drawing up invitations to notables. In one epistle to Carlos Fuentes, he quotes *Macbeth* and urges the writer to present himself in the jungle. Fuentes responded promptly, thanking Marcos for helping him to understand that there are two distinct Mexicos (Fuentes has lived outside of the country for years) but begging off the invite, deferring in favor of "The Group of San Angel," an elite luncheon club of influential writers and politicians who had begun to meet to eat and develop a blueprint for a "pluralistic" (coalition) government as a ploy to circumvent post-electoral cataclysm.

¡Locura!

"My job is to make war and write letters," Marcos penned Carlos Monsivais, the elegant chronicler of the convulsions of the civil society, and a major influence on Mexican essayists. Should he address "Monsi" with the familiar "tu" ("you) or the more respectful "usted"? Monsivais, who is uncertain around militaries and particularly ones that occupy far-off jungles, attended the Convention under protest, on assignment from *Proceso*.

The Sup says he rewrote the invitation to Enrique Krauze (*Century of Caudillos*) five times—Krauze declined to attend the CND, questioning the Zapatistas' democratic credentials. To the Uruguayan Eduardo Galeano, Marcos sent an invitation that echoed that writer's unique vignette style. To Elena Poniatowska (*Nights of Tlatelolco*, *Tinisima*) the Subcommander wrote a note in archaic Spanish, pleading that "she place her rosy foot in Zapatista lands." Other invitations went to novelist-diplomat Fernando Del Paso (negative), musician Guillermo Briseño (but of course), painter Alfredo Gironella (an emphatic si) and so many cultural heavies that writer Daniel Cazes feared he would be one of the only Mexicans not so honored (his invitation arrived in the next mail). On the international scene, Marcos pounded out invitations to Noam Chomsky, Nelson Mandela, and the Polish journalist Rysward Kapuscinsky. Don Samuel was asked to attend but could not—probably under orders from the CEM. His Vicar, Gonzalo Ituarte, went instead. Manuel Camacho was apparently not convened. To each, Marcos dramatically urged that they "jump from the side of death to the side of hope."

The National Democratic Convention advanced towards realization July 9th with the Chiapas state convention, held in three Indian languages in an Ocosingo coffee warehouse under the watchful eye of the military. The

CND would be convened August 6th-9th, two weeks before the presidential elections, in San Cristóbal and "Aguascalientes." The CND was being sponsored by the EZLN, the Chiapas state convention, and "The Caravan of Caravans," to be known in all subsequent documents as "the three parts." The civil society was encouraged to meet and select delegates from the "ejidos" and the unions and the schools and the barrios and the colonias throughout the country and beyond—chicanos organized in Texas and California. The unattached were urged to form groups and select their representatives. Delegates would then present their proof of selection to one of the three conveners for accreditation. Meetings were held to firm up the arrangements— ultras and electoralists duked it out in the UNAM's Che Guevara Auditorium. Buses were rented. Antonio García de León reminded *La Jornada* readers that in 1910, at the end of the Díaz dictatorship, 5,000 "civil clubs" were suddenly formed all over Mexico to overthrow the old despot.

Preliminary resolutions were hammered out in work groups—the demands centered on "the disarticulation of the state party" and the substitution of "a government of transition." Despite the rumors, the CND would endorse no candidate but encouraged full electoral participation, a position that sidestepped the ultras' insistence on abandoning the electoral track.

As the CND loomed closer, Marcos himself seemed more and more attached to the possibilities of the vote, hinting to *El Financiero*'s crack "cronista" Jaime Aviles that the Convention might support Cárdenas but that Cárdenas would reject the endorsement. Marcos condemned those who might write his name in—"I'm a poet not a president," calling the gesture "active absentionism" that could only benefit the PRI.

Down in the jungle, Marcos's poetry was taking shape. Several thousand members of the Zapatista base, the milicianos, and the combatants, hung their rifles on tree branches and began to assemble "Aguascalientes," once "La Realidad," the site of the first safehouse, the release of Absalón, the encounter with Cuauhtémoc Cárdenas, and countless other Zapatista adventures. "The professionals of violence are also professionals of carpentry," Bellinghausen noted on *La Jornada*'s over-inked pages. Under the baton of Comandante Tacho, a theater seating 6,000 delegates, five "inns" or "Hiltons," cookhouses, toilets, even a library, were being constructed. Electricity was contracted ($7,000 USD) from Guadalupe Tepeyac, ten minutes down the road. The cutting and stripping of thousands of trees to shape the amphitheater's benches, caused consternation among the protectors of the Lacandón rainforest. Stop "The Devastation of the Lacandón Jungle" pleaded a paid protest taken out in *La Jornada* August 1st, by an Arizona natural resources student, accusing Marcos of destroying the jungle, the "patrimony of all Mexicans."

While Tacho's troops chopped and hammered, Major Moïsés calculated the depths of the latrines—how many times a day would convention-goers defecate and what might be the volume, Moy questioned Bellinghausen. Marcos himself enthusiastically showcased the arena for a visiting Poniatowska (she had trained for four months to come to the jungle). The Zapatistas had spent 40,000 new pesos ($13,000 USD) to put "Aguascalientes" together, money accumulated from war taxes that had been ear-marked to buy arms. "Are you really soldiers?" the Poniatowska asked. "Soldiers yes, but simpático ones." "Que horror!" shrieked Elena, commanding the Zapatistas to throw all their arms into the sea. Marcos assured her that "yes, we want to disarm—do you think we want to live like this in a jungle with our ski masks on for the rest of our lives?" The Mexico City writer was calmed.

A good chunk of the Zapatista investment had been in 4,000 meters of nylon material to roof the amphitheater. To Marcos, the huge swath was a great sail and "Aguascalientes" an enormous pirate ship, staffed by "stern sailors," its prow pointed into the jungle sea. The "cronistas" began to compare the Sup's vision to that of Werner Hertzog's *Fitzcarraldo*.

* * *

The arrival of thousands of convention-goers in San Cristóbal broke the tourist hex that the New Year's uprising had put on the old stone city. Now Ciudad Real was once again awash with visitors, even if they were Indians and lefties, militant farmers, trade unionists, rockeros, chicanos, gringos, gachupines, and chilangos, chilangos, chilangos—most convention-goers were from the Federal District. The political tourists jammed the hotels and restaurants, emptied the stores of comestibles, overwhelmed the street vendors and artisans and newsboys. "Marcos should have a convention every weekend," one grateful "taxista" told me.

Despite the flailing final attempts of the Ultras to disrupt the Convention's direction, five enormous work groups were assembled and voted up platforms urging participation in the August 21st elections and an active and massive defense of the vote thereafter. Much of the internal polemic was out of earshot of the press which was barred from witnessing the workings of the sessions, an act of arbitrary anti-democracy imposed upon the "Democratic National Convention" by "the three parts." 11 distinct media, led by Televisa, and all of them particularly disdainful in their treatment of Zapatista viewpoints, were banned permanently from the Convention—the ejection of Bruno López from "Aguascalientes" because his employer, Univisión, is part of the Televisa empire, particularly irked reporters.

Nonetheless, Zapatista press management had more democratic aspects—independent and corporate media were subject to regulations designed to prevent major Mexican and U.S. outlets from getting a jump on the small fry—no satellite transmission units, cellular phones or private vehicles would be allowed into the jungle. Some big-time reporters, their edge diminished, went home in disgust.

The great caravan assembled before dawn on Sunday, August 7th and the trip to the jungle, despite the acute discomforts of transit, was first-class "locura" every millimeter of the way. All along the side of the road down to the Lacandón, families gathered to cheer the caravan on, holding up cardboard signs that expressed their hand-lettered support of the EZLN and calling upon the government to permit them "Elections Without Pressures." In Comitán, cops raised Vs of victory and soldiers boarded the buses, not to brusquely search the occupants but to wish them "a safe trip." "Marcos! Marcos!" gleefully screamed a tyke running alongside our bus in Las Margaritas.

After the Margaritas military checkpoint, the pace slowed to a bellycrawl—it took 23 hours just to traverse the 78 kilometers to Guadalupe Tepeyac. Buses mired in the mud or fell into ravines or their transmissions gave up the ghost. Zapatista milicianos climbed aboard and searched luggage for contraband. As the hours passed, each bus became its own circle of conspiration. Intimacies were exchanged in the dark and tempers frayed and the jungle dawn came up live vermilion soon enough on Monday morning. In Guadalupe Tepeyac, there were bananas and marimbas and refrescos and breakfast enough to revive convention-goers for the trek to "Aguascalientes."

At the gateway to the rustic convention center, long lines of delegates, invitees, and the press sizzled and keeled over in the blazing sun as first Zapatista troops, then CEU coeds, frisked each entrant one by one, confiscating six packs and can openers and thousands of Swiss Army knives. Once inside the perimeter, the ambiance was that of an impending rock concert. Marcos's sail shimmered under the jungle rays. Thousands of little high-tech tents dotted the hillsides and hammocks were slung up in the "posadas." The urban safari-goers hauled backpacks and sleeping bags and every tin of tuna fish in Mexico's southeast. The campesinos, equipped with their "cobijas" (blankets) and their "morales" (shoulder bags), brought the tortillas.

The National Democratic Convention was not unlike a Fuller Brush salesmen's convention—only the profession being convened at "Aguascalientes" was that of social activism. Every few steps, this reporter would bump into a combatant "maestro" from Oaxaca's teachers union or a campesino from Michoacán, veterans of the "damnificado" movement from the 1985 Mexico City earthquake, fraud fighters in Guerrero state elections, Gay "luchadores," Chicano militants, human rights warriors, old faces and friends who I have interviewed over long years close to the ground here. While comrades hailed and embraced, Marcos and other Zapatista luminaries had their photos snapped with convention-goers, Tacho fiddled nervously with the great sail. The Convention was to begin at dusk. The buzzing of humans outdroned the mosquitoes.

August 8th, 1994 was a propitious day to hold such a revolution-starred event—the 121st, the 117th, the 115th, or the 111th birthday of Saint Emiliano Zapata, depending on whose history you swallow. As evening fell, the multitudes gathered under the great sail and the Zapatistas gave voice to the Convention, first Tacho, who presented the EZLN's bases of support, "those who kept our secret, who brought us pinole and tostadas in the mountain." 300 men and women, most masked by paliacates, marched slowly past the flag-bedecked podium, their measured tread stroking the earth like the Zapatistas' collective heartbeat that the base represents. Then the presidium was named: dozens of notables, including Antonio García de León, Pablo González Casanova—the ex-UNAM rector, Rosario Ibarra, the poet Juan Bañuelos, the historian Lorenzo Meyer, *La Jornada* publisher Carlos Payán, the actress Ofelia Medina, Poniatowska, *El Tiempo*'s Concepción Villafuerte. Hundreds of Zapatistas troops marched in, presenting arms. Each weapon had a white strip of cloth attached to the muzzle.

"Welcome aboard!" Marcos took the helm, "through my voice speaks the voice of the Zapatista Army of National Liberation." The Subcomandante's discourse was directed at the soldiers with their muzzled guns: "the war will not come from us!" he breathed, it was up to the government to give Mexico elections without fraud. "We have raised this Tower of Hope and, for a time, we have put aside our weapons, our rancor, our pain for our dead, our conviction as warriors, to hold this meeting, this first step towards true peace..." The Subcomandante told of the Zapatistas' very first military operation, how they were invited to take the ejido of the Old Antonio, and how when they had gotten there, climbing in stealthily over the mountains, the people were already assembled on the basketball court and applauded their coming, the first dialogue between his military and the civil society. The Convention was "the celebration of broken fears. Yes to the beginning of the end of this long nightmare that, grotesquely, we call the history of Mexico...we expect from this convention a collective call to the nation to struggle for what belongs to us, for our place in history..." The delegates, the reporters, the dignitaries on the stage, were fixed on the Subcomandante but the audience was all of Mexico and it was in the palm of his hand. "For us nothing, for everyone, everything!" Then Marcos gave "Aguascalientes" to the Convention, gave the Convention to the Convention, announcing that the EZLN was retiring from the CND but would obey its dictates, whatever they might be. The flag of the nation Marcos presented to Rosario Ibarra, whose own guerrilla son had disappeared in Monterrey at about the same time that the "Pepes" began sending their brigades to Chiapas. And then, pale and trembling (Jaime Aviles reports), Marcos, followed by Tacho and Major Mario, disappeared into the increasingly turbulent jungle night.

The first storm struck just as the Subcomandante was making his exit. From the first drop of the downpour, it was evident that the sail would not hold water and that Marcos's great ship had no anchor. The second "tormentón" lifted the sail off its moorings, snapping the hawsers that held it in tension and sending 4,000 meters of soaking nylon cascading in soft billows over thousands of trapped convention-goers. The electricity went next, further panicking the populous of "Aguascalientes." Now the rain was drenching, unending, the worst "aguacero" of the season— four times, the torrent washed over the jungle clearing, turning "Aguascalientes" into a dangerous swamp. I stood under half a shingle and spoke of the God of the poor with two old-timers from Michoacán. Friends came and said all the "old people" were to be gathered in the library— despite the slur, this reporter, a young senior citizen, followed his would-be rescuers to the only shelter on the premises.

In the library, lined with donated volumes, poets and artists huddled forlornly or collapsed in half-sleep, occasionally punctuated by drowsy dialogue about relative ages and a careful review of Marcos's offer of peace in return for a clean election. In the dawn, the survivors emerged to a sea of mud and a sail-less barque—the Convention had seemingly shipwrecked on the shoals of a jungle storm. Yet, in spite of the carnage wreaked upon "Aguascalientes," behind the damp remnants of the stage, the two great Mexican flags draped as backdrop, had held their place, like a red, green, and white beacon to remind us of what shore we had landed upon.

The first rays' bright warmth and shared cups of coffee aroused camaraderie. Carlos Monsivais leaned heavily on a stick, dangling a sprained ankle, and ruminating on the Woodstock parallel—the Convention coincided with the 25th anniversary of that generationally-charged craziness. One by one, the delegates hobbled back to the disabled amphitheater. Pablo González Casanova extolled the revival of spirits, the teams that were already clearing away the debris: "this morning, we are roofless, without food, without even a mirror in which to see our faces....this shows us that solidarity is not enough—now we know how it is to wake up like this every day."

To escape a second killer storm, the Convention would be curtailed after approval of the resolutions, the Presidium had decided. Although the Ultras kept the chants alive until the end, the Convention ultimately resolved that everyone go home and disarticulate the state party, encouraging a big vote for the candidate who would uphold the Convention's platform. Four days later, before 200,000 in Mexico City's Zócalo, Cuauhtémoc Cárdenas embraced the CND's program.

As thousands of convention-goers broke camp for the long journey home, Marcos returned to the stage to joust one more time with the press. The Zapatistas were now under the command of the Convention, he stressed—they would use their influence with other armed groups to maintain peace while the elections unfolded, a reiteration of the offer to Salinas for an embargo on armed struggle in return for a fair election (in which a PRI victory would be unacceptable.) Despite the harrowing night and the pervasive mud, the Convention had been a huge success, the Sup said, "almost an orgasm." Should he remove his ski mask, he asked thousands of lingering supporters. No-o-o-o, they lowed, one respondent blowing a loud "cacho," the cow's horn trumpet of Tzeltal villages.

The Convention was not over, Marcos reminded his people now go home and make this "locura" live locally. Reluctant to leave but charged with energies for August 21st and beyond, the Nahuas and Tlapanecos of La Montaña, the Purépecha nation of Michoacán, the Mixtecs and the Mixes of Oaxaca, the widows of the Costa Chica, the Chile Frío banda de guerra, the Yaquis and the Yuppies and the Men of Corn, the CEU "historicos," young workers, old social warriors, professors and painters and entertainers, politicos, campesinos, PRDistas, periodistas, and even the Ultras, slowly returned to their ejidos and schools, jobs and fields and barrios, with a sense that history was just beginning and that August 21st might indeed be the first day of the Mexico that had been born again in this damp, Zapatista-infested jungle.

The End
of the
Beginning

Way back in 1968, a watershed year on the left, Amado Avendaño, then a young and impecunious lawyer, got hitched to Concepción Villafuerte, sold his car, and sank the sales price in the start-up of the then-weekly *El Tiempo*. Avendaño's political career had a similarly threadbare genesis. Amado's decision to run for the governorship of Chiapas as the candidate of the much-heralded but depressingly underfunded "civil society," sprang from the conviction that "now that the Zapatistas have interrupted" the doing of politics as usual, "those of us who have not yet put on the ski mask" have to do our part. But the civil society, whose "unarmed belligerence" Avendaño sought to encapsulate, has, by definition, no party of its own. Cárdenas's PRD is about as close to a non-party with official registry as one can get. In late May, after Cárdenas's fractious visit with the Zapatistas, Avendaño and his supporters packed the state PRD convention and walked off with the nomination, thereby forcing Chiapas party piecards Jack Demosthenes and Cherubim Mayorga to stalk out in an huff.

Avendaño, a former PRIista municipal president of San Cristóbal, co-founder of the Fray Bartolomé Human Rights Center, and a sometimes attorney who had defended Padre Joel Padrón when Patrocinio locked him up in Cerro Hueco, was a weird candidate from the outset. His goofy, smiling demeanor is often at odds with the seriousness of his discourse. "I have to be congruent between what I say and what I do," Amado once told me, sitting on

377

his leaky living room couch while kids whizzed by on trikes—such congruence is a poor quality for a politician. From the first minute of his campaign, Amado made it abundantly clear that he was not some power-hungry PRDista but that the Party of the Aztec Sun was merely lending him its registration to campaign against Absalón's old partner in crime, Eduardo Robledo. The office for which both were competing was, in itself, a surrealistic niche—"Chiapas is ungovernable," Amado insists. The anti-politico politico's plan was to win, occupy the governor's mansion just long enough to write a new constitution and alter the state's system of systematic injustice, and go home, a true government of "transition."

Despite its eccentric underpinnings, Amado Avendaño's campaign for high office was remarkably like the standard model. He kissed babies and made speeches and attended political breakfasts—although the locations of these endeavors were more exotic than his rival Robledo's. On July 14th, Avendaño became the first candidate to actively campaign in the Zapatista zone. The Guadalupe Tepeyac meeting was opened by the usual EZLN military salute. Amado's stump speech was translated into Tzeltal and Tojolabal. On the platform with the newshound-turned-candidate was PRD senate hopeful Irma Serrano—a former "exotic dancer" and "amante" of President Díaz Ordaz—who was born at La Soledad just down the road from Tepeyac. Serrano was pictured in the middle of the jungle wearing a suit made of "unidentified animal skins," read the caption.

93,000 Mexicans were thought to reside in the Zapatista zone, 28,000 of them with photo credentials. Despite its mixed line on elections, the EZLN had been declaring since January that it would not impede the August 21st elections anywhere in the nation, a geographical swatch that presumably included its own territory. On July 30th, the former CNDH Ombudsman Jorge Madrazo, now Camacho's replacement as peace commissioner, announced agreement between the Zapatistas and the Federal Electoral Institute (IFE) to install 65 polling stations ("casillas") inside the rebel zone, one corner of Chiapas's ninth federal electoral district. A mixed government-civil society electoral commission was created with the prima actress Ofelia Medina (celebrated for her portrayal of Frida Kahlo) as president. Poet Juan Bañuelos and sociologist Xochitl Leyva were added to the body. One stipulation of the new electoral commission: Zapatista fighters could not vote with their pasamontañas on unless their photo-credential showed them wearing a ski mask.

Then, early on Monday morning, July 25th, the Avendaño bandwagon came to a crushing, tragic halt. Campaigning across the state in and around Tapachula, Amado had received an urgent summons from interim PRI governor Javier López Moreno to attend an "important" political breakfast in Tuxtla, to discuss the upcoming elections. Although Amado had stopped attending these functions because he felt they only benefited the PRI's awkward efforts to appear to be a democratic institution, he told Doña Concha on the phone Sunday night that he would go up to the state capital in the morning.

Before dawn, the editor and five members of his campaign committee piled into the family Suburban and set out from Tapachula for Tuxtla Gutiérrez on the coastal highway. At 5:40 A.M., a dozing Jaime Aguilar, a young videographer filming the trip, remembers opening his eyes just as a huge, license-less, green Kenworth trailer-truck struck the Suburban head-on on a straight-away between Pijijíapan and Tonalá, near the Ranch of the Seven Cigarettes. Two Avendaño cousins and Agustin Rubio, Amado's campaign manager, were killed instantly. Amado himself was critically injured, receiving a fractured skull and a crushed thorax in the crash. Both Rubio, a former state CIOAC director forced to leave Chiapas in 1988 because of threats on his life, and Avendaño, had repeatedly been plagued with anonymous phonecalls advising them to desist their political activities or suffer the consequences.

Recovering from serious injuries, Aguilar told *La Jornada* several days later that the Kenworth had deliberately crashed into the Suburban. He also recalled seeing a white pick-up with polarized windows pass the Avendaño vehicle twice before the fatal crash. The circumstances were certainly suspicious—the 75-ton Kenworth had no license plates either on the cab or the trailer. According to the cab insignia, the titular owner of the rig was one Ramón Rodríguez of Chihuahua, Chihuahua. (Mr. Rodríguez was "out of the country" when reporters tried to reach him). Moreover, the driver of the Kenworth had vanished from the crash scene by the time Federal Highway Police reached the site, driven off, one eyewitness reported, by Immigration agents towards Tapachula on the Guatemalan border. The truck, unaccountably, had been deadheading cargoless towards that border town, a costly run that southern Mexican trucking execs find hard to digest. An expired driver's license, subsequently discovered by the Mexican Attorney General's investigators in the cab (the highway patrol found nothing) listed a fake Mexico City address for "Luciano Tress Virgín." In San Cristóbal, Doña Concha immediately labeled the crash an attempt on her husband's life, accusing unidentified Patrocinio henchmen still in state government, of setting up Amado for the kill. They knew where he was going, they knew what route he was taking, they knew what time he would be traveling, she concluded. A furious López Moreno denied the charges but ordered a full-scale investigation.

"Everything points to an accident," lamented Secretary of the Interior Jorge Carpizo, concerned that the crash would exacerbate electoral tensions. The "accident" was "not a rare occurrence" in the history of how things happen in Chiapas, Don Samuel told the local press.

State and federal authorities seemed particularly determined to erase all evidence of possible political assassination—the roadway where the accident occurred was repaved the next day, recalls Amado Jr., who escaped the crash relatively unscathed. The Mexico City journalism student also recalls that federal authorities, rather than concerning themselves with locating the missing driver, took time out to search the victims' luggage.

Clinging to life, the candidate was helicoptered to Mexico City where he was visited by Carpizo, Cárdenas, Superbarrio, the head of the Mexican hospital system, and, ultimately, Carlos Salinas himself, all while Avendaño was still in a coma. On July 27th, Chiapas authorities ran a re-creation of the crash to sustain their theory that the mishap had been a tragic accident. On July 30th, the "driver," Tress Virgín's alleged son, was taken into custody in the federal district and immediately consigned to prison in Tapachula for the crime of "imprudence." Case closed.

With just three weeks to go till election day, Amado's campaign seemed doomed by the "accident." Accusations flew fast and furiously. Cárdenas called the moment a dark one in the nation's political life. Ernesto Zedillo responded by labeling PRD charges of attempted assassination "political opportunism." Cárdenas shot back, "the only beneficiary of the death of Luis Donaldo Colosio is Ernesto Zedillo—now that's political opportunism..." Other suspicious transportation "accidents" had befallen opposition candidates before. The plane crash of former PRI president

Carlos Madrazo 20 years ago after he had launched an independent candidacy, was recalled as was the auto accident death of 1988 PAN presidential standard-bearer Manuel Clouthier several months after that disputed election. Irma Serrano had nearly been killed in a car crash on this same stretch of highway when she ran for senator in 1991.

Public incredulity was not assuaged by the "driver"'s incarceration. For months, the ghost Kenworth had apparently been navigating the nation's highways, sailing through highly patrolled toll booths without license plates from one end of Mexico to the next. Not once had the gypsy truck ever been stopped by authorities. Out beyond Guadalupe Tepeyac, transforming La Realidad into "Aguascalientes" for the Convention, Marcos was more than alarmed. "Chiapas is a state that has more police than Indians who know how to read and write," he ironized, wondering where all the cops had gone on the morning of the crash and agreeing with Doña Concha that the "accident" had been a deliberate one. With just weeks to go until election day and days to the Convention, the EZLN went back on "red alert."

* * *

On July 6th, six years to the day after the nefarious fraud that had robbed him of the presidency, Cuauhtémoc Cárdenas jammed an indoor bullring on the edge of the capital with 20,000 ebullient aficionados and 400 million dots of confetti (Aviles). From that gala night onwards, the Ingeniero's campaign, which had been dawdling in deep space, gathered steam. In the middle of the month, Cuauhtémoc stumped the explosive Guerrero coast, headed inland through his home state of Michoacán, doing 25,000 supporters a day from Acapulco all the way to the Meseta

Tarasca. At the end of July, the son of the Tata drew huge crowds in Tabasco and southern Veracruz—30,000 in Villahermosa and Coatzacoalcos, mostly disgruntled oil-workers who poured out in defiance of union prohibitions. The Engineer's August 7th "closing" in Morelia, the Michoacán capital, drew 50,000 on the same weekend as Marcos's "locura" was unraveling in Chiapas. Back in Mexico City, Cárdenas toured the capital's 16 delegations, bringing out tens of thousands each day. Cuauhtémoc's August 13th magnum rally packed the Zócalo with 150,000 to 200,000 supporters, his biggest public gathering since the PRI had cheated him out of victory in '88, two and a half times what El Jefe Diego drew that afternoon to the same plaza and equal to what Ernesto Zedillo drummed out the next day with one significant qualification—Cárdenas's people were convinced, Zedillo's obligated to attend. The monumental crowd, howling "que se muera el PRI!" and bathed in yellow and black, the colors the PRD had chosen to replace the green, white, and red (the colors of the flag) that the Institutionals claimed for their own, heard the Ingeniero, Doña Rosario, and the pudgy party prez Porfirio Muñoz Ledo each endorse the Democratic National Convention's resolutions. The immensity of the meeting lifted PRD spirits and reportedly put the fear of god into the PRI. Cárdenas wrapped up his campaign four days before election day in Chiapas, Tapachula, in the steamy Park of the Marimbas, 25,000 sweaty fanatics chanting his name and Marcos's in tandem. In ten months of campaigning, Cuauhtémoc Cárdenas had traveled the length and breadth of the republic several times over, held over a thousand meetings, and claimed face-to-face contact with two million voters. As August 21st loomed, the Engineer appeared to be cresting, finishing big, just as in 1988. Those close to Cuauhtémoc were convinced that he was going to win. Their enthusiasm was contagious.

To be sure, there were a lot of folks who said such thinking was delusionary. The pollsters, for example, poo-pooed the PRD's prospects. Poll-taking was the first fall-out from NAFTA to penetrate the Mexican election indus-try—gringo pundits named Harris and Belden and Mitofsky probed the land for preferences. The credibility accorded their findings was one measure of how close Mexico had grown to Washington political hucksterism in the past six years.

Since the Great Debate, the polls had placed Cárdenas a distant third, fluctuating between nine and 17% of the sample, and in the 11-14% range during the final weeks of the campaign. The Engineer frowned when quizzed about the numbers: "they are unreal, they want to make me dis-appear"—and recalled 1988 when he was supposed to have been down from 60 to 14% going into the final week, according to the calculations of the polltakers. Indeed, designed and paid for to service clients like the PRI, the pollsters seemed more interested in influencing the outcome of the presidential race than truly taking the pulse of the public.

Down the August homestretch, Zedillo zoomed above 40% after having run neck and neck with Diego since May. The Jefe seemed to have purposely sealed his own fate when he sat down for ten days in July at the height of the horse race and just stopped campaigning completely. His handlers claimed that he was preparing for another TV debate with Zedillo but that never happened. *Chisme* had him terminally ill with stomach cancer. The *New York Times* and *Newsweek* said that Jefe Diego was suffering from "a nervous disorder"—that, psychologically, he was frightened of winning the presidency. Although the PANista's poll ratings continued to hover around 27-30%, the number of his rallies and their attendances dwindled fearfully. Some said the fix was already in. The electoral playing field was made even more unlevel when two candidates collude to defeat a third, Lorenzo Meyer noted in *Reforma*.

"There could be many surprises on August 22nd" Epigminio Ibarra warned on the pages of the rival *La Jornada*. "In the basement of the nation, a dynamic has been unleashed that is not measurable in the polls..."

But the polls were not the only sign in the electoral zodiac that a Cárdenas victory was an impossible dream. The election process itself was being organized and administered by the newly-created Federal Electoral Institute (IFE) out of a multi-million-buck set of bunkers in the south of the capital and the IFE was staffed and directed by the same PRI hacks who had fabricated the historic flim-flam back in '88. Indeed, director Arturo Núñez had been the PRI's lead rep to the IFE's predecessor CFE on the night the system crashed—Núñez even bragged to international reporters swilling it up at a free-bee four-course breakfast at the fashionable Camino Real hotel in June 1994, that, six years ago, the PRI had "opted" to close down the computers because the results were not "representative," i.e., Cárdenas was way ahead. Now, despite the placement of six citizen councilors on the IFE's governing General Council—the celebrated "citizenizing" of the Institute—the PRI continued to control the electoral machine via the mandates of General Council president and Secretary of the Interior Jorge Carpizo and the allegiances of thousands of technicians, bureaucrats, and "vocales" in Mexico's 300 federal election districts.

The PRD and the IFE skirmished right up to election day about the validity of voter registration lists—even debating this heady matter on the national tube.

Cárdenas's representative to the General Council, Samuel Del Villar, insisted that 15-20% of the listed names were invalid and that an equal percentage of PRD voters had been shaved ("rasurado") from the "padrón" (registry). A professor who demonstrated how simple it was to acquire more than one voter i.d. was threatened with prison by Carpizo (whose Secretariat runs the jails)—Fernando Bazua sought sanctuary in Washington instead. To counter PRD insinuations, the Secretary of the Interior displayed a hastily-drawn audit, coordinated by a longtime U.S.-based PRI contractor that concluded the "padrón" was 97% correct—Mckinsey & Co. had a history of doing business with Manuel Bartlett, the official who had occupied Carpizo's chair when the big fraud came down six years back down the pike. The PRI and the PAN and the six satellite parties funded by the PRI-government to steal votes from the opposition, voted the voting lists up. Then the PRD discovered that almost a million and a half names on the Mexico City voting lists—a fifth of the electorate—had the same three names (in Chiapas, the homonyms ran 34%). Carpizo responded by offering to put Del Villar, the bearer of this bad news, behind bars, but had to eat his words when the IFE's own investigation proved the information to be true.

The "homonyms" were not the only words Jorge Carpizo had to swallow during the run-up to August 21st. On June 24th, the Interior Secretary, who had been appointed by Salinas to bring integrity to an outlaw electoral process, mysteriously resigned his office, citing harassment by an unnamed party as the cause of his sudden retirement. The stock market promptly plummeted 2% of its total value. Then, 48 hours later and on the heels of a Salinas-generated drive to urge his reconsideration, Carpizo withdrew his resignation. The unnamed "party" responsible for his momentary powder-taking was never named—Carpizo begged reporters not to delve because such delving might reveal "impartiality." Ernesto Zedillo immediately lashed out at the PRD as being the party that had hounded poor Jorge into retirement. Cárdenas responded that the Interior Secretary's temper tantrum had been directed at PRI plans to steal the election. Insiders indicate that the culprit was the Institutional Party—Carlos Hank's "Atlacomulco Group" had been pressuring the PRI's 28 remaining state governors for vote quotas, a dinosaurian tradition. On June 26th, to seal the deal on Carpizo's return, Salinas reassured the nation that, no matter who won, he would turn over power to the winner December 1st.

PRD hallucinations of impending victory clashed seriously with the financial reality of the campaign. The PRI outspent Cárdenas 20 (and probably 400) to one to put Zedillo over on the public. Under the first election-spending regs ever inscribed on the books here, the PRI's top-line was $42 million USD but in 1993, during a PRI fundraising orgy at the home of banker emeritus Antonio Ortiz Mena (Salinas's uncle by marriage), then-party president Genaro Borrego had dunned the nation's new billionaires to cough up $625 million, to be earmarked for the 1994 campaign. On the other side of the money, Cuauhtémoc spent a little over $2 million USD in his bid for the presidency, about what the ruling party ante'd up for just one senatorial campaign.

The Institutionals filled their coffers (a) by demanding kickbacks from tycoons to whom their party had given away the country during the Salinas years and (b) through local fund-raising committees that often raked the loot in via car raffles, a popular political sport here. In one PRI-run Mexico City raffle, party organizers won for themselves 10 out of the 24 Cavaliers being offered (dryly noted in *Reforma* on August 13th).

With such naked bamboozlements to consider, it was little wonder that the nation was skeptical about the fairness of the upcoming elections. An Alianza Civica (Civic Alliance) survey done in June indicated that 46.5% of those interviewed thought fresh fraud was in the offing August 21st. Over 50% feared post-electoral violence would soon consume Mexico.

Partially funded by the highly suspect U.S. National Endowment for Democracy, the Civic Alliance proved a rare independent voice throughout the electoral process. Monitoring the electronic media was one valuable Alliance function—its surveys indicated that Zedillo was assigned about 45% of all TV and radio newstime (more on Televisa's "24 Hours")—not counting what Salinas and the PRI-government were getting every night, anyway. The rest of Zabludowsky's newshole was divided between the other eight parties, 45 seconds a candidate, with Marcela Lombardo, the grandmotherly Popular Socialist (0.66% of the final tally) allotted the same equal time as Cuauhtémoc and Diego, who together would take half the official vote. Commercial breaks on the newscasts were monopolized by Zedillo, the PRI, "Solidarity," and "Procampo" spots, a seamless skein of Institutional Party propaganda. The Civic Alliance calculates that the PRI was spending a million new pesos a day on the electronic media at the end of the campaign.

Government pay-outs further stacked the deck against the opposition. The Procampo payment calendar had been drawn up by Agriculture Secretary Carlos Hank, Zedillo's main man, to coincide with the August 21st elections. June-to-August checks to 3.2 million Mexican farmers totaled over $3 billion USD—a 360 new peso ($115 USD) subsidy payable upon presentation of one's voter i.d., such as was the practice in Mexico state where Hank holds maximum sway. The bonanza was designed to capture perhaps 10 million votes from the poorest farm families in Mexico—each family being calculated at, at least, three votes. Cárdenas could only offer the campesinos democratic change.

As in '88, when Cuauhtémoc's chief electoral aide Xavier Ovando was gunned down three nights before the election (still unsolved), the 1994 outing had an ugly face to it. On July 11th, a CEU student, shaking a can for Cárdenas in front of the Tasqueña bus station in the south of the capital was kidnapped and tortured by men driving a car marked "Judicial Police." On July 25th, the same day as the partially successful attempt on Avendaño's life, Pablo Ramírez Lobato, a young PRD leader in Yautepec Morelos, was gunned down by PRIista rivals. On July 30th, Professor Gabino Aparicio, a Cárdenas organizer in Puebla, was run down while crossing the street in the state capital. On the same day, Party president Muñoz Ledo's son and a companion were kidnapped for several hours in southern Mexico City. Ricardo Reyes, who occupied the same position in the Cárdenas campaign in 1994 as Ovando had in 1988, received repeated death threats. The home of PRD IFE advisor César Yañez was twice burglarized.

By hook or by crook, the PRI was not going to lose August 21st. The ruling party had put the whole electoral bureaucracy, the media, the federal government, 28 state governors, and 2,128 mayors, representing 88% of the nation's cities, on its payroll. Ignacio Pichardo, handpicked by Hank to run the PRI, called for a "full car" ("carro completo"): all 64 senators, 300 deputies, and the presidency (he wasn't far off the mark). At his closing rally in the Zócalo, Ernesto Zedillo had to talk fast as his "followers," who had been obligated to attend under penalty of fines of up to three days' pay, abandoned the plaza so quickly and in such numbers that the candidate was soon ranting to a nearly-deserted square. "Vamos a ganar!" ("We're going to win!") Zedillo shouted for the umpteen billionth time on the campaign trail. Triumphalism had been his major theme. "We say we're going to win so often as a psychological favor to the opposition, to get them used to our triumph so that it won't hurt as much," the PRI candidate smirked to reporters.

* * *

Election morning broke sultry over the Zapatista zone. The rays of the jungle sun penetrated and dissipated the valley fogs. The flat iron slabs that pass for churchbells in Zapatista hamlets like Patihuitz and San Miguel, Guadalupe Tepeyac and the Ejido Morelia (not technically inside the zone), rang out to summon the electorate to the vote. The EZLN had dismantled its roadblocks and withdrawn to the mountains the night before. The rebels would not vote or interfere with the process in any way—an August 18th proclamation pledged the Zapatistas not to retaliate with arms if and when fraud was discovered.

María Lorenzo Ruiz was first on line in San Miguel, ready to vote at 7 A.M. But the ballot boxes had never arrived from Tuxtla. Caralampio Santis, a local polling place official, substituted cookie boxes instead, cut a hole in each and covered the opening with plastic so that the balloting would be "transparent," then opened the converted cookie boxes on both ends to demonstrate they had not come "pregnant"—packed with votes—a popular PRI shell game. The indelible ink frightened María Lorenzo, who had never voted before. "I'm 60 years old and this is the first time in my life I've ever had a ballot in my hand" said a farmer behind her on line. "Before the PRI would say that a lot of votes came from here but it was a trap— we never had a casilla here before."

The ballots ran out in San Miguel by noon—this was a special polling place reserved for those "in transit." Some had walked three days from Montes Azules to cast a ballot. A list was drawn up and those who had no ballot gave their preference. On the Ejido Morelia, the shortage of ballots was just as acute. The "casilla" had received just 506 ballots when it required 1,500 to accommodate 12 surrounding communities. Meanwhile at La Laguna, an ARIC-PRI enclave, 1,500 ballots had been sent for just three settlements, denounced the frustrated voters of Morelia. The election officials at La Laguna were reportedly wearing PRI tee-shirts and caps. To satisfy the hundreds who could not vote at Morelia, a communal assembly was convened and preferences voted publicly up. Meanwhile, overhead, military and police spotter aircraft flew continual overflights, searching for trouble spots.

Despite the air surveillance and the electoral anomalies on the ground, early on the morning of August 22nd, Ofelia Medina arrived back in San Cristóbal with the Zapatista ballot boxes. 65 casillas and two specials had been set up in the zone. 19,000 out of 28,000 registered voters had exercised their right to suffrage—many could not vote because the ballots had run out or the military had confiscated or destroyed their credentials back in January. 70% of the vote in Zapatista land had been cast for Cárdenas, Amado Avendaño, and the PRD, 14,000 votes. The rest went to Zedillo, Robledo and the ARIC-PRI. The results provided the first accurate census of political allegiances in the Zapatista-controlled zone. The ballot boxes were handed over to Don Samuel to be transported down to Tuxtla.

Outside of rebel territory, the voting process had not been quite so tranquil. In the special casilla set up in San Cris's 31st of March plaza, 600 frustrated citizens threatened to burn the ballot boxes if they weren't allowed to vote—the 300 ballots allocated to the polling station had been used up early by soldiers from Rancho Nuevo. At 4 P.M., the Army took up positions in front of the abandoned ballot boxes after election officials fled in panic. Down in Tuxtla, the riot police used tear gas to repel angry voters similarly denied suffrage, who launched stones, bottles, and corncobs at Government Palace windows in retaliation. Across the state in Tapachula, a lack of ballots also stirred pitched battles with the state and local police.

From one end of Mexico to the next, the special casillas turned into tinderboxes. In Tijuana, furious voters blocked traffic, and in Juárez, international bridges. Civil unrest was afoot outside specials in Monterrey, Guadalajara, Cuernavaca, and Cancún. Mobs marched on the IFE bunker in the extreme south of Mexico City, tried to vault the steel fence, and were driven off by troops, "granaderos" (the capital's Tac Squad), and police dogs.

Ironically, the assignment of only 300 ballots to each special polling place had been the PRD's idea. Fearful that a surfeit of ballots in the specials would be abused by PRI "alchemists," Cárdenas's reps to the IFE had fought to limit the number distributed in the 679 such casillas set up around the country. The PRI government, ever alert to exploit electoral loopholes, had simply sent "carrousels" (motorized multiple voters) of public employees to exhaust the supply early.

Driving the Valley of Chalco in the misery belt just outside the capital on election morning, one could not deny the hugeness of the turnout—ultimately quantified at 35 million voters, 77% of the electorate in a nation where usually less than half the eligible voters ever cast a ballot. Many were voting for the first time. In Santiago Cuatenco, under the Popocatepetl volcano, old Indian women were instructed by the President of the casilla how to mark the insignia of the PRI. Such illegalities went unchecked—in ten polling places visited, only one featured a PRD representative.

Chalco is about as deep as "México Profundo" gets. A million barely-employed Mexicans live in its cinder block hovel and raw sewage ditch colonies—the men work as bootblacks or wipe windshields on Mexico City streets, the women are often domestic servants. Most everyone here migrated from somewhere else, Oaxaca or Guerrero or Chiapas, refugees from the decapitalized countryside. In 1988, Cuauhtémoc Cárdenas won the valley of Chalco two to one. In 1989, Carlos Salinas established the "Solidarity" program here so that Cárdenas would never win Chalco again.

In Xico, "the cradle of Solidarity" where the poorest of Chalco's poor are hidden, Doña Lupe, a "lideresa" (leader) of the local "ambulantes" (street vendors) was up early, knocking on what passes for front doors here, turning out the vote for the PRI. "Colosio, yes, he was good—it's a pity that they killed him," she told *El Financiero*, doubling her ballot and stuffing it through the slot of the "urna." "This Zedillo for whom I have just voted, it's sad—he will be a puppet of those above him..."

In the dusty Chalco plaza that afternoon, under the great Solidarity billboard, hundreds of voters, erased from voting lists in their local polling places, seethed in the heat. Some suggested that the "urnas," abandoned by queasy officials, should be torched. Others protected them. The housewives clustered all around me were frantic with anxiety. They had to have their voting cards punched or local PRI authorities would not allow them to enroll their children when school began two weeks hence. The moment defined the August 21st fracaso for me. There is just no legal way to win an election from a state party that barters votes for school enrollment, free milk programs, a job, a wedge of waterproofed cardboard for your roof, even a place to bury your dead—the PRI controls the public graveyards throughout Mexico. Cuauhtémoc Cárdenas had banked everything on winning the vote of the poor but the poor, precisely because they are the weakest and most disprotected constituency in the Mexican construct, are the most susceptible to the pressures and manipulations of the PRI government.

* * *

The depth of the Cárdenas defeat was evident early. No longer would it take days for the votes to be counted and a winner declared. In 1994, NAFTA brought exit polls and quick counts to the electoral banquet here. A few minutes after the 6 P.M. poll closing, the *Washington Post* had numbers: Cárdenas had lost by 30%, Diego by 20. In accordance with IFE dictates, public release of the early returns was prohibited but out on Insurgentes Norte, in the PRI's mausoleum compound where just five months previous he had stood above Luis Donaldo's bier, Ernesto Zedillo was already giving the international press triumphal interviews, intimating magnanimously that his government might just include members of the defeated opposition. At 11 P.M., the National Chamber of the Radio and Television Industry (CNIRT), which had reserved first rights on broadcasting its own quick count, gave Zedillo upwards of 50%—the same slice the Chamber had awarded him in its pre-election day polls. Cárdenas was in the mid-teens. Around midnight, it was evident to even his most diehard supporters that Cuauhtémoc had not been elected president. In a packed-to-the-gunnels 19th floor press conference at the Sheraton on Reforma, the Ingeniero reminded reporters that the PRD had gone into the election under protest. He did not say that he had lost but he did not say that he had won either. Contrary to the IFE's claims of election day tranquility, there had been many irregularities. Many in attendance who had followed behind the Engineer for years, were close to tears. The candidate ended the session defiantly—he had invited his people to the plazas of the country at noon the next day and he was going to the Zócalo whether or not the authorities tried to bar his presence.

At 12:10, with not 15% of the casillas yet counted, El Jefe Diego took to the tube to virtually concede defeat, announcing that he was returning to private life. And just before 3:00 in the morning, Jorge Carpizo, as president of the IFE'S General Council which had been in session since the polls opened, called out the official preliminary results: 47.1% for Zedillo, 31.25% for Fernández de Cevallos, and 15.49% to Cárdenas. The numbers had been running since early evening and did not stop running for days, precisely what the IFE had been assigned to do. It had been the absence of numbers in 1988, the notorious system crash, that had so thoroughly poisoned the air. Now, what the numbers actually said was not as important as their uninterrupted flow across the giant screens. The drift was crystal clear. After seven years on the road to this election day Armageddon, Cuauhtémoc Cárdenas's crusade for democratic change had run head-on into the same 75-ton Kenworth truck that had taken Amado Avendaño not quite out of the Chiapas governor's race.

REBELLION FROM THE ROOTS

* * *

The incredulity and impotence was palpable on the faces of those gathered on the Zócalo the next noon. Knots of Cárdenas's people, many of them Convencionistas as well, formed circles and debated what to do next. Now that the electoral option had crashed, picking up the gun had appeal. Others argued for peaceful resistance. The Ingeniero and an enraged Rosario Ibarra spoke to 30,000 supporters from a splintered truck bed. The battle over the ballots in the special casillas had proved that the voting lists were tainted, just as the PRD had been warning for months now. Cárdenas insisted "fraud isn't defeat—its fraud! I'm not claiming victory—I don't know who won." Cuauhtémoc's options were not numerous. Once again, he summoned his people to the Zócalo, the following Saturday, for a maximum protest rally to "clean up" the election. "The electoral game just doesn't work," spat a Mario Saucedo, leader of the PRD's Trisecta, the most radical current, and an old urban guerrillero himself, and stalked out of the Zócalo. 500 snarling Cardenistas launched a 13 mile hike down Tlalpan Avenue towards the IFE where they fought the Granaderos for hours. The long-predicted post electoral resistance appeared to have kicked in.

There is little question that fraud, as it had been in 1988, was pervasive at all levels of the August 21st election. The Civic Alliance, which sent 15,000 volunteer observers to 20 states, calculated that voters with valid credentials were erased ("rasurado") from voting lists in 65% of the 96,000 casillas installed all over the country. Over one million votes were annulled by PRI-selected election officials. 50,000 votes were invalidated because they were cast for Marcos or Camacho or Colosio or the late comedian Cantinflas (who, wags wag, had been the real winner in many previous Mexican elections). An estimated half million citizens had been deprived of their votes because of PRI "carrousels" in the special casillas. Del Villar claimed over 3,000 polling stations registered more votes than voters, the famous PRI "tacos." The indelible ink to prevent multiple voting washed off with industrial detergents. In a third of the casillas, noted the Alianza, the ballot was not secret—Alliance observers filmed PRI officials marking ballots for voters in La Montaña. In Altamirano, Chiapas, observers filmed the military filming voters—Alliance observers paired off with "internationals" from Global Exchange, an increasingly visible player in Mexico's NGO orbit.

Operating out of offices on Reforma with 30 phonelines rented on the NED grant, the Alliance served as the key clearing house for thousands of incidents of electoral chicanery. Predictably, Alianza phone lines were cut for four hours on election day. Bomb threats repeatedly kept Alliance workers away from their desks. Alianza observer training sessions in Guerrero and Tabasco states were raided by local police searching for guerrillas and weapons.

Much of the manipulation that occurred August 21st did so silently, on computers moving results around between secret bunkers. Covert computation centers were discovered by the opposition in Puebla and Hermosillo (Sonora), Jalapa (Veracruz) and the state government palace in Chilpancingo, Guerrero. Down the street from me in the old quarter of Mexico City, a friend's sons were hired by PRIistas to transmit numbers from neighborhood casillas to a mysterious receiving center that was not the IFE.

Indeed, something weird was happening with the IFE's computerized tallies. 9% of the polling places, 8,000 casillas, were never registered on the PREP preliminary reporting system. There appeared to be a parallel computation system located outside of IFE headquarters ("Cenarrep II"). 48 hours after the election, a breathless Carpizo announced that a sinister attempt to introduce a virus into IFE computers had been thwarted.

As the "actas"—the tally sheets verifying the preliminary results modemed from the polling stations—poured into the basement of the IFE bunker, reporters from *La Jornada* and *El Financiero* began to peruse them. The anomalies were staggering—at one Nueva Casa Grande, Chihuahua casilla, 400 voters cast ballots but 1,200 ballots were extracted from the ballot box. When the reporters sought to photograph the "actas," IFE bigwigs clamped down—flashbulbs might cause the ink to fade on the pages. Besides which everything was hunky dory, insisted Jesús Collado, in charge of the Cadel center where the documentation was being concentrated. When Collado pulled three acts at random from the stacks to demonstrate their legitimacy, two of them manifested flagrant irregularities. The IFE subsequently closed down the basement center to public viewing.

Despite the many faces of the fraud, the international press saw no problems with the election. To the *New York Times*, the elections had been "the cleanest in memory." Democrat and Republican National Institute electoral "visitors" agreed that everything had been on the up and up. Former National Democrat Party fundraiser Paul Kirk called the irregularities "irrelevant." U.S. Ambassador James Jones told a press conference that such irrelevancies wouldn't change the final results. Bill Clinton promptly tendered his congratulations to Ernesto Zedillo. So did Fidel Castro. So did (huh!) Nelson Mandela.

Jim Jones's Yanqui pragmatism was not off the wall. The truth is that if all the votes stolen and subverted by the

PRI's election day mischief were laid end to end, Cuauhtémoc Cárdenas would still not be the president of Mexico today. Sure, despite the fact that the PRI had been preparing to bury him and his party every minute of every day since July 6th, 1988, the Ingeniero had received 300,000 more votes than he did six years previous. The bad news is that he had lost the election to Ernesto Zedillo by 10 million votes. The PRI steamroller had flattened Cárdenas's crusade for democracy three to one and reduced the PRD to bystander status in the new congress with just 78 out of nearly 600 seats.

The numbers were daunting—even among the poor, Cuauhtémoc's natural constituency, Cárdenas ran behind Zedillo—and Diego, whose party is a conservative, unabashedly upper middle class one. "The results show that tens of thousands of poor people, the victims of the PRI and its policies, voted for the official party," lamented Marco Rascón the morning after in *La Jornada*, "Deep Mexico is deeply divided."

"PUEBLO PUTO!" read the letters scrawled upon a Coyoacan district wall the day following the election: "The People are Whores!" The sentiment pulsated like a newly-sewn scar.

Since polls closed August 21st, the analysts have been finecombing the results for clues as to why, on the threshold of a new democratic dawn, the people of Mexico turned once again to its old tormentor for succor. Better an old familiar evil than an new unknown good, they explain, citing a hoary adage to explain why a party suspected by many of murdering its own candidate could have obtained 50% of the popular vote.

To not a few Mexicologists, the "vote of fear" was the linchpin of the PRI's gargantuan victory. "I'm afraid," one little kid said to another in the Zedillo commercial.

"Why are you afraid?" asks his companion. "Because my daddy's afraid..."

Of what was the Mexican electorate so fearful? If Ernesto Zedillo isn't elected president, the country's number one banker Roberto Hernández warned the nation in July, instability was on the agenda. A Cárdenas victory would mean capital flight, devaluation, bankruptcy, and destabilization, Hernández admonished the wealthy. Three years previous, Carlos Salinas had gifted Roberto Hernández with the newly re-privatized Banamex, the nation's most profitable banking institution, sold to his syndicate at a bargain basement price.

Going broke was not all that the Mexican people appeared to fear was coming after August 21st. High profile kidnappings (such as that of Mr. Hernández's business partner Alfredo Harp Helú) and assassinations (Cardinal Posadas, Colosio) were adjudged to be unnerving the public, a sense of uncertainty that the PRI exploited to the max. Indeed, ex-special prosecutor Miguel Montes's final report hinting that Mario Aburto was a crypto PRDista may well have scented Cárdenas's fate. Moreover, insinuated the alarmists, Cárdenas would be responsible for postelectoral turmoil if he wasn't solidly slapped down by the electorate. "If you don't vote for Zedillo, there may not be an afterwards," read one mass-produced PRI window sign.

Public insecurity was further exacerbated by the guerrilleros that were supposed to be lurking in the hills of Guerrero where 20,000 "cuernos de chivos" were alleged to be stashed. A four-part Jornada investigation in late July didn't do much to diminish paranoias. Heavily armed rebels roamed the sierras of Puebla, Hidalgo, Veracruz, Oaxaca and Michoacán where the fireworks would begin at dawn on August 22nd according to much-published rumors that now appear to have been deliberate government plants. Even the Pentagon was forecasting generous post-electoral violence.

And then there was Cárdenas's mad-dog colleague, Subcomandante Marcos, promising mayhem in the jungles of Chiapas. "If the PRI doesn't opt for its honorable suicide August 21st, we're going to put it before the firing squad," was one of the Sup's more chilling contributions to the pre-electoral debate. "Zedillo owes Marcos at least a cabinet post for all the votes he brought him," commented *El Financiero* columnist Angel Viveros in a post-electoral observation.

* * *

Despite Marcos's brash broadsides issued rapid-fire prior to election day, the Zapatistas were eerily silent for 72 hours after the fall. The Subcomandante and the EZLN had bet heavily on the outcome, had laid their weapons aside and agreed to follow the rules and regulation of peaceful redress of grievances when and if the fraud came down. Now, many in the civil society the Zapatistas had pledged to follow were looking to the EZs for guidance.

The CCRI's initial communiqué was business-like: the troops had resumed their positions. "The elections in our zone were completed tranquilly, something we cannot say for others." The General Command's observations were confined entirely to the post-electoral situation closest to home—the EZLN underscored that Amado Avendaño had won the governor's seat (the PRI was calling it 51 to 34% for Robledo) and encouraged civil mobilization to defend the victory, as agreed upon by the CND. "The supreme government has bet on a great lie in order to demobilize us," the communiqué advised, advising resistance.

Marcos sent his own message out in the same bundle; an odd note, full of postscripts that blame the "gringos" for bringing the PRI's "carro completo" (sic), cites a chapter in *Don Quixote*, makes a puzzling reference to one "Maríana," and then relates how the old Antonio would always shoot mountain lions through the eye so as not to damage the pelt. The mountain lion "pads on cloud-shod paws" and kills "by looking" at its prey. Hmm. A third communiqué a week later was more to the point: Robledo must abandon his pretense of victory to avoid a bloodbath. Marcos sweetened the pot by offering to send the proclaimed governor cigarettes while he served his sentence in Cerro Hueco.

* * *

Six days after the election, Cuauhtémoc Cárdenas drew 100,000 followers to the Zócalo. Six years previous, after the PRI government had snatched victory from him in the vote count, the Ingeniero had summoned this same sea of brown faces to this same plaza. The faces were still brown, still the color of this earth, still the color of Mexico. But they were fewer now and they did not seem to want to burn down the National Palace as in '88 when firebombs were tossed at its great doors. The chant "El Pueblo votó y Cárdenas ganó!" ("The people voted and Cárdenas won!") sounded hollow in the leaden August air. Now he could not say that he had won, the Ingeniero told his people. He was retiring as a candidate after seven years of relentlessly plying this ungrateful land. The best of Mexico had voted for him (and, by implication, the worst had not). Now the PRD must reconsider its commitment to the electoral track—if the August 21st election was not cleaned up and the government separated from the process, the Party of the Aztec Sun would withdraw from all future elections. The PRD would defend its votes with mobilization but only where there was a chance of victory. Chiapas was mentioned, but just in passing. Now it was time to go home. The speech was moving only because it sounded so much like a goodbye. The people were not much stirred and only the announcement that a baby boy had been born to a farm woman from Michoacán behind the stage during the speech, lifted spirits. "You are all the godparents," the proud father told the dissolving gathering.

I walked Tata Santiago, Tata Miguel, and Tata Marcelino back to the bus they had expropriated up in the meseta to bring them to the capital to hear what the Ingeniero had to say. The Purépecha farmers were tense and thoughtful. "I'll never vote again," declared Marcelino, "para qué?" One of the compañeros worried that the plastic loader he had just bought for his .22 was already coming apart. "Bueno, Juanito, cuídate bien" ("Ok, Johnny, take good care"). We embraced. We have known each other a long time, 30 years of social struggle that has borne us sporadic victories and a lot of sour fruit. Now the compañeros were going home to their muddy mountains and rusty .22s with a fading belief in transforming this country anyway except by the gun. It was not a happy ending to a beginning that is already thoroughly soaked in the bitter blood of this country.

* * *

Despite the Tatas' pessimism, much has changed in Mexico since the Zapatista Army of National Liberation padded into San Cristóbal after midnight on that frigid New Year's eve, a distant, frozen memory now. The civil society has grown stronger and the Indian peoples more determined than ever to take their proper place in history right now. Marcos and the Zapatistas have shown their countrymen and women that audacity—and poetry—can alter the balance between the basement of Mexico in which

18 million citizens continue to live in extreme poverty and the penthouse where Salinas's 24 new billionaires lap up the neo-liberal luxury. But the longest-ruling state party in the known universe, the "perfect dictatorship," as Vargas Llosa once labeled it, continues to usurp power and intends to do so long into the 21st century. Despite all the drama that has convulsed this year of living dangerously, for too many Mexicans, democratic change still remains on ice in the deep freeze of history.

The images of these past months unspool so rapidly that I have a hard time holding them up to the light of permanence. One that keeps coming back to me is that of the last minutes of Marcos's convention deep in the Lacandón jungle. "Z-a-a-a-p-a-a-a-t-a-a-a Viiiiiiveeee!" hollered the old campesino leader Efrén Capiz, who had been kept off the stage for hours because he is not a big fan of the electoral option so popular at the CND. Hunched in front of the twin flags that had miraculously endured the great storm the night before, Capíz began his incantation: "Zapata lives and lives!" he urged the damp convencionistas, "y la lucha sigue y sigue. Y sigue y sigue y sigue y sigue y sigue y sigue y sigue y sigue y sigue y sigue y sigue," thundered the old farmer, gathering strength, his fists pumping at the unkind heavens, "and goes on and goes on and goes on and goes on and goes on and goes on and...." Capíz did this for a long time, maybe ten minutes, until the Convention's exasperated presidents finally nudged him away from the microphone.

He had made his point.

Index

A

abortion-on-demand law, 75
Aburto Martínez, Mario, 310, 316-319, 323-324, 327, 400
ACIEZ. *see* Independent Alliance of Campesinos-Emiliano Zapata
Acosta, MariClaire, 135-136
Adrazo, Carlos, 382
AFL-CIO, 47
Agrarian Reform, 258, 259
Aguascalientes, 365, 369, 372, 374
Aguayo, Sergio, 40, 128, 130, 131, 135
Aguilar, Caralampio, 257-258
Aguilar, Jaime, 379-380
Aguilar Camín, Hector, 128, 320
Aguilár Talamontes, Rafael, 339
Aguirre Beltrán, Gonzalo, 57
Aguirre Franco, Felipe, 158
Alejandra, Dr., 114, 286
Alianza Civica. *see* Civic Alliance
Alvarado, Pedro de, 64
Americas Watch, 122, 126
Amnesty International, 113, 126, 130-132, 158
Ana María, Comandante, 19
ANCIEZ. *see* Emiliano Zapata National Alliance of Independent Farmers
Aparicio, Gabino, 389
Araujo, Hugo Andrés, 276
Arellano Félix brothers, 303, 305
ARIC. *see* Rural Association of Collective Interest
Aridjis, Homero, 265, 320
Arizmendi, Felipe, 225-226
Armed Forces of National Liberation (FALN), 273
Army, Mexican. *see* Mexican Federal Army
Aspe, Pedro, 321
assassinations, 312-313, 327, 381, 400
Aubanel, María, 326
Autonomous University. *see* Universidad Nacional Autónoma de Mexico
Avendaño, Amado, 8-11, 18, 82, 104, 110, 297, 349, 377-380, 401
Aviles, Jaime, 368, 374
Aztec-Mexicas, 57-58, 61

B

Bailey, John, 44
Balboa, Juan, 157, 264
Bañuelos, Juan, 373, 379
Barbach, Ann Louise, 297, 299, 316, 342
Barbosa, Maximiliano, 177

Index

Bardacke, Frank, 167

Barragán, Marcelino, 158, 272

Barrios, Gutiérrez, 313

Bartlett, Manuel, 336, 386

Bartolomé de las Casas. *see* Las Casas, Bartolomé de

El Barzón, 177

Batel, Celeste, 314

Bazua, Fernando, 386

Bellinghausen, Herman, 73, 119, 186, 236, 259, 369

Benítez, Federico, 308, 326-327

Blom, Franz, 253

Boff, Cleodoves, 218, 224

Boff, Leónardo, 218, 224

bombings as acts of sabotage, 104-106

Bonfils, Guillermo, 59, 64, 67

Borrego, Genaro, 387

Briseño, Guillermo, 367

Bruce, Leo, 89

Buendía, Manuel, 322-323

Burguete, Araceli, 69, 158

Burston-Marsteller, 47

Bush, George, 46, 133

C

Cabañas, Lucio, 94, 105, 175, 271

Calderón, Othón, 123

Calles, Plutarco Elias, 313

Calva, José Luis, 240, 241

Camacho Solís, Manuel, *198. see also* National Action Party (PAN)

at Colosio funeral, 313-315

as conciliator to ELZN, 147-149, 162-165, 171-172

at EZLN peace talks, 229, 232-235, 329

mayor of Mexico City, 163-164

peace accord, works on, 344, 356-360

political ambitions, 167-169, 246-247, 304, 360

release of Castellanos Domínguez, 182-185

response to EZLN demands, 246

Camero, Hector, 275

Camp, Roderic I., 44, 95, 101, 121

Campa, Valentín, 152

Canadian Interfaith delegation, 125-126

Candelaria, María, 66

Canek, Jacinto, 54, 63

Canoen Mundo, Marcelo, 173

Cantu, Eloy, 102

Capiz, Efrén, 404

Caravan for Peace, *193*, 213-214, 364

Caravan of Caravans, 364-365, 368

Cárdenas, Cuauhtémoc, *199. see also* Party of the Democratic Revolution (PRD)

at Colosio funeral, 314
contacts with EZLN, 178, 347-353
debate, 344-346
election defeat, 391, 394-396, 399, 402-403
election results (1988), 74, 335-336
embraces CND program, 375-376
presidential campaign (1988), 74, 95, 148, 152, 334-339, 389, 393
presidential campaign (1994), 333-335, 382-387, 389, 402-403
support of EZLN, 333, 338
Cárdenas, Cuauhtémoc, jr., 342
Cárdenas, Juan Carlos, 89, 90-91
Cárdenas, Lázaro, 70, 275, 334-335, 342, 349, 351
Carpizo, Jorge, 31, 129, 131-132, 146-147, 165, 321, 381, 385-387
Carranza, Venustiano, 69, 71, 201-202
Carrasco, Bernabé, 219
Carrasco, Deodorio, 174
Carrasco, Pita, 365
Casey, William, 37, 38, 43
Castañeda, Jorge G., 31, 35, 135, 287
Castellanos, Rosario, 156
Castellanos Domínguez,
Absalón, 71, 113, 130-131, 150, 155-172, 179-185
Castellanos Domínguez, Ernesto, 159-160, 260
Castellanos Herrerias, Absalón, 181
Castes, War of the, 64, 67
Castillo, German, 305, 306, 309
Castillo, Herberto, 342, 349
Castillo Perraza, Carlos, 332
Castro, Fidel, 398
Cathedral of Paz. see San Cristóbal, Cathedral of
Caves, Men of the, 278-279
Cazes, Daniel, 367
CCRI. see Clandestine Revolutionary Indigenous Committee
CENCOS, 152
Center for Constitutional Rights, 125
Center for Investigation and National Security (CISEN), 307, 311
Center for the Study of Armed Movements, 286
Central Independiente de Obreros Agrícolas y Campesinos. see CIOAC
Central Intelligence Agency, 43, 44
CEOIC. see State Council of Campesino and Indigenous Organizations
Cerro Hueco, 131-132

Cevallos, Diego Fernández de, 332
CFE. *see* Federal Electrical Commission
Chamulas, 65-67, 69, 81
Chiapas. *see also* Zapatista Army of National Liberation
death count in war, 150-151
demographics, 71-73
description by Marcos, 77-79
elections and voting, 73-74, 242
history, 64-65, 68
land distribution, 69-70, 212, 240-241. *see also* Mexican Constitution. Article 27
March for Peace, 151
penal code, 242
political insurrection, 210-212
rebellion, roots, 18-19, 53-71, 271-272
supernatural beliefs, 66-67, 69
Chilam Balam, 63, 71
Chinameca, 201-205
Chomsky, Noam, 136, 367
Chrétien, Jean, 310
CIDH. *see* InterAmerican Human Rights Commission
CIES. *see* Southeast Investigation and Study Center
Cincinnati Plan, 221
CIOAC, 33, 70, 76, 210, 354
CISEN. *see* Center for Investigation and National Security
Citizens' Defense Group (UDCO), 79, 214
Citizens' Fair Trade Campaign, 125
Ciudad Real. *see* San Cristóbal de las Casas
Civic Alliance (Alianza Civica), 388, 396-397
civil society. *see* Mexico. civil society
civilian population casualties, 94, 96, 104, 110, 123, 130, 135, *189*, *194*
Clandestine Revolutionary Indigenous Committee (CCRI), 19, 30, 110-111, 171, 179, 208, 232, 315-316, 340. *see also* Marcos, Subcomandante; Zapatista Army of National Liberation
Clandestine Revolutionary Indigenous Committees (CCRI), 287-288
Clara Ruiz, Manuel, 28
Clark, Ramsey, 104, 124-125, 126
Clark Alfaro, Victor, 324
Clinton, William, 46, 103
Clouthier, Manuel, 382

Index

CNC, 113, 276

CND. *see* National Democratic Convention

CNDH. *see* National Human Rights Commission

CNIRT. *see* National Chamber of the Radio and Television Industry

CNN, 44

CNPA. *see* Zapatista Coordinating Body of the Plan of Ayala

CNPI. *see* National Coordinating Body of Indian Peoples

cocaine. *see* drug traffic

COCEI, 174

Coello Trejo, Javier, 159, 181

COFALASA, 260

Collado, Jesús, 398

Colosio, Luis Donaldo. *see also* Institutional Revolutionary Party (PRI)
  assassination, 304-312
  investigation of death, 322-328
  political campaign, 144-145, 168-170, 236
  political heir of Salinas, 12, 148

Columbus, Christopher, 53, 56, 61

Columbus Lighthouse, 57

Comillas, Marquis of, 254

Commissioner of Peace and Reconciliation. *see*

Camacho Solís, Manuel

Common Front of Social Organizations, 80

CONAC-LN, 354, 358, 364

Concha, Miguel, 152-153

Confederación Nacional Campesino. *see* CNC

CONPAZ, 101, 117, 127-128, 139

Constantino Kanter, Jorge, 213, 214, 244, 320

Continental Wholesale Florists, 263

Corazón a Corazón, 364

Córdoba Montoya, José María, 31, 225, 226, 322

Corripio Ahumada, Ernesto, 225-226

Cortez, Hernán, 57, 58

Covarrubias, Pepe, 76

Crane, Tom, 117, 118, 122

CREACH, 81

Cuauhtémoc, 57-58

Culej, Manuel Moshen, 124-125

D

Danzos Palomino, Ramón, 152

De Voss, Jan, 253

Declaration of the Lacandón Jungle, 17, 86, 107, 290

Declaration of the Lacandón Jungle, Second, 360-361

DeGyves, Leopoldo, 174

Del Paso, Fernando, 367

Del Villar, Samuel, 386, 397

Díaz, Porfirio, 201, 254

Díaz, Socorro, 34

Díaz Cuscat, Pedro, 67

Díaz Ordaz, Gustavo, 271, 272

Domínguez, Belisario, 155

Domínguez, Genaro, 58, 222

Dominican Republic, 56-57

Doyle, Kate, 41

Drug Enforcement Administration (U.S.), 41, 42

drug war, 39, 40-42

drug wars, 95, 139

Duby, Trude, 253

E

Echeverría, Luis, 259-261, 273-274, 314

Economist Intelligence Unit, 144

election day (1994), 390-394

election fraud, 336, 340, 350, 386-389, 390-394, 395-398

electorate voting, 392-393, 399-400

electronic media and campaigns, 339, 388

Elias (teacher), 68-69

Emiliano Zapata National Alliance of Independent Farmers (ANCIEZ), 25, 80-82

Encounter of Two Worlds, 55

Enríquez Cabot, Juan, 164

Estévez, Dolia, 38, 43, 45, 135

Estrada, José Luis, 29-30

European Community-Mexico trade pact (1991), 135

E.Z.L.N. *see* Zapatista Army of National Liberation

F

Fabio Beltrones, Manlio, 321

Fábregas Puig, Andrés, 172

FALN, 273

Farabundo Martí Liberation Front, 107, 108, 281

Federal Electoral Institute (IFE), 243, 385, 394, 395, 397-398

Federal Electrical Commission, sabotage of, 104-105

Federal Voters Registry (RFE), 335-336

Fellowship of Reconciliation, 123, 126

Fenner, Justus, 15-16

Fernández de Cevallos, Diego, 344-346, 384, 395, 399

Figueroa, Rubén, jr., 176

Flores, Liliana, 300

Flores Montiel, Ignacio, 76

FMLN, 107, 108, 281

Foreign Broadcast Information Service, 44

Foreign Press Association, 127

Franco, Aguirre, 225-226
Fray Bartolomé de las Casas Human Rights Center, 24, 116, 127-128, 377
Fray Bartolomé de las Casas Indigenous Congress, 261
Fray Francisco de la Vittoria Center, 152
Free Enterprise Study Center, 223
Fuentes, Carlos, 128, 178, 321, 366

G

Galeano, Eduardo, 367
Galindo, Ignacio, 67, 85
Gallardo, José Francisco, 121, 133
Gálvez, Andulio, 71, 158
Gamaz, Arturo, 271, 278
Gantin, Bernard, 224
García, Amalia, 342
García, Armando, 91-92
García, Domiro, 305
García de León, Antonio, 66, 156, 211, 368, 373
Garduño, Roberto, 69, 92, 132
Garrido Canabal, Tomás, 74, 75
Gay Cultural Circle, 76
Geneva Convention, 104, 111, 123, 126, 163
Gilly, Adolfo, 347, 348, 349, 351, 352, 353
Gironella, Alfredo, 367

Glickman, Dan, 44-45
La Gloria, 66
Godínez, Miguel, 25, 26, 50, 86, 87, 122, 123, 130
Golden, Tim, 109, 209, 257, 292, 358
Golonchán, massacre at, 70-71, 157
Gómez, Pablo, 352
Gómez, Salvador, 66
Gómez Checheb, Augustina, 67
Gómez Maza, Paco, 363
Gómez Morín, Manuel, 331
Gómez Urquiza, José, 335
Gonzales Torres, Jorge, 341
González, Pablo, 202
González Blanco Garrido, Patrocinio, 31-32, 74-76, 80, 81, 145-146, 264
González Casanova, Pablo, 373, 375
González de Alba, Luis, 301-302
Gordillo, Aaron, 33
Gore, Albert, 47
Gore-Perot NAFTA debate, 136-137
Gortari, Carlos Salinas de. *see* Salinas, Carlos
Granados Chapa, Miguel Angel, 320
Group of San Angel, 366
Guajardo, Jesús, 202-204
Guatemala, 40, 42, 43, 44, 65, 107-108

Index

Guatemalan Guerrilla Army of the Poor, 55
Guerrero (state), 175-177
Gutiérrez, Gustavo, 218
Gutiérrez Barrios, Fernando, 76, 170
Guzmán, Chapo, 42, 305

H

Hahns Arias, Hans Karl, 29
Hank González, Carlos, 241, 314, 321, 322, 387, 388-389
Hank Rhon, Carlos, 263
Hank Rhon, Jorge, 263
Harp Helú, Alfredo, 400
Henríquez, Elio, 33, 34, 81, 205-206
Henriquéz, Juan, 247
Hernández, Antonio, 33, 75, 80, 173
Hernández, Lázaro, 214, 280
Hernández, Manuel, 159
Hernández, Roberto, 400
Hernández Galicia, Joaquín, 95, 285
Hernández López, Marcos Jerónimo, 296
Herrerias, Elsy, 155, 161
Hertzog, Werner, 370
Hidalgo, Miguel, 294
Hinojosa, Oscar, 209
Hirsch, Schulamis, 18
homosexuals, 76, 299
Horton, John, 37-38
hospital, Solidarity, 73

human rights defended, 100-101, 115, 117, 120-121, 122, 128, 133, 146
Human Rights Watch, 122
Humberto, Comandante, 245-246

I

Ibarra, Epigmenio, 110, 205, 366, 385
Ibarra de Piedra, Rosario, 152, 274, 349, 350, 373, 374, 383, 396
Ibarrarán, Pablo, 92
IFE. *see* Federal Electoral Institute
Immigration Control Act, 138
IMSS-Coplamar clinic, 91, 93, 123
Independent Alliance of Campesinos-Emiliano Zapata (ACIEZ), 280
Independent Proleterian Movement (MPI), 354
Indians of Mexico. *see* Mexico: indigenous peoples
Indigenous, Black, and Popular Resistance, 55, 56
Institute for Cultural Ecology, 266
Institute for International Strategic Studies, 94
Institutional Revolutionary Party (PRI). *see also* Colosio, Luis Donaldo;

Salinas, Carlos; Zedillo, Ernesto
  campaign finances, 387-388
  Chiapas votes, 73-74
  control of Federal Electoral Institute, 385-386
  longest ruling state party, 12, 404
  presidential candidates, 312, 320-322, 343
  re-organization, 146-147
  work against Cárdenas, 338-339
InterAmerican Human Rights Commission (CIDH), 135
International Coffee Organization, 280
International Red Cross, 126, 180, 229
International Treaty Council, 126
Irma, Captain, 288-289, 291
Ituarte, Gonzalo, 11, 357, 367

J
Javier Garrido, Luis, 236
John Paul, (Pope), 56-57, 224
Johnson, David, 103
Jones, James, 137, 398
Jornadas (Workdays) for Peace and Reconciliation, 209-215, 228, 230-245
journalists. see press and media
Juan Carlos de Borbón, 55

Juárez, Benito, 60
Juarista National Army, 244

K
Kapuscinsky, Rysward, 367
Kirk, Paul, 398
Kleist, Trina, 295, 355
Krauze, Enrique, 248, 367

L
La Jornada, 33, 105
Lacandón, 251-267
Lacandón jungle
  agriculture, 257-258
  Las Cañadas, 258-259, 262, 278-279
  ecological reserve, 261-262, 263
  environmentalism, 265-267
  history, 251-255
  land distribution, 260-261, 265
  logging and forests, 253-255, 260, 264
  Mexican Revolution, 254
  settlers, 255-257, 258
Lacon-Tums, 64, 65, 252
LaFalce, John, 133
Las Casas, Bartolomé de, 14, 53-54, 65, 218
Latell, Brian, 37, 38, 45
Lázaro, Yolanda, 307, 308
Leñero, Vicente, 86, 93, 208, 209, 285
Léon, García de, 338
Leyva, Xicoténcatl, 303, 322

Index

Leyva, Xochital, 262
Leyva, Xochitl, 379
liberation theology, 218-224, 277
Liga Comunista 23rd de Septiembre, 271, 273
Línea Proletaria, 276-277
Llaguno, Pepe, 219
Llosa, Vargas, 404
Loaza, Soledad, 224
Lomas Taurinas colony, 306-307
Lombardo, Marcela, 388
Lona, Arturo, 219
Long, Thomas, 100, 110
López, Bruno, 97, 371
López Angel, Domingo, 80, 173
López Moreno, Javier, 241, 379
López Ortiz, Juan, 90
López Portillo, José, 32, 261-262, 299, 314
Lorenzo, Augustín, 98
Lucero Navárrez, Humberto, 123

M

Macías, Rodolfo, 318
Madero, Pablo Emilio, 341, 349
Madrazo, Jorge, 118, 119, 129-130, 379
Madrid, Miguel de la, 148, 157, 314, 323, 337
Mandela, Nelson, 367, 398

March, Ignacio, 265
Marcos, Subcomandante, 190, 192. see also Zapatista Army of National Liberation
  amnesty proposal, response to, 165-167
  Battle of Rancho Nuevo, 84-86
  on Colosio killing, 312
  communique, 171, 205, 223, 365
  interviews, 206-207, 208, 282-283
  invitations to CND, 367
  letter to Clinton, 103
  on NAFTA, 20-21
  name chosen, 278
  at peace talks, 214-215
  Plaza of 31st of March, 17-19, 20
  Política Popular brigade, 278
  self-description, 294-302
  spokesperson for EZLN, 301
  threatens PRI, 401-402
Marín, Felipe, 253
Marín, Luis, 64, 65
Martin del Campo, Jesús, 108
Martínez, Paulino, 361
Martínez Soriano, Felipe, 105
Martínez Verdugo, Arnaldo, 292
Marxist Leninism, 261, 292
Marxist-Leninism, 273

Index

masks, 18, 111, 300-301

Matsui, Robert, 134

Mayoral, Rodolfo, 323, 324

Mayoral, Vicente, 310-311, 323, 324

Mayorga, Cherubim, 352, 377

Mazariegos, Diego de, 62, 64, 81, *187*

McCaughan, Michael, 116-117, 296

McGehee, Ralph, 43

Mckinsey & Co., 386

Meade Treviño, Walter, 296

Medellin Council of Latin American Bishops, 218, 275

media coverage, 48-50, 97, 99, 182-183, 205-206, 231-233, 237, 248, 292, 370-371. *see also* Televisa

Medina, Ofelia, 373, 379, 391

Menchaca, Gastón, 9, 11

Menchú, Rigoberta, 55, 56, 126-127, 314

Méndez Arceo, Sergio, 219

Messina, Enrique, 318

Mexican Academy for Human Rights, 128

Mexican Academy of Human Rights, 158

Mexican Air Force, 19, 86, 95, 97-100, 102-104, 109, 113. *see also* Mexican Federal Army

Mexican Communist Party, 177, 292

Mexican Constitution. Article 4, 240

Mexican Constitution. Article 27, 212, 224, 236, 239, 241, 293

Mexican Federal Army. *see also* Mexican Air Force
friendly fire, 28, 100
and human rights, 24, 120-121
killing of police officers, 41, 129
and Ocosingo, 223
supply route to EZLN, 364
training in U.S., 41

Mexican Federal Judicial Police, 41

Mexican Green Environmental Party (PVEM), 341

Mexican military structure, 94-95

Mexican Miracle, 12, 39, 60, 133, 141-143

Mexican revolution (1910-1919), 54-55, 68, 69, 202, 254, 271, 290

Mexican Socialist Party, 334

Mexican Stock Exchange, 106, 120, 141-142

Mexico
civil society, 151, 208, 360-361, 377, 403
economy, 142-144
environmentalism, 262, 263, 265-266, 267

genocide of indigenous peoples, 14, *53-55*, 57
indigenous peoples, 57-60, 239
line of credit from U.S., 321
religion, 221-222, 277-278
women, status of, 288-292
Meyer, Franz, 184
Meyer, Lorenzo, 373, 385
Meza Yeladequi, Jesús, 108, 132, 186
Millán, Porfirio, 23
Minnesota Human Rights Advocates, 50, 126
Mirón, Benito, 354
missionaries, U.S., 221-222
Moctezuma, Pedro, 278
Moguel, Julio, 279
Monsivais, Carlos, 367, 375
Montaña, Gerardo, 305
Montaño, Jorge, 136
Montes, Miguel, 322-327, 400
Montes Azules Biosphere, 261-262, 263
Montoya, Córdoba, 310
Morales, Ignacio, 256
Morales, Mardonio, 221, 224, 227, 256, 276
Morelia (ejido), 113-119, 138-139
Morelos, José María, 175
Moreno, Humberto, 257
Moreno, Samuel, 8
Moreno Toscano, Alejandra, 164, 182

Morquecho, Gaspar, 111, 366
Morris, Walter, 186
Mota Sánchez, Ramón, 310
MPI. *see* Independent Proleterian Movement
Mulroney, Brian, 46
Mundo Maya, 60, 80
Muñoz, Alejandro, 115, 296
Muñoz, Jack Demosthenes, 352, 377
Muñoz Ledo, Porfirio, 334, 349, 383
Mutter, Andrew, 259, 266
Muyrán, Patricia, 213

N

Na'Bolom Institute, 253
NAFTA, 11-12
  and human rights, 125, 133
  impact on farmers, 20-21, 241-242
  and Mexican Stock Exchange, 141
  pro and anti struggle, 47-48
  and U.S. Congress, 30, 45-48, 50-51
narcotics. *see* drug wars
National Action Party (PAN), 303-304, 331-332, 335, 339, 340, 352. *see also* Camacho Solís, Manuel
National Anthropological Museum, 60
National Chamber of the Radio and Television Industry (CNIRT), 394

National Coordinating Body
of Indian Peoples (CNPI),
58, 61, 175
National Democratic
Convention (CND), 361,
363-376, 383
National Human Rights
Commission (CNDH), 22,
41, 116, 118, 119, 128-130,
136, 150, 324
National Indigenous Institute,
58, 70, 79, 115, 156, 174,
180
National Security Archives,
41
National Small Property
Owners Confederation,
212-213
Negroponte, John, 39, 137
North American Free Trade
Agreement. see NAFTA
Núñez, Arturo, 385

O

Obregón, Alvaro, 312-313
Ocana, Gilberto, 132
Occeli, Cecilia, 13, 75
Ocosingo, 87-94, 92-93, 93-
94, 123, 256
Ocotál. see San Isidro Ocotál
OID. see Organization of
Ideological Direction
Ojarasca, 73
Olympic Games, 1968
(Mexico), 121, 158, 272
Olympic Games, 1992

(Spain), 55-56
The Ombudsman. see
Madrazo, Jorge
Organization of American
States, 135
Organization of Ideological
Direction, 276
Orive, Adolfo, 274-277
Ortega, Margarita, 303
Ortiz Arana, Fernando, 313,
321
Ortiz Lara, Sergio, 325
Ortiz Mena, Antonio, 74-75,
387
Osuna, Mercedes, 9
Ovando, Xavier, 389

P

Padrón, Joel, 22, 223, 377
PAN. see National Action
Party
PARM, 340
Party of the Authentic
Mexican Revolution
(PARM), 340
Party of the Aztec Sun. see
Party of the Democratic
Revolution (PRD)
Party of the Cárdenist Front
for National
Reconstruction, 339
Party of the Democratic
Revolution (PRD). see also,
Cárdenas, Cuauhtémoc
anti-democratic sins, 351-
352

Index

beginnings, 334, 336

colors, 383

convention and Avendaño, 377

at EZLM peace talks, 342, 347-348

finances of campaign, 387

in Michoacán, 175

seats in congress, 399

voter registration, 385-386

Party of the Mexican Revolution, 335

Party of the Poor, 94, 105, 273

Payán, Carlos, 128, 373

Paz, Octavio, 178, 248, 300, 320

Pazos, Luis, 223, 285, 320, 359

PDM. *see* UNO-Mexican Democratic Party

Pelosi, Nancy, 133

PEMEX, 266

Pérez Canchola, José, 317, 318-319

Pérez Díaz, Maríano, 353

Pérez Stuart, José, 285

Perot, H. Ross, 47, 49, 170

Petrich, Blanche, 27, 42, 88, 122, 123, 205-207, 290, 352

Physicians for Human Rights, 117, 122

Pichardo, Ignacio, 389

Plaza of Three Cultures killings, 272-273

Política Popular movement, 274, 275, 276, 278

poll-taking, 346, 358, 384

Poniatowska, Elena, 367, 369, 373

Popular Forces of National Liberation, 261

Popular Socialists (PPS), 340, 388

Posadas, Juan Jesús, 30-31, 49, 146, 219, 305

Pozas, Ricardo, 213

PPS. *see* Popular Socialists

PRD. *see* Party of the Democratic Revolution

presidential debate, Mexican, 344-346

press and media, U.S., 48-50

PRI. *see* Institutional Revolutionary Party

Prigione, Giralamo, 224-225, 305

prisoner exchange. *see* Zapatista Army of National Liberation

Procampo, 388

Proceso, 32-33

PROCUP. *see* Revolutionary Party of Workers and Farmers

Pronasol. *see* Solidarity anti-poverty program

Protestants in Mexico, 221-222

PSUM. *see* Unified Socialist Party

Index

PUA. *see* Union America Party

PVEM. *see* Mexican Green Environmental Party

Q

Quincentennial anniversary, 55-56, 61-62

Quincentennial observance, Indians', 55-57, 61-62

R

racism, 59-60, 270

Ramírez, Carlos, 103, 149, 181, 320, 332-333, 352

Ramírez Lobato, Pablo, 389

Ramóna, Comandante, 233, 242, 290

ranchers, private armies of, 256

Rancho Nuevo, 83-86, *189*, *194*

Rascón, Marco, *399*

rebellion. *see* Chiapas: rebellion

refugees, 101, 127, 255

resources, war for, 263

Reveillo Bazán, Antonio, 13, 121, 149, 165

Revolutionary Agrarian Law, 241, 265-266

Revolutionary Law of Women, 290-291

Revolutionary Party of Workers and Farmers-Popular Unity (PROCUP), 105

Reyes, Ricardo, 389

Reyes Aguilar, Rodolfo, 89, 90-91

RFE. *see* Federal Voters Registry

Ricardo Pozas Caravan for Peace, 213, 214

Ríos Montt, Efrain, 157

Rius (Eduardo Del Rio), 298

Rivapalacios, Rodolfo, 308, 323, 324-326, 327

Rivera, David, 92

Rivera, Diego, 60

Robberson, Tod, 326

Robbins, Sandina, 96, 237

Robledo, Eduardo, 159, 172, 378, 401, 402

Rodgers, Ross, 49-50, 51

Rodriguez, Ramón, 380

Rodríguez, Richard, 319

Rojas, Carlos, 174

Rojas, Gonzallo, 296

Rojas, Marcos, 296

Rolando, Major, 186, 269-270, 293, 296-297, 328

Román, José Antonio, 225

Román Robles, Cayetano, 253

Romero, Marco Antonio, 23

Romo, Fernando, 226, 227

Romo, Pablo, 22, 24, 223, 228, 296

Rubio, Agustin, 379-380

Ruffo, Ernesto, 303, 324

Ruiz, Gaudencio, 173

Ruiz, Margarito, 173

Ruiz, Pablo, 84
Ruiz, René, 155, 160, 161, 162, 179
Ruiz, Samuel, *198*
  abortion law, 75
  as EZLN mediator, 162
  helps Lacandón settlers, 261
  and human rights, 101, 125
  inciter of rebellion, 21, 80, 139, 226, 227
  liberation theologian, 218, 219-226, 277
  Línea Proletaria, 277
  meets with EZLN, 356-357
  at peace talks, 228, 232, 247
  release of Castellanos Domíniguez, 182, 184
Ruiz Anchondo, Patricia, 235
Ruiz Cortines, Adolfo, 255
Rural Association of Collective Interest (ARIC), 220

S

Sabines, Juan, 157
Sabines Pérez, Julio, 264
Saint Vincent de Paul nuns, 213
Salcedo, Roberto, 246, 357
Salinas, Carlos. *see also* Institutional Revolutionary Party (PRI)
  amnesty for EZLN proposed, 165
  cabinet shakeup, 141
  ceasefire offer, 99, 107, 110, 111, 149-150, 207
  Chiapas votes, 73-74
  confrontation with Zapatistas postponed, 35
  dealings with Chiapas, 145, 146, 211
  dedicates hospital, 73
  denies rebellion, 210
  election (1988), 335, 336
  fires Secretary of Interior, 76
  Mexican Miracle, 12, 39, 60, 133, 141-143
  and NAFTA, 35, 46
  names Colosio successor, 148, 170
  New Years day (1994), 11-14
  turn over power, 387
  use of military, 120, 122
Salinas, Carlos M. (Amnesty International), 131-132
Salinas de Gortari, Raúl, 276
El Salvador Indian massacre (1932), 55
San Cristóbal, Cathedral of, 209, 217-218, 228
San Cristóbal de las Casas, 14-15, 77, *197*
San Cristóbal Municipal Archives, 16, *196*
San Isidro Ocotál, 23-25
Sánchez, Tranquilino, 323
Sánchez Galicia, Jesús. *see* Meza Yeladequi, Jesús

Index

Sánchez Ortega, José Antonio, 311, 324, 326

Sandinistas, 37, 280-281

Santis, Caralampio, 390

Santis, Severino, 114-119

Santis Gómez, Ermelindo, 114-119

Santis López, Sebastián, 114-119

Santler, Helmet, 101

Sarmiento, Sergio, 320, 359

Saucedo, Mario, 342, 396

Scheer, Robert, 136-137

Scherer, Julio, 32, 33

SEDENA, 86, 99, 100, 103-104, 122

Serra Puche, Jaime, 242

Serrano, Irma, 352, 378, 382

Setzer Marseille, Elmar, 31, 76, 145

Shattuck, John, 137

Sisa, Bartolina, 54

slavery, 65, 68

Snow, Clyde Collins, 117-118, 122

El Sol, 107, 108

Solidarity anti-poverty program, 72, 73, 84, 169, 240, 242, 306, 393

Solorzano family, 89

Sosa, Yon, 261

Southeast Investigation and Study Center (CIES), 262, 263, 265

Southern Army of Liberation, 289

State Council of Campesino and Indigenous Organizations (CEOIC), 173, 210, 353-354, 356

State Forestry Patrol, 23, 264

Stavenhagen, Rodolfo, 129

Stockwell, John, 43

Stone, Les, 284

Suárez Culebro, Romeo, 26

Suárez Rivera, Adolfo, 163

Susana, Captain, 291

T

Talavea, Carlos, 219

Televisa, 21-22, 62, 178, 234. see also media coverage

Tidball-Binz, Morris, 131-132

El Tiempo, 8-9

Tierra y Libertad (encampments), 275

Tlaxcalteca Codex, 58

TLC. see NAFTA

Todos Unidos Contra Acción Nacional (TUCAN), 308, 323, 325

Torral, José, 313

Torres, Camilo, 218

Torricelli, Robert, 45, 131, 132, 134-135, 137, 359

Toscono, Alejandra, 357

Tratado de Libre Commercio. see NAFTA

Traven, Bruno, 251, 254

Trejo, Jorge, 88, 92, 94, 223

Tress Virgín, Luciano, 380,

381

TUCAN. *see* Todos Unidos Contra Accíon Nacional

Tupac Katari, 54

Turek, Elizabeth, 101

Turok, Antonio, 10, 181-182, 206

Tzeltal republic, rebellion of, 66

U

UDOC. *see* Citizens' Defense Group

UNAM. *see* Universidad Nacional Autónoma de Mexico

UNESCO biosphere program, 262, 263

Unified Socialist Party (PSUM), 158

Union America Party (PUA), 318

Union of Democratic Journalists (UPD), 76

Union of Ejidos, 257, 277

Union of Unions, 261, 277

Universidad Nacional Autónoma de Mexico (UNAM), 147, 164, 213, 272-275, 275

UNO-Mexican Democratic Party (PDM), 341

UPD. *see* Union of Democratic Journalists

URNG (Guatemala), 43, 107-108

U.S. aircraft used by Mexican military, 102-103, *191*, 246

U.S. National Endownment for Democracy, 388

V

Valadés, Diego, 147, 212, 318, 319

Vancouver Plywood Co., 255

Vázquez, Genaro, 175, 271

Vázquez, Matilde, 91-92

Vázquez Raña, Mario, 107

Vázquez-Sánchez, Miguel, 262, 266

Vega Domínguez, Jorge de la, 156

Velázquez, Fidel, 169-170

Velver Payán, Jaime, 286

Vigueras, Carlos, 137-138

Villa, Francisco, 87, 201

Villafuerte, Concepción, 8-9, 373, 377

Visher Garrido, Peter, 108-109, 296

Viveros, Angel, 401

voter registration, 379, 385-386, 394, 396. *see also* election fraud

W

War of the Castes, 64, 67

Warman, Arturo, 129

Watson, Alexander, 137

White Guards, 71, 88, 158, 214, 222, 276, 284

Wilkerson, S. Jeffrey, 266

Index

Womack, John, 203, 293

woman's status, 288-292

Workdays for Peace and Reconciliation. *see* Jornadas for Peace and Reconciliation

working class vs. ruling class, 48

World's Fair, Seville (1992), 55-56

X

Xi'Nich, 62, 79, 80

Y

Yañez, César, 389

Z

Zabludowsky, Jacobo, 21, 62, 223, 296, 388

Zapata, Emiliano, 15, 69, 175, 201-205, 241

Zapatista Army of National Liberation, *188, 195. see also* Clandestine Revolutionary Indigenous Committee; Marcos, Subcomandante

accused of sabotage, 105

agreement with Federal Electoral Institute, 379

amnesty proposal, 165

armed reformists, 283, 286

Battle of Rancho Nuevo, 83-86

belligerent status, 162-163, 181, 243, 360

Castellanos Domínguez sentence, 183-184

CCRI. *see* Clandestine Indigenous Revolutionary committee

ceasefire offer, 99, 110-111

children in ranks, 20, 262

co-optation by PRI, 147-148

communal assemblies, 249, 281, 287

declaration of war, 10, 13

demands, petition of, 185, 231, 235-236, 237

demands, political, 242-243

democratic organization, 281, 283, 287

drug smuggling, accused of, 42, 43

and ecology, 265-267, 369

electoral posture, 339-340, 378-379

free zones, 180

full strength, 285-286

health campaigns, 282

impact on economy, 119-120, 122, 141-144

impact on electoral mode, 144-145

impact on political parties, 331-332

knowledge of, by Mexican authorities, 25-35

knowledge of, by U.S., 38

leadership identification,

107-108
merchandising of, 237-238
NAFTA, effect on, 30, 35, 38, 136-137
negotiations for peace, 230-245
no vote on peace accord, 359
Ocosingo, Battle of, 88-94
origins, 17, 25, 259
peace accord negotiations, 357-358
peace delegates, 230-231, 244
peace negotiation promises, 242-243, 246
peace talk safety measures, 228-229
peace talks in Cathedral, 208-215
philosophy, 292-294
Pledges for Peace and Reconciliation, 241
pliego petitorio summary, 245-246
prisoner exchange, 179-186
program, eleven word, 17
rebellion begins, 7-11
red alert, 316, 353, 356, 382
religious services, 294
and socialism, 280, 292
stages of growth, 279
support spreads, 172-179
training camp, 27
weapons, 283-285

women combatants, 288-292
Zapatista Coordinating Body of the Plan of Ayala (CNPA), 70
Zedillo, Ernesto, 313, 321, 322, 343-346, 360, 384, 390, 394. *see also* Institutional Revolutionary Party (PRI)
Zorrilla Pérez, José Antonio, 322-323